I0084121

The New Era of Socialism with Chinese Characteristics

Global Relevance

The New Era of Socialism with Chinese Characteristics

Global Relevance

Jiang Hui

New Classic Press

2025

NEW CLASSIC PRESS
Published by New Classic Press (UK) ★
5th Floor, 99 Mansell Street, London, E1 8AX, UK,
Great Britain ★ Established in the year 2008 ★
Seeking business opportunities worldwide

The New Era of Socialism with Chinese Characteristics Global Relevance

Written by Jiang Hui
Translated by Tong Xiaohua
Used by Permission of Jiangxi People's Publishing House Co., Ltd. (China)
Original Chinese edition © Jiangxi People's Publishing House Co., Ltd., 2022
First published in English in the United Kingdom of Great Britain and Northern
Ireland
by New Classic Press in 2025

ALL rights reserved

It shall not be reproduced or issued without the prior written permission

ISBN 978-1-917143-49-3

10 9 8 7 6 5 4 3 2 1

DESIGNED BY SRA BERKS

Without limiting the rights under copyright reserved above, no part of this
publication may be reproduced, stored in or introduced into a retrieval system, or
transmitted, in any form or by any means (electronic, mechanical, photocopying,
recording, or otherwise), without the prior written permission of both the copyright
owner and the above publisher of this book.

The publisher's policy is to use paper manufactured from sustainable forests.

Contents

Introduction

The New Era of Socialism with Chinese Characteristics— Global Relevance

I

As we navigate the third decade of the 21st century, a profound and increasingly acknowledged truth and trend emerge: the world is experiencing transformative shifts unseen in a century, with China at the forefront as a pivotal catalyst for these changes. In this New Era, China, under the leadership of the century-old Communist Party of China (CPC), has ascended to the world's center stage, achieving feats that have captivated global attention. These achievements have empowered the Chinese people, who endured over a century of subjugation and humiliation, to rise with dignity. They have propelled the Chinese nation, with its over 5,000 years of civilization, toward modernization in all respects. Furthermore, they have carved out a successful path for socialist thought, which has spanned over 500 years, in the world's most populous country. Consequently, the People's Republic of China has made significant strides to keep pace with the times, and the rejuvenation of the Chinese nation now shines with promise.

The miraculous development and significant contributions of the New Era of socialism with Chinese characteristics represent not only a glorious chapter in China's historical progress but also a remarkable creation in the annals of the development of human society. The establishment of scientific theories in this New Era has given rise to contemporary Chinese Marxism and 21st-century Marxism. The triumphs of socialism with Chinese characteristics in the New Era serve as a guiding banner and a mainstay for global socialism. The pioneering of China's modernization path in this New Era provides a model and a new choice for many other developing countries striving for modernization. Moreover, China in this New Era has emerged as a contributor to global development and a leader of our times, offering Chinese wisdom to solve global challenges and presenting Chinese approaches for humanity's quest for a better social system.

The New Era heralds the creative transformation and innovative development of Chinese civilization, infusing it with vibrant energy. This era crafts a new form of human progress, making significant contributions to the advancement of global civilization. These monumental initiatives have addressed numerous challenges in the development of human society, offering Chinese approaches for the pursuit of superior social systems. The New Era of socialism with Chinese characteristics is a time when all Chinese people work together to realize the Chinese Dream of National Rejuvenation. It is also an era in which China continues to make substantial contributions to humanity. The remarkable achievements in this New Era hold profound significance not only in the development history of the Chinese nation and the People's Republic of China but also in the broader context of global socialism and human society.

In light of these historic achievements and transformative changes, we can confidently assert that China in the New Era, now at the center stage of the world, is deeply intertwined with the 21st-century global landscape. While uplifting its own people, China's development increasingly contributes to global progress. General Secretary Xi Jinping incisively remarked, "Proceeding from reality in all it does, the CPC has led the Chinese people to the path of socialism with Chinese characteristics. History and our experience have proved and will continue to prove that this is the path that works and the path that pays off. We will continue to follow this path to ensure that development is pursued both for our own good and for the benefit of the world."[1]

The extraordinary achievements of China in the New Era lay a robust foundation for building a great modern socialist country in all respects and provide valuable lessons for other developing countries seeking modernization. China's development offers approaches for reforming and optimizing the global governance system, contributes to the creation of an inclusive and coexistent world civilization, and provides significant support and momentum for the revitalization of global socialism. It also presents a Chinese model that challenges the Western notion that "a strong country must seek hegemony," making substantial contributions to world economic development and human advancement.

Anything unique to one nation is of great significance to the rest of the world. Through the outstanding achievements and significant contributions of China in the New Era, we must delve deeply into the profound global influence and increasingly evident world significance of this transformative period. We need to explore the contemporary and international relevance of China's development and contributions, as well as the universal and global significance of the Chinese path and

---

1 Xi Jinping, "Strengthen Cooperation among World Political Parties to Benefit the People: Keynote Speech at the CPC and World Political Parties Summit," *People's Daily*, July 7, 2021.

Chinese theory. As the world's largest socialist state and the most populous developing country, China has achieved a monumental leap from "catching up with the times" to "leading the times." The CPC, with over 95 million members, leads a country of more than 1.4 billion people, making it the world's largest ruling party with substantial global influence. Such an era, such a country, and such a Marxist party, with their historic achievements and monumental contributions, will undoubtedly be celebrated as key chapters in the epic history of the Chinese nation and as miraculous milestones in the annals of human development.

A century ago, British philosopher Bertrand Russell predicted in his work *The Problem of China* that "China, by her resources and her population, is capable of being the greatest power in the world after the United States." He envisioned China playing a pivotal role on the global stage and bringing new hope to humanity in times of great need. Nearly half a century ago, British historian Arnold Toynbee, in his seminal work *A Study of History*, suggested in a conversation with Japanese social activist Daisaku Ikeda, themed "The Twenty-First Century and the Future of Humankind," that humanity's hope lies in the East. Toynbee believed that Chinese civilization would offer endless cultural treasures and intellectual resources for the world's transformation and the future of human society in the 21st century. He explicitly predicted that the country most qualified and likely to pioneer a new civilization for humanity was China, and that Chinese civilization would unify the world. As we navigate through the third decade of the 21st century, observing contemporary China and the world today, we cannot help but admire the historical foresight of these two Western philosophers.

Today, a growing number of discerning individuals around the world recognize that it is time to take China seriously. China has become an integral part of life in various regions across the globe, shouldering responsibilities commensurate with its status, crafting its own chapter of destiny, and collaborating in the writing of the world's destiny. In constructing their society, the Chinese people are also developing a set of values distinct from those of the West. We increasingly realize that China's development path and values, characterized by unique Chinese features, also possess broad global significance and universality. They embody an organic unity of nationality and globality, particularity and universality. The great innovations and miracles of New Era China have profound contemporary and global significance, making them a major subject worthy of in-depth study in the present era.

II

Based on this awareness and deep reflection, this book aims to comprehensively and systematically summarize and distill the valuable experiences of the socialism with Chinese characteristics in the New Era. It seeks to reveal the intrinsic logic and fundamental principles of China's development in this New Era and to thoroughly explain the theoretical, practical, contemporary, and global significance of its historic achievements and transformative changes. The book integrates theory and practice, history and reality, and domestic and international perspectives. It coordinates the overarching strategy of the rejuvenation of the Chinese nation with the profound changes unseen in a century on the global stage. By examining and understanding New Era China within the context of historical eras, global trends, and international structures, the book deeply analyzes significant issues with contemporary and global perspectives, such as "China's New Era and Global Changes" and "China's New Era and the 'Great Historical Era.'" It examines the intricate and mutually influential relationship between China's New Era and the world's significant transformations from a sweeping historical vantage point.

In managing these two overarching contexts, the book astutely captures both the changing and unchanging aspects of the development environment in New Era China. It accurately identifies the historical opportunities and major challenges that China faces in this New Era, scientifically 'assessing China's position and role in the contemporary world. It elucidates how the Chinese Communists of the New Era, standing at the forefront of the times and leading the era, guide the Chinese people to create new historical achievements amid the historical trend of "the rise of the East and the decline of the West," the competition between two social systems, and the transformative changes in economic globalization, world multipolarity, and the international landscape.

The book asserts that the tremendous transformation of the Chinese nation—from standing up, growing rich, to becoming strong—marks the irreversible progress toward achieving national rejuvenation. In the context of the unprecedented changes in the world, New Era China emerges as a builder of world peace, a contributor to global development, a defender of international order, a leading force of contemporary progress, a major driving force behind global changes, a leading advocate for human peaceful development, a shaper of a new international order, and a significant contributor to human advancement. The global significance of socialism with Chinese characteristics in the New Era will continuously expand, deepen, and become more evident as the historical development of humanity progresses.

The book also delves into the global significance of the New Era of socialism with Chinese characteristics from several critical dimensions: making original contributions to the development of 21st-century Marxism, advancing world socialism to a Vnew stage, pioneering a new path for human modernization, and providing innovative solutions to global problems. Through these significant contributions and their global implications, New Era China profoundly interprets and fully substantiates the three whys: Why does the CPC always deliver? Why does Marxism always work? Why does Chinese socialism always shine?

Theoretical contributions

Xi Jinping Thought on Socialism with Chinese Characteristics for a New Era stands as contemporary Chinese Marxism and 21st-century Marxism. It epitomizes the essence of Chinese culture and spirit in this era, representing a scientific theory that not only guides China but also exerts a profound influence on the world. This thought innovatively applies the fundamental tenets of scientific socialism, offering a scientific summary of the experiences and lessons from the global socialist movement, thereby enriching and evolving scientific socialism with new theoretical content. It is both a theoretical achievement of the new leap in the adaptation of Marxism to the Chinese context, guiding the Chinese nation toward its rejuvenation, and the latest theory of 21st-century Marxism, making original contributions to the development of Marxism.

Institutional and practical contributions

socialism with Chinese characteristics in the New Era vividly demonstrates the superiority of the socialist system. Presently, a prominent feature of capitalist development is the emergence of various systemic drawbacks. In stark contrast, the CPC advances comprehensive deepening of reforms, continually developing and refining the system of socialism with Chinese characteristics. This results in unique governance and institutional advantages. As socialism with Chinese characteristics continues to evolve, our system will become increasingly mature, the superiority of our socialist system will further manifest, and our path will become ever broader. The tremendous achievements of the New Era of socialism with Chinese characteristics present Marxism and socialism with a refreshed image to the world, bringing about significant shifts in the historical evolution and competition between socialism and capitalism, favoring Marxism and socialism.

Contributions to human development

New Era China has pioneered a modernization path unprecedented in human history. Chinese modernization boasts unique connotations and significant characteristics, alongside global significance and exemplary roles. It has forged a new form of human advancement, offering a new option for developing countries seeking modernization. In promoting the building of human community with a shared future, amid unprecedented global changes, Chinese Communists have skillfully addressed the era's profound questions: "What kind of world should we build, and how should we go about it?" This approach provides Chinese wisdom, Chinese approaches, and Chinese strength for addressing major human problems and constructing a world of lasting peace, universal security, common prosperity, openness, inclusiveness, cleanliness, and beauty. New Era China has emerged as a crucial force in promoting human development and progress, steering humanity in the 21st century toward the right direction of development and advancement.

III

Any major historical activity or event that propels the development and progress of human society carries profound international and global implications. Lenin once pondered the question of "In What Sense We Can Speak of the International Significance of the Russian Revolution," specifically addressing the extent to which the Russian October Revolution of the early 20th century bore international relevance. He explicitly noted that, following the Russian October Revolution, "considerable international experience" had accumulated. Lenin clearly articulated that "certain fundamental features of our revolution have a significance that is not local, or peculiarly national, or Russian alone, but international."[1] He precisely defined the main content and characteristics of the international significance of the Russian Revolution: "taking international significance to mean the international validity or the historical inevitability of a repetition, on an international scale, of what has taken place in our country."[2] Lenin emphasized the issues of "international experience" and "international significance" just two and a half years after the October Revolution, in his work "'Left-Wing' Communism: An Infantile Disorder," written between April and May 1920.

The passage of natural time does not diminish the significant implications of great historical events. The October Revolution in then-backward Russia was the most advanced revolution in human history, namely the proletarian or socialist revolution. Some contemporaries believed that a revolution in advanced Western Europe would be more typical than the Russian Revolution, viewing Russia as a special exception. Lenin refuted this erroneous view, firmly asserting that the October Revolution, the most advanced revolution in human history, inevitably had international significance beyond Russia, possessing "the historical inevitability of a repetition on an international scale." The subsequent flourishing of socialism from one country to many after the October Revolution fully validated the historical foresight of the great revolutionary and thinker, Lenin.

From this historical perspective, using the materialist conception of history, the historic achievements and transformative changes of socialism

---

1   V. I. Lenin: "'Left-Wing' Communism: An Infantile Disorder," https://www.marxists.org/archive/lenin/works/1920/lwc/ch01.htm.
2   Ibid.

with Chinese characteristics in the New Era, and their significant global implications for the development of human society, are the inevitable result of China's great historical creation. China is increasingly moving to the center stage of the world, influenced by the "historical inevitability" in the intertwined historical context of the New Era of China and profound changes unseen in a century.

General Secretary Xi Jinping remarked, "Contemporary China is experiencing the most extensive and profound social transformation in its history, while also engaging in the most ambitious and unique innovation practices in human history."[1] The grand endeavors and historical innovations of New Era China are intrinsically Chinese yet universally significant; they embody distinct Chinese characteristics while holding global relevance. From its inception, the CPC has been dedicated to seeking happiness for the Chinese people and rejuvenation for the Chinese nation, while also striving for human progress and global harmony.

In 1921, on the eve of the Party's founding, Mao Zedong, with a visionary global perspective, recognized the worldwide significance of China's revolutionary cause: "China's problems are fundamentally world problems. If the transformation of China does not consider world transformation, it will be narrow and hinder the world."[2] During the era of reform and opening up, Deng Xiaoping confidently predicted, "By the middle of the next century, when we approach the level of the developed countries, then there will have been really great changes. At that time the strength of China and its role in the world will be quite different. We shall be able to make greater contributions to mankind."[3] General Secretary Xi Jinping repeatedly emphasized, "To make new and greater contributions

---

1   Xi Jinping, *Speech at the Seminar on Philosophy and Social Sciences*, Beijing: People's Publishing House, 2016, p. 8.
2   Mao Zedong: *Collected Works of Mao Zedong*, Beijing: People's Publishing House, 1993, vol. I, p. 1.
3   Deng Xiaoping, *Selected Works of Deng Xiaoping*, Beijing: Foreign Languages Press, 1994, vol. III, p. 146.

for humanity is the CPC's abiding mission."[1] The New Era of socialism with Chinese characteristics is a time of continually making greater contributions to humanity. Under the leadership of the CPC Central Committee, with General Secretary Xi Jinping at its core, the Chinese people have created the great miracle of "China's governance," a historic achievement that not only leads the times but also transforms the world.

Only what is national can be global, and only by leading the times can one reach the world. The role of New Era China on the world stage, its fulfillment of global responsibilities, and its demonstration of global significance are an intricate unity of historical inevitability and historical initiative.

While the development of history follows certain laws, people are not completely passive within it. By grasping the laws and trends of historical development, seizing opportunities for historical transformation, and acting proactively and effectively, we can make better progress and contribute more significantly. On the new journey of building a great modern socialist country, the CPC unites and leads the Chinese people in holding high the banners of peace, development, cooperation, and mutual benefit. It promotes the development of new international relations, the building of a human community with a shared future, and the high-quality development of the Belt and Road Initiative (BRI), offering new opportunities to the world through China's new development.

The continuous evolution of socialism with Chinese characteristics has forged a new path to modernization and a new form of human advancement, expanding the routes for developing countries to achieve modernization and providing a new choice for them. It offers a new model for human advancement. The global significance of the New Era of socialism with Chinese characteristics echoes what Lenin referred to as "the

---

1 *Documents from the 19th CPC National Congress*, Beijing: People's Publishing House, 2017, p. 46.

historical inevitability of a repetition on an international scale."

The "historical inevitability" nurtured and embodied by New Era China is the result of the natural historical process and objective historical laws that are not altered by human will. Its significance in "repetition on an international scale" refers to its major impact on the world and its macro-historical significance for the development of human society. The global significance of the New Era of socialism with Chinese characteristics breaks the myth of so-called "universal values" as "the only choice," providing Chinese wisdom and Chinese approaches for the development of human society and the exploration of better social systems. It offers a new direction, a new choice, and a bright future.

The great success and global relevance of the New Era of socialism with Chinese characteristics will increasingly be demonstrated and affirmed in the annals of Marxist development, the chronicles of world socialist progress, the narrative of the evolution of human society, and the saga of human advancement. Conducting in-depth research into the global relevance of this New Era of socialism with Chinese characteristics is both timely and aligned with the prevailing trends. Such endeavors are bound to yield fruitful results. This book represents an initial foray into this critical research area and aspires to inspire a wealth of high-quality studies, befitting the grandeur of our era.

Part One

The New Era in China and the Momentous Changes in the World

Social development is a harmonious unity of objective regularity and subjective initiative. Correctly understanding and grasping the domestic and international environments of our development, scientifically analyzing the direction and trends of social changes, and accurately judging our historical conjuncture are essential prerequisites for seizing opportunities and promoting development. Throughout its century-long struggle, our Party has consistently adhered to the fundamental tenets of Marxism to analyze and grasp historical trends, correctly handle the relationship between China and the world, and skillfully seize and utilize various historical opportunities to drive fundamental and all-around progress and leaps in our development. Coordinating the grand strategy of the rejuvenation of the Chinese nation with the momentous changes in the world, referred to as the "two factors of overriding importance," is the defining macro backdrop for China's development in the New Era. It is also the basic point for analyzing all major issues, planning all work, and making scientific decisions.

As socialism with Chinese characteristics navigates through a New

Era, the world is undergoing the most profound and unprecedented changes in a century. As General Secretary Xi Jinping stated, "China is at present in its best period of development in modern times, while the world is undergoing the most profound and unprecedented changes in a century. These two realities are intertwined and mutually influential."[1] This major judgment by the Party Central Committee, with General Secretary Xi Jinping at its core, encapsulates a profound understanding of the logical, historical, and practical aspects of the times. General Secretary Xi emphasized, "[L]eading officials should have two factors in mind: One is the strategic goal of achieving national rejuvenation, the other is the world experiencing a level of change unseen in a century. This is the prerequisite to planning our work."[2] Grounding reforms, development, stability, domestic affairs, foreign affairs, national defense, and all aspects of Party, state, and military governance in the context of the "two factors of overriding importance" is the fundamental requirement for realizing the progress and development of contemporary China.

I. The New Era: A Milestone in China's Development

To accurately understand our current historical conjuncture and development stage is the primary issue to be addressed in the socialist revolution, development, and reform. Social development is a dynamic process, characterized by quantitative changes leading to qualitative transformations. Quantitative changes lay the groundwork for qualitative shifts, and qualitative changes are the inevitable culmination of quantitative progress. Precisely assessing our present stage of development and

---

1   Xi Jinping, *On Building a Human Community with a Shared Future,* Beijing: Central Party Literature Publishing House, 2018, p. 539.
2   Xi Jinping, *The Governance of China,* Beijing: Foreign Languages Press, 2020, vol. III, p. 99.

clearly recognizing the historical context of our social advancement are fundamental premises for our Party's commitment to and development of socialism with Chinese characteristics in the 21st century.

In his political report to the 19th CPC National Congress, General Secretary Xi Jinping articulated: "With decades of hard work, socialism with Chinese characteristics has crossed the threshold into a New Era. This is a new historic juncture in China's development."[1] The primary foundation for this significant political judgment is that, since the 18th CPC National Congress, under the leadership of the Party Central Committee, with General Secretary Xi Jinping at its core, the Party and the country have embarked on comprehensive and pioneering exploration and practice. Building on the extensive exploration and practice accumulated by the Party and the country over many years, we have achieved historic accomplishments and experienced historic transformations. These advancements have resulted in a new historic leap, propelling socialism with Chinese characteristics into a new era.

Xi Jinping remarked, "[T]his era is one for socialism with Chinese characteristics, not for some other models.".[2] This New Era represents a pivotal stage in the evolutionary journey of socialism with Chinese characteristics—a period that bridges the past with the future, cherishing the legacy while paving the way for new horizons. From the perspective of the development process of socialism with Chinese characteristics, the New Era is an innovative evolution grounded in the inheritance of the Party and the country's previous explorations and practices. It signifies a progression from the founding period to entering the new century, from standing on a new starting point to crossing the threshold into a New

---

1   Xi Jinping, *Secure a Decisive Victory in Building a Moderately Prosperous Society in All Respects and Strive for the Great Success of Socialism with Chinese Characteristics for a New Era: Report at the 19th National Congress of the Communist Party of China*, Beijing: People's Publishing House, 2017, p. 10.
2   Xi Jinping, *The Governance of China*, Beijing: Foreign Languages Press, 2020, vol. III, p. 92.

Era. This progression showcases the historical unity of continuity and development, as well as the comprehensive and phased characteristics of social advancement.

As Xi Jinping pointed out: "Upholding and developing socialism with Chinese characteristics is a significant endeavor. Deng Xiaoping laid down the basic ideas and principles for it. The Party's third generation of central collective leadership with Jiang Zemin at its core and the Party Central Committee led by General Secretary Hu Jintao both wrote splendid chapters in this great endeavor. Now, it is our generation's task to continue undertaking this great endeavor."[1] From this vantage point, the New Era is an auspicious epoch in which the Party Central Committee, with General Secretary Xi Jinping at its core, unites and leads the entire Party and the Chinese people. By keeping pace with the times, upholding fundamental principles and breaking new ground, we continue to author the grand narrative of upholding and developing socialism with Chinese characteristics. We are crafting the magnificent chapter of the Chinese nation's journey from standing up, becoming rich, to becoming growing strong, striving to achieve new victories in socialism with Chinese characteristics.

Crossing the threshold into the New Era of socialism with Chinese characteristics is both the inevitable result of our country's historic achievements and transformations and the necessary response to profound changes in the principal contradiction within contemporary Chinese society. This New Era endows the Party and the country's cause with fresh theoretical guidance, contemporary significance, historical tasks, developmental goals, and practical requirements, thereby providing a temporal and fundamental basis for scientifically formulating the

---

1 *Documents Produced since the 18th CPC National Congress*, Beijing: People's Publishing House, 2017, vol. I, p. 114.

Party's principles and policies. The New Era is a significant milestone in the development of socialism with Chinese characteristics and is an extraordinary period in the 100-year history of our Party, the 70-plus years of the People's Republic of China, and the 40-plus years of reform and opening up.

1. The New Era marks a new conjuncture

"Only by clearly discerning the heart of the matter can we uncover the true principles that guide us." The 19th CPC National Congress made the significant political judgment that "socialism with Chinese characteristics has crossed the threshold into a new era," indicating a new historical conjuncture in contemporary China's development. This judgment was based on a scientific understanding of the profound changes in the global, national, and Party contexts and represents a major strategic consideration affecting the overall development of our country. It reflects the Party's distinctive character of advancing with the times and its deep understanding of the laws governing Communist Party rule, socialist development, and the development of human society, showcasing a high level of confidence in upholding and developing socialism with Chinese characteristics.

According to Marxist historical materialism, understanding social development and changes in the era is not a matter of subjective judgment but requires delving into the changes in the objective material conditions of society and the modes of production. Marx stated, "Just as our opinion of an individual is not based on what he thinks of himself, so can we not judge of such a period of transformation by its own consciousness; on the contrary, this consciousness must be explained rather from the contradictions of material life, from the existing conflict between the social productive forces and the relations of production."[1] Engels also remarked, "[I]n every historical epoch, the prevailing mode of economic production and exchange, and the social organization necessarily following from it, form the basis upon which it is built up, and from that which alone can be explained the political and intellectual history of that epoch."[2] These important statements provide us with the worldview and methodology to scientifically understand the characteristics of the era, analyze its essence, and make scientific judgments about it, serving as the "golden key" for better understanding the New Era.

The 19th CPC National Congress declared that "socialism with Chinese characteristics has crossed the threshold into a new era," a significant strategic determination that influences the entire trajectory of our country's development. This judgment is grounded in a scientific understanding of the profound changes occurring on global, national, and Party levels. It reflects the new historical conjuncture in our Party and country's cause. Using "socialism with Chinese characteristics has crossed the threshold into a new era" to denote the new historical conjuncture China's development reflects both the historical continuity of our Party's leading the people in diligent exploration in practice and theory around this central theme over the past four decades of reform and opening up, and the monumental leap forward achieved by harnessing significant strategic and historical opportunities, thus advancing with the times.

Since the 18th CPC National Congress, our Party has spearheaded theoretical innovation and guided the creative exploration and practice of the Party and the people. Building on the major achievements in our country's development since the founding of the People's Republic of China, especially since the introduction of the reform and opening

---

1   https://www.marxists.org/archive/marx/works/1859/critique-pol-economy/preface-abs.htm.
2   https://www.marxists.org/archive/marx/works/download/pdf/Manifesto.pdf.

up policy, the Party and the country's cause has undergone historic transformations. The principal contradiction in our society has evolved into the gap between imbalanced and insufficient development and the people's growing expectation for a better life. We are in period in which the timeframes of the Two Centenary Goals converge: achieving a moderately prosperous society in all respects and embarking on the new journey of fully building a modern socialist country, thereby advancing toward the Second Centenary Goal. China is increasingly moving to the center stage of the world, achieving a great leap from standing up, getting rich, to becoming strong.

The world is undergoing major developments, transformation, and adjustment, but peace and development remain the call of our day.

The trends of global multi-polarity, economic globalization, IT application, and cultural diversity are surging forward; changes in the global governance system and the international order are speeding up; countries are becoming increasingly interconnected and interdependent; relative international forces are becoming more balanced; and peace and development remain irreversible trends.

And yet, as a world we face growing uncertainties and destabilizing factors. Global economic growth lacks energy; the gap between rich and poor continues to widen; flashpoints arise often in some regions; and unconventional security threats like terrorism, cyber-insecurity, major infectious diseases, and climate change continue to spread. As human beings we have many common challenges to face.

The changes in our international status and environment have delineated a fresh historical juncture in our development. Historic transformations vividly illustrate our crossing the threshold into the New Era, while the shift in the principal social contradiction acts as its decisive factor. The new tasks and objectives of this period of historical convergence clarify the goals and missions of the New Era. Defining our development's new historical juncture within the context of the New Era helps to further unify thought, consolidate strength, and advance the great cause of socialism with Chinese characteristics from a new historical starting point.

Since the 18th CPC National Congress, General Secretary Xi Jinping, in leading the entire Party and the Chinese people in advancing the great practice of socialism with Chinese characteristics in the New Era, has demonstrated extraordinary theoretical courage, outstanding political wisdom, and a profound sense of mission as a Marxist politician, thinker, and strategist. With a deep affection for the people embodied in the phrase "I will fully commit to the people and never fail them," he has responded to the new demands of the times and practice and to the new expectations of the people. He has unwaveringly upheld the great banner of reform and opening up in the New Era, proposed the Two Centenary Goals and the Chinese Dream of National Rejuvenation, and overseen the great struggle, great project, great cause, and great dream. He has ensured coordinated implementation of the Five-Sphere Integrated Plan and the Four-Pronged Comprehensive Strategy, adhered to a people-centered philosophy of development, and strengthened confidence in the path, theory, system, and culture of socialism with Chinese characteristics. He has contributed to the decisive victory in building a moderately prosperous society in all respects and the commencement of a new journey toward fully building a modern socialist country. He has led the formulation of the 4th Five-Year Plan for Economic and Social Development and Long-Range Objectives through the Year 2035, writing a new chapter in upholding and developing socialism with Chinese characteristics. The New Era is an extraordinary time for promoting theoretical innovation and practical breakthroughs.

The entry of socialism with Chinese characteristics into the New Era holds profound significance in the history of the People's Republic of

China, the history of the Chinese nation, the history of world socialism, and the history of human development. This New Era signifies that the Chinese nation, which endured great hardships throughout modern times, has made a has achieved a tremendous transformation: it has stood up, grown rich, and is becoming strong, heralding a bright prospect for national rejuvenation. It signifies that scientific socialism in 21st-century China has gained powerful vitality, with the great banner of socialism with Chinese characteristics being held high in the world. It also signifies that the path, theory, system, and culture of socialism with Chinese characteristics are continuously developing. This has expanded the channel for developing countries to achieve modernization, provides new choices for those countries and peoples who wish to accelerate development while maintaining their independence, and offers Chinese wisdom and approaches to addressing global challenges.

2. The New Era exhibits new characteristics

The entry of socialism with Chinese characteristics into the New Era not only continues the historical trajectory but also introduces new characteristics that keep pace with the times, embodying rich connotations and profound significance.

From the historical trajectory of socialism with Chinese characteristics, the New Era emerges as a momentous epoch that bridges past achievements and future aspirations, continuing the quest for great victories under new historical conditions. This unique path was not only pioneered during the period of reform and opening up but also built on the prolonged struggles and foundations laid by our Party and nation. It is the result of relentless exploration and sacrifice by successive generations of central collective leadership, who have united the entire Party and the Chinese people.

Since the founding of the People's Republic of China, and especially since the advent of reform and opening up, our Party has steadfastly united and relied on the people, demonstrating self-reliance and hard work. Together, they have established the path of socialism with Chinese characteristics, creating unprecedented economic miracles of rapid development and long-term social stability. This transformation has fundamentally altered the destiny of the Chinese people and nation, irreversibly ending the era of internal strife and poverty that plagued China in modern times, and ushering in a historical process of continuous growth and national rejuvenation. This resurgence has positioned the Chinese nation, with its over 5,000-year-old civilization, to stand tall and renewed among the world's peoples.

As President Xi Jinping stated, "Since the introduction of the reform and opening up policy, we have reviewed our historical experience and constantly made difficult explorations, and we have finally found the right path to achieve the rejuvenation of the Chinese nation and our achievements have attracted the world's attention. This path is socialism with Chinese characteristics." As socialism with Chinese characteristics is in the New Era, we must steadfastly adhere to and develop this theme, continuously adapting to new demands and persisting in our exploration and efforts. This will allow socialism to exhibit even greater vitality and promise in China.

From a strategic and developmental perspective, the New Era marks a grand epoch of achieving decisive victories in building a moderately prosperous society in all respects, and moving forward to build a modern socialist country in all respects, and ultimately a great modern socialist country. The 19th CPC National Congress proposed a two-step strategic plan to build China into a great modern socialist country by the middle of this century, based on the achievement of a moderately prosperous society in all respects. Today, the First Centenary Goal of building a moderately prosperous society in all respects has been successfully accomplished. The journey toward the Second Centenary Goal of building a great modern socialist country in all respects has now begun. The Chinese nation has thus entered the New Era, marked by its historic transformation from standing up, to growing rich, to becoming strong.

From the perspective of building a better life for the people

The New Era is a great era of united struggle by the Chinese people to continuously create a better life and gradually achieve common prosperity for all. Achieving common prosperity is a fundamental principle and essential requirement of socialism. Leading the people to create a better life and ensuring that all people share the fruits of reform and development has been the unwavering goal of our Party. General Secretary Xi Jinping pointed out, "Our people love life and wish to have better education, greater job security, more decent incomes, more reliable social security, a better standard of health care services, more comfortable living conditions, and a more beautiful environment. They want their children to grow up well and have better jobs and more fulfilling lives. The people yearn for a better life, and our goal is to help them achieve it."[1] In the New Era, we must adhere to the fundamental purpose of serving the people wholeheartedly, practice the development philosophy centered on the people, and take the realization, maintenance, and development of the fundamental interests of the overwhelming majority of the people as the highest standard. We must continue to improve the level of social welfare and enhancement, promote social fairness and justice, strive to enable all people to enjoy a happier and healthier life, and promote more significant and substantial progress in the well-rounded development of individuals and the common prosperity of all people.

---

1 *Documents Produced since the 18th CPC National Congress*, Beijing: Central Party Literature Publishing House, 2014, vol. I, p. 70.

From the perspective of achieving national rejuvenation

The New Era is a great era for all Chinese sons and daughters to work together to realize the Chinese Dream of National Rejuvenation. Seeking happiness for the Chinese people and rejuvenation for the Chinese nation is the original aspirations and mission of the Chinese Communists. General Secretary Xi Jinping stated: "Since the very day of its founding, the Party has made seeking happiness for the Chinese people and rejuvenation for the Chinese nation its aspiration and mission. All the struggle, sacrifice, and creation through which the Party has united and led the Chinese people over the past hundred years has been tied together by one ultimate theme—bringing about the great rejuvenation of the Chinese nation."[1]

The great achievements of the new-democratic revolution have created the fundamental social conditions for the rejuvenation of the Chinese nation; the great achievements of the socialist revolution and development have laid the fundamental political premise and institutional foundation for the rejuvenation of the Chinese nation; the great achievements of reform, opening up, and socialist modernization have provided a vibrant system guarantee and rapid development of material conditions for the rejuvenation of the Chinese nation. In the New Era, the historic achievements and transformations in the Party and national undertakings have provided a more complete institutional guarantee, a more solid material foundation, and a more proactive source of inspiration for realizing the rejuvenation of the Chinese nation. The realization of the rejuvenation of the Chinese nation has entered an irreversible historical process.

From the perspective of China's relationship with the world

In the New Era, China is moving closer to the center stage of the

---

1   Xi Jinping, *Speech at a Ceremony Marking the Centenary of the Communist Party of China,* Beijing: People's Publishing House, 2021, p. 3.

world and making ever-greater contributions to humanity. The Chinese people have always linked their future and destiny closely with those of people from other countries, and the CPC has consistently seen it as its mission to make new and greater contributions to humanity. Since the founding of the People's Republic of China, we have consistently adhered to an independent foreign policy of peace, upheld the Five Principles of Peaceful Coexistence, unwaveringly pursued a path of peaceful development, practiced an open strategy of mutually beneficial cooperation, and steadfastly safeguarded the basic norms governing international relations and international fairness and justice.

Since the introduction of the reform and opening up policy, China has transitioned from being relatively closed to engaging in comprehensive openness, actively participated in the process of economic globalization, promoted the development of an open world economy, and facilitated the transformation of the global governance system. We have clearly opposed hegemonism and power politics, made significant contributions to human development, and actively contributed to the noble cause of human peace and development. In the New Era, the relationship between China and the world has undergone profound changes. Our interactions, exchanges, and integration with the international community are unprecedentedly close, and we have become recognized as a builder of world peace, a contributor to global development, and a defender of international order. We continue to contribute Chinese wisdom, Chinese approaches, and Chinese strength to reforming and improving the global governance system, to the great cause of world peace and development, and to building a human community with a shared future. China upholds the banner of peace, development, cooperation, and mutual benefit, remains committed to the path of peaceful development, promotes the development of a new type of international relations, and advances the high-quality development of the

BRI. Through China's new development, we will benefit the world and propel the wheels of history toward a bright goal.

From the perspective of advancing the great new project to strengthen the Party

In the New Era, the Party has undergone tremendous changes. Since the 18th CPC National Congress, under the leadership of the Party Central Committee with General Secretary Xi Jinping at its core, we have embodied the character of a Marxist party with the courage for self-reform. With determination and courage, we have advanced the full and strict self-governance of the Party, unwaveringly fought against corruption, maintained a zero-tolerance stance with no restricted areas and full coverage, and ensured officials do not dare to be, are not able to be, and do not want to be corrupt. The anti-corruption struggle has achieved overwhelming victories. Incorporating full and strict self-governance of the Party into the Four-Pronged Comprehensive Strategy, we have achieved an organic integration of Party self-governance and state governance. This has led to historic and pioneering achievements in the full and strict self-governance of the Party in the New Era, generating all-encompassing and profound impacts.

We have upheld and improved the Party leadership system and the national supervision system, and strengthened checks and oversight on the exercise of power, we have incorporated the system of full and strict self-governance of the Party as an essential component of the Party's leadership system. This has been integrated into the system of socialism with Chinese characteristics and the national governance system through comprehensive planning, providing fundamental guidelines for advancing full and strict self-governance of the Party in depth. Adhering to the principle of systems- and regulations-based Party self-governance, we have established the sound mechanisms led by the strengthening of the political foundations for the Party to comprehensively advance the Party's various aspects of development. We have also improved the systems for the Party to supervise officials, select and appoint competent personnel, and create long-term mechanisms for resolving the Party's own issues, opening up an unprecedented new landscape for Party self-supervision and self-governance.

On the new journey, we must continue to be guided by the strengthening of the foundations for the Party, advance the great new project to strengthen the Party, adhere to the principle that full and strict self-governance of the Party is always ongoing, and continuously promote the Party's self-reform. This ensures that the Part Party never betrays its nature and mission, and that it continues to be a strong leading core in the historical process of the New Era.

3. The new thought leads the New Era

The era is the mother of thought, and practice is the source of theory. "All epoch-making systems have as their real content the needs of the time in which they arose."[1] The New Era fosters the new thought ideas, and this new thought shapes the New Era. The New Era of socialism with Chinese characteristics is an era that demands and is certain to produce theory and thought. The great thought of this great era, guiding the great practice, is Xi Jinping Thought on Socialism with Chinese Characteristics for a New Era. This great thought and theory is the Marxism of the 21st century, a scientific theory that leads China and influences the world, and it represents a new leap in the adaptation of Marxism to the Chinese context, holding significant and far-reaching significance for the era, history, and the world.

Represented by Xi Jinping, Chinese Communists have responded to

---

1 https://www.marxists.org/archive/marx/works/1845/german-ideology/ch04b.htm.

the changes of the times, stood at the forefront of the era, and voiced the pioneering ideas of the times. From the combination of theory and practice, they have systematically addressed major contemporary issues such as what kind of socialism with Chinese characteristics to uphold and develop, how to go about it, what kind of socialist modernized country to build, how to go about it, what kind of long-term ruling Marxist party to build, and how to go about it. This has led to the creation of Xi Jinping Thought on Socialism with Chinese Characteristics for a New Era. This great thought creatively applies the basic principles of scientific socialism, scientifically summarizes the experiences and lessons of the world socialist movement, and enriches and develops scientific socialism with new ideological content. This great thought is not only the theoretical achievement of a new leap in the adaptation of Marxism to the Chinese context, guiding the Chinese nation toward rejuvenation, but also represents the latest theory of Marxism in the 21st century, making original contributions to the development of Marxism.

Addressing and solving the major theoretical and practical problems posed by the times is an important mission and fundamental characteristic of scientific theory. Marx and Engels once said that our theory "is a historical product, which at different times assumes very different forms and, therewith, very different contents."[1] The world is constantly changing, and China is also constantly evolving. The breadth and depth of changes in our era and in China far exceed the imagination of the earlier writers of Marxist classics. General Secretary Xi Jinping pointed out: "The fundamental principles of Marxism are universal truths with eternal intellectual value, but the earlier writers of Marxist classics did not exhaust the truth; instead, they continuously paved the way for seeking and

---

1 Engels, *Dialectics of Nature*, Moscow: Progress Publishers, 1934, p. 43.

developing the truth."[1]

The consistent successes of our Party in revolution, development, and reform stem from our steadfast commitment to integrating the fundamental tenets of Marxism with the specific characteristics of our era and China's national conditions. This commitment has enabled us to continually respond to the significant challenges presented by contemporary times and practice, thereby advancing the adaptation of Marxism to the Chinese context. Throughout this historical journey, we have also developed a coherent and evolving body of Marxist theories that adapt to the changing times.

General Secretary Xi Jinping noted: "The Party's history embodies an ongoing process of adapting Marxism to the Chinese context and exploring innovative theories and ideas."[2] Over the past century, our Party has sought truth from facts while freeing the mind, and broken new ground while maintaining its orientation and consolidating its foundations. In this way, it has broadened the dimensions of Marxism with Mao Zedong Thought, Deng Xiaoping Theory, the Theory of Three Represents, the Scientific Outlook on Development, and the Thought on Socialism with Chinese Characteristics for a New Era, providing sound guidance for the Party and the people. Xi Jinping Thought on Socialism with Chinese Characteristics for a New Era observes, interprets, and leads the times through the lens of Marxism, maintaining the organic unity of Marxism's universality and its national character. It examines the theoretical and practical needs for the innovative development of Marxism with a profound historical and broad global perspective, promoting the development of Marxism with the vivid and rich practice of contemporary China. It stands as a banner and model

---

1   Xi Jinping, *Speech Marking the 120th Birthday of Mao Zedong*, Beijing: People's Publishing House, 2013, p. 17.

2   Xi Jinping, *Speech at the Preparatory Meeting for the Education Campaign on CPC History*, Beijing: People's Publishing House, 2021, p. 12.

for the innovative development of Marxism in the 21st century.

The 19th CPC National Congress, standing at the height of history and the times, established the historical status of Xi Jinping Thought on Socialism with Chinese Characteristics for a New Era. This not only achieved the advancement of the Party's guiding thought with the times but also provided an effective guide for the further development of the Party and the nation. This historic decision and contribution reflect the Party's high degree of political and theoretical confidence and maturity. Xi Jinping Thought on Socialism with Chinese Characteristics for a New Era inherits and develops Marxism-Leninism, Mao Zedong Thought, Deng Xiaoping Theory, the Theory of Three Represents, and the Scientific Outlook on Development. It is the latest achievement in the adaptation of Marxism to the Chinese context, crystallizing the practical experiences and collective wisdom of the Party and the people, and serves as an action guide for the entire Party and the people in striving for the rejuvenation of the Chinese nation. It must be upheld and continually developed.

Xi Jinping Thought on Socialism with Chinese Characteristics for a New Era not only embodies the latest achievements of contemporary Chinese Marxism but also effectively constructs the latest theoretical form of Marxism in the 21st century. This thought deepens the understanding of the laws governing the Communist Party's rule, socialist development, and the development of human society. It integrates Marxist philosophy, political economy, and scientific socialism, making original contributions to enriching and developing Marxism. For instance, it upholds the world outlook and methodology of dialectical materialism and historical materialism, creatively applying the viewpoints of practice, contradiction, the people, and well-rounded development, thereby enriching and developing Marxist philosophy. It proposes new development philosophies, builds a modern economic system, and advances supply-side structural reform, enriching and developing Marxist political economy. It identifies the transformation of the principal contradiction in Chinese society, developing the theory of socialist development stages. It advocates for the improvement and development of the socialist system with Chinese characteristics and advances the modernization of the national governance system and capacity, enriching and developing the theory of socialist modernization, among other contributions. These new concepts, ideas, and strategies of significant theoretical and practical importance constitute the new content of Marxism in the 21st century.

Xi Jinping Thought on Socialism with Chinese Characteristics for a New Era has generated widespread appeal and influence worldwide, gaining broad recognition and high praise. Many believe that this thought is rich with the CPC's century-long practice and exploration experiences, using Marxism to observe, interpret, and lead the times. With a profound historical perspective and a broad global vision, it examines the theoretical and practical needs for the innovative development of Marxism and drives the development of Marxism with the vivid and rich practice of contemporary China.

This great thought effectively answers the questions posed by our times, by the people, by history, and by practice. It deepens the understanding of the laws governing the Communist Party's rule, socialist development, and the development of human society with a new historical and contemporary perspective. It has achieved a new leap in the adaptation of Marxism to the Chinese context and represents a new leap for Marxism in the 21st century.

II. The Momentous Changes in the World: Transformations of the Era and History

Throughout human history, world development has always been the result of the intertwining and interaction of various contradictions. Examining the history of world civilization, humanity has continuously progressed through successive revolutions, including the Agricultural Revolution, the Industrial Revolution, and the Information Revolution. Each of these transformations has had profound impacts on human life, triggering significant shifts in societal thoughts. As economic globalization deepens, the current world order is undergoing major changes, with the international balance of power becoming more equitable. The challenges and opportunities ahead are unprecedented, and the future development of the world is likely to be highly uncertain.

Currently, the world is experiencing a period of significant development, transformation, and adjustment. Countries are becoming increasingly interconnected and interdependent, and the trend of peace and development is irreversible. However, instability and uncertainty remain prominent. The global economy faces insufficient growth momentum, regional sensitive issues arise frequently, and traditional and non-traditional security concerns intertwine, presenting humanity with numerous common problems and challenges. Standing at the height of the era and history, General Secretary Xi Jinping made the significant strategic judgment that "the world today is undergoing momentous changes of a kind unseen in a century," profoundly revealing the profound changes and distinct characteristics of the contemporary world. We must take Xi Jinping Thought on Socialism with Chinese Characteristics for a New Era as our fundamental guideline, deeply understanding and grasping the main features, profound implications, trends, and evolving patterns of the changes in the world today, and maintain a clear and profound understanding of these great changes.

1. Changes in the world economic landscape

Over the past century, the global economic center and key pillars of the world economy were predominantly located in Western Europe and North America for a long time. Since the turn of the new century, "global multipolarity, economic globalization, the digitalization of society, and cultural diversity have deepened, while the transformation of the global governance system and international order has accelerated. Emerging market countries and developing nations have risen rapidly, leading to a more balanced international distribution of power."[1] The collective rise of emerging market countries has increasingly become a vital force driving global economic growth. Although Western capitalist countries have largely sustained a recovery momentum through re-industrialization, the global economic recovery has exhibited a "thriving in the South, sluggish in the North" trend.

The accumulation speed in areas such as capital, talent, and technology in emerging economies and developing countries is continuously accelerating, making them a driving force in promoting global trade and investment growth. A large number of emerging market countries and developing countries are rapidly developing. Coupled with the severe impact of the 2008 global financial crisis on the virtual economy of the US and Europe, the global economic focus is gradually shifting from the West to the East, and the focus of world economic development is gradually returning to the field of the real economy.

---

1 *Documents Produced since the 19th CPC Central Committee*, Beijing: Central Party Literature Publishing House, 2019, vol. I, p. 640.

In the foreseeable future, the international economic landscape and balance of power will undergo accelerated changes. The World Economic Outlook report released by the International Monetary Fund in April 2021 shows that the global GDP in 2020 was $84.54 trillion, with a total population of 7.662 billion and a per capita GDP of $11,033. According to statistics, in 2020, China's GDP reached $14.73 trillion, marking a growth of 2.3%, while the United States saw a GDP decline of 3.3%, bringing its GDP to $20.95 trillion. The ratio of China's GDP to that of the United States rose to 70.3%, surpassing 70% for the first time in history. During its post-World War II peak, the Soviet Union's GDP reached only about 40% of the US GDP. Japan's GDP once reached 70% of the US GDP, but at its peak, Japan's GDP—calculated using pre-Plaza Accord exchange rates—was around 30% of the US GDP, with the increase to 70% primarily driven by a sudden appreciation of the yen. Therefore, China is likely the first country since World War II to have its GDP reach 70% of that of the United States.

From 2010 to 2020, the economic share of BRICS countries in the global economy rose from 17.83% to 24.28%. In recent years, the contribution of emerging market countries and developing countries to world economic growth has reached 80%. Based on exchange rate-weighted calculations, the economic volume of these countries accounts for nearly 40% of the world. If emerging market countries can maintain their current development speed in the foreseeable future, it is expected that by around 2028, the economic volume of emerging market countries and developing countries will approach half of the world's total. According to the 2019 Joint Media Statement of BRICS Informal Leaders' Meeting, Brazil, Russia, India, China, and South Africa, the BRICS countries, have been the main drivers of global growth over the past decade or so, now accounting for one-third of global economic output; it is expected that by

2030, BRICS countries will continue to account for more than half of the world's economic growth.

Economic globalization is an inevitable trend in historical development. General Secretary Xi Jinping pointed out: "[E]conomic globalization is a result of growing social productivity, and a natural outcome of scientific and technological progress—not something created by any individuals or any countries. Economic globalization has powered global growth and facilitated movement of goods and capital, advances in science, technology and civilization, and interactions among peoples."[1]

Not only do developed countries benefit from economic globalization, but developing countries can also leverage their advantages to develop rapidly in the globalization process. However, the economic globalization we have seen so far has mainly been driven by international financial capital, leading to many unequal, unfair, and unreasonable phenomena in the international economic order. Economic globalization has indeed brought new problems, but these issues are not caused by the globalization process itself. Instead, they stem from the excessive profit-seeking and severe lack of regulation of the dominant international financial capital. These are new manifestations and issues of the fundamental contradictions of capitalism in globalization. The financial crises in Mexico in the 1990s, the Asian financial crisis, the financial crises in Argentina and other Latin American countries in 2001, each became progressively more severe. The recent 2008 global financial crisis, which was the longest-lasting, most widespread, and most impactful, indicates that the globalization model and global economic and financial governance system led by developed countries are facing structural adjustments. In the context of weak global economic recovery, there has been a rise in "anti-globalization" movements led by Western countries, particularly the United States. Trade

---

1   Xi Jinping, *The Governance of China*, Beijing: Foreign Languages Press, 2017, vol. II, p. 520.

protectionism, isolationism, and populism are spreading, posing more severe challenges to world peace and development. Especially during Donald Trump's presidency, the unilateral initiation of trade wars further fueled the tide of "anti-globalization," leading economic globalization into a period of deep adjustment and rebalancing.

As the world's largest developing country and a major socialist country advancing toward modernization, China is both a beneficiary and a contributor to globalization, bearing the responsibility of leading the development of economic globalization. In response to the rising tide of trade protectionism, unilateralism, and new manifestations of anti-globalization, Xi Jinping has called on the world to "build an open world economy and oppose trade protectionism," and has pledged that "China will not close its door to the world; we will only become more and more open." This is not just a verbal commitment but is backed by concrete actions. In recent years, China has proposed the BRI, promoted the development of free trade zones, held the China International Import Expo, upheld and practiced 21st-century multilateralism, and proposed a globalization development strategy for building a human community with a shared future. These efforts benefit most countries and people around the world and have gained recognition and support from most countries and people globally.

Since the beginning of the 21st century, a new round of technological revolution and industrial transformation has been emerging, with global technological innovation displaying many new development trends and characteristics. Major technological innovations are reshaping the global economic structure. General Secretary Xi Jinping pointed out: "History has proven that engineering and technological innovation drive the rapid rotation of the wheels of history, providing an inexhaustible source of power for the progress of human advancement. It has propelled humanity from ignorance to civilization, from nomadic civilization to agricultural civilization, and industrial civilization, leading us into the information age."[1]

This new round of technological and industrial revolution brings new opportunities for the development of human society, while also presenting unprecedented challenges. Artificial intelligence, big data, cloud computing, quantum information, biotechnology, new material technology, and new energy technology are now widely infiltrating almost all fields. This new wave of technological revolution and industrial transformation is gathering momentum, fostering numerous new industries, new business forms, and new models, promoting a significant leap in overall social productivity, accelerating industrial upgrading, and leading the global economy to leapfrog development, bringing about profound changes in global development and human production and lifestyle. This will inevitably change the comparative and competitive advantages of different countries, providing unprecedented opportunities for emerging market countries and developing countries to achieve leapfrog development. Xi Jinping noted: "If we do not recognize change, respond to change, or seek change, we may fall into a strategic passivity, miss development opportunities, and even miss an entire era."[2]

Currently, all major developed countries are accelerating their pace of seeking new economic growth areas through technological innovation. The new technological revolution also provides enormous opportunities for late-developing countries. Whether China can meet the challenge and plan ahead depends mainly on whether it can accurately recognize changes, effectively respond to changes, and actively seek changes, achieving

1   Xi Jinping, "Harness Engineering and Technology to Benefit Humanity and Shape the Future: Keynote Speech at the 2014 International Conference on Engineering and Technology, *People's Daily*, June 4, 2014.
2   Xi Jinping, "Striving to Build China into a World Leader in Science and Technology," *People's Daily*, June 1, 2016.

?substantial progress in innovation-driven development.

The outbreak of the COVID-19 pandemic in 2020 accelerated the development of the new trend of the "rise of the East and decline of the West" in the international landscape. Various signs indicate that the collective rise of emerging market countries and developing countries is unstoppable, making the global development map more comprehensive and balanced. The rise of emerging countries will tighten the connections between these nations, solidifying the foundation for world peace. It is foreseeable that the focus of world economic growth will shift from the US and Europe to emerging market countries, with spillover effects to other developing countries and regions.

According to data released by the General Administration of Customs of the People's Republic of China, the total value of China's goods trade with ASEAN in the first quarter of 2020 reached 991.34 billion yuan, a year-on-year increase of 6.1%. Of this, China's exports to ASEAN were 539.43 billion yuan, an increase of 2.4%, while imports from ASEAN were 451.91 billion yuan, an increase of 10.9%. ASEAN has historically emerged as China's largest trading partner.

About a hundred years ago, the United States became the world's largest creditor nation and capital exporter, shifting the global economic center from the eastern shore of the Atlantic to the western shore, marking a major change in economic geography. The current shift from the Atlantic to the Asia-Pacific, involving a much larger population and broader coverage, is incomparable to the previous shift. This transformation is truly unprecedented in a century.

With the rise of developing countries, especially emerging economies, the global economic landscape is no longer what it was at the end of World War II. At the end of World War II, the economic scale of developing countries was very small, and even by 1980, the GDP of developing and emerging economies accounted for less than 25% of the world's total at current prices. However, by 2020, this proportion had risen to 40.6%. The International Monetary Fund predicts that the actual GDP growth rate of developing countries and emerging economies will recover from -3.3% in the previous year to 6.0% in 2021, while developed countries will recover from -5.8% to 3.9%. The trend of dual-speed growth, where the annual growth rate of developing countries and emerging economies is more than 2 percentage points higher than that of developed economies, will continue during the world economic recovery phase, indicating that the importance of developing countries and emerging economies in the global economic landscape will continue to rise.

As of the end of 2018, the two countries with the highest economic growth rates and the largest economic volumes among the BRICS nations were China and India. China had a real economic growth rate of 6.6%, with a GDP of US$13.608 trillion, accounting for approximately 15.86% of the global economy. In 2020, China's GDP surpassed 100 trillion yuan, with a per capita income exceeding US$10,000. India, in 2018, had an economic growth rate of over 7%, with a GDP of US$ 2.726 trillion, accounting for about 3.18% of the global economy. Overall, China and India are expected to maintain relatively high economic growth rates in the coming period, with their economic volumes and global shares having further room for growth.

The other three BRICS countries had lower economic growth rates and GDP volumes in 2018. Brazil's real economic growth rate in 2018 was 1.1%, with a GDP of US$1.869 trillion, accounting for 2.18% of the global economy. Russia's real economic growth rate was 2.3%, with a GDP of approximately US$1.658 trillion, accounting for 1.93% of the global economy. South Africa grew by 0.8%, with a GDP of about US$366.3 billion, accounting for approximately 0.43% of the global economy. Thus, in 2018, the combined GDP of the BRICS countries was about US$20.23 trillion, accounting for approximately 23.58% of the global economy.

In 2018, the global population was approximately 7.594 billion, with a per capita GDP of about US$11,300. Among the five BRICS countries, only Russia had a per capita GDP exceeding US$10,000, slightly above the global average. China's per capita GDP was close to US$9,800, Brazil's about $8,900, South Africa's over US$6,000, and India's just over US$2,000. Thus, the average per capita GDP of the BRICS countries in 2018 was about $6,400, approximately 56.6% of the global average. Excluding China, the average per capita GDP of the other four countries was only about $3,800, which is not only far below that of developed countries in Europe, America, and Japan but also significantly lower than the global average.

2. Changes in the world political landscape

The world is currently witnessing the deepening of political multipolarity. After the end of the Cold War, the bipolar world order disintegrated, concluding the US-Soviet rivalry and gradually giving rise to a political landscape where the United States emerged as a "superpower," while Europe, Russia, China, and Japan became "multiple powers." This shift marked the onset of a new phase of political multipolarity. As we entered the early 21st century, the formation of an international multipolar political order has been accelerating. The Western developed countries, once united by capital and interests, now appear increasingly fragmented, with divergent stances on major global governance issues.

With the collective rise of emerging market countries and developing countries, the relationship between Western developed countries, represented by the US and Europe, and developing countries, represented by China and India, which account for about 85% of the world's population, is becoming more balanced. This shift provides a strong foundation for the deepening development of world multipolarity. As Xi Jinping pointed out in his speech at the general debate of the 70th Session of the United Nations General Assembly in 2015: "The movement toward a multipolar world and the rise of emerging markets and developing countries have become an irresistible trend of history."[1]

With technological advances driving social informatization and cultural diversification, the interconnection between countries has become closer, providing more substantial material and technological conditions for the deepening development of world multipolarity.

In recent years, the global political landscape has been undergoing a historically accelerated evolution, characterized by the intertwining of various contradictions and the competition among different forces and plans. During Donald Trump's presidency, the US government prioritized its own interests above those of other countries, under the banners of "America First" and "America's priority." This led to the continuous withdrawal from international agreements and organizations such as the Trans-Pacific Partnership (TPP), the Paris Climate Agreement, the Intermediate-Range Nuclear Forces Treaty, the Iran Nuclear Deal, and the United Nations Human Rights Council. The US also fiercely criticized NATO and the United Nations, at times even threatening to withdraw from the World Trade Organization WTO, contravening the long-established rules of free trade.

During the global impact of the COVID-19 pandemic, countries like the US not only failed to enhance international cooperation under the "crisis-driven" model but were also keen on shifting blame to other countries and the World Health Organization. The US even announced

---

1 *Documents Produced since the 18th CPC National Congress*, Beijing: Central Party Literature Publishing House, 2016, vol. II, p. 695.

its withdrawal and defunding of the WHO, effectively undermining cooperation and policy coordination in health security and economic support. Domestically, some US politicians became "servants" of the COVID-19 virus in its war against humanity.

The insufficiency of international cooperation driven by self-interest, coupled with the failure of crisis-driven cooperation leading to inadequate international macroeconomic policy coordination, highlights the further decline in the efficiency and capability of global governance. This has accelerated the evolution of the national political landscape. The US also launched a Section 301 investigation against China under the guise of intellectual property rights and initiated investigations into major global economies in the name of national security, creating trade frictions in key industries such as automobiles, steel, and aluminum.

This situation has prompted major European countries to focus on their own interests, compounded by Brexit and anti-immigration and anti-globalization sentiments in some European countries, impacting the traditional political standing of the European Union. On the surface, this appears to reflect US dissatisfaction with the current international order. However, it essentially indicates that the US' dominant position in the global political landscape is beginning to wane, a trend that is likely to become more pronounced with the rise of emerging and developing countries. The international political landscape is experiencing the most profound and complex changes since World War II, particularly since the demise of the Soviet Union.

As the relative power of Western countries such as the United States and Europe declines, a large number of emerging market countries and developing countries, represented by the BRICS nations, are collectively rising. This irreversible trend not only propels world peace and development but also makes these countries the main driving force.

China, as the largest developing country, adheres to a path of peaceful development, striving for global peace and development, and is increasingly becoming a key force in maintaining world peace and development.

The profound shifts in the global landscape have driven major countries, particularly Western nations like the United States, to accelerate the adjustment of their strategies and relationships in a bid to preserve their global dominance. This has made the international situation more complex and volatile. While nations fiercely compete across various fields, they also prioritize leveraging international mechanisms and rules, vying for influence and a greater voice in shaping global regulations.

Currently, traditional security threats such as regional conflicts and disputes, terrorism, nuclear proliferation and nuclear security, and cybersecurity are intertwined with non-traditional security threats. This necessitates enhanced global governance to maintain world peace, development, and collective security. The dynamic changes in international power and the deep evolution of the international landscape and relationships are ongoing.

Following the outbreak of the COVID-19 pandemic, Western political parties have experienced declining cohesion, organizational shrinkage, weakened social functions, and ineffective national governance. This has led to political polarization and the rise of populist parties, highlighting inefficiency and decay as prominent flaws in contemporary capitalist party systems. The pandemic has further exacerbated longstanding issues in Western societies, such as wealth disparity and racial discrimination.

In contrast, during the pandemic, our Party has utilized inter-party communication channels to conduct external promotion in various forms, levels, and perspectives. This has guided foreign parties, political organizations, think tanks, and media to actively voice support, objectively and fairly assessing China's sacrifices and contributions to the global fight against the pandemic and the institutional advantages behind these efforts. We have firmly refuted the false statements of a few political forces, showcasing our Party's highly responsible attitude toward global public health security and highlighting our commitment to building a human community with a shared future.

The changing global political ecology has also led to new trends in international cultural exchanges and ideological confrontations. The struggle in the ideological and cultural fields has become more intense, with competition among different systems, development paths, and values becoming the main focus. Especially today, after several centuries of the dominance of "Western-centrism," the inertia of Western countries like the United States imposing their historical culture and social systems on others cannot change overnight. This leads to increasingly prominent ideological arrogance, prejudice, and hostility surrounding historical culture and social systems, potentially intensifying the "clash of civilizations." The deeper driving force behind contemporary international exchanges is cultural interaction and integration, where the interaction of different cultures is becoming more frequent, and the international ideological struggle is growing sharper and more complex. In international competition, the Chinese path may be labeled by Western countries with a stronger tint of systemic and ideological rivalry.

In the realm of global cultural exchanges and confrontations, on one hand, more and more countries are learning from each other through exchange and mutual learning, leveraging their strengths to explore development paths and social systems, thereby significantly promoting the prosperity of world culture and the progress of human advancement. On the other hand, some Western countries adopt cultural hegemony strategies in international cultural exchanges, promoting Western cultural values, ideologies, institutional models, and development paths as "universal standards," coercing developing countries into accepting Western values and systems. They particularly intensify ideological infiltration against socialist countries, planning and instigating "color revolutions."

Countries around the world should achieve peaceful coexistence on the basis of mutual respect and seeking common ground while reserving differences, promoting exchange and mutual learning to inject momentum into the progress of human advancement. As Xi Jinping pointed out: "Each country is unique, with its own history, culture and social system, and none is superior to others. What is important is whether a country's social system fits its national conditions, enjoys public endorsement and support, serves to deliver political stability, social progress and better lives, and contributes to human progress."[1] This statement represents the fundamental principle for ideological exchanges, interactions, and integration between countries and must be jointly upheld.

In addition, a country can achieve significant development in competition only by genuinely safeguarding its ideological and cultural security, promoting its core values, and exploring institutional models and development paths that suit its national conditions.

We must firmly seize the power to lead, strengthen our voice, and effectively manage our ideology. We must continuously adapt Marxism to the Chinese context in keeping with the times, and increase its appeal to the people, and actively cultivate and practice the core socialist values. We should not forget our origins, absorb foreign ideas, and look toward the future, building a socialist ideology that has strong cohesion and leading power. This will better construct the Chinese spirit, Chinese values, and Chinese strength, contribute Chinese wisdom to the development and progress of human advancement, and provide intellectual guidance for the

---

1   Xi Jinping. "Light Up Our Way Forward with Multilateralism: Special Address at the World Economic Forum Virtual Event of the Davos Agenda," *People's Daily*, January 26, 2021.

well-rounded development of the people.

3. Changes in the pattern of international relations

From the perspective of world historical development, countries, regardless of size, strength, or wealth, should be equal and mutually respectful. However, major countries are the main forces on the international historical stage, and the direction of the world pattern is generally determined by the relationships between major countries. This is an undeniable fact. Whether it was the struggle for maritime supremacy between the Netherlands, Spain, and Portugal during the Age of Exploration or the confrontation between the US and the Soviet Union after World War II, these events reshaped the global power structure and international pattern of their times.

In the current era, the gap in overall strength between emerging market countries and developing countries and developed countries represented by the United States is continuously narrowing. In particular, with China's increasing strength and closer ties with the world, it has gradually become an important player influencing the international pattern. From 2007 to 2020, the proportion of the United States' economic output in the world's total economy decreased from 25.22% to 24.77%, while China's economic output increased from 6% to 17.42%. Harvard University professor Graham Allison stated in his book *Destined for War: Can America and China Escape Thucydides's Trap?*, "The world has never seen anything like the rapid, tectonic shift in the global balance of power created by the rise of China."[1] "China's economic network is spreading across the globe, altering the international balance of power in a way that causes even longtime US allies in Asia to tilt from the US toward China."[2]

---

1 Graham Allison, *Destined for War: Can America and China Escape Thucydides's Trap?*, Boston and& New York: Houghton Mifflin Harcourt, 2017, p. 9.
2 *Ibid.*, p. 33.

Some Western scholars, influenced by traditional Western theories of great power relations, emphasize that a country's rise in power will inevitably lead to struggles for world hegemony. In his book *Destined for War: Can America and China Escape Thucydides's Trap?*, Graham Allison analyzes the Thucydides's Trap theory, describing how, in the past 500 years, 12 out of 16 emerging powers have clashed with established powers during their rise, with only 4 avoiding conflict. John Mearsheimer, a professor at the University of Chicago, bluntly states in his book *The Tragedy of Great Power Politics*: "[T]he great powers that shape the international system fear each other and compete for power as a result. Indeed, their ultimate aim is to gain a position of dominant power over others, because having dominant power is the best means to ensure one's own survival."[1] "[I]nternational politics has always been a ruthless and dangerous business, and it is likely to remain that way."[2]

Some Western politicians are unwilling to see China rise and grow stronger. They view China's rise and development through the lens of Western historical experience, seeing China's state system and governance model as challenges and alternatives to Western systems. They spare no effort to distort, smear, and suppress China's development path and social system. For instance, they label the socialist system with Chinese characteristics as "capitalist socialism," "state capitalism," or "new bureaucratic capitalism," and malign China's rise as "new imperialism." They also distort the successful practice of the BRI as "new colonialism" and launch trade wars to suppress China's economic and high-tech development. Their fundamental purpose is to overthrow the leadership of the CPC and the socialist system, delaying or obstructing the historical process of the rejuvenation of the Chinese nation.

---

1   John Mearsheimer, *The Tragedy of Great Power Politics,* New York and London: W. W. Norton & Company, 2001, p. xi.
2   *Ibid.,* p. 2.

In the face of potential profound adjustments in major country relations, it is crucial for China to safeguard national sovereignty, security, and development interests and to promote world peace and development. A very important aspect of this is to build a new type of major country relations and skillfully manage the international situation. China's diplomacy is principled, values friendship, upholds justice, and seeks fairness.

China has consistently advocated for major country relations that avoid conflict and confrontation, emphasize mutual respect, pursue cooperation for mutual benefit, and jointly follow the path of peaceful development. As early as February 2012, then Vice President of China, Xi Jinping, pointed out during his visit to the United States: "Entering the second decade of this century, China-US relations are at a new historical starting point. We should... expand the convergence of interests and areas of mutually beneficial cooperation between our two countries, promote continuous progress in the China-US cooperative partnership, and strive to shape the cooperative partnership into a new type of major country relations for the 21st century."[1] Since the 18th CPC National Congress, building a new type of major country relations has become a highlight of China's major country diplomacy. China has also prioritized achieving non-conflict, non-confrontation, mutual respect, and mutually beneficial cooperation among major countries as a key direction of its foreign policy.

Building a new model of major country relations can avoid falling into the self-imposed Thucydides's Trap. In his speech at the reception in Seattle, Washington State, the United States on September 22, 2015, General Secretary Xi Jinping responded: "There is no Thucydides's Trap in the world, but if major countries repeatedly make strategic misjudgments,

---

1   Xi Jinping, "Work Together to Create a Better Future for China-US Cooperative Partnership: Speech at the Welcome Banquet by American Friendly Groups," *Guangming Daily*, February 17, 2012.

they may create such a trap for themselves."[1] Constructing a new type of major country relations is an unprecedented endeavor, with no ready-made experience or models to follow, so encountering some difficulties and even setbacks is normal. However, as long as the major countries can start from the fundamental interests of all humanity, exercise courage, and strive toward building this new model of major country relations, they can certainly secure greater benefits for the people living in our shared global village amid these significant changes.

4. Changes in the global governance structure

Currently, the shifting economic and political landscape of the world is driving a profound reshaping of the global governance system.

In today's world, new issues urgently needing resolution have emerged in the field of global governance. The issues of peace, development, governance, and trust are closely interrelated and collectively form the four major challenges facing humanity in our era. Geopolitical hotspots are emerging one after another, hegemonism and power politics still persist, the shadows of terrorism and armed conflicts linger, and unilateralism and protectionism are on the rise. Multilateralism and the multilateral trade system are under severe attack, while famines and pandemics appear intermittently. Traditional and non-traditional security issues are complexly intertwined. These problems are influencing the direction of the global governance system.

On January 25, 2021, General Secretary Xi Jinping, in his special address at the World Economic Forum Virtual Event of the Davos Agenda, pointed out that this era faces four major challenges:

The first is to step up macroeconomic policy coordination and jointly

---

1   "Speech at the Reception in Seattle, Washington State, the United States," *People's Daily*, September 24, 2015.

promote strong, sustainable, balanced and inclusive growth of the world economy.

The second is to abandon ideological prejudice and jointly follow a path of peaceful coexistence, mutual benefit, and mutually beneficial cooperation.

The third is to close the divide between developed and developing countries and jointly bring about growth and prosperity for all.

The fourth is to come together against global challenges and jointly create a better future for humanity.

Whether these issues can be properly resolved is related to the development space of countries around the world, the prosperity and stability of the entire world, and the fate of the people of all countries, who have never been so closely connected as they are today. As the biggest variable in global governance, the United States continues to emphasize "America First," is unwilling to continue providing or selectively provides global public goods, and has begun to call for the re-establishment of international rules.

Following their rise, emerging market countries and developing countries hope for a more refined global economic governance system that better meets the development needs of global productivity and is more conducive to the common development of all countries. They desire to promote equality in rights, opportunities, and rules among countries in international economic cooperation, to advance the democratization and rule of law in global governance rules, and to increase their representation and voice in global governance. They are working to make the global governance system more balanced in reflecting the wishes and interests of the majority of countries.

In recent years, the economic growth rate of emerging market countries has significantly outpaced that of the Western powers of Europe and America. Their influence, voting power, and say in organizations such as the World Trade Organization, the International Monetary Fund, and the World Bank have seen substantial improvements. China has taken the lead by proposing the BRI and initiating the establishment of new multilateral financial institutions such as the Asian Infrastructure Investment Bank. These are important steps toward the correct direction of reforming the global economic governance system.

After the global financial crisis in 2008, the G20 established its role as the "main forum for international economic cooperation," ensuring the international community strengthens macroeconomic policy coordination and introducing a series of major measures, helping the world economy gradually emerge from the shadow of the global financial crisis. The G20 has also actively promoted reforms in IMF quotas and World Bank voting rights, established a more representative Financial Stability Board, and supported the WTO in playing a central role in the multilateral trading system. The G20 includes both developed and emerging market countries, and the consultation among all members demonstrates that emerging market countries are making significant contributions to improving global economic governance.

One of the momentous changes of a kind unseen in a century is the collective rise of emerging market countries and developing countries, represented by China, which fundamentally alters the world landscape and the existing order. As the largest developing country, China adheres to the path of peaceful development, is dedicated to promoting peace and development worldwide, and firmly upholds the international order and system centered on the purposes and principles of the United Nations Charter. China promotes the concept of global governance based on achieving shared growth through discussion and collaboration, increasingly becoming a pivotal force in maintaining world peace and development.

China is an active participant and beneficiary of the international development system, as well as a constructive contributor. In October 2013, China proposed the establishment of the Asian Infrastructure Investment Bank, which was a constructive move to assume more international responsibility, improve the existing international economic system, and provide international public goods. In December 2015, the Asian Infrastructure Investment Bank Agreement met the legal conditions for entry into force, and the was officially established. As the initiator of the AIIB, China unwaveringly supports its operation and development. Besides paying its share of the capital on time, China also contributed US$50 million to the Project Preparation Special Fund established by the AIIB, effectively increasing infrastructure investment in Asia. This move mobilizes various resources, especially private sector funds, into the field of infrastructure development, promotes regional connectivity and economic integration, improves the investment environment of developing member countries in Asia, creates job opportunities, enhances long-term development potential, and brings a positive boost to economic growth in Asia and even worldwide. The formal establishment and operation of the AIIB is of great significance to the reform and improvement of the global economic governance system. It aligns with the trend of adjustment and evolution in the world economic landscape and makes the global economic governance system more just, reasonable, stable, and effective.

In recent years, China has also been striving to make the global governance system more just and reasonable, advancing the democratization of international relations, establishing a new type of international relations centered on mutually beneficial cooperation, and building a human community with a shared future. With China's rising strength, the country actively participates in formulating governance rules in emerging fields such as oceans, polar regions, cyberspace, outer space, nuclear security, anti-corruption, and climate change. China promotes the reform of unjust and unreasonable arrangements in the global governance system and gradually undertakes more responsibilities within its capacity. China's contributions to the United Nations' assessed contributions[1] and peacekeeping assessments have significantly increased.

From 2013 to 2015, China contributed 5.148% of the United Nations' regular budget, ranking third among member states after the United States 22% and Japan 9.68%. For the period 2016–2018, China's contributions rose to 7.921% of the UN regular budget and 10.2% of the peacekeeping budget. In the period 2019–2021, China surpassed Japan for the first time, becoming the second-largest contributor to the UN regular budget, just behind the United States. China's share of the UN regular budget increased to 12.01% approximately US$336 million, and its share of the peacekeeping budget rose to 15.22%.[2] This demonstrates China's commitment to the correct view of righteousness and benefit, originating from the grand cause of world peace and development. It further showcases China's role as a major country, which strives to contribute Chinese wisdom and strength to the improvement of global governance.

III. The Interplay of China's New Era and the Unprecedented Global Changes

China has entered the New Era, and the world is undergoing unprecedented changes of a kind unseen in a century. The New Era of China and these global changes are influencing each other simultaneously

---

1 UN budget adjustment rules: The United Nations General Assembly's Fifth Committee, responsible for budgetary matters, reviews and adjusts the scale of assessments every three years to reflect the latest economic conditions of member states. The assessment rate is based on each member's economic capacity, primarily the share of Gross National Income (GNI) in the global economy over the past three and six years, with considerations for total external debt and per capita national income allowing for certain reductions.
2 "China's Share of UN Contributions Rises to Third Globally," *The Beijing News*, December 25, 2015.

and are deeply intertwined, leading to profound changes in the relationship between China and the world. In this global transformation, China is not a bystander but an active participant and a leading force with significant influence. General Secretary Xi Jinping profoundly stated, "History indeed has its laws, but this does not mean that people are completely passive. As long as we follow the general laws and trends of history, and leverage opportunities for change accordingly, we can achieve greater success."[1] Understanding the characteristics and major trends of the evolving global changes, correctly handling the relationship between China and the world, focusing on the big picture, seizing the trends, and accomplishing significant tasks are the inevitable requirements of the development of the times.

1. The rise of the East and the decline of the West is the main trend of major changes

The world today is undergoing momentous changes of a kind unseen in a century, with the trend of the rise of the East and the decline of the West becoming increasingly prominent. The development of socialism with Chinese characteristics has led to a profound transformation in the historical evolution and competition between two ideologies and two social systems worldwide, favoring Marxism and socialism. This major trend has profound historical significance not only for the development of socialism in China but also for the development of world socialism and human progress.

In the unprecedented global changes, Western capitalist developed countries led by the United States still hold significant economic, technological, financial, and military advantages. Although China has

---

1 Xi Jinping, "Speech at the Preparatory Meeting for the Education Campaign on CPC History," Beijing: People's Publishing House, 2021, p. 13.

achieved a shift from following and running alongside to leading in some major technologies, it still faces critical bottlenecks in many core technologies, being constrained by others. Since 2018, the United States has utilized its advantages in chip technology to curb and suppress Chinese companies like ZTE and Huawei. The main theme of the unprecedented global changes is the rise of the East and the decline of the West, presenting China with significant strategic opportunities as well as unprecedented risks and challenges. The most critical challenge is that the United States and other Western countries have openly regarded China as their main competitor, strategically encircling, rule-binding, development-delaying, and image-smearing China.

In 2020, China's GDP was US$14.73 trillion, accounting for 17.5% of the world economy, nearly ten times its share in 1978, when it was 1.8%. The US economy accounted for 24.6% of the world economy in 2020, down from 27.4% in 1978. China's total GDP in 2020 surpassed that of the European Union for the first time. Preliminary data released by Eurostat showed that the GDP of the 19 Eurozone countries fell by 6.8% in 2020 compared to the previous year, while the GDP of the 27 EU countries fell by 6.4%. Excluding the UK, the nominal GDP of the 27 EU countries was about US$15.58 trillion in 2019. Based on Eurostat's calculation of a 6.4% decline in GDP in 2020, the total GDP of the 27 EU countries was US$14.58 trillion in 2020. From 2021 to 2035, the GDP of China and the US will approach parity, intensifying the competition between the two countries, with challenges becoming more frequent and severe. Currently, the US leverages trade and technology to coerce China into compliance, but the systemic competition between China and the West, represented by the US, is long-term. Despite the US adopting unilateralism and trade protectionism, the trends of world multipolarity, economic globalization, social digitalization, and cultural diversity are inevitable and irreversible.

Cooperation based on competition will be the main theme of future Sino-US relations. Facing these unprecedented global changes, China must seize opportunities, meet challenges, and be bold in fostering new opportunities amid crises and opening up new horizons on a shifting landscape.

Currently, China is in its best development period since modern times, while the world is undergoing unprecedented changes of a kind unseen in a century. These two dynamics are interwoven and mutually impactful. With the changing world landscape and the transition from old to new international orders, the competition between two social systems in the long river of history has shown a trend of one rising and the other falling, highlighting the advantages of the socialist system. At the same time, we must recognize that the competition between these two social systems in the unprecedented global changes is long-term, complex, and sometimes very intense. Western capitalist countries, led by the United States, are unwilling to see the development and growth of China, viewing China's development path and model as a significant challenge and alternative to the Western institutional model and values. The reality is that the "effective governance of China" stands in stark contrast to the "disorder in the West." Some Western capitalist countries are plagued with chaos, sluggish economic growth, widening wealth gaps, severe political polarization, constant party disputes, frequent violent incidents, and increasing social fragmentation, plunging the capitalist system into unprecedented difficulties. This also indicates that a prominent feature of the unprecedented global changes is the obvious trend of the rise of the East and the decline of the West. How to make this trend a trend for the rise of socialism and the decline of capitalism is a major issue for the development of world socialism in the 21st century.

2. China's development as the main driving force of major changes

As the world's largest developing country and socialist country, China has always upheld the banner of peace, development, cooperation, and win-win outcomes. It has consistently adhered to the shared values of all humanity, including peace, development, fairness, justice, democracy, and freedom. China is committed to maintaining world peace and promoting common development, aiming to build human community with a shared future, becoming a positive force in promoting the transformation of the global political and economic order toward fairness and reasonableness.

"To constantly make new and greater contribution to humanity is a solemn promise made by our Party and our people a long time ago."[1] As early as 1956, Mao Zedong pointed out that by the 21st century, China would undergo significant changes, "China will become a powerful socialist industrial country," and "China should make greater contributions to humanity." Since the founding of the People's Republic of China, China has actively advocated the Five Principles of Peaceful Coexistence, opposed hegemonism, and strived to fulfill its international responsibilities in bringing about a fairer and more reasonable international order. Since the introduction of the reform and opening up policy, with the rapid development of China's economy, China's contribution to the international community has grown increasingly significant. Data shows that since 2002, China's average contribution to world economic growth has been close to 30%. During the global financial crisis since 2007, under immense pressure and difficulties, China, as a responsible major country, insisted on maintaining the stability of the yuan without devaluation, kept the yuan exchange rate against the US dollar basically stable, orderly promoted the market-oriented reform of the yuan, and opened up the domestic financial

---

1　Xi Jinping, *Speech at the Ceremony Marking the 95th Anniversary of the Founding of the CPC*, Beijing: People's Publishing House, 2016, p. 20.

market. These actions made significant contributions to stabilizing the world economy, acting as a major stabilizer and important engine for global economic growth.

After the 18th CPC National Congress, General Secretary Xi Jinping solemnly declared at a press conference: "Our responsibility is to rally and lead the whole Party and the Chinese people, take up this historic baton and continue working hard for the great renewal of the Chinese nation, so that we will stand rock-firm in the family of nations and make fresh and greater contribution to humanity."[1] Since then, he has repeatedly emphasized that we will uphold the banner of peace, development, cooperation, and win-win outcomes, unswervingly follow the path of peaceful development, adhere to the strategy of opening up for mutual benefit, and commit to developing friendly cooperation with countries around the world, fulfilling international responsibilities and obligations. We will continue to work with the people of all countries to advance the noble cause of human peace and development. At the 2015 High-Level Forum on Poverty Reduction and Development, General Secretary Xi Jinping summarized China's contributions to the global community since the founding of the People's Republic of China. He pointed out: "Over the past sixty-plus years, China has provided nearly 400 billion yuan in aid to 166 countries and international organizations, dispatched over 600,000 aid personnel, among whom more than 700 brave Chinese sons and daughters sacrificed their precious lives for the development of other countries. China has announced seven times the unconditional cancellation of government interest-free loan debts owed by heavily indebted poor countries and least developed countries to China. China has actively provided medical assistance to 69 countries in Asia, Africa, Latin America and the Caribbean,

---

1 *Documents Produced since the 18th CPC National Congress*, Beijing: Central Party Literature Publishing House, 2014, vol. I, pp. 69–70.

and Oceania, and has helped over 120 developing countries meet their Millennium Development Goals."[1] Moreover, since the 18th CPC National Congress, China has proposed the BRI, adhering to the principles of peace, development, cooperation, and win-win outcomes, and the principle of achieving shared growth through discussion and collaboration. By integrating its advantages in production capacity, technology, and capital with market advantages, China has signed cooperation documents with more than 160 countries and international organizations. This not only spurred economic development in countries along the route, offering opportunities for them to get on board its express train of development but also promoted global economic growth, pioneered a new type of economic globalization, and expanded new space for international cooperation.

Currently, China has truly become an important engine of global economic growth. According to the 2019 National Economic and Social Development Statistical Bulletin published by the National Bureau of Statistics and its interpretation, in 2019, China's contribution to world economic growth reached about 30%, continuing to be the main driving force for global economic growth. In 2020, facing the sudden outbreak of the COVID-19 pandemic, China not only swiftly took action to control the situation domestically and actively engaged in international exchanges and cooperation but also, despite facing tremendous pressure in its own pandemic prevention and control, provided assistance to the international community in various ways as much as possible.

Furthermore, organizations such as the Shanghai Cooperation Organization and BRICS, which include China, are playing increasingly important roles in promoting the transformation of global political and economic order. As the largest developing country and the largest socialist

---

1 *Documents Produced since the 18th CPC National Congress*, Beijing: Central Party Literature Publishing House, 2016, vol. II, p. 721.

country, China has fully demonstrated the image of a responsible major country in the international community. It has taken pragmatic actions in multiple key issues such as international climate change and peacekeeping, showcasing the demeanor of a responsible major country. The concept of building a human community with a shared future, proposed by General Secretary Xi Jinping, has been explicitly included in United Nations documents and has gained broad recognition from the international community, providing Chinese wisdom and approaches for global governance.

Today, as China moves closer to the center stage of the world, the Chinese Communists, with General Secretary Xi Jinping as the main representative, actively promote the building of human community with a shared future, continually making new and greater contributions to world peace and development, and providing Chinese approaches and wisdom for humanity's exploration of a better social system. China has proposed the BRI and actively cooperated with countries along the route, building public platforms for regional and global cooperation and providing global public goods. Efforts to improve infrastructure in developing countries, build roads and railways, and establish institutions such as the Asian Infrastructure Investment Bank and the Silk Road Fund are all examples of China's active assumption of major country responsibilities, effectively combining national interests with major country responsibilities and international interests. Everything the CPC and the Chinese government do is for the happiness of the people, the rejuvenation of the nation, and the pursuit of a harmonious world.

General Secretary Xi Jinping pointed out: "The CPC The Party cares about the future of humanity, and wishes to move forward in parallel with all progressive forces around the world. China has always worked to safeguard world peace, contribute to global development, and preserve international order."[1] As Socialism with Chinese Characteristics enters the New Era, China is increasingly approaching the center stage of the world. The relationship between China and the world has never been as closely intertwined as it is today, and China's influence on the world has never been as comprehensive and profound. Faced with the significant and profound changes of the 21st century and the unprecedented global transformation, General Secretary Xi Jinping, with a profound historical perspective and global vision, has deeply grasped the trends of China and the world's development. He proposed the concept of building a human community with a shared future, which embodies wise reflections and unique insights on major issues of human development. Promoting the building of human community with a shared future is the Chinese wisdom and approach provided by the Chinese Communists in the New Era to scientifically answer the question of our times: "What kind of world should we build, and how should we go about it?" It has become a clear banner for China to lead the trend of the times and the direction of human advancement's progress.

The goal of building a human community with a shared future is to organically integrate China's development with that of other countries worldwide. This approach not only focuses on the long-term development and destiny of human society in the current era but also aims to address many of the common challenges humanity faces. While steadfastly pursuing its own development path, China also aligns with the broader historical trends and follows the laws governing the development of human society. In addition, China offers vibrant and practical wisdom and approaches to the world, aimed at rectifying global imbalances and inadequacies in development, and addressing deficits in development,

---

1   Xi Jinping, *Speech at a Ceremony Marking the Centenary of the Communist Party of China,* Beijing: People's Publishing House, 2021, p. 16.

peace, governance, and trust. By applying its unique path and development philosophy, China is leading and shaping a new future for human society's development, providing new ideas and making fresh contributions to the common progress of humanity.

IV. Coordinating the Domestic and International Situations and Correctly Grasping Changes and Constants

At present and for a period to come, China's development remains in an important period of strategic opportunity, but both opportunities and challenges are evolving. We must coordinate the domestic and international situations, using a comprehensive, dialectical, and long-term perspective to discern the changes and constants in our development environment. We must correctly handle major relationships in all aspects, be adept at creating opportunities in crises, and open new prospects amidst changes. We should seize opportunities, respond to challenges, maximize benefits, minimize harm, and advance courageously. General Secretary Xi Jinping clearly articulated: "This education campaign will help all Party members to be clear about China's strategy of realizing national rejuvenation within the context of a wider world that is undergoing change on a scale unseen in a century, to establish a comprehensive and balanced view of history, to understand the dynamics of evolution and the laws of history by analyzing history, the times and the world from a broader perspective, and to devise systematic, forward-looking and innovative strategies as appropriate."[1]

---

1   Xi Jinping, *Speech at the Preparatory Meeting for the Education Campaign on CPC History,* Beijing: People's Publishing House, 2021, p. 14.

1. Change and stability in the international environment

The world today is undergoing momentous changes of a kind unseen in a century. This is a major strategic judgment made by General Secretary Xi Jinping, using a broad global vision and deep historical perspective to determine the trends in world development. It provides us with contemporary insight, historical coordinates, and realistic grounds to understand the complex international situation. We must recognize both the main characteristics and overall landscape of the unprecedented changes in our external development environment, and accurately grasp its development trends, rich connotations, driving forces, and direction of evolution.

The theme of peace and development has not changed, but the world has entered a period of turmoil and transformation, with a significant increase in instability and uncertainty in the international environment. General Secretary Xi Jinping pointed out: "We firmly believe that peace and development are the themes of our times and the questions of our times. The international community needs to bear historical responsibility with unity, wisdom, and courage to answer these questions and demonstrate accountability in our era."[1] Currently, the global COVID-19 pandemic and the unprecedented changes of a kind unseen in a century are interacting, with people's aspirations for development, peace, unity, and progress growing stronger. At the same time, it must be noted that the world entering a period of turmoil and transformation is a primary characteristic of these major changes. The accelerated advancement of new technological revolutions and industrial transformations brings technological progress and productivity leaps, which will profoundly alter human production and lifestyles, influencing the international balance of power and the global

---

1   *Documents Produced since the 19th CPC National Congress*, Beijing: Central Party Literature Publishing House, 2019, vol. I, p. 640.

political and economic landscape. The extensive and far-reaching impact of the COVID-19 pandemic has created setbacks in economic globalization, with unilateralism, protectionism, and hegemonism posing threats to world peace and development. The United States, in its effort to maintain world hegemony, strives to contain the rise of developing countries, particularly by openly declaring China as a main competitor and exerting extreme pressure in fields such as technology and trade. Under the impact of the pandemic, the world economy is sluggish and even faces severe recession. Populism and xenophobia are on the rise, and conflicts in the ideological domain are intensifying. Overall, the international economic, technological, cultural, security, and political landscapes are undergoing profound adjustments, with multiple factors intertwining and acting together, exacerbating the instability and uncertainty of the international environment.

The fundamental direction toward economic globalization has not changed, but economic globalization has encountered setbacks and countercurrents, with significant changes in the contradictions and driving forces it faces. Economic globalization is an objective requirement of the development of productivity and an inevitable result of scientific and technological progress. It is an irreversible historical trend, consistent with economic laws and the interests of all countries.

General Secretary Xi Jinping emphasized that "economic globalization is an objective reality and a historical trend." "The world will never return to isolation, and no one can sever the ties between countries."[1] The vast ocean of the global economy cannot shrink into isolated lakes and rivers. The long-term trajectory and fundamental direction of economic globalization remain unchanged. However, economic globalization is currently facing

---

1   Xi Jinping, "Speech at the General Debate of the 75th Session of the United Nations General Assembly," *People's Daily*, September 23, 2020.

strong headwinds and undergoing profound transformations. During economic downturns, various contradictions become more pronounced or even intensified—such as those between fairness and efficiency, growth and distribution, technology and employment. The wealth gap is widening, the global extreme poverty rate has risen for the first time in 20 years, and economic imbalances are worsening across the world. Some countries are turning inward, international trade and investment are contracting sharply, and the flow of people, goods, and capital is being severely disrupted. Global industrial and supply chains have been deeply affected.

Historically, countries like the United States and other Western nations were the primary engines driving economic globalization. Today, some of these very nations have become significant obstacles to its progress, even fueling anti-globalization movements that are sowing chaos and creating challenges for global economic governance. In contrast, China is emerging as a major force advocating for the liberalization and facilitation of international trade and investment, steering economic globalization toward a more equitable and reasonable direction.

In sum, the changes and constants in the process of economic globalization present both formidable challenges and new opportunities for China's development in the evolving global landscape.

The fundamental trend of world multipolarity has not changed, but the global landscape is undergoing profound adjustments, with significant changes in the international balance of power. The general direction toward world multipolarity and the democratization of international relations has not changed, and there is an increasingly strong call for the establishment of a more just and reasonable new international political and economic order. At the same time, the international balance of power is experiencing unprecedented changes, and the global landscape is entering a period of transformation and reshaping. The old systems and orders are difficult to sustain, while new systems and orders have yet to form. International forces are realigning, leading to a profound adjustment in the global landscape, with the trend of the rise of the East and the decline of the West becoming increasingly evident. China's continuous rapid development has become a major force driving the evolution of the global landscape. Against the backdrop of the pandemic and economic downturn, the contrast between China's effective governance and the West's disorder has become more pronounced. It is also necessary to recognize that hegemonism and power politics still persist, harming international fairness and justice. These phenomena not only hinder the fundamental resolution of various conflicts and contradictions but also erode the foundations of world peace. The competition for dominance in global governance and the formulation of international rules is becoming increasingly fierce. The governance deficit, trust deficit, peace deficit, and development deficit remain the main issues that humanity urgently needs to address.

The great transformation unseen in a century is a change in the world, an era, and history, bringing unprecedented opportunities and challenges to our country's development. The key is to accurately grasp the new contradictions and challenges in this great transformation, to be adept at recognizing the changes and constants in an increasingly complex international environment, and to respond appropriately. This means maintaining composure and resolve amidst changes, seeking opportunities within these changes, taking proactive actions, positively responding to the impacts and challenges brought by changes in the external environment, preventing and resolving various risks and hidden dangers, enhancing the country's comprehensive strength and risk resistance capability, and creating an external environment and conditions conducive to our country's development.

2. The changes and constants in the domestic environment

The 14th Five-Year Plan marks the beginning of a new journey to build a modern socialist country in all respects, and our country has entered a new development stage. We must deeply understand the connotations and characteristics of this new development stage, correctly recognize and deeply grasp the changes and constants in the domestic environment, address the main contradictions in development with higher standards, better implement the new development philosophy, build a new development dynamic, and achieve high-quality development. We must recognize that our country is still in the primary stage of socialism, while also acknowledging that it has entered a new development stage. Fully understanding the historical conjuncture and development stage of the Party and the people's cause is the fundamental basis for our Party to clarify the central tasks of each stage and formulate policies, and it is also an important experience for our Party to continuously achieve victories in revolution, development, and reform.

Since the 18th CPC National Congress, General Secretary Xi Jinping frequently emphasized that the primary stage of socialism is the greatest national condition and reality of contemporary China. "It is imperative not only in accelerating the economy, but also in speeding up political, cultural, social and ecological development; not only when our economy was small, but also when it is large; and not only when planning long-term development, but also during daily work."[1] At the Fifth Plenary Session of the 19th CPC Central Committee, General Secretary Xi Jinping reiterated: "This is based on a sound assessment of the stage, environment, and conditions for our country's development: that China is still in the primary stage of socialism and will remain so for a long time to come; that China is still the largest developing country in the world; that development remains

---

1   Xi Jinping, *The Governance of China*, Beijing: Foreign Languages Press, 2018, vol. II, p. 11.

the CPC's top priority in governance."[1]

On the other hand, during the long-term primary stage of socialism, as our country's development progresses and its composite national strength improves, different historical periods will inevitably have distinct characteristics and primary tasks. The 19th CPC National Congress made a significant political judgment that socialism with Chinese characteristics has entered the New Era based on changes in the principal contradiction in our society. Currently, our country is entering a new development stage, which is a phase within the primary stage of socialism. At the same time, it is a new starting point after decades of accumulation, marking a new phase where our Party leads the people in achieving a historic transformation from standing up, getting rich, to becoming strong. This is of profound historical significance in the history of the rejuvenation of the Chinese nation and the history of socialist development. In the new development stage, facing new development environments and conditions, we must steadfastly adhere to the new development philosophy, accelerate the development of a new development dynamic that focuses on domestic circulation and features positive interplay between domestic circulation and international circulation, and promote higher quality, more efficient, more equitable, more sustainable, and safer development of the economy.

We must recognize that the long-term positive fundamentals of our country's development have not changed, but also acknowledge the more complex problems and severe challenges faced in the new development stage.

On one hand, our country continues to have various advantages and conditions for development. The basic trend of sustained, healthy, and stable economic growth has not changed, and the overall momentum of

---

1   *Documents of the Fifth Plenary Session of the 19th CPC Central Committee,* Beijing: People's Publishing House, 2020, p. 80.

long-term improvement remains unchanged. After years of development, our country has accumulated substantial material foundations, rich human resources, vast market space, strong development resilience, and a stable social environment. These are the important foundations and fundamental guarantees for promoting economic development and resisting various risks. In 2020, our country achieved significant strategic results in fighting the COVID-19 pandemic and economic recovery, becoming the only major economy in the world to achieve positive economic growth, with the economic aggregate surpassing 100 trillion yuan. Our composite strength and international influence have improved in the face of adversity, fully demonstrating the advantages and governance efficiency of the socialist system with Chinese characteristics.

On the other hand, our development also faces many difficulties and challenges. The economy is influenced by cyclical and structural factors, short-term and long-term issues are intertwined, and there are multiple impacts from external shocks and the COVID-19 pandemic. Issues of unbalanced and inadequate development remain prominent, and reforms in key areas and critical links are still arduous. The capacity for innovation does not meet the requirements for high-quality development, the agricultural foundation is still not solid, there are large gaps in urban-rural and regional development and income distribution, ecological and environmental protection tasks are still heavy, there are still gaps in ensuring people's livelihood, and weaknesses persist in social governance. The tasks of constructing a new development dynamic, cultivating new growth drivers, invigorating development vitality, creating new international competitive advantages, and expanding development space remain daunting and challenging.

We must recognize both the overarching and long-term nature of the principal contradiction in our society, as well as the new characteristics and requirements brought about by changes in this contradiction in the new development stage. Entering the New Era, the change in the principal contradiction in our society is a historic shift that affects the overall situation and imposes many new demands on the work of the Party and the country. The principal contradiction in society has fundamental, overarching, and long-term impacts, spanning the entire process of building a modern socialist country. Solving this principal contradiction cannot happen overnight; it requires both proactive efforts and sustained persistence. The key is to address the primary and major aspects of contradictions based on the new characteristics and problems of different development stages, focusing on solving prominent issues, consolidating foundations, leveraging strengths, addressing weaknesses, and enhancing deficiencies to promote comprehensive, coordinated, and sustainable economic and social development.

From the two aspects of the principal contradiction in society, during the 14th Five-Year Plan period, issues of unbalanced and inadequate development remain prominent, constraining the overall level of development. The increasingly diverse, multi-layered, and multifaceted needs of the people for a better life are not yet fully met, making the development tasks complex and demanding. Currently, the people's expectations have evolved in general from satisfying basic needs to improving the quality of life, and their demands at different levels and in various areas are becoming more diverse. Thus, the focus of resolving contradictions has shifted to high-quality development. People's demands have not only increased, but some previously less pressing issues now require urgent resolution. The principle of ensuring and improving people's livelihood in the course of development remains unchanged. The focus should be on enhancing the systematic and targeted approach to solving problems of unbalanced and inadequate development, thereby improving the quality of life for the people.

The domestic environment in the new development stage is complex and intricate, demanding a deep understanding of the new characteristics and requirements brought about by changes in the principal contradiction in society. We must correctly recognize and handle the relationship between changes and constants, accurately grasp new opportunities, and calmly respond to new challenges. It is vital to see our unique political, institutional, developmental, and opportunity advantages, and acknowledge the many favorable conditions for economic and social development. In addition, we must recognize the prominent contradictions, increased risks, and challenges in development, and the many difficulties and problems we face. We must remain steadfast and overcome all obstacles, continuously advancing toward our established goals, and striving to write a new chapter in China's development.

3. Coordinate the domestic and international situations and focus on doing our own work well

The profound and complex changes in the domestic and international environments require us to adopt a comprehensive, dialectical, and long-term perspective to correctly understand and respond to various contradictions and challenges. The most important and crucial task at present is to better coordinate the overall strategy of the rejuvenation of the Chinese nation with the unprecedented changes in the world not seen in a century. We must follow the directives of the CPC Central Committee and the plan of the Fifth Plenary Session of the 19th CPC Central Committee, to understand and grasp the laws of development, carry forward the spirit of struggle, adopt a worst-case scenario mentality, accurately recognize changes, respond to them effectively, and proactively seek changes. We must seize opportunities, face challenges, and open up new prospects.

Adhere to the overall leadership of the Party and improve the systems and mechanisms for the Party's leadership in economic and social development

Adhering to the Party's leadership in all work is the first basic strategy for upholding and developing socialism with Chinese characteristics in the New Era. The Fifth Plenary Session of the 19th CPC Central Committee identified the adherence to the Party's overall leadership as the primary principle that must be followed for economic and social development during the 14th Five-Year Plan period. General Secretary Xi Jinping emphasized, "Whether we can steer the world's second-largest economy well, and whether we can maintain sustained and healthy economic and social development, fundamentally depends on whether the Party plays its core role in leading economic and social development effectively."[1] The more severe and complex the situation becomes, the more contradictions, risks, and challenges increase, the more we need a strong core of leadership to ensure the steady progress of our economy and the harmony and stability of our society. We must fully leverage the greatest advantage of the Party's leadership, improve and refine the systems and mechanisms for the Party's leadership in economic and social development, and ensure that the Party fully exerts its roles in setting the direction, planning the overall situation, formulating policies, and promoting reform in economic and social development. We must also ensure that the Party's leadership is implemented in all fields, aspects, and stages of economic and social development.

Maintain and utilize the important period of strategic opportunity, and be skilled at turning crisis into opportunity and challenges into opportunities

---

1   *Documents Produced since the 18th CPC National Congress*, Beijing: Central Party Literature Publishing House, 2016, vol. II, p. 834.

"Opportunity may knock just once; grab it before it slips away." As we entered the 21st century, our Party judged that the first 20 years of this century would be an important period of strategic opportunity that we must seize tightly and can make great achievements. We seized this important period of strategic opportunity, deepened reforms, expanded opening up, promoted development, and achieved historic accomplishments and transformations. The Fifth Plenary Session of the 19th CPC Central Committee conducted a comprehensive analysis of the domestic and international situation and made a new important judgment: that our country's development is still in an important period of strategic opportunity both now and in the foreseeable future, but both opportunities and challenges have evolved with new developments. At present, The opportunities are more strategic and promising; the challenges are more complex and bear on our overall situation. The challenges are unprecedented, but they can turn into extraordinary opportunities if we respond with ingenuity. Our successful response to the COVID-19 pandemic is an example of turning crisis into opportunity. We must dialectically understand the relationship between opportunities and challenges, enhance our awareness of risks and opportunities, and capture and create opportunities while responding to risks and challenges. We should not only be adept at riding the trend and taking proactive actions but also be courageous in facing challenges head-on, steering through headwinds, and turning crises into opportunities to ensure a good start in the building of a modern socialist country in all respects.

Adhere to a systematic approach and promote comprehensive and coordinated socialist modernization

Since the 18th CPC National Congress, General Secretary Xi Jinping consistently emphasized the importance of systematic thinking, comprehensive planning, integrated coordination, and balanced consideration, focusing on key areas to drive overall progress. The Fifth Plenary Session of the 19th CPC Central Committee regards "adhering to a systematic approach" as a crucial principle for economic and social development, which holds significant practical importance. The more complex and volatile the situation, the more risks and challenges there are, the more we need systematic planning and coordinated promotion. According to the central plan, we should strengthen forward-looking thinking, comprehensive planning, strategic layout, and overall promotion, balancing both domestic and international situations, handling both development and security matters well, and maintaining a unified national strategy. We should leverage the unique advantages of the CPC's leadership and the socialist system with Chinese characteristics, and the new nationwide system that concentrates resources to accomplish major tasks, ensuring that the whole nation moves in unison and works together. We must fully mobilize all positive factors and better utilize the enthusiasm of the central and local governments and various sectors to achieve a unified development of quality, structure, scale, speed, efficiency, and security.

Enhance awareness of opportunities and risks, maintain strategic confidence, adopt a worst-case scenario mentality, and promote the spirit of struggle

General Secretary Xi Jinping stated: "To achieve the goals we have set, we must have both the strategic confidence to unperturbed by the cloud that obscures our vision and the enterprising spirit of 'not reaching the Great Wall, we are not true heroes.'"[1] In the face of major crises and challenges, we must uphold the stability and continuity of our strategic policies, and maintain strategic confidence and historical resilience; otherwise, we risk becoming indecisive, wavering, drifting with the current,

---

1   *Documents Produced since the 18th CPC National Congress*, Beijing: Central Party Literature Publishing House, 2014, vol. I, p. 701.

and losing our footing. It is essential to plan comprehensively and with a long-term perspective, integrating the management of both immediate issues and broader trends, the present and the future. We must adjust our strategies in response to changing circumstances and firmly grasp the strategic initiative. Adopting a worst-case scenario mentality means preparing for the worst while striving for the best possible outcomes. We must enhance our awareness of potential dangers, consistently prevent risks and challenges, and avoid any strategic or subversive errors. Particular emphasis should be placed on preventing and resolving major risks and challenges that could delay or disrupt the process of national rejuvenation.

We must clearly recognize the long-term, complex, and arduous nature of the great struggle on the path to national rejuvenation, promote the spirit of struggle, and enhance our fighting capabilities. This entails being both courageous in struggle and confrontation, as well as adaptive and flexible in our approach. We must take the initiative, act proactively, and continue to secure new victories in the cause of socialist modernization.

Always stand on the right side of history and actively promote the building of human community with a shared future

Amid the momentous changes of a kind unseen for a century in the world and during a period of upheaval and transformation, China's fundamental stance is to always stand on the right side of history. This involves adhering to the logic of historical progress and striving for prosperity, peace, and brightness for the majority of people worldwide. General Secretary Xi Jinping pointed out: "Protectionism is on the rise in today's world, but we need to stand on the right side of history. We should uphold multilateralism and democracy in international relations, pursue development in a spirit of open and win-win cooperation, strive to make economic globalization open, inclusive, balanced and beneficial to all, and foster an open world economy."[1] We must consistently treat the correct handling of the relationship between China and the world as a major issue, promote positive interactions between China's development and world development, better unify domestic development with opening up to the outside world, connect China's development with global development, and align the interests of the Chinese people with those of people worldwide. We should advocate for a fairer, more efficient global governance system. Adhering to the path of peaceful development, regardless of the challenges humanity faces or changes in the world situation, China will steadfastly remain a builder of world peace, a contributor to global development, and a defender of international order. We will unswervingly promote the establishment of a new model of international relations and the building of human community with a shared future, striving for the rejuvenation of the Chinese nation and contributing more to world peace and development.

The world is currently experiencing unprecedented changes, but time and momentum are on our side. This is the source of our confidence and determination. At the same time, we must clearly recognize that although our country's development remains in an important period of strategic opportunity both now and in the foreseeable future, both opportunities and challenges have evolved. The magnitude of opportunities and challenges is unprecedented, and overall, opportunities outweigh challenges. We must continue to be humble and cautious, work hard, mobilize all positive factors, unite all forces that can be united, and fully focus on our tasks, persistently achieving our established goals.

General Secretary Xi Jinping clearly demands: "On the journey ahead, we must demonstrate stronger vigilance and always be prepared for potential danger, even in times of calm. We must adopt a holistic approach

---

1   Xi Jinping, *On Grasping the New Development Stage, Implementing the New Development Philosophy, and Building a New Development Dynamic*, Beijing: Central Party Literature Publishing House, 2021, p. 353.

to national security that balances development and security imperatives, and implement the national rejuvenation strategy within a wider context of the once-in-a-century changes taking place in the world. We need to acquire a full understanding of the new features and requirements arising from the change to the principal contradiction in Chinese society and the new issues and challenges stemming from a complicated international environment. We must be both brave and adept in carrying out our struggle, forging new paths and building new bridges wherever necessary to take us past all risks and challenges."[1]

In this New Era, the rejuvenation of the Chinese nation has entered an irreversible historical process, but it will not be achieved easily or with mere fanfare. At this critical juncture, there can be no pause, hesitation, or observation from the sidelines. We must press ahead with determination and continue to strive. With the strong leadership of the CPC, the effective guidance of Xi Jinping Thought on Socialism with Chinese Characteristics for a New Era, and the united efforts of the Chinese people, the goal of the rejuvenation of the Chinese nation is bound to be achieved.

---

1   Xi Jinping, *Speech at a Ceremony Marking the Centenary of the Communist Party of China,* Beijing: People's Publishing House, 2021, pp. 17–18.

Part Two

The New Era of China and the "Great Historical Epoch"

To keep pace with, shape, and lead the times, and to continuously advance the progress of human society, it is essential to gain a comprehensive understanding of the epoch, recognize its fundamental nature and characteristics, and identify its key trends of development. General Secretary Xi Jinping put forward a significant judgment with a broad historical perspective and profound historical insight:

"Despite the tremendous differences between now and the days of Karl Marx, world socialism's 500 years of history shows that we are still where Marxism has said we should be."[1]

This insightful discourse, with its deep historical vision, precise grasp of historical development dynamics, and accurate understanding of the essence and characteristics of the epoch, provides significant guidance for us to scientifically comprehend the fundamental nature and main characteristics of the current historical epoch. It helps us correctly grasp the laws and development trends of the development human society, establish a proper view of the times, the world, and history, deeply understand the

---

1   Xi Jinping, *The Governance of China*, Beijing: Foreign Languages Press, 2017, vol. II, p. 68.

origins and future direction of socialism with Chinese characteristics within the larger historical epoch, and better comprehend the historical and global significance of the New Era of socialism with Chinese characteristics. This allows us to better uphold and develop socialism with Chinese characteristics in the New Era and continue adapting Marxism to the Chinese context and the needs of our times.

I. The Basic Connotation and Criteria for the Great Historical Epoch

General Secretary Xi Jinping's significant judgment is clear and explicit: "We are still where Marxism has said we should be." What exactly does it mean to say, "we are still where Marxism said we should be"? What is the standard for dividing historical epochs? To answer these questions, we must first look at the development of Marxism and clarify this major issue based on the fundamental thoughts and views of authors of Marxist classics regarding historical epochs.

1. We are still where Marxism has said we should be

The epoch discussed by authors of Marxist classics is primarily a social-historical category from the perspective of historical materialism. Marx, Engels, and Lenin used the concept of "epoch" in different ways and from various angles. For instance, in the works of Marx and Engels, we find expressions such as "historical epoch," "revolutionary epoch," "social epoch," "cultural epoch," "primitive epoch," "prehistoric epoch," "ancient Greek and Roman epoch," "medieval epoch," "feudal epoch," and "bourgeois epoch." In Lenin's works, terms like "patriarchal system epoch," "bourgeois democratic parliamentary epoch," "epoch of proletarian dictatorship," "epoch of proletarian political rule," and "epoch of imperialist wars" are used.

Overall, the use of the term "epoch" in these contexts sometimes refers to a clearly marked historical period or stage, while at other times it refers to a social-historical period defined by distinct production relationships and economic-social forms, with clear class characteristics and modes of governance. The phrase "where Marxism said we would be" primarily refers to the latter. Thus, the core content of the Marxist view of epochs should include the following two aspects:

1) Clear Production Relations and Economic-Social Form

The economy is the deepest foundation of any epoch, with the level of development of productive forces being the most fundamental and decisive factor. Marx pointed out:

"It is not the articles made, but how they are made, and by what instruments, that enables us to distinguish different economic epochs. Instruments of labor not only supply a standard of the degree of development to which human labor has attained, but they are also indicators of the social conditions under which that labor is carried on."[1]

It is clear that Marx approached the understanding of historical epochs primarily from the perspective of "economic epochs" and from the standpoint of the use of means of labor, i.e., the level of development of productive forces. Marx also noted that:

"Social relations are closely bound up with productive forces. In acquiring new productive forces men change their mode of production; and in changing their mode of production, in changing the way of earning their living, they change all their social relations."[2]

Engels further emphasized:

"[E]conomic production, and the structure of society of every

---

1   https://www.marxists.org/archive/marx/works/1867-c1/ch07.htm.
2   https://www.marxists.org/archive/marx/works/subject/hist-mat/pov-phil/ch02.htm.

historical epoch necessarily arising therefrom, constitute the foundation for the political and intellectual history of that epoch."[1]

It is evident that both Marx and Engels fundamentally understood epochs through the lens of productive forces and production relations, and the transformations in production methods that result from their interaction. This is the most essential content of the Marxist view of epochs and serves as the fundamental basis for understanding historical epochs. By deeply examining and analyzing the capitalist mode of production, Marx developed the theory of surplus value, revealing the secret of capitalist exploitation. He uncovered the fundamental contradiction of capitalism: the socialization of production versus the private capitalist ownership of the means of production. Marx delved into the irreconcilable and antagonistic nature of this contradiction, which permeates the entirety of capitalism, and concluded that:

"Its [The bourgeoisie's] fall and the victory of the proletariat are equally inevitable."[2]

At the same time, he made it clear that:

"No social order ever perishes before all the productive forces for which there is room in it have developed; and new, higher relations of production never appear before the material conditions of their existence have matured in the womb of the old society itself."[3]

These two statements form the theoretical basis for Marx's concept of the great historical epoch, outlining the transition from capitalism to socialism.

2) A Social-Historical Period Defined by Class Struggle and Systems of Rule

Marx and Engels believed that the emergence of classes and class

1 https://www.marxists.org/archive/marx/works/1848/communist-manifesto/preface.htm.
2 https://www.marxists.org/archive/marx/works/1848/communist-manifesto/ch01.htm.
3 https://www.marxists.org/archive/marx/works/1859/critique-pol-economy/preface-abs.htm.

struggle was not the result of human invention, nor could it be altered by the subjective will of individuals. Rather, it was an objective phenomenon that came into being as human society reached a certain stage of development, and it runs through the entire process of class society. As social economies advanced and modes of production and exchange evolved, human society inevitably divided into different classes, with class conflicts centered around economic interests. As Marx and Engels famously stated:

"The history of all hitherto existing society is the history of class struggles... In the earlier epochs of history, we find almost everywhere a complicated arrangement of society into various orders, a manifold gradation of social rank."[1]

Since the dissolution of primitive communal ownership, human history has, in a certain sense, remained a history of class struggles, an epoch of class rule, where different classes strive to protect their interests. To distort or deny the existence of class and class struggle is to misunderstand the essence of human society and its developmental laws, making it impossible to accurately grasp the nature of the times or to drive social progress.

The development of production methods continuously gives rise to different classes that own the means of production, leading to various forms of class struggle and thus different periods of class rule. From this perspective, certain historical periods can be named after their ruling classes. For example, the feudal period can be called the epoch of the landlord class, and the capitalist epoch can be seen as the epoch of the bourgeoisie.

Marx and Engels pointed out that:

"Our epoch, the epoch of the bourgeoisie, possesses, however, this distinct feature: it has simplified class antagonisms. Society as a whole is

1   https://www.marxists.org/archive/marx/works/1848/communist-manifesto/ch01.htm.

more and more splitting up into two great hostile camps, into two great classes directly facing each other—Bourgeoisie and Proletariat."[1]

Marx and Engels used the transformation of modes of production and systems of class rule as the primary criteria for understanding historical periods. This approach often allows for social forms and historical epochs to be viewed as intertwined. Such an "epoch" is comprehensive and intrinsic, reflecting the overall trends and laws of social development—a "great historical epoch," as Lenin termed it.

Lenin upheld and expanded upon this view of epochs. He saw changes in modes of production, alongside shifts in class relations and production relations, as the foundation for defining an epoch. To Lenin, an epoch is not merely a local or national phenomenon but rather a reflection of the broader condition of human society as a whole.

Even though "in each of them [important historical epochs] there are and will always be individual and partial movements, now forward now backward; there are and will always be various deviations from the average type and mean tempo of the movement,"[2] the overall direction, key characteristics, and movement of an epoch are fundamentally determined. To accurately identify the nature of an epoch, one must view it from the perspective of the total development of social history and the global landscape.

The essence of an epoch is embodied in the interconnectedness of history and the broader global framework, and its defining characteristics are the necessary expressions of this interconnectedness. Although Marx, Engels, and Lenin lived in different historical periods, and the specific traits of their times were sharply contrasting, they all existed within the overarching "great historical epoch" of capitalism. Thus, Lenin, in

---

1   *Ibid.*
2   https://www.marxists.org/archive/lenin/works/1915/mar/x01.htm.

his understanding of the times, adhered to the fundamental trajectory, development trend, general direction, and key features of this "great historical epoch." This adherence to the larger historical framework laid the foundation for Lenin's comprehensive analysis of the imperialist epoch, further enriching and advancing the Marxist view of historical epochs.

2. The scientific basis for dividing historical epochs

The scientific division of historical epochs is one of Marxism's key methods for revealing the laws governing the development of human society. It is essential for thoroughly understanding, navigating, and interpreting the times and serves as the foundation for formulating strategies, lines, principles, and policies. In Marxist theory, the division of historical epochs is a fundamental and crucial question. This process is not merely a matter of segmenting time; it requires a thorough analysis to identify the core social characteristics of distinct historical periods with clear features. This involves looking beyond the "natural time" visible on the surface and delving into the deeper "historical time," to construct a temporal framework that reflects the essential nature, main contradictions, and developmental trends of a given historical period.

Different criteria for dividing epochs lead to different understandings of history. For instance, based on technological advancements, history can be divided into the Stone Age, Bronze Age, Iron Age, Steam Age, Electrical Age, and Internet Age. From the perspective of industrial development, history may be divided into the Agricultural Age, Industrial Age, Post-Industrial Age, and Information Age. Economically, one could speak of the epoch of the natural economy, the commodity economy, and the product economy. Politically, there are divisions such as the Autocratic epoch and the Democratic epoch. In terms of civilization, history can be divided into the Age of Savagery, the Age of Barbarism, and the Age of

Civilization. Some of these criteria are singular, while others are composite; some focus on natural attributes, while others emphasize social attributes. Certain classifications are based on specific domains of society, while others consider society's broader development.

Marxist theory divides historical epochs based on historical materialism. Marx and Engels, from a macro-historical perspective, revealed the laws of the development of human society by examining the dialectical relationship between productive forces and relations of production, between the economic base and superstructure. This method, which identifies the essence, main contradictions, and core characteristics of different epochs, serves as the fundamental standard for dividing historical epochs.

Marx's classic exposition of this concept appears in the "Preface to *A Contribution to the Critique of Political Economy*" (1859), where he writes:

"At a certain stage of development, the material productive forces of society come into conflict with the existing relations of production or— this merely expresses the same thing in legal terms – with the property relations within the framework of which they have operated hitherto. From forms of development of the productive forces these relations turn into their fetters. Then begins an era of social revolution. The changes in the economic foundation lead sooner or later to the transformation of the whole immense superstructure."[1]

Marx further explains:

"In broad outline, the Asiatic, ancient, feudal and modern bourgeois modes of production may be designated as epochs marking progress in the economic development of society."[2]

In this way, Marx applied historical materialism to outline the

---

1 https://www.marxists.org/archive/marx/works/1859/critique-pol-economy/preface.htm.
2 *Ibid.*

fundamental criteria for dividing historical epochs. Based on this analysis, he identified four major stages of the development of human society: primitive society, slave society, feudal society, and capitalist society. Due to the contradictions inherent in capitalism, Marx predicted that it would eventually collapse as the "last antagonistic form of the social production process," leading him to assert:

"With this social formation therefore, the prehistory of human society comes to a close."[1]

Marx's analysis also includes the historical trajectory of transitioning from capitalist society to socialist and communist societies, thereby introducing a fifth stage of human development: communist society. In this framework, the criteria for dividing historical epochs coincide with those used to differentiate social formations.

When distinguishing between different historical epochs, Marx emphasized the unity between the level of productive forces, production relations, and social relations, with particular focus on production and social relations. In *The Poverty of Philosophy*, Marx stated:

"Social relations are closely bound up with productive forces. In acquiring new productive forces men change their mode of production; and in changing their mode of production, in changing the way of earning their living, they change all their social relations. The hand-mill gives you society with the feudal lord; the steam-mill society with the industrial capitalist."[2]

This underscores that Marxism's concept of an "epoch" is not limited to economic, technological, or cultural dimensions, but is fundamentally a political, social, and historical category.

Building on Marx's method of historical materialism and class analysis,

---

1   https://www.marxists.org/subject/economy/authors/eldred-roth/ap-habermas.htm.
2   https://www.marxists.org/archive/marx/works/subject/hist-mat/pov-phil/ch02.htm.

Lenin refined the criteria for dividing historical epochs by emphasizing the role of class struggle. He argued:

"We cannot know how rapidly and how successfully the various historical movements in a given epoch will develop, but we can and do know *which class* stands at the hub of one epoch or another, determining its main content, the main direction of its development, the main characteristics of the historical situation in that epoch, etc."[1]

In this view, the advanced class of a particular epoch—one aligned with the epoch's development and driving societal progress—is the decisive force shaping the epoch's characteristics, its dominant features, and trajectory. Lenin's focus on class thus adds a concrete dimension to Marx's emphasis on productive forces and production relations, providing a more detailed application of this standard in class-based societies.

Lenin not only provided a profound explanation of the nature of different epochs and the criteria for distinguishing them, but he also, based on the specific conditions of capitalist development and proletarian revolutionary struggle of his time, conducted a scientific analysis of the key contradictions, developmental trends, and the future prospects for socialist revolution within the capitalist epoch. Using Marxist theory, Lenin systematically identified the defining characteristics of the epoch, dividing capitalism's development into three historical stages:

1. The first stage (1789–1871), spanning from the French Revolution to the Franco-Prussian War, marked the rise and complete triumph of the bourgeoisie, representing the ascendant phase of the capitalist class.

2. The second stage (1871–1914), from the Franco-Prussian War to the outbreak of World War I, was the period during which the bourgeoisie consolidated its dominance but began its decline, while new class forces gradually gathered strength.

---

1   https://www.marxists.org/archive/lenin/works/1915/mar/x01.htm.

3. The third stage (from 1914 onward) ushered in the age of imperialism, a period characterized by conflicts and instability driven by imperialist powers.

Lenin famously noted, "We are undoubtedly living at the juncture of two epochs."[1] At this new " juncture of two epochs," new social and class dynamics were emerging. "From a rising and progressive class the bourgeoisie has turned into a declining, decadent, and reactionary class. It is quite another class that is now on the upgrade on a broad historical scale."[2]

In *Imperialism, the Highest Stage of Capitalism*, Lenin further analyzed the intensification of contradictions of monopoly capitalism, identifying it as "the most powerful driving force of the transitional period of history, which began from the time of the final victory of world finance capital."[3] It was here that Lenin introduced the concept of the "transitional period of history."

After the October Revolution of 1917, Lenin identified the revolution as a defining moment, describing it as "the beginning of a world-wide change of two eras in world history—the era of the bourgeoisie and the era of socialism, the era of capitalist parliamentarism and the era of the Soviet state institutions of the proletariat."[4] This marked one of the earliest expressions of what later Marxist literature would describe as "the epoch of transition from capitalism to socialism."

Following Lenin's analysis, the international communist movement largely adhered to his understanding of the epochs. In *The Foundations of Leninism*, Stalin described the contemporary epoch as one of imperialism and proletarian revolution. The 1957 Moscow Declaration, passed during

---

1   *Ibid.*
2   *Ibid.*
3   https://www.marxists.org/archive/lenin/works/1916/imp-hsc/ch10.htm.
4   https://www.marxists.org/archive/lenin/works/1919/mar/28.htm.

the International Meeting of Communist and Workers Parties from 12 socialist countries, stated that the main content of the epoch was "the transition from capitalism to socialism initiated by the Russian October Revolution." This formulation gained widespread acceptance among communist parties worldwide, becoming the most widely recognized interpretation of the current epoch, grounded in historical reality.

Xi Jinping, when referring to "where Marxism has said we should be," draws on Marxist historical materialism, which is based on the dialectical relationship between the forces of production and relations of production, and between the economic base and the superstructure. His analysis, grounded in the contradictions of capitalism and the dynamics of class struggle, points to the epoch of transition from capitalism to communism—the "great historical epoch" as defined by Lenin, beginning with the October Revolution and representing "the historical epoch of transition from capitalism to socialism." Despite the vast and profound changes over the course of 500 years of global socialism and 170 years of the international communist movement, the essential nature of the epoch and the trajectory of the development of human society remain unchanged. We are still where Marxism has said we should be.

II. Upholding the Dialectical Unity of the Nature and Characteristics of the Epoch

Maintaining the unity between the fundamental nature of the epoch and its defining characteristics (or themes) holds significant practical and methodological value for understanding and interpreting the times both comprehensively and scientifically.

1. The unity between the "great historical epoch" and the "smaller epochs"

Lenin's major contribution to the Marxist theory of historical epochs was not limited to preserving Marx's method of analyzing the "great historical epoch." His true innovation lay in his ability to combine this method with a scientific understanding of the broader direction and trends of the "great epoch" of capitalism, while also analyzing the specific historical conditions and features of his time. Lenin's analysis illuminated the transition from free-market capitalism to monopoly capitalism (also known as "imperialism"), the coexistence of imperialist rule and proletarian revolution, the parallel development of capitalist and socialist societies, and the simultaneous processes of socialist revolution and socialist construction. By addressing these complex, transitional phenomena, Lenin creatively introduced a method that integrated the analysis of both the "great epoch" and the "smaller epochs."

In his essay "Under a False Flag," Lenin first applied Marxism's analytical method of the "great historical epoch" to define the transitions between different periods of history. He emphasized that "the historic events that are unfolding before our eyes can be understood only if we analyze, in the first place, the objective conditions of the transition from one epoch to the other."[1] He believed that major historical events, such as the proletariat overthrowing bourgeois rule and socialism replacing capitalism, can only be understood by examining the fundamental changes in the objective conditions of an epoch. The transformation of a "great historical epoch" is a broad, macro-level perspective on the development of human society.

This method aligns with Marxism's theory of social evolution and serves as a foundational, comprehensive, and directional approach to analyzing historical periods, providing valuable guidance on large-scale societal changes. However, Lenin also recognized that the transformation of

---

1   https://www.marxists.org/archive/lenin/works/1915/mar/x01.htm.

a "great historical epoch" is a complex, dynamic, and evolving process. This process naturally gives rise to many specific, unique situations that require careful, detailed analysis. It is necessary to examine the concrete conditions of each stage of development and each country to formulate the correct strategies and policies.

Lenin further stressed, "Only on that basis, i.e., by taking into account, in the first place, the fundamental distinctive features of the various "epochs" (and not single episodes in the history of individual countries), can we correctly evolve our tactics; only a knowledge of the basic features of a given epoch can serve as the foundation for an understanding of the specific features of one country or another."[1] Here, Lenin's reference to "various epochs" and "given epoch" essentially points to "smaller epochs," which evolve within the broader "great historical epoch." For example, Lenin stated, "Imperialism, or the domination of finance capital, is that highest stage of capitalism."[2] Moreover, he argued that the imperialist epoch was also the epoch of proletarian revolution, declaring: "Imperialism is the eve of the social revolution of the proletariat."[3]

Lenin's analysis of the shift from the "War Communism" policy to the "New Economic Policy" after the October Revolution demonstrates the application of Marxism's "great historical epoch" and "smaller epoch" analytical methods. By combining these two approaches, Lenin was able to contextualize human society's broader development within specific historical circumstances, thus achieving a dialectical unity between the "great historical epoch" and the "smaller epochs." This comprehensive and detailed analysis enabled Lenin to uncover the underlying patterns of bourgeois rule, make accurate judgments about Russia's specific historical context, and develop strategies that helped guide the success of the Russian

---

1   *Ibid.*
2   https://www.marxists.org/archive/lenin/works/1916/imp-hsc/ch03.htm.
3   https://www.marxists.org/archive/lenin/works/1916/imp-hsc/pref02.htm.

socialist revolution and its subsequent development.

From this, we can see that when Marxism refers to an "epoch," it is discussing a "great epoch." Yet, each "great epoch" noted by Marxist theorists is not static. These epochs may exhibit different stages of development due to qualitative or phase-specific changes. As a result, a historical epoch can be subdivided into several "smaller epochs," each defined by the dominant characteristics and key issues of its respective developmental stage. Today, we remain in the "great epoch" of transition from capitalism to socialism—a period characterized by its distinctive production relations and socioeconomic structures, as well as its clear class nature and forms of governance. This "great epoch" is shaped by fundamental social contradictions that reflect its essence.

However, within this "great epoch," different stages of development feature distinct primary contradictions, creating a series of interconnected "smaller epochs" that reflect varying themes and characteristics. This shows that fundamental social contradictions define the "great epoch," while the primary contradictions of societal development define the "smaller epochs." It is essential not to confuse or oppose these two concepts but to recognize both their differences and their interconnections. By understanding the dialectical unity between the "great historical epoch" and the "smaller epochs," we can grasp both the overarching trends of the "great epoch" and the specific features of the current stage. In doing so, we can better guide and respond to the demands of our time.

Therefore, a comprehensive understanding of the present epoch requires recognizing the dialectical unity of its fundamental essence and defining characteristics.

2. The relationship between the essence and characteristics of an epoch

The essence of an epoch refers to its fundamental nature, which is rooted in the dominant mode of production, the balance of class forces, and the nature of social institutions. To determine the nature of a historical period, one must examine the contradictions between material conditions and the mode of production. As Marx stated, "Just as one does not judge an individual by what he thinks about himself, so one cannot judge such a period of transformation by its consciousness, but, on the contrary, this consciousness must be explained from the contradictions of material life, from the conflict existing between the social forces of production and the relations of production."[1] Engels echoed this sentiment in the preface to the English edition of *The Communist Manifesto*: "[I]n every historical epoch, the prevailing mode of economic production and exchange, and the social organization necessarily following from it, form the basis upon which is built up, and from which alone can be explained the political and intellectual history of that epoch."[2] In Marxist theory, the term "great historical epoch" refers to the essential and fundamental nature of a specific period in history. At this most fundamental level—through the lens of society's historical development—we derive broad historical concepts like the "capitalist epoch" and the "socialist epoch." From this perspective, it is also concluded that today's epoch remains, in essence, a historical period transitioning from capitalism to socialism.

The characteristics of an epoch, on the other hand, refer to the distinctive realities and key traits that emerge during different stages of development within such a "great historical epoch." These characteristics are reflected across political, economic, cultural, and social dimensions, highlighting the fundamental essence of the time. They encompass such factors as the epoch's central theme, its primary contradictions, major issues, class relations, international relations, global power structures,

---

1 https://www.marxists.org/archive/marx/works/1859/critique-pol-economy/preface.htm.
2 https://www.marxists.org/archive/marx/works/1848/communist-manifesto/preface.htm.

and the developmental stages of different social systems, along with their interrelations. For example, within the capitalist epoch, there have been distinct phases—free-market capitalism, monopoly capitalism, state monopoly capitalism, and finally, international financial monopoly capitalism. Each phase has been marked by its own set of dominant issues and contradictions. However, it is crucial to understand that these main contradictions and issues do not encompass all the problems of the time. One cannot simply equate the characteristics or themes of an epoch with the contradictions and issues it faces. Contradictions are present everywhere and at all times, both major and minor. Their nature, influence, and role in the course of an epoch's development vary significantly.

Therefore, while it is vital to grasp the primary contradictions and issues of an epoch, this does not mean secondary ones should be overlooked. Instead, we must both major and minor problems and both major and minor aspects of a problem, while focusing on major issues and major aspects of a problem. To fully comprehend the theme of an epoch, it is necessary to integrate it with an understanding of its broader issues.

There is a clear distinction—and an even stronger connection—between the essence and characteristics of an epoch. These are two dialectically unified aspects of the same historical period. The essence of an epoch is fundamental and decisive, guiding the overall direction, expression, and extent of its defining characteristics. To accurately understand the characteristics of an epoch, one must base this understanding on its essence. Only from this vantage point can we rise to the historical and contemporary heights needed to look to the future, exploring the distinctive features, laws, and trends of an epoch within its vast, long-term historical context.

The characteristics of an epoch represent the concrete expression of its essence during different historical stages, especially in how the epoch's primary tasks, main contradictions, and historical missions manifest. While maintaining clarity about an epoch's essence, we must also carefully analyze its characteristics, unifying short-term objectives with long-term goals, specific problems with broader challenges, and occasional phenomena with inevitable trends. In doing so, we gain a deeper understanding of the past, maintain a firm stance in the present, and move forward with clear strategic insight. This approach enables us to address the specific challenges of the epoch and guide its development in the right direction.

The essence and characteristics of an epoch are therefore inseparable and intertwined. Only by organically combining these two aspects can we form a scientific and accurate understanding of the times, grasp the trajectory and laws of historical development, and respond appropriately to the epoch's challenges. This in turn allows us to devise policies and strategies that align with the trends of our time.

Conversely, separating the essence of an epoch from its characteristics leads to errors in understanding history, fostering either dogmatism or formalism. Focusing solely on particular changes or localized features without recognizing the broader, inevitable patterns that reflect the epoch's essence and underlying laws can result in confusion and misdirection. We may be deceived by superficial appearances, become complacent with the status quo, or lose both the motivation and direction to continue progressing. Without a clear understanding of historical trends, we risk making fundamental errors that could derail human society's progress. Conversely, rigidly adhering to past interpretations of an epoch's essence without considering evolving realities and contradictions can result in outdated thinking. When theory becomes disconnected from present-day practice, we fail to address the epoch's primary contradictions and cannot provide solutions to the new challenges of our time.

It is therefore essential to adopt a pragmatic and forward-looking approach in understanding the pulse of our epoch. By doing so, we align ourselves with the tide of progress, responding to the demands of the times. Thus, the organic unity of an epoch's essence and characteristics is vital to accurately understanding the present, guiding future development, and formulating sound policies and strategies.

In the historical period of transition from capitalism to socialism, two major social systems have long coexisted and competed, each phase exhibiting distinct characteristics and themes. Lenin identified the late 19th and early 20th centuries as the "epoch of proletarian revolution," and up until the 1970s, the dominant theme of the time remained "war and revolution." After the 1980s, however, Deng Xiaoping introduced the notion that the theme of the epoch had shifted to "peace and development." Thus, while the fundamental essence of our epoch has not changed—it remains, as Marxism defines, the epoch of transition from capitalism to socialism—the theme has evolved, moving from war and revolution to peace and development. In other words, while war and revolution, and peace and development, are distinct stages in this historical process, they both reflect the same underlying transition.

In today's world, within the dynamic between war and revolution and peace and development, peace and development have become the primary aspect. Among the various social contradictions of our time, peace and development stand out as the main contradiction, playing a dominant role in guiding the progression of our epoch. However, this does not imply that war and revolution have disappeared. They remain significant issues, and we cannot overlook their presence or impact as we assess the characteristics of this epoch. Likewise, during periods when war and revolution were at the forefront, the importance of peace and development was never entirely absent. To properly understand the dialectical relationship between these opposing forces is essential for a scientific grasp of the epoch. Therefore, while recognizing that we are still in the transition from capitalism to socialism, our ability to correctly understand the epoch's characteristics is crucial for the future of socialism and the progress of human society.

At the turn of the 20th century, Lenin, observing the new developments in capitalism, proposed that imperialism represented the highest stage of capitalism—a monopoly stage. He argued that capitalism had entered the age of imperialism, and identified war and revolution as the defining themes of the time. This profound insight guided communist parties worldwide, enabling them to lead socialist revolutions and support national liberation movements in colonial and semi-colonial countries, which resulted in major victories. After Lenin's death, Stalin carried forward Lenin's views, stating: "Leninism is Marxism of the era of imperialism and the proletarian revolution. To be more exact, Leninism is the theory and tactics of the proletarian revolution in general, the theory and tactics of the dictatorship of the proletariat in particular."[1] He further clarified: "[W]e are now living in an epoch of wars and revolutions."[2] Stalin's view of the epoch's defining features remained consistent with Lenin's, and it played a pivotal role in helping proletarian parties across the world devise correct lines, policies, and strategies. These insights propelled global proletarian revolutions and national liberation movements, leading to the establishment of socialist states and independent nations, fundamentally altering the global political landscape by dismantling the imperialist-colonial order. This shift laid the foundation for the modern epoch, in which the theme of peace and development took center stage. The Chinese Communists inherited and developed these insights, significantly influencing China's revolution, development, and reform efforts.

---

1 https://www.marxists.org/reference/archive/stalin/works/1926/01/25.htm.
2 https://www.marxists.org/reference/archive/stalin/works/1930/aug/27.htm.

3. The CPC's scientific understanding of the essence and characteristics of the epoch

Since its inception, the CPC has maintained a clear understanding of the essence of this epoch as a period of transition from capitalism to socialism. However, the Party's understanding of the specific characteristics of each phase has involved both successes and lessons learned.

Mao Zedong, in light of both China's and the world's circumstances, carried forward and developed Lenin's critical judgment regarding the themes of revolution and war during this historical period. Beginning in the 1870s, capitalism gradually transitioned from free competition to monopoly capitalism, and the world entered the age of imperialism. By this time, the major capitalist powers had already divided the world amongst themselves, and economically backward nations became colonies, semi-colonies, or dependent states. China, too, following the Opium Wars, was reduced to a semi-colonial, semi-feudal society. Despite the efforts of many dedicated patriots to explore ways to save the nation and achieve the rejuvenation of the Chinese nation, all attempts ultimately failed. Historical practice proved the incompetence of the feudal land-owning class, the limitations of the peasant class, the weakness and compromise of the bourgeoisie, and the dependence and corruption of the big bourgeoisie and bureaucratic capitalists. These factors revealed that, in the age of imperialism, the paths of reform, restoration of the monarchy, and adopting Western capitalist models were not viable for China in its semi-colonial, semi-feudal state.

At a time when the Chinese people were lost in confusion and uncertainty, the salvoes of the October Revolution brought us Marxism-Leninism. It was then that the Chinese began to think of using Marxism-Leninism to address the pressing issues of the times, seeking to resolve China's predicament. They came to realize that mere cooperation and reform could neither transform China nor the world. It was only through revolution, through the armed seizure of power, that the "three great mountains" of feudalism, imperialism and bureaucrat-capitalism could be overthrown, leading to national independence and rejuvenation.

In 1937, Mao Zedong, in his "On Contradiction," embraced Stalin's continuation of Lenin's view of the epoch, further clarifying that "Leninism is the Marxism of the era of imperialism and proletarian revolution." He pointed out that during the imperialist period, the contradiction between the proletariat and bourgeoisie "became intensified, the contradiction between monopoly and non-monopoly capital emerged, the contradiction between the colonial powers and the colonies became intensified, the contradiction among the capitalist countries resulting from their uneven development manifested itself with particular sharpness.... Leninism is the Marxism of the era of imperialism and proletarian revolution precisely because Lenin and Stalin have correctly explained these contradictions and correctly formulated the theory and tactics of the proletarian revolution for their resolution."[1]

In 1939, in the "Outline of the Second Imperialist War," Mao Zedong wrote: "Capitalist economies have reached their limit; an epoch of great change and revolution has arrived. The present age is a new epoch of war and revolution... and we are living in this epoch."[2] He also emphasized that the people's liberation movement and national liberation struggles formed the "frontlines of revolution" and the "camp of revolution,"[3] further incorporating the national liberation movements in colonial and semi-colonial countries into the broader scope of the proletarian revolution—a significant contribution by Mao to Lenin's theme of war and revolution.

1   Mao Zedong, *Selected Works of Mao Tse-tung,* Beijing: Foreign Languages Press, 1967, vol. I, p. 325.
2   *Mao Zedong's Military Writings,* Beijing: People's Publishing House, 1993, p. 478.
3   Peking University Law Department (eds.), *Selected Statements by Mao Zedong on International Issues,* Beijing: World Affairs Press, 1959, p. 80.

Thus, under the leadership of Mao Zedong, the CPC consistently upheld the dialectical unity between the essence of the epoch and its characteristics. They combined the theme of war and revolution with the essence of the transition from capitalism to socialism. By integrating Marxism-Leninism with the practical realities of China's revolution and war, they achieved the great victories of the new-democratic revolution and the socialist revolution, establishing a socialist state and realizing the most profound and transformative social changes in China's history.

Following the establishment of the People's Republic of China, some Western capitalist countries and domestic reactionary forces attempted to overthrow the new government. After World War II, many newly established socialist and developing countries also faced instability. First, the postwar world saw the emergence of two opposing blocs: the Western capitalist camp led by the United States and the socialist camp led by the Soviet Union. The Cold War between these two blocs was intense, and China, still in its infancy as a new nation, had to confront Western blockades, the Korean War, the Vietnam War, the Sino-Soviet Zhenbao Island conflict, the Soviet "nuclear threat," the Sino-Indian border dispute, and other severe international conflicts. Second, the Kuomintang, which had retreated to Taiwan, continued to rely on imperialist forces, attempting to counterattack the mainland, posing a threat to the achievements of the socialist revolution.

Thus, up until the 1970s, the CPC's assessment that the epoch was still characterized by war and revolution was largely accurate. During this period, even amidst the backdrop of war and revolution, the Party never abandoned its pursuit of peace and development. China established an independent and relatively complete industrial and national economic system, independently developed its nuclear bombs, missiles and the artificial earth satellite, proposed the Five Principles of Peaceful

Coexistence, regained its legitimate seat at the United Nations, established diplomatic relations with over 140 countries, and improved its relations with Western nations such as the United States. These achievements clearly demonstrate that, during this complex period of both domestic and international challenges, the CPC not only upheld the theme of war and revolution but also skillfully navigated the dialectical relationship between war, revolution, peace, and development.

Since the late 1960s and early 1970s, the prolonged Cold War between the U.S. and the Soviet Union illustrated that neither side could decisively overpower the other through war and revolution. This stalemate led to significant reorganization and polarization within both camps, resulting in signs of de-escalation in their confrontations and rapid global economic growth, heralding a new epoch defined by peace and development. However, during this period, our Party misjudged the dynamics of domestic class struggle and failed to grasp the characteristics of the times, which hindered our ability to effectively implement the major judgments made at the Eighth National Party Congress regarding primary social contradictions. This misalignment exacerbated class struggles and resulted in a policy framework "taking class struggle as the key link," leading to serious repercussions for both the Party and the people and offering profound lessons for our understanding of the epoch's themes.

Since the onset of reform and opening up, our Party has accurately identified the essence of the times and successfully recognized and transitioned to the new thematic focus of the epoch, laying the ideological and theoretical foundation for formulating reform policies. Deng Xiaoping's insights into the essence of the epoch exemplify the application of Marxist theory to understand global trends and address Chinese issues. In the 1980s, Deng clearly articulated that "peace and development are the two outstanding issues in the world today," fostering a consensus within the Party on the concept of "contemporary themes" and correctly distinguishing between the essence of the epoch and its thematic concerns. This organic combination has enabled China, on its path of reform and socialist modernization, to maintain its socialist direction while aligning with the currents of development.

Deng first introduced the concept of "issues of the times" ("themes of the times") during a meeting with the delegation from the Japanese Chamber of Commerce and Industry on March 4, 1985, stating, "[T]he two really great issues confronting the world today, issues of global strategic significance, are: first, peace, and second, economic development. The first involves East-West relations, while the second involves North-South relations. In short, countries in the East, West, North and South are all involved."[1] His statements were echoed at the 13th National Party Congress in 1987, where peace and development were reiterated as "the two outstanding issues of the world today," and were officially designated as "the theme of our times" at the 14th Congress in 1992. This theme has been consistently emphasized in subsequent Party congresses, reaffirming a longstanding consensus. The political report of the 19th National Congress reiterated this theme, stating, "The world is undergoing major developments, transformation, and adjustment, but peace and development remain the call of our day."[2]

The integration of the essence and characteristics of our era (the thematic focus of our times) is of great practical significance for the successful advancement of socialism with Chinese characteristics along the right path. Embracing the themes of peace and development is crucial for our country to seize strategic and historical opportunities for accelerated growth. However, it is essential to recognize that the essence of our

---

1 Deng Xiaoping, *Selected Works of Deng Xiaoping*, Foreign Languages Press, Beijing, 1994, vol. III, p. 111,
2 *Documents of the 19th CPC National Congress*, Beijing: People's Publishing House, 2017, p. 47.

era remains unchanged; we are still where Marxism has said we should be—an epoch marked by the transition from capitalism to socialism. Acknowledging this allows us to maintain our firm ideals and confidence in the inevitable triumph of socialism. While affirming the essence of our times and understanding the inevitable historical trends, we must also align ourselves with contemporary developments, heed the era's voice, and address its emerging challenges. The progression of our era knows no bounds; we must not only keep pace but also take the lead. As General Secretary Xi Jinping aptly stated, "We should advance in accordance with the logic of historical progress and develop in line with the trends of our time."[1]

In summary, since the reform and opening up, we have consistently adhered to the theme of "peace and development," focusing intently on construction and wholeheartedly pursuing development. This commitment has created a favorable peaceful external environment for reform, opening up, and socialist modernization. We have seized strategic opportunities to accelerate our growth, leading to a rapid enhancement of our composite national strength and an unprecedented elevation of our international status.

Concurrently, we have maintained that the essence of our era remains unchanged. Amid the ever-shifting international landscape, we have preserved our strategic resolve, recognized the evolving characteristics of our times within the broader trends of historical development, and steadfastly upheld the Four-Sphere Confidence through a deep understanding of social development laws. For example, after the upheaval in Eastern Europe in the 1990s, theories such as "the failure of socialism" and "the end of history" gained considerable traction. At this critical juncture, Deng

---

1   Xi Jinping, *On Building a Human Community with a Shared Future,* Beijing: Central Party Literature Publishing House, 2018, p. 539.

Xiaoping firmly asserted that the overall trend of social and historical development is irreversible: "[I]n China socialism will not change. China will surely follow to the end the socialist road it has chosen. No one will be able to overwhelm us. As long as China doesn't collapse, one fifth of the world's population will be upholding socialism. We are full of confidence that socialism has a bright future."[1] This confidence stems from a profound understanding of the essence of our era.

Furthermore, we recognize that the transition from capitalism to socialism is a long and complex historical process, and we uphold the unity of the Party's highest program and basic program. This reflects our commitment to uniting the essence of our times with its characteristics (the thematic focus of our times). As General Secretary Xi Jinping stated: "Our experience has made it clear, time and again that Marx and Engels' analysis of the fundamental contradictions of capitalist society is still relevant, and the historical materialist view that capitalism will inevitably perish and socialism will inevitably triumph remains valid. This is the irreversible general trend of social and historical development, although the path may be winding."[2]

General Secretary Xi Jinping has emphasized that when observing the world, we must avoid being dazzled by superficial distractions or obscured by fleeting clouds. Instead, we should employ the telescope of historical laws to scrutinize our surroundings. By grasping the laws of the development of human society, the development of socialism, and the governance of the ruling party, we can navigate the currents of our time and become pioneers of progress. "Any philosophy which is successful in one country is of significance to the world. It must show the way to the

1   Deng Xiaoping, *Selected Works of Deng Xiaoping*, Foreign Languages Press, Beijing, 1994, vol. III, pp. 310–311.
2   *Documents Produced since the 18th CPC National Congress*, Beijing: Central Party Literature Publishing House, 2014, vol. I, p. 177.

people in modern times. We should upgrade Marxism on the basis of the realities of modern times. We should use Marxism to better observe, interpret, and lead the times, make clear our current mission, and know the course of history and the direction for the future."[1]

We must continue to utilize Marxism to observe, interpret, and lead the times, enriching its application with the vibrant practices of contemporary China. By adopting a broad perspective, we can absorb exemplary achievements from human civilization, ensuring we innovate while upholding our foundational principles during reform. This will allow us to continuously surpass our previous selves. In doing so, we deepen our understanding of the governance laws of the Communist Party, the principles of socialist construction, and the dynamics of the development of human society, thereby forging new frontiers for contemporary Chinese Marxism and 21st-century Marxism. This reflects a profound understanding of the essence and characteristics of our epoch, providing correct answers to the questions posed by our times.

III. Contemporary Socialism and Capitalism

By unifying the essence and characteristics of the epoch, and integrating theory with practice, history with reality, and domestic with international perspectives, we can conclude that at the dawn of the 21st century, we are still where Marxism has said we should be. While the essence of this epoch remains unchanged, it presents new characteristics distinct from those of the past. We find ourselves within the historical transition from capitalism to socialism, as described by Marxist theory, with peace and development remaining central themes. However, neither of these issues has been fundamentally resolved, and they manifest in various

---

1   Xi Jinping, *The Governance of China,* Beijing: Foreign Languages Press, 2017, vol. II, p. 69.

new forms and characteristics.

Modern capitalism has reached the imperialist stage, characterized by international financial monopolies, where internal contradictions are intensifying on a global scale. In today's world, peace, development, cooperation, and mutual benefit remain the defining trends of our era. The balance of global power continues to shift in ways that favor peace and progress, yet humanity still faces numerous challenges. The mission to uphold world peace and advance shared development remains a formidable and enduring task.

It is essential to observe and analyze the new transformations and emerging tendencies within contemporary capitalism with both a global perspective and a historical lens. We must delve into the evolving dynamics of world socialism in the 21st century, examine the new challenges and trends it confronts, and assess the current state of competition between global capitalism and socialism. Only through a comprehensive and historical understanding of these developments can we fully grasp the new characteristics and directions of our time.

As General Secretary Xi Jinping emphasized during the 43rd group study session of the Political Bureau of the 18th CPC Central Committee:

"The world is evolving more rapidly than ever before, giving rise to many profound and complicated problems and theoretical questions. Accordingly, we need to enhance our research on modern capitalism, analyze what changes are happening and the nature of these changes, and acquire a better understanding of the law governing the profound and complicated changes in capitalism and international political and economic relations."[1]

In this New Era, we must rigorously explore the relationship

---

1   Xi Jinping, *The Party's Public Communication Work*, Beijing: Central Party Literature Publishing House, 2020, p. 287.

between socialism with Chinese characteristics and global socialism. We must investigate the contributions China can make to the development of socialism worldwide in the 21st century, and highlight the global significance of China's path, theory, system, and culture. In doing so, we will ensure that scientific socialism remains relevant and feasible in contemporary China, allowing it to flourish with renewed vitality in the 21st century.

1. The fundamental forces of contemporary global socialism

The principal forces of socialism today include proletarian parties, socialist movements, and various socialist ideologies and schools of thought. Foremost among these are the communist and workers' parties of different nations, which steadfastly defend the interests of the working class and are committed to the ultimate ideals of socialism and communism. These parties constitute the most vital elements of contemporary world socialism.

Over the past 30 years, the development of communist parties worldwide has been marked by two pivotal milestones:

First, the political upheavals in Eastern Europe during the late 1980s and early 1990s inflicted severe setbacks on communist parties. Some parties dissolved or rebranded, and many faced an existential crisis.

Second, the 2008 global financial crisis exacerbated the fundamental contradictions of capitalism, exposing a resurgence of structural crises. The once-proclaimed "end of history" was decisively repudiated, offering communist parties new opportunities for growth, though not without the onset of new challenges.

In examining the types and distribution of Communist organizations, we can categorize them as follows:

First, there are the Communist Parties governing in real socialist countries. This includes the Communist organizations in nations such as China, Vietnam, Cuba, Laos, and DPRK. These parties have maintained long-term governance and actively explore paths for socialist construction, reform, and development that are suited to their national contexts. Their economic and social advancements have garnered global attention, demonstrating the superiority of the real socialist system through tangible achievements. The CPC is the largest Marxist ruling Party in the world, with the highest membership of any political Party globally. China, the most populous country in the East, adheres to and develops socialism with Chinese characteristics. Currently, China is the world's second-largest economy, with the CPC and its model of socialism becoming pivotal to the development of world socialism in the 21st century. There are approximately 100 to 110 million members of Communist parties in real socialist countries worldwide. As of June 5, 2021, the CPC reported a total membership of 95.148 million, along with 4.864 million grassroots organizations. Other ruling Communist parties include the Communist Party of Vietnam, with around 5.2 million members; the Communist Party of Cuba, with about 700,000 members; the Lao People's Revolutionary Party, with 350,000 members; and the Workers' Party of Korea, which reportedly has around 4 million members, although some sources suggest this number could be as high as 9.1 million.[1]

Second, we find the Communist organizations in developed capitalist countries. These include Communist parties in Western Europe, North America, Oceania, and parts of Asia, notably Japan. Overall, these parties have faced significant challenges in recent years, leading to a decline in their overall strength. Many have struggled to adapt amidst external pressures and internal divisions, yet there have been sporadic signs of growth. Among

---

1   https://www.upi.com/Top_News/World-News/2021/01/06/North-Koreas-no-mask-Party-Congress-raises-questions-about-statistics/640160994771 2/.

these, the Japanese Communist Party is the largest, boasting approximately 305,000 members and 24,000 Party branches. Its newspaper, *Akahata,* first published in 1928, reaches an audience of 1.13 million readers. In the United States, there are several Communist organizations, with the largest being the Communist Party USA, established in 1919. To strengthen its organizational capacity, the Party has implemented measures in recent years, such as simplifying membership procedures and actively recruiting young people, currently totaling around 3,000 members. In Oceania, the Australian Communist Party has a history spanning over a century, while New Zealand established a new Communist organization in 2018. However, both the older and newer parties hold very limited influence in their respective political landscapes.

Western Europe, as the birthplace of socialist thought and movements, remains a focal point for the international communist movement and world socialism. This region is characterized by the presence of numerous countries, many of which host multiple Communist parties—approximately 50 in total. However, most of these parties have memberships ranging from a few hundred to a few thousand. Notably influential parties include the French Communist Party, which currently has around 100,000 members, although only about 47,000 actively pay dues, allowing it to remain a significant political force in France.

In Italy, following the transformation of the former Italian Communist Party amid the upheavals in Eastern Europe, the re-established Italian Communist Movement has undergone several splits and reorganizations. Today, three major Communist factions hold influence: the Communist Party of Reconstruction, with about 9,000 members; the Italian Communist Party (originally the Italian Communist Party), which started with 10,000 members in 2016 but has seen significant attrition, now comprising just over 3,000 members; and the Communist Party

(Italy), founded in 2009, which has experienced rapid growth from 1,000 members at its inception to approximately 4,000 today. Among these, the Communist Party (Italy) is currently the most dynamic and influential. The Portuguese Communist Party has about 50,000 members, with over 3,000 new members joining in recent years—67% of whom are under 50 years old—helping to partially reverse the party's trend of aging. Meanwhile, the Spanish Communist Party, a traditional bastion of European communism, has seen a significant decline, now numbering around 10,000 members. The Communist Party of Greece and the Progressive Party of Working People of Cyprus have maintained stable memberships, hovering around 30,000 and 15,000, respectively.

Third, the Communist Parties of the former Soviet Union and Eastern Europe. At present, the development of communist organizations across this region varies widely. For example, the communist parties of Russia, Belarus, Kazakhstan, and the Czech Republic have shown resilience, having withstood the severe trials following the Eastern European upheavals, securing a foothold and seeking new paths for growth. Among the former Soviet republics, the Communist Party of the Russian Federation remains the largest communist organization. Despite a series of fluctuations since the collapse of the Eastern Bloc, the party has faced significant challenges in the 21st century. In recent years, both its influence and membership have waned, with the latest figures from its official website indicating a membership of 162,000. Nevertheless, the party has advanced the theory of "Renewed Socialism" and has actively engaged in various struggles against the ruling right-wing government, positioning itself as the most prominent opposition force in the national political arena.

In Eastern Europe, the Communist Party of Bohemia and Moravia stands as the region's largest communist entity. For nearly three decades, it has maintained a stable presence in parliament, though in recent years the party has experienced a marked decline. By 2019, its registered membership had fallen to 34,622, and it now faces the significant challenge of an aging membership base. Moreover, due to shifting domestic political landscapes, internal divisions, and anti-communist repression, several communist forces in the former Soviet and Eastern European regions have seen a steep decline. For instance, the Party of Communists of the Republic of Moldova, which had twice held power before the financial crisis, has seen its membership drop from over 30,000 to just 11,000. Some communist parties, such as the Communist Party of Ukraine and the Communist Party of Georgia, have been banned, witnessing a drastic fall in their ranks from tens of thousands to mere thousands.

Fourth, the Communist Parties of other developing countries. In the wake of the Eastern European upheavals, several parties in developing countries have persisted in retaining their communist identity and activities. These parties continue to explore paths and strategies of struggle that align with their national characteristics and developmental realities, with some achieving notable success. For instance, the Communist Party of India (Marxist), with over 1 million members, is currently the largest communist party in non-socialist countries. The South African Communist Party, with a membership of 285,000, is the largest communist organization on the African continent. Nepal's communist organizations have also garnered considerable attention. Over the past few decades, various communist factions have risen to power multiple times, and communists currently control the Nepali government. However, the proliferation of numerous communist parties within the country has led to persistent internal conflicts and divisions.

Beyond these communist parties, there exists a multitude of other left-wing parties and organizations around the world. Although they may not explicitly adhere to Marxism or scientific socialism as their guiding ideology, they share a common opposition to capitalism, neoliberalism, right-wing bourgeois parties, hegemonism, and colonialism. Some advocate for the establishment of a form of socialism, such as the socialist movements and theories of Latin American left-wing parties in the early 21st century, which have drawn global attention. Among them, Venezuela's "21st Century Socialism" has had a significant impact both in theory and practice. Despite facing substantial difficulties following the death of President Chávez, it continues to exert an important influence on both the theoretical and practical fronts.

Additionally, various socialist schools of thought have emerged beyond traditional party boundaries, including market socialism, eco-socialism, socialism based on economic democracy, and feminist socialism.

In conclusion, the early 21st century has seen world socialism emerge from the lows following the Eastern European upheavals, rebounding after enduring severe setbacks. It is now forging ahead, defending its positions while innovating in response to contemporary developments and seizing opportunities amidst new capitalist crises. We can confidently say that this marks a period of gradual recovery, seeking revitalization through transformation. As General Secretary Xi Jinping aptly stated, "Although there may be twists and turns in the development of world socialism, the overall trend of human social progress remains unchanged and will not change."[1]

2. Main characteristics of the developmental changes of world Communist parties

First, while certain political practices shine, their overall disadvantaged position remains unchanged. During the downturn of the world socialist

---

1   *Documents Produced since the 19th CPC Central Committee,* Beijing: Central Party Literature Publishing House, 2019, vol. I, p. 425.

movement, some Communist parties have managed to play relatively important roles in their national politics. Certain parties have consistently been major political forces competing for power. For instance, since the 1990s, two Communist parties in Nepal have governed multiple times, and at the end of 2017, the leftist alliance formed by the Communist Party of Nepal (Unified Marxist-Leninist) and the Communist Party of Nepal (Maoist Centre) achieved a sweeping electoral victory. The Progressive Party of Working People in Cyprus briefly became the only ruling Communist Party in an EU member state in the 21st century and remains the largest opposition Party today.

Some parties have maintained their influence within the ruling structures. For example, after the end of apartheid in 1994, the South African Communist Party, in coalition with the African National Congress and the Congress of South African Trade Unions, has remained one of the ruling parties, holding significant sway in the national political landscape. The CPRF, as the largest surviving Communist Party in the former Soviet bloc, has retained a degree of influence within the national government, particularly in recent years, witnessing a notable resurgence. In the September 2021 elections for the State Duma, the CPRF garnered over 20% support. The Communist Party of Belarus, despite having only about 6,000 members and limited parliamentary representation (gaining eight seats in 2016), has been able to significantly influence national policy decisions.

Certain parties have achieved remarkable breakthroughs. For instance, the Workers' Party of Belgium, which had been marginalized since its establishment in 1968, underwent a strategic shift in 2008 toward a development path combining "principle" with "flexibility," leading to a rapid rise. In 2014, the Party made history by securing two federal parliamentary seats and 52 local council positions. By 2018, its local representation surged to 157, and in 2019, the Party set a record with 12 federal and 4 Senate seats, placing fifth among 12 parties with elected representatives nationwide, while its membership grew from 2,800 in 2007 to over 19,000 today. Similarly, the Communist People's Party of Kazakhstan has seen its influence expand, moving from years of absence in parliament before the financial crisis to winning seven seats in two consecutive national elections.

Furthermore, while some parties may not achieve notable success at the national political level, they wield significant influence within local governments. For instance, the Communist Party of India (Marxist) has long governed the states of West Bengal, Tripura, and Kerala. Although it has lost power in the first two, it continues to firmly hold leadership in Kerala. The French Communist Party, despite a marked decline in recent years, still maintains a degree of influence at the local level. In the 2020 French municipal elections, the Party secured 223 mayoral positions[1] and formed governing partnerships in key cities such as Marseille, Lyon, and Bordeaux.

However, overall, the current developments among Communist parties worldwide reveal a fragmented and uneven distribution, lacking a cohesive, large-scale impact. The sporadic and non-continuous growth of these parties in various countries following the crisis is quite evident. Some parties experience temporary surges in support, only to see a swift decline thereafter. For example, the Spanish Communist Party nearly doubled its support in 2011 compared to pre-crisis levels (from 3.8% to 6.9%), yet in the 2015 elections, it plummeted to a historic low of 3.7%, largely due to the rise of left-wing populist parties. Additionally, several Communist parties have faced repeated setbacks in recent elections. Since 2008, the

---

1   "It has also been reported that the number of mayoral positions won by the French Communist Party is 233, see *Libération* at https://www.liberation.fr/politiques/2020/07/02/aux-municipales-l-ancrage-communiste-en-pleine-mutation_1793100.

support for Italy's three main Communist parties has struggled to hover around 1%, failing to cross the parliamentary threshold and thus holding no seats in the national assembly. Following the retreat of the "pink tide" in Latin America, Communist parties in Peru, Chile, and Brazil have gradually lost their governing partnerships. Influenced by both domestic and international factors, the Japanese Communist Party, the Communist Party of Bohemia and Moravia, and others have also witnessed varying degrees of decline in support and representation in recent elections.

Second, a trend toward unity has strengthened, yet significant contradictions and divisions remain.

Since the late 1990s, Communist parties worldwide have been exploring effective forms of mutual connection and cooperative struggle.

At the international level, increasingly mature communication and exchange mechanisms have emerged. For instance, the International Meeting of Communist and Workers' Parties has convened twenty-one times, becoming a vital platform for sharing experiences and coordinating actions among parties operating independently. Regional organizations, such as the European Left Party, the "Communist Alliance—CPSU," aimed at restoring the Soviet Communist Party and allied nations, and the Visegrad Conference of Communist and Workers' Parties from Central and Eastern Europe, have also established communication channels for coordination. However, in practice, significant differences in views and strategies within some of these coordinating bodies have caused tensions, nearly leading to a split in the International Meeting of Communist and Workers' Parties. Moreover, more ideologically radical parties, like the Greek Communist Party, have questioned the nature and direction of the European Left Party, prompting the formation of a parallel organization— the Initiative of Communist and Workers' Parties.

Domestically, some Communist parties that had split due to historical differences and ideological disputes are actively seeking to reconcile and consolidate power. There are notable successes, such as the merger of several Maoist parties into the Communist Party of Nepal (Maoist Centre) in 2016. In May 2018, this Party formally merged with the Communist Party of Nepal (Unified Marxist-Leninist), establishing the most powerful Party in Nepal's history. However, there are also failures, such as the difficult unification process between the Communist Party of Italy and the Reconstructed Communist Party, which ultimately led to the formation of a new Italian Communist Party by the former in 2016. Even successful collaborations today are fraught with instability and uncertainty, potentially leading to renewed divisions. For instance, just two years after the 2018 merger of the Communist Party of Nepal, disputes over leadership positions in late 2020 caused a split between the Maoist Centre and the Unified Marxist-Leninist party.

In recent years, collaboration between Communist parties and other leftist movements has intensified. This is evident at the national governance level, such as the longstanding "tripartite governing alliance" between the South African Communist Party, the African National Congress, and the Congress of South African Trade Unions, as well as alliances formed between some Latin American Communist parties and major leftist parties. Furthermore, electoral cooperation is apparent between Communists and various radical left parties, such as the French Communist Party with La France Insoumise, the Spanish Communist Party with Podemos, and the Portuguese Communist Party with the Left Bloc. In these alliances, however, Communist parties often find themselves in subordinate or dependent roles. Additionally, some Communist parties are actively exploring effective means for broad left-wing unity in light of current political realities. For instance, the Central Committee of the Communist Party of the Russian Federation convened in October 2020, emphasizing the importance of strengthening unity among leftist parties and trade unions to form a patriotic leftist front, aiming to build a political alliance with long-term goals to expand its influence and protect the rights of Russian workers and national interests.

Moreover, Communist parties around the globe have forged several coordinating organizations through various conferences. For instance, the Lebanese Communist Party organizes the Arab Left Forum, which fosters ongoing connections among Communist and leftist parties in the Arab world. Similarly, the European Social Forum and the Saint Paul Forum in Latin America provide platforms for regular participation, bridging interactions between Communist parties and their leftist counterparts.

Third, while these parties actively seek pathways for development, they face numerous challenges.

Since the upheavals in Eastern Europe and the subsequent financial crisis, Communist parties in different regions have embarked on distinct journeys toward socialism, shaped by their unique national contexts. They aim to enrich socialist theory and advance practical applications, achieving notable successes while confronting significant obstacles.

In countries like Vietnam, Cuba, Laos, and DPRK, ruling Communist parties have gradually pursued economic and political reforms since the late 1980s to address issues arising from socialist practice. These reforms seek to unveil the principles governing socialist construction and development in economically underdeveloped nations. While these four parties share a commitment to preserving the fundamental systems and trajectories of socialism, they exhibit unique characteristics in their specific reform measures, resulting in a diverse developmental landscape. Currently, the ruling positions of these parties remain relatively stable, and their governance capabilities continue to strengthen. However, they confront various risks and challenges, such as external pressures, internal transformations, the need for a nuanced understanding of market economies, addressing wealth disparity and corruption, and navigating the complexities of ownership and state-owned enterprise reform. In response, these parties consistently introduce new insights and initiatives, with some making bold strides while others adopt a more cautious approach, all engaged in a process of theoretical and practical exploration.

Communist parties striving for survival and development within capitalist systems are committed to discovering pathways to socialism grounded in their domestic realities. Over the past few decades, their explorations have generally followed two main trajectories. The first, represented chiefly by the Maoist Communist Party of Nepal and the Communist Party of India (Maoist), seeks to seize power through armed struggle to establish socialism. However, with the Maoist Party of Nepal shifting toward parliamentary politics in 2008 and the Indian Maoist Party facing military repression as a designated terrorist organization, this approach has waned in influence. The second path sees the majority of Communist parties actively participating in parliamentary struggles, either as a means to advocate for workers' interests or as a strategy for transitioning to socialism. While a few have managed to ascend to power through electoral competition, no successful precedents exist for achieving institutional transformation via peaceful, democratic means.

Currently, many Communist parties face developmental challenges, such as declining influence and political marginalization. To counter these trends, some have undertaken significant strategic adjustments. A notable example is the Spanish Communist Party, which has long been a proponent of moderate European communist theory. However, entering the 21st century, the party's support and societal impact have steadily diminished. In an effort to regain its footing, the Spanish Communist Party has engaged in profound self-reflection regarding its "European

Communism" approach for over three decades, shifting from moderation to a more radical stance. It has redefined its guiding ideology, reinstating Leninism at its core, replacing the democratic operation principle it had followed for 40 years with democratic centralism, and pivoting from a focus on parliamentary seat contests to more proactive anti-neoliberal actions outside of parliament. Additionally, some Communist parties have shown a fervent desire for reform and development. For instance, in recent years, the French Communist Party has engaged in internal debates about its decline and the prospects of 21st-century communism, proposing to maintain its distinct Party identity and clear communist image while seeking strategic revitalization through a Communist Manifesto for the 21st Century.

Fourth, the repression by anti-Communist forces has prompted Communist parties to unite in resistance.

Following the upheavals in Eastern Europe, anti-Communist sentiments have flourished in certain regions, leading to a continued deterioration of the external environment faced by these parties, which often suffer restrictions and repression. This predicament has become increasingly pronounced in recent years. In the former Soviet bloc, parties such as the Communist Party of Ukraine, the Communist Party of Poland, the Communist Party of Moldova, and the Communist Party of Georgia have faced various forms of assault and persecution, including violent searches, arrests, and unjust trials. Some Communist organizations have been disbanded, their leaders imprisoned, and their publications silenced. Even parties with a degree of standing in parliamentary politics encounter significant challenges from administrative authorities; for instance, Milos Jakeš, a former general secretary of the Communist Party of Czechoslovakia, has been prosecuted for civilian deaths resulting from border shootings between 1976 and 1989.

In recent years, one of the most significant challenges facing foreign Communist parties has emerged from a series of anti-Communist resolutions passed by regional European institutions. Starting with the European Committee's 2006 resolution that "strongly condemned the crimes of totalitarian Communist regimes," followed by the European Parliament's 2009 designation of August 23 as a day of remembrance for the crimes of Nazism and Communism, and culminating in the September 18, 2019 resolution titled "The Importance of European Memory for Europe's Future," which labeled the 1939 Molotov-Ribbentrop Pact as a direct cause of World War II while calling for the removal of all "totalitarian" monuments throughout Europe, including those honoring the Soviet Red Army—these resolutions have ignited a significant backlash in the Western world. Communist parties in multiple countries have vehemently denounced these resolutions as "reactionary," mobilizing through rallies, statements, and protests to express solidarity with their beleaguered counterparts.

This adverse external environment has constricted the survival space for these parties, exacerbating the challenges they face during periods of decline. Yet, it has also sparked a spirit of resistance and determination among Communists, fostering greater cooperation among various parties as they unite to defend the history, theory, and future of Communism.

Fifth, attention has been paid to China's development and path.

Another notable phenomenon among global Communist parties is their increasing focus on China's development and its unique path. As the world's largest socialist nation, China is emerging as a cornerstone of global socialist development, thanks to its remarkable achievements and sense of responsibility. The theory and practice of the CPC have become immensely attractive and influential to numerous foreign Communist parties. With intensified bilateral Party interactions and successful multilateral events, such as the "Ceremony Marking the 200th Anniversary of Marx's Birth," there is a growing trend within the international communist movement to "look east."

Some foreign Communists have praised the accomplishments of socialism with Chinese characteristics, asserting that the CPC has pioneered a new path for human development. Former East German Chancellor Modrow noted, "China, under the innovative leadership of the Communist Party, provides an attractive alternative to the crisis-ridden capitalist system through its modernization path rooted in socialism... China proves that human development and coexistence can be organized in a better way." Many Communists actively reflect on the CPC's successful experiences, crediting its achievements to its innovative adherence to and development of Marxism. Former Secretary-General of the Italian Communist Party, Diliberto, emphasized, "The most important lesson from the CPC lies in its creation of an original and profoundly beneficial theoretical system of Marxism. This system embodies the distinctive character of Marxist theory—grounding all concepts in reality, linking theory to practice, and testing and evolving truth through practical application." Gennady Zyuganov, leader of the Communist Party of the Russian Federation, argues that China's emergence as a leader in socialist construction stems directly from two factors: "First, the CPC is a Party armed with advanced theory; second, it excels at learning from the masses and history."

Moreover, the majority of Communist parties actively support the construction of a community with a shared future for humanity and endorse initiatives like the Belt and Road Initiative. Former Secretary-General of the Italian Communist Party, Paolo Ferrero, remarked that the human community with a shared future is an initiative proposed by the CPC to tackle contemporary global challenges, reflecting the party's sense of responsibility toward both the Chinese people and the world. He stressed that all Communist parties should enhance communication and cooperation to promote this shared future. Many Communist parties have sincerely expressed their desire to learn from China's invaluable experiences in reform and governance, indicating their intent to draw from the CPC's effective practices in Party building and governance while underscoring the significance of China's practical experiences. For instance, Massimiliano Ay, Secretary-General of the Swiss Communist Party, stated that China's current explorations can be viewed as a crucial experimental phase in the development of global socialism, serving as a concrete practice of socialism in the 21st century. The CPC's developmental experience holds global significance, as its remarkable achievements in building socialism not only empower China to continue on the right path but also inspire Communist parties in other nations.

Sixth, the development of other leftist forces

Based on the current state of other left-wing movements, the situation can be summarized as follows: they possess a "favorable moment" but lack "popular support"; they have shifted towards radicalism but lost their sharpness; they are taking active steps but lack clear direction; they seek unity yet remain largely fragmented and divided. The "favorable moment" refers to the rare conditions and environment in the Western world since World War II that are conducive to the development of left-wing theory and practice. Capitalism has faced its greatest financial crisis since the post-war period, resulting in crises of values, legitimacy, and belief. The COVID-19 pandemic, in particular, has had a profound impact on both the political and economic aspects of capitalism, prompting deep reflection within Western societies. Capitalism and the right wing have been dealt a heavy blow, shifting from the aggressive advances following the Eastern European upheavals to defensive postures. Public dissatisfaction and resistance are also at their most intense and concentrated since World

War II, with the focus of struggle even targeting the capitalist system itself. Thus, this represents a rare "favorable moment" for the left to rise again and pursue significant development—a once-in-a-century historical opportunity.

However, in the face of such an auspicious opportunity, the Western left feels a profound sense of inadequacy, struggling to bear the weight of history. Although they have been inspired and emboldened by the capitalist crisis, reigniting hopes for a leftist revival, they have encountered new setbacks in an environment where "the whole world turns left," experiencing electoral defeats. For instance, the intense social upheavals and enduring contradictions in Western European countries have led disillusioned citizens to abandon long-established right-leaning social democratic parties. Meanwhile, alliances formed by right-wing forces have won successive victories, while social democratic parties have faced widespread defeats. Even radical leftist Communist organizations, which should have garnered support from the middle and lower classes suffering from the crisis, have found this support elusive. The longstanding vilification of Communism in Western society and the marginalization of Communist parties have rendered their theoretical and policy propositions unrecognized and unaccepted by the majority.

In this vacuum, far-right parties such as France's National Front, Austria's Freedom Party, Sweden's Democrats, Spain's Vox, and Greece's Golden Dawn have attracted some support from the middle and lower classes. Additionally, issue-oriented parties that are neither left nor right, like Italy's Five Star Movement, have emerged. Some new radical leftist parties, ideologically positioned between Communism and social democracy, have made substantial strides. For instance, Greece's Radical Left Coalition became the first radical left Party to gain power through elections in Europe, while Spain's Podemos rapidly ascended to become the third-largest Party in the country within a few years of its founding. However, the development of such parties often proves unstable; for example, the Radical Left Coalition in Greece was ousted after one term, and Podemos has shown signs of decline after an initial phase of rapid growth. Maintaining developmental continuity is a common challenge faced by these types of parties.

Overall, amid the crisis of capitalism, the Western left possesses a "favorable moment" and, to some extent, "geographical advantage," given the conditions for international and domestic activities. However, the most glaring deficiency is the lack of "popular support," characterized by weakened organizational strength and fragmentation, which hampers their ability to secure broad support from the populace. The difficulties and dilemmas confronting the Western left manifest in several specific areas.

1) Loss of Identity: "In Name but Not in Substance"

For an extended period, Western politics has downplayed ideological distinctions. Under the influence of right-wing theorists proclaiming the "end of ideology" and the "end of history," left-wing intellectuals have increasingly doubted the relevance and efficacy of their own theoretical frameworks. Many on the left, swayed by the supposed "absolute triumph" of liberal democracy, have either fallen silent or embraced the so-called "Third Way," which seeks to transcend the traditional left-right divide. Even the more radical elements of the left have largely abandoned revolutionary aims and instead maintain only a nominally "radical" posture. Consequently, the left as a whole has been marginalized, often assimilated into the broader liberal democratic order, losing much of its distinct identity and edge. Although the global financial crisis has prompted a reevaluation of these trends, the task of reestablishing a clear leftist identity remains one of the most pressing issues today.

2) Lack of Theoretical and Strategic Preparation

Over the past three decades, the Western left has proposed various innovative or modernized theoretical strategies. However, under the hegemony of neoliberalism, much of this "innovation" has involved either the rejection of traditional leftist principles or the softening of the left's ideological sharpness, often resulting in a tepid reformism. At times, leftist theorists have even adopted, directly or indirectly, the concepts and frameworks of right-wing liberalism. As a result, reformism, pragmatism, opportunism, and cynicism have become deeply entrenched within leftist intellectual circles. The so-called "modernization" of leftist thought has thus proven inadequate for weathering the storms of social upheaval or for guiding systemic change. As one British leftist remarked:

"Some leftist forces have gradually drifted to the right, supporting neoliberal governments. Others, obsessed with maintaining their 'purity,' have rendered any attempt at political reorganization a waste of time. If this continues, the left will confine itself to distributing pamphlets, holding meetings, criticizing everyone else, and congratulating itself on its 'unsullied purity'—all utterly meaningless activities. If this is the case, we might as well retreat into our small groups and leave the task of social transformation to the right and the far-right."[1]

When crises strike capitalism, the left, lacking long-term theoretical reserves and strategic foresight, finds itself unable to lead or harness the growing wave of anti-capitalist sentiment. Instead, it is often overtaken by the rapid pace of unfolding events, left struggling to keep up.

3) Excessive Critique, Insufficient Constructive Solutions

The global financial crisis provided the left, particularly communist and other radical factions, with an opportunity to reinvigorate their critical theories, exposing the inherent contradictions and dangers of capitalism. They effectively diagnosed the root causes of the crisis, laying bare the

---

1 Quoted from *Contemporary World and Socialism*, 2008, no. 4, pp. 190–191.

systemic flaws. Following the outbreak of COVID-19, the left continued its critique of capitalism and neoliberalism, using the logic of capital to reveal the true nature of capitalism under crisis conditions. In general, the critical theories of the left have played a meaningful role, offering a form of "social correction." However, when it comes to offering solutions to the crises and addressing concrete socio-economic problems, the left has struggled to formulate coherent, long-term, and systemic programs that meet both the practical demands of the moment and the interests of the wider populace. Their proposals remain fragmented, lacking a clear and cohesive agenda, and the left continues to operate without a unified theoretical or organizational foundation capable of guiding sustained development.

4) Desire for Unity, But Persistent Division

Since the collapse of Eastern Europe, the Western left has sought to unite its forces, both to overcome its marginalization and to counter the globally unified forces of transnational capital and neoliberalism. These efforts have included attempts to form broad "left-wing united fronts" that encompass a variety of leftist factions, as well as various forms of internal coalitions and forums within specific leftist movements. While some of these efforts have achieved notable successes, the left remains deeply fragmented. Its internal composition is diverse, and many factions continue to operate independently, leading to significant internal divisions. Particularly among the radical left, conflicts and contradictions are commonplace, which has weakened the overall strength of the movement.

3. New opportunities and challenges for global socialism

At the dawn of the 21st century, the development of global socialism faces both unique opportunities and formidable challenges. Among the opportunities are the following:

First, the deepening crisis of capitalism has begun to shift the political landscape. The dominance of neoliberalism and the stronghold of right-wing parties are showing signs of retreat. For leftist parties, including communist organizations, this represents a significant and favorable change in the political environment, providing a more conducive context for their survival and growth.

Second, the ongoing crisis of capitalism has validated many of the critiques and proposals long advanced by socialist and progressive forces. For decades, these voices were marginalized or drowned out, but the current crisis has revived interest in their ideas. The resurgence of "Marxist fever" in the West and around the world is a testament to this renewed relevance.

Third, after three decades of struggle, adjustment, and reflection following the collapse of Eastern Europe, many socialist forces, including communist organizations, have regained a foothold on the global stage. They have engaged in numerous struggles and initiatives against capitalism, demonstrating resilience and adaptability. Through theoretical reflection and practical experience, these movements have gradually adjusted to the changing international and domestic environments, shifting from a position of decline and passivity to one of active engagement. This process has laid a foundation of organizational strength and has prepared a base of support for the future development of global socialism.

Fourth, in the face of the coordinated and powerful assault by right-wing forces on a global scale, Communist and leftist movements have increasingly bolstered their ties and cooperation. Over time, they have transitioned from the isolated struggles that followed the Eastern European upheavals to broader efforts aimed at unifying leftist forces. This shift has fostered a significant organizational advantage in the global socialist movement, which now operates on a more cohesive and substantial scale.

Fifth, 30 years after the demise of the Soviet Union and the drastic changes in Eastern Europe, time has allowed for the crystallization of valuable lessons. These lessons, which reflect historical truths, embrace objective rationality, and reveal deep systemic patterns, are of profound importance. They provide essential historical insight for the revival and future development of world socialism in the 21st century.

Sixth, the extraordinary achievements of socialism with Chinese characteristics in the early 21st century stand as a high point within a broader global decline of the socialist movement. These triumphs have inspired Communist parties and progressive forces around the world, giving them renewed hope for the resurgence of socialism in the 21st century. Without question, China's success serves as the most tangible, solid, and reliable "base" and "foothold" for the development of world socialism in this epoch.

World socialism in the 21st century faces several new and pressing challenges:

1) From a global perspective, the fundamental balance of power between capitalism and socialism remains unchanged—capitalism remains strong, while socialist forces are relatively weak. Capitalism continues to grow more aggressive, and in non-socialist countries, socialist parties and movements remain fragmented and underpowered.

2) In many countries—particularly in crisis-stricken Western nations—Communist and socialist parties remain marginalized or outright excluded from national political life. Their policies and viewpoints struggle to influence government decisions, leaving them on the periphery of the political stage.

3) Most Western socialist parties and movements still have a relatively weak influence on social movements. Their ability to capitalize on capitalist crises is limited, and they lack the experience and strategies needed to

effectively propose solutions to these crises. As a result, they find it difficult to lead mass movements that are dissatisfied with the economic order and opposed to capitalist domination.

4) Although a vast global working class has objectively formed and continues to grow, it remains in a state of "in-itself" existence, lacking a clear, unified class consciousness. The working class remains fragmented and often in competition with itself, which severely hampers the potential for deeper and more effective socialist movements worldwide.

4. New features and trends in the development of contemporary world socialism

At the dawn of the 21st century, amidst ongoing capitalist crises, the development of world socialism faces both promising opportunities and daunting challenges. Indeed, one might argue that the new and old problems of socialism have become increasingly entangled, creating a complex and evolving landscape.

To ignore these new issues and challenges is to fall into blind optimism, while failing to recognize the new features, bright spots, and opportunities in socialism's development is the outlook of a historical conservative. Even though the global power structure characterized by "capital strong, socialism weak" and "West strong, East weak" persists, the balance of power and the conditions of competition between global capitalism and socialism have undergone significant changes.

A key milestone in the resurgence of socialism during the first half of the 21st century will be the demonstration of socialism's broader institutional superiority over capitalism. Looking back over several centuries of socialist development, we can observe:

▪ In the 19th century, the center of the world socialist movement was in Europe. According to Marx and Engels, the revolutionary center shifted from Britain to France and eventually to Russia. This period was characterized by the creation, dissemination, and application of Marxist theory, which gradually became dominant. In practice, this epoch saw the broad development and maturation of the socialist and workers' movements.

- In the 20th century, the center of world socialism shifted to Russia, and the main theme of the epoch was revolution, the seizure of power, and the establishment of a new social system. This was realized in the victory of the Russian October Revolution and the creation of several socialist states.

- In the 21st century, the center of world socialism has shifted to China, and the historical theme of this epoch is the continuous improvement and development of the socialist system amidst competition between two social orders. Socialism is now demonstrating its institutional superiority and proving its profound advantages.

The most concentrated and striking manifestation of the capitalist crisis in the early 21st century is the inefficiency and decline of the capitalist system itself. Francis Fukuyama, who once famously proclaimed the "end of history," now discusses the "decline of the capitalist system." In *Capital in the Twenty-First Century*, Thomas Piketty explores the dysfunction and failure of the capitalist economic model. Numerous Western theorists are now addressing the collapse of long-revered values like democracy, freedom, and equality—principles once thought to be the eternal cornerstones of capitalism.

In stark contrast to the decline of capitalism, China is advancing the perfection and development of its socialist system through comprehensive reforms, making socialism more mature and stable. By the middle of the 21st century, the key task and historical theme for global socialism will be to secure broader institutional advantages over capitalism. This will mark the most important milestone in the revival of world socialism in the 21st century.

The longstanding competition between global capitalism and socialism is approaching a historic turning point, one that will favor the resurgence of world socialism. China is on track to surpass the United States in terms of total economic output, becoming the world's largest economy. This shift will bring about a fundamental change in the balance of power between the two dominant social systems. As it stands, unless there is a significant historical disruption, China's overtaking the U.S. economically is only a matter of time.

From the perspective of the competition between these two systems, the moment when China—the world's largest socialist country—surpasses the most advanced capitalist nation the U.S. sometime in the 21st century, will be a historic milestone. It will signify a pivotal shift in the global power dynamic between socialism and capitalism. While China may still be in the primary stage of socialism at that point, with its per capita GDP and income levels lagging behind those of developed capitalist nations, this comparison does not diminish the profound historical significance of China's rise.

In the history of world socialism, the Soviet Union once sought to surpass the U.S., but its efforts ultimately ended in failure with the demise of the USSR—a process that provided many lessons for future generations. Today's "catching up" is fundamentally different from the mass movements of the past, such as the Great Leap Forward or the efforts to "overtake Britain and the U.S." On this new historical footing, China's surpassing of the U.S. in economic terms carries deeper significance. For the first time in human history, a socialist country will hold the top position in the global economy, offering undeniable proof of the superiority of the socialist system.

This development also signals the beginning of a major shift in the global power structure, challenging the longstanding dynamics of "the West strong, the East weak" and "capitalism strong, socialism weak." As a result, the relationships, order, and structure between East and West, between socialism and capitalism, will be reshaped and redefined under new power dynamics and competitive conditions.

The criteria for assessing the state and progress of socialism must integrate both the number of socialist countries and the extent to which socialist ideals are realized. When evaluating whether world socialism is in a "low" or "high" tide, it is insufficient to simply count the number of socialist countries ruled by Communist parties. We must also consider qualitative factors, such as the degree to which socialist values— those reflecting the essence of socialism—are being realized, and how convincingly the superiority of the socialist system is demonstrated.

Admittedly, the number of socialist countries is the most direct and visible metric. After the upheavals in Eastern Europe, the number of socialist countries governed by Communist parties dropped from 15 to five, a significant setback for socialism. However, relying solely on this quantitative measure to assess the current state of socialism is simplistic and misleading. As history evolves and the global socialist movement progresses, the criteria for evaluating socialism's development must become more comprehensive and nuanced.

In countries governed by Communist parties, we must examine whether the core principles of socialism are being fulfilled—such as the development of productive forces, the realization of common prosperity, and the establishment of fairness and justice. Additionally, we should evaluate the depth and scope of each country's efforts to explore its own path to socialism, as well as the influence these countries have on the developing world. Their global influence and ability to shape international discourse are also key indicators.

In capitalist countries, we should assess whether socialist elements are becoming more prominent—whether workers' living standards are improving, social rights are being realized, and whether anti-capitalist socialist and progressive forces are gaining strength.

In sum, a well-rounded and nuanced evaluation of the global socialist movement is essential. While we certainly hope to see an increase in the number of socialist countries governed by Communist parties, we must also recognize the long-term, complex, and sometimes tumultuous nature of socialism's development. It is essential to examine each substantive achievement and historical leap forward in the socialist movement with specificity, historical awareness, and objectivity.

5. Changes and new challenges in contemporary capitalism

The fundamental contradictions of capitalism inevitably lead to periodic economic crises, and each crisis brings with it new contradictions and forces a significant adjustment within the capitalist order. The long history of capitalism, particularly since World War II, shows that technological revolutions and post-crisis adjustments have driven significant changes within contemporary capitalism.

However, the financial crisis of 2008, followed by the recent impact of the COVID-19 pandemic, has revealed a series of new contradictions and challenges in capitalism's economic, political, and social structures.

Contemporary capitalism, after weathering multiple crises and subsequent adjustments, has undergone profound transformations compared to its earlier forms, particularly pre-World War II. State ownership of capital and corporate ownership have become pivotal, assuming dominant roles within capitalist property structures. The relationship between labor and capital has deepened: once a formal dependence, it has now become a substantive one, with capitalists tightening their control over workers. Moreover, measures such as lifetime employment, employee stock ownership, and social welfare programs have been introduced to soften the tension between labor and management. A significant shift has also occurred in the division between ownership and control of capital: capitalists now hold shares in companies but seldom manage them directly. Instead, hired professional managers oversee the operations and governance of enterprises. In terms of economic regulation, while market mechanisms still play a role, governments now actively intervene in economic affairs. The nature of economic crises has also shifted, with cyclical and structural crises becoming intertwined and financial crises erupting with increasing frequency. Imperialism, too, has advanced into a new phase of financial monopolistic imperialism.

These changes are driven by several factors: the development of productive forces—especially the technological revolution—and the persistent struggle of the working class to protect its interests, which has forced adjustments in capitalist production relations. Additionally, reformist parties within the capitalist system have advocated for changes, while the rise and development of socialism, alongside its early institutional advantages, have influenced capitalism's evolution. These changes are objective realities; they reflect the broader laws of the development of human society and the internal dynamics of capitalism. To ignore them would be a mistake. To some extent, these adjustments have mitigated economic crises within capitalism and have objectively fostered the growth of socialist elements within capitalist societies. In the broader sweep of human history, these changes represent significant progress. Acknowledging them is essential for a deeper understanding of capitalism's essence and trajectory, and for advancing the global socialist movement.

Yet, despite these new and seemingly positive developments, they remain partial shifts within the framework of capitalism. These adjustments do not represent a fundamental change in the nature of capitalist production relations. The essence of capitalism—centered on capital—remains intact. The fundamental contradictions of capitalist society continue to persist, and the cyclical eruption of economic and financial crises remains unresolved. Marxism's scientific critique of capitalism's nature and development has not been rendered obsolete. Since the 2008 global financial crisis, and particularly in the wake of the COVID-19 pandemic, the underlying nature and problems of contemporary capitalism have been starkly revealed.

First, the financialization, hollowing out, and debt accumulation in Western developed economies have become more evident. Western countries, exploiting their monopolistic financial positions, have seen their financial sectors expand and inflate at breakneck speeds. By 2010, the scale of financial derivatives in the U.S. and Europe had ballooned to $680 trillion, 50 times the U.S. GDP and ten times the total global GDP. Meanwhile, the real economy has been severely hollowed out. Despite U.S. President Donald Trump's efforts to reverse this trend through tax cuts and trade wars, the hollowing out of the real economy, driven by financial monopolies, has persisted. The trade deficit with China has continued to widen, and the disconnect between stock markets and the real economy has only deepened. When the COVID-19 pandemic struck, Western nations—particularly the United States, the world's most powerful economy with the most advanced healthcare system—were thrown into chaos, with severe shortages of basic medical supplies revealing the hollow core of their real economies. At the same time, Western countries' reliance on debt-fueled consumption and high social welfare spending has left them burdened with unsustainable debt. The 2008 global financial crisis led to further debt expansion as developed Western nations sought to mitigate its fallout. Following the global outbreak of COVID-19 in 2020, the U.S. Federal

Reserve implemented an unprecedented policy of unlimited quantitative easing. These measures have only exacerbated the severe debt burdens of Western economies, setting the stage for the next financial crisis.

Second, the rise of populism, partisan conflict, and democratic dysfunction in the political landscape of Western developed countries has become increasingly apparent. Following the eruption of the 2008 global financial crisis, various populist forces rapidly gained momentum in Europe and the United States. Western-style elections have become deeply influenced by populism, with an increasing number of parties and constituents catering to these sentiments, complicating the selection of capable leaders. The election of former U.S. President Donald Trump, who championed "America First," embraced unilateralism, frequently withdrew from international agreements, and enacted a series of anti-globalization measures, alongside events such as Brexit, exemplifies this trend. Such actions have exacerbated political polarization within Western nations.

In their quest for power, political parties in the West have increasingly prioritized their interests over those of the nation and its citizens. The intensification of partisan rivalry often leads to extreme measures designed to appease voters. After the outbreak of the COVID-19 pandemic, U.S. politicians, fixated on electoral gains, neglected the urgent need for effective pandemic control and instead focused their efforts on attacking the previous Obama administration, China, and the World Health Organization. This neglect not only exacerbated the health crisis but also revealed the essence of Western governments as serving capital and a select group of vested interests rather than the broader populace.

Moreover, the Western model of democracy, once a source of pride, has further exposed its hypocritical, shortsighted, and self-serving nature in times of crisis. Far from improving, this system has increasingly become a chronic ailment in contemporary Western governance, sacrificing social welfare, public health, and the wellbeing of the people for the sake of capital interests and the so-called "freedoms" and "democracy" of individuals. The failure to effectively control the rapid spread of COVID-19 in the United States serves as a stark illustration.

Third, contemporary capitalist society is marked by deepening divisions, widening wealth disparities, and escalating social conflicts. The resurgence of extreme populism in Western countries has driven political extremism, further fracturing public opinion and reducing social cohesion. For instance, under Trump's administration, drastic measures such as restricting immigration, constructing border walls, and overturning the healthcare reforms of the Obama epoch have intensified divisions among political parties, public opinion, and society at large. In the fierce competition of an economy centered on capital interests, the polarization of wealth accumulation has inevitably widened the gap between rich and poor. Instead of narrowing this divide, contemporary capitalism has exacerbated it amid crises and difficulties. Data from a 2018 U.S. think tank indicated that in 2015, the income of the wealthiest 1% was 26 times that of the remaining 99%. Such social inequity inevitably intensifies social conflict, leading to an increase in collective unrest in Western nations. Movements like "Occupy Wall Street" in the U.S., the "Nuit Debout" and "Yellow Vests" protests in France, and various forms of unrest sparked by the Floyd incident continue to unfold, with large-scale violence, shootings, and riots becoming increasingly frequent.

6. Capitalist crisis and world socialism

The capitalist crisis of the early 21st century has raised fundamental questions about the future of capitalist development. During the upheavals in Eastern Europe and the collapse of the Soviet Union, discussions abounded regarding the "crisis of socialism." Some celebrated the demise, others hurried to pen the "obituary of socialism," and some confidently declared "the end of history." It was a grand and fervent anti-socialist chorus! Yet, merely a few decades later, viewed from a broader historical perspective, that "moment" has revealed a twist of fate as history humorously placed the "crisis" within the "room" of capitalism.

Of course, history is never so simplistic. Behind such metaphorical "jokes" lies the objective, rigorous, and serious operation of historical laws, which inevitably carve paths for themselves through various contingencies.

Economic crises provide a crucial lens through which to observe and study capitalism. Since the outbreak of the 2008 global financial crisis, the crises affecting capitalism have manifested with diverse contents, characteristics, and forms, each carrying different implications, impacts, and trends. Many, including defenders of capitalism, have remarked that "this time is different." Thus, where does capitalism currently find itself in crisis? Does it have any chance of survival? How should we properly understand the relationship between the development of socialism and the crisis of capitalism?

First, where lies the crisis of capitalism?

History is far from a mere cycle of repetition. For over 300 years, the capitalist system has seemingly endured a constant ebb and flow between prosperity and crisis. Yet, the dialectics of historical development relentlessly drive substantive change, revealing itself through the illusion of stability, sudden contingencies, and ongoing gradual transformations. Each crisis enriches our understanding of capitalism's fate, adding new dimensions to the quest for historical solutions that transcend the capitalist framework. What, then, constitutes the "different"? What implications does this hold for both capitalism and socialism?

The crisis increasingly highlights the waning historical legitimacy of the capitalist mode of production. At its essence, capitalism is propelled by an insatiable quest for capital accumulation and an unending demand for profit. As Marx articulated in *Capital*, quoting British trade unionist T.J. Dunning: "Capital eschews no profit, or very small profit, just as Nature was formerly said to abhor a vacuum. With adequate profit, capital is very bold. A certain 10 per cent. will ensure its employment anywhere; 20 per cent certain will produce eagerness; 50 per cent, positive audacity; 100 per cent will make it ready to trample on all human laws; 300 per cent, and there is not a crime at which it will scruple, nor a risk it will not run, even to the chance of its owner being hanged. If turbulence and strife will bring a profit, it will freely encourage both."[1] Today, this mode of production seeks ever-greater profit through speculation instead of organized production, dismantling the real economy in favor of the virtual, replacing civil governance with blatant exploitation. It is no longer merely a matter of violating laws or inciting discord; it is now a perilous pursuit by the wealthiest 1% to obliterate entire societies in their quest for exorbitant profits. Such actions inevitably jeopardize the very foundations of capitalism itself. It is little wonder that American investor Jeremy Grantham lamented, "Capitalism threatens our very existence."

For the global socialist movement, the crisis presents new conditions that may favor its development, yet it does not guarantee socialism's revival. Just as the capitalist crisis of the 1970s did not lead to the advancement of world socialism but rather to its decline, capitalism emerged from its crises to expand globally in the following three decades. The dialectics of history reveal that capitalism and development coexist, marked by the dual realities of diminishing historical legitimacy and a resilient capacity for self-adjustment. The prevailing trend during any period is shaped by the interplay of various conditions, yet the historical inevitability of socialism ultimately supplanting capitalism remains intact.

---

1   https://www.marxists.org/archive/marx/works/1867-c1/ch31.htm.

Second, what insights does the capitalist crisis provide for socialism?

From the preceding analysis of the capitalist crisis, we can draw three key conclusions regarding its relationship with the socialist movement:

1) During times of capitalist crisis, the principles of Marxism concerning the connection between capitalist crises and socialist revolutions retain significant practical relevance. However, the application of these principles must adapt to the evolving conditions of the epoch and the changing social landscape. Crises create opportunities and conditions for the socialist movement that differ from those in normal times, yet they do not inherently lead to an upsurge in socialist revolution. The outcome is contingent upon a confluence of subjective and objective factors. The idea that one can exploit a crisis for a decisive strike toward a global socialist transformation is a naïve misjudgment. Historical realities demonstrate that Marxism's analysis of the fundamental contradictions within capitalist society remains relevant; the historical materialist perspective of the "two inevitabilities" has not lost its validity. However, the transition from capitalism to socialism is a long, intricate, and multifaceted historical journey.

2) In the nearly century-long journey of transformation and adjustment, contemporary capitalism exhibits crisis response capabilities, innovative potential, regulatory strategies, adaptability, and governance tactics that are markedly different from those in the epoch of Marx and Engels. The manifestations, scale, cycles, intensity, and impact of capitalist crises have shifted, leading to complex and profound changes in their influence on socialist movements and revolutions. As we have entered the phase of international monopoly capitalism in the 21st century, the power and reach of the international monopolistic bourgeoisie have been solidified and strengthened. Capitalism's capacity for self-regulation and innovation remains formidable, placing it in a position of relative superiority, thus

likely maintaining the global socialist movement in a prolonged state of decline. As General Secretary Xi Jinping aptly stated, "We must deeply understand the self-regulatory capabilities of capitalist societies, fully acknowledge the objective reality that Western developed countries have long held advantages in economic, technological, and military fields, and earnestly prepare for the enduring cooperation and struggle between these two social systems. For an extended period, the primary stage of socialism must continue to engage in both long-term cooperation and struggle with capitalism, which possesses more advanced productive forces. It is essential to earnestly learn from and draw upon the beneficial achievements of civilization created by capitalism. Additionally, we must confront the reality of being criticized for the shortcomings in our socialist development when compared to the strengths of developed Western countries."[1]

Marx and Engels posited that capitalist economic crises are inherent to the capitalist mode of production, revealing all contradictions within capitalist economies and societies. Crises inflict severe hardships on the proletariat and the broader working population. Moreover, they ignite stronger resistance from the exploited and oppressed, propelling the socialist movement against the bourgeoisie to greater heights. Historically, such dynamics ultimately lead to the overthrow of bourgeois rule by the proletariat and the establishment of a new socialist mode of production and society. Generally speaking, the occurrence of capitalist crises inevitably creates conditions conducive to the development of socialism. However, whether these conditions manifest as effective social movements and yield the desired outcomes is contingent upon the interplay of various social forces and factors.

While crises generate opportunities and conditions distinct from

---

1   Xi Jinping, *A Holistic Approach to National Security*, Beijing: Central Party Literature Publishing House, 2018, p. 22.

stable periods, they do not guarantee a resurgence of socialist revolution. Marx and Engels believed that severe economic crises in capitalism would precipitate peaks of socialist movement activity, asserting that every factor mitigating the effects of previous crises contained the seeds of even more intense future crises. However, following their deaths, significant transformations occurred both in the epoch and within capitalism itself. The capitalist system underwent considerable change, leading to enhanced crisis response capabilities, innovation, regulation, adaptability, and strategies of governance that starkly contrast with those of the Marx-Engels period. The mechanisms, scale, cycles, intensity, and consequences of capitalist crises have evolved, complicating their effects on socialist movements and revolutions.

For instance, the capitalist crisis of the 1970s did not catalyze the growth of world socialism; instead, it marked a decline in the global socialist movement. In contrast, capitalism managed to recover from its crises, resulting in a global expansion over the subsequent 30 years. The ongoing crisis of capitalism in the early 21st century has inflicted significant damage, yet socialism has yet to emerge as a widely recognized alternative solution. Currently, capitalism finds itself entrenched in the phase of international monopoly capitalism, with the influence and power of the international monopolistic bourgeoisie further reinforced. Capitalism's self-regulatory and innovative capacities remain robust, positioning it advantageously, while the global socialist movement must navigate a long and arduous path to regain its momentum.

3) It is necessary to understand the complexity and long-term nature of the socialist cause amidst capitalist crises. The current circumstances and social conditions evoke Engels' reflections and profound analyses regarding the revolutions of 1848 prior to his passing. In the introduction to Marx's *The Class Struggles in France, 1848 –1850*, written in 1895, he noted:

"History ... has made it clear that the state of economic development on the Continent at that time was not, by a long way, ripe for the elimination of capitalist production; it has proved this by the economic revolution ... all on a capitalist basis, which in the year 1848, therefore, still had a great capacity for expansion."[1] He further remarked, ". If even this mighty army of the proletariat has still not reached its goal, if, far from winning victory by one mighty stroke, it has slowly to press forward from position to position in a hard, tenacious struggle, this only proves, once and for all, how impossible it was in 1848 to win social transformation merely by a surprise attack."[2]

Today, as the capitalist crisis continues to spread, even intensifying in certain countries and regions, the notion that capitalism will swiftly collapse amid this turmoil— or that one can capitalize on the crisis to mount a single, decisive blow for a global socialist revolution— remains equally unattainable. Yet, amid this crisis, Marxists and revolutionaries must adeptly harness historical agency, leveraging the circumstances arising from the capitalist crisis to actively promote a new path toward the revitalization of world socialism, rather than passively waiting for all objective and subjective conditions to align before taking action. The development of world socialism is a natural process determined by the laws of human history. Simultaneously, the dialectical unity of objective historical necessity and the subjective agency of historical actors is crucial. The effectiveness of historical laws, the full utilization of historical conditions, and the timely seizing of historical opportunities depend on the proactive and conscious actions of these agents. In the context of the 21st-century capitalist crisis, how socialist parties and movements navigate the relationship between historical objectivity and human agency will be pivotal in determining

---

1   https://www.marxists.org/archive/marx/works/download/pdf/Class_Struggles_in_France.pdf.
2   *Ibid.*

whether world socialism can achieve revitalization.

7. New dynamics in the relationship between contemporary capitalism and socialism

History shows that every major crisis in capitalism inevitably leads to significant adjustments and transformations within the system, profoundly influencing the state and strategic adaptations of world socialism. In this sense, capitalist crises present critical opportunities to observe and study the development, strength, conditions, opportunities, and strategies of socialism. To clarify, we will broadly compare the changes in world capitalism and socialism following three major capitalist crises since the 20th century.

The period following the 1929 capitalist crisis saw the Soviet Union, as the core of socialist power, seize an excellent opportunity for rapid economic development, becoming the world's second industrial power after the United States. The socialist system began to reveal its unique advantages. Globally, socialism expanded from one country to multiple nations, achieving a remarkable victory and subsequently forming a world socialist bloc in the post-war period. Conversely, the capitalist world, led by the United States, sought to alleviate various contradictions of capitalism through reforms such as the New Deal enacted by President Franklin D. Roosevelt. By learning from Soviet experiences in nationalization and planned economy, capitalism navigated the crisis relatively successfully, ultimately establishing a world capitalist bloc and entering a "Golden Age" of postwar development. After their respective adjustments and developments following the crisis, the two social systems emerged in a state of equilibrium, cooperating to achieve victory in the anti-fascist war while simultaneously establishing a prolonged Cold War characterized by polar opposition between the two ideological camps.

In the aftermath of the capitalist crisis of 1973, following years of stagnation, Western capitalism, plagued by "stagflation," underwent a significant transformation through the "Reagan Revolution" in the United States and Thatcher's "New Deal" in Britain. These initiatives, combined with a new wave of technological revolution and the advance of economic globalization, set the stage for over 30 years of rapid capitalist expansion. Meanwhile, the Soviet Union and other socialist countries, instead of capitalizing on the crisis to strengthen themselves, fell into their own severe crises due to systemic rigidity and a failure to implement timely, forward-looking reforms. The culmination of these internal weaknesses, along with other factors, led to the collapse of the Soviet Union and the upheavals in Eastern Europe, plunging world socialism into a historical low point.

In this contest, global capitalism gained the upper hand. However, a remarkable exception emerged: socialist China, far from being defeated like the Soviet Union and Eastern Europe, rose to prominence. Through overcoming various difficulties and crises, China carried out successful reforms and pioneered the path of socialism with Chinese characteristics. This path led to achievements that attracted worldwide attention, creating a localized high tide within the broader low ebb of global socialism, and in doing so, preserving and revitalizing the socialist cause. As Deng Xiaoping insightfully remarked: " So long as socialism does not collapse in China, it will always hold its ground in the world."[1]

After the 2008 capitalist crisis, the political and economic strength of developed capitalist countries, including the United States, began to decline relatively, and their ability to dominate the world became increasingly constrained. The myth of capitalism's "end of history," which had emerged after the Eastern European transformations, was shattered. The aggressive expansion of capitalism, which had surged forward globally,

---

1   Deng Xiaoping, *Selected Works of Deng Xiaoping*, Beijing: Foreign Languages Press, 1994, p. 334.

began to retreat. At the same time, the balance of power between global capitalism—represented by the United States and Western Europe—and global socialism—represented by China—underwent significant changes.

Although the overall pattern of "strong capitalism and weak socialism" remained, capitalism was clearly on the defensive, while the forces of global socialism, led by China, were on the rise. This crisis marked the beginning of a new era in the competition between the two major social systems and in world historical development. It signaled a shift in the long cycle of capitalist development, which was now entering a significant period of decline, while world socialism, though still in a general low tide since the Eastern European upheavals, began to experience a new upward trajectory, driven by the remarkable achievements of socialism with Chinese characteristics. This crisis heralded a new stage in the competition between the two systems and a fresh phase in world history, with new dynamics and a new structure.

By comparing the three distinct periods surrounding the three major capitalist crises, we can more clearly trace the broad contours of change in the longstanding contest between global capitalism and global socialism over the past century. From a comparative perspective, in the 70-plus years between the capitalist crisis of the 1930s and the early 21st century, global capitalism experienced a cycle of decline, resurgence, and subsequent downturn. Meanwhile, global socialism underwent a process of rise, decline, and then gradual recovery. In the short decades since the collapse of the Soviet Union and the upheavals in Eastern Europe, the "invisible hand" of history has produced a remarkable and unexpected reversal, vividly demonstrating Lenin's observation: "It is said that history is fond of irony, of playing tricks with people, and mystifying them."[1]

This situation offers a vivid, real-world test of both the necessary

---

1   https://www.marxists.org/archive/lenin/works/1914/jun/x01.htm.

and contingent forces at play in historical development. And perhaps the greatest surprise delivered by the "hand of history" is that amidst this "magical reversal," it opened the door to the "room with a view"—the path of socialism with Chinese characteristics. As General Secretary Xi Jinping pointed out: "Especially after the demise of the Soviet Union and the upheavals in Eastern Europe, pessimistic voices about China were rampant on the international stage, with various 'China collapse' theories never ceasing. However, not only did China not collapse, but its comprehensive national strength has increased day by day, and the living standards of its people have continuously improved. 'The scenery here is uniquely beautiful.'"[1]

In conclusion, we can assert that the world is undergoing a major transformation of a kind unseen in a century. Yet, from a broader historical perspective, we remain within the epoch that Marxism has illuminated—an era in which human society is still transitioning from capitalism to socialism. In this historical period, the theme of peace and development remains unchanged, though the content and scope of this theme have undergone profound changes, exhibiting new characteristics and trends. The key contradictions and various tensions within global development are increasingly prominent, and the coexistence and competition of different forces have taken on new features. The trend of "the East rising and the West declining" is becoming ever more pronounced. As the world's largest developing country and the largest socialist nation, China is steadily moving to the center of the global stage, having progressed from lagging behind the times to catching up with the times, and now to leading the times. China is increasingly becoming a crucial force in shaping the global landscape. From the perspective of socialist development, the 21st

---

1   Xi Jinping, *Stay True to the Original Aspirations and Founding Mission of the Party,* Beijing: Party Building Books Publishing House and Central Party Literature Publishing House, 2019, pp. 66–67.

century stands as an era of great socialist revival, a century of resurgence. In this New Era, China's socialism has emerged as the guiding light and the backbone of global socialism. As China continues its historic journey toward national rejuvenation, it will contribute even greater achievements to the advancement of the times, the prosperity of the world, and the progress of humanity.

Part Three

China's New Era Explains the Three Whys

Since its founding one hundred years ago, our Party has consistently upheld Marxism as Marxism is the fundamental guiding thought upon which our Party and country are founded, and has continually advanced the adaptation of Marxism to the Chinese context. Marxism has profoundly changed China, and China has greatly enriched and developed Marxism. History has proven that the choice of Marxism by history and the people is entirely correct. It is entirely correct for the CPC to inscribe Marxism on its banner, and it is entirely correct to persist in combining the fundamental tenets of Marxism with China's specific realities, continuously advancing the adaption of Marxism to the Chinese context and the needs of our times.

The great success of socialism with Chinese characteristics in the New Era is attributed to the effective guidance of Marxism, the correct leadership of the CPC, and the relentless efforts of the Chinese people. The scientific theory of Marxism, the grand cause of socialism, and the leadership of the CPC have organically integrated in the extraordinary historical context of the New Era. This integration has forged the glory of the era through the new practice of the four greats—the great struggle for national development, the great project to strengthen the Party, the great cause of Chinese socialism, and the great dream of national rejuvenation.

The historic achievements and transformative changes in socialism with Chinese characteristics in the New Era deeply explain the three major questions of our time: Why does the CPC always deliver? Why does Marxism always work? Why does Chinese socialism always shine? Only a great era can successfully answer the questions of the times.

General Secretary Xi Jinping, in a series of important discussions, not only profoundly answered these three fundamental questions of our time but also scientifically explained the close, complementary, and organic unity among them. He clearly articulated: "The capability of our Party and the strengths of socialism with Chinese characteristics are attributable to the fact that Marxism works."[1]

From the combination of history and reality, theory and practice, deeply understanding General Secretary Xi Jinping's important discussions and profound explanations, and comprehensively grasping why China in the New Era has successfully answered these three fundamental questions, is crucial for understanding the significance of socialism with Chinese characteristics in the New Era, both in its contemporary and global contexts.

I. Why Does the CPC Always Deliver?

As a Marxist party, the CPC embodies the qualities of an advanced political organization, distinct in its historical significance. Its unique strength is deeply rooted in the Chinese soil, originating from the Chinese

---

1   Xi Jinping, *Speech at a Ceremony Marking the Centenary of the Communist Party of China,* Beijing: People's Publishing House, 2021, p. 13.

people, serving the Chinese people, and relying on the Chinese people. The CPC's capability are manifold:

- It continuously realizes the people's aspirations for a better life by representing the fundamental interests of the overwhelming majority of the people.

- It uses well-defined theory as its foundation and continuously creates and innovates the adaptation of Marxism to the Chinese context as its guide.

- It maintains its vanguard nature, constantly solidifying its class support and expanding its public support.

- It strengthens its governance capabilities by continuously enhancing its leadership and organizational skills.

- It persistently promotes the great project to strengthen itself in tandem with the great cause of socialism, leading great social revolution through great self-reform.

- It sustains vitality and vigor by maintaining its advanced and pure nature through continuous self-reform.

1. Clear program and goals

Engels pointed out that the program of a working-class party, "whatever may be its first shape, must develop in a direction which may be determined beforehand."[1] From its inception, the CPC, under the guiding light of Marxism, clearly set communism and socialism as its goals, striving to build a new Chinese society. Mao Zedong stated: "We Communists do not conceal our political views. Definitely and beyond all doubt, our future or maximum program is to carry China forward to socialism and communism. Both the name of our Party and our Marxist world outlook unequivocally point to this supreme ideal of the future, a future

---

1   https://marxists.architexturez.net/archive/marx/works/1887/01/26.htm.

of incomparable brightness and splendor."[1] General Secretary Xi Jinping noted: "We must recognize that our current efforts and the continuous efforts of many generations to come are all directed toward ultimately achieving the great goal of communism."[2] Regardless of how circumstances change or what difficulties and obstacles are encountered, our Party has never wavered in its determination and will to achieve this goal.

The Constitution of the CPC includes both the highest program for striving toward the ultimate ideal and the basic program and phased goals for achieving this grand ideal in the current stage. It clearly articulates: "The realization of communism is the highest ideal and ultimate goal of the Party." It also explicitly stipulates: "The highest ideal of communism pursued by the Chinese Communists can be realized only when the socialist society is fully developed and highly advanced." General Secretary Xi Jinping pointed out: "Socialism with Chinese characteristics represents the unity of the Party's highest and basic programs. We must strive with all our efforts toward the current stage's goals, but we must not lose sight of the lofty goal of communism. If we lose our lofty goal as Communists, we will lose our direction and become driven by pragmatism and utilitarianism."[3] The strength of our Party primarily lies in its strong political will in pursuing ideals, and the unwavering belief in ideals and convictions among the Party members and officials. They are firmly committed to the path of socialism with Chinese characteristics while holding the lofty ideal of communism, resolutely implementing the Party's basic line and program during the primary stage of socialism, and consciously becoming steadfast believers and faithful practitioners of the lofty ideal of communism and the common ideal of socialism with Chinese characteristics.

---

1   Mao Zedong, *Selected Works of Mao Tse-tung*, Beijing: Foreign Languages Press, 1967, vol. III, p. 232.
2   Xi Jinping, *Stay True to the Original Aspirations and Founding Mission of the Party*, Beijing: Party Building Books Publishing House and Central Party Literature Publishing House, 2019, p. 73.
3   *Documents Produced since the 18th CPC National Congress*, Beijing: Central Party Literature Publishing House, 2014, vol. I, p. 116.

At different historical stages, our Party has always proposed inspiring goals based on the will of the people and the needs of career development, uniting and leading the people in striving for them. For instance, the Two Centenary Goals were formed and perfected through the great historical creation led by generations of Communists in China, aiming at national rejuvenation. Led by Mao Zedong, the Chinese Communists, after a bloody struggle, established the People's Republic of China, making the Chinese nation stand up. After the founding of the People's Republic, Mao Zedong proposed the vision of transforming China into a prosperous and strong country, requiring 50 to 100 years, and set forth the grand goal of the Four Modernizations. The remarkable achievements in the development of the People's Republic laid the institutional and material foundation and made all necessary preparations for the development of the country and the gradual realization of the century-long goals. During the reform and opening up period, led by Deng Xiaoping, the Chinese Communists formally established the strategic goal of quadrupling the gross national product by the end of the 20th century to achieve a moderately prosperous society, and proposed the three-step development strategy. Throughout the over 40 years of great struggle in reform and opening up, the Two Centenary Goals were gradually established and continuously improved. The 16th CPC National Congress proposed the goal of building a higher-level moderately prosperous society benefiting over a billion people in the first 20 years of the 21st century, and the 17th National Congress put forward new requirements for building a moderately prosperous society in all respects.

Since the 18th CPC National Congress, with General Secretary Xi Jinping at its core, the Central Committee has proposed that the rejuvenation of the Chinese nation is the greatest dream of the Chinese people since modern times. At this new historical starting point, the Party continues to advance the realization of the Two Centenary Goals. These goals are closely linked with the Chinese Dream, merging into a grand overarching objective, and becoming the spirit and clear guidance for the unity and progress of over 1.4 billion Chinese people. The great dream promotes and complements the great struggle, the great project, and the great cause. Driving forward and achieving these four greats forges new glories for the Party and the country. The Two Centenary Goals concretely and clearly outline the practical direction, strategic steps, and major tasks for realizing the Chinese Dream, with significant progress and notable results. The people gain the most and share the broadest benefits, leading to national strength, social progress, and the historic leap of the Chinese nation from standing up, growing rich, and becoming strong. This great dream is forged and practiced through great endeavors.

The 19th CPC National Congress not only set clear requirements for achieving the First Centenary Goal but also divided the attainment of the Second Centenary Goal into two stages. It defined the objectives and strategic arrangements for these two stages: by 2035, to basically achieve socialist modernization; and by 2050, to build a great modern socialist country. The strategic plan made at the 19th National Congress for the development of socialism with Chinese characteristics in the New Era provide a timetable and roadmap for achieving the Two Centenary Goals. Following this strategic plan, the Fifth Plenary Session of the 19th Central Committee adopted the 4th Five-Year Plan for Economic and Social Development and Long-Range Objectives through the Year 2035, which further outlined the goal of basically achieving socialist modernization by 2035. The Chinese nation has become prosperous through reform and opening up, and under the Party's leadership, the Chinese people are steadily realizing common prosperity. The Two Centenary Goals serve as a continuous source of inspiration, motivating the people to strive, channel their efforts, and unite their collective strength to progress.

2. Guided by the evolving Marxism adopted to the Chinese context

Guiding thought is the life and soul of a political party, forming the foundation for the party's line, principles, and policies. The theoretical basis and fundamental principles of the guiding thought possess relative stability. Any changes or replacements usually signify substantial shifts within the party. However, the specific content of the guiding thought is not static. A truly advanced political party must continuously adapt to the development of the times and social changes, focusing on the specific practices of its country and nation. It must actively engage in intellectual and theoretical innovation, continually infusing the guiding thought with new contemporary content and national characteristics.

The fundamental reason why the CPC remains vibrant and youthful is its adherence to the ever-evolving Marxism adopted to the Chinese context. In terms of guiding thought, the CPC has consistently upheld Marxism as the foundational guiding principle for the founding and governance of the state. The Party has always emphasized the study, research, and application of Marxism, treating Marxism adopted to the Chinese context as the shining banner that guides its continual progress. It firmly opposes the diversification of guiding thoughts while promoting theoretical innovation in line with China's national conditions and the characteristics of the times. This involves using an up-to-date Marxism to guide new practices, rejecting both the denial of Marxism and the dogmatic approach to it.

Over the past 100 years, the Party has continually enriched and developed Marxism through practical application, accurately addressing contemporary issues, and consistently advancing the adaptation of Marxism to the Chinese context and the needs of our times. This has led to new theoretical realms within Marxism and produced significant theories, including Mao Zedong Thought, Deng Xiaoping Theory, the Theory of Three Represents, the Scientific Outlook on Development, and Xi Jinping Thought on Socialism with Chinese Characteristics for a New Era. These theories have provided effective theoretical guidance for the development of the Party and the people's cause, and have secured advantages and future prospects for the practice of socialism with Chinese characteristics.

Mao Zedong, as the founder of the People's Republic of China, was among the first to explore the laws of adapting Marxism to the Chinese context within the CPC. During the bidirectional process of adopting Marxism to the Chinese context and applying Marxism in China, he developed theories suitable for China's national conditions, encompassing the new democratic revolution and the socialist revolution. He created Mao Zedong Thought, which integrated the universal principles of Marxism-Leninism with the specific realities of the Chinese revolution. The emergence of Mao Zedong Thought vividly illustrated the progressive and innovative nature of Marxism in the context of evolving times, significantly enriching the theoretical treasury of Marxism.

The new revolutionary circumstances, markedly different from the times of Marx, Engels, and Lenin, necessitated responses to the path of the proletarian revolution intertwined with national liberation movements and democratic revolutions. Mao Zedong clearly recognized the necessity of developing Marxism. He stated, "During Marx's lifetime, he could not foresee all the problems that would later arise, nor could he solve all those problems at that time. The problems of the Russian revolution could only be solved by Lenin; the problems of China can only be solved by the Chinese people."[1] He courageously broke away from the revolutionary form of urban insurrection centered on Soviet Russia, mobilizing the

---

1   Mao Zedong, *Collected Works of Mao Zedong*, Beijing: People's Publishing House, 1999, vol. VIII, p. 5.

people of workers and peasants to pursue a revolutionary path of encircling the cities from the countryside and seizing power through armed struggle. Under his leadership, the Chinese people achieved victory in the new-democratic revolution and established a new China where the people run their own country. Had Mao Zedong rigidly adhered to certain specific conclusions of Marxism without innovating it, and persisted in the path of urban insurrection, the Chinese revolution would have continued to grope in darkness, possibly suffering even greater failures.

Deng Xiaoping, as the chief architect of China's reform and opening up, led the Chinese people in boldly correcting "Left" errors. He shifted the Party's focus to economic development, upheld the policy of reform and opening up, and decisively seized historical opportunities. This initiative pioneered a new path of building socialism with Chinese characteristics, allowing the Party and the people to stride forward in step with the times and infusing Marxism with new vitality. Deng Xiaoping once emphasized that integrating the fundamental tenets of Marxism-Leninism with China's realities and forging our own path is essential, as it stems from "[t]he lesson we have learned from our setbacks."[1] He emphasized, "Scientific socialism develops in the course of actual struggle, and so do Marxism-Leninism and Mao Zedong Thought. We will not, of course, backtrack from scientific socialism to utopian socialism, nor will we allow Marxism to remain arrested at the level of the particular theses arrived at as long as a century ago. This is why we have often repeated that it is necessary to emancipate our minds, that is, to study new situations and solve new problems by applying the basic tenets of Marxism-Leninism and Mao Zedong Thought."[2]

In this era whose theme is peace and development, the global

1 Deng Xiaoping, *Selected Works of Deng Xiaoping*, Beijing: Foreign Languages Press, 1994, vol. III, p. 101.
2 Deng Xiaoping, *Selected Works of Deng Xiaoping*, Beijing: Foreign Languages Press, 1995, vol. II, p. 187.

landscape continues to undergo significant changes, with rapid advances in scientific and technological revolutions, the emergence of economic globalization, and the formation of a new pattern of political multipolarity. Our Party has profoundly understood the fundamental characteristics of this era, focusing on its features, deeply summarizing the historical experiences of the socialist movement, and continuously advancing the process of adapting Marxism to the Chinese context. This practice once again demonstrates the progressive and innovative qualities of Marxism.

In the New Era, to achieve the rejuvenation of the Chinese nation, the CPC Central Committee, with General Secretary Xi Jinping at its core, has combined the fundamental tenets of Marxism with China's specific realities and the best elements of Chinese traditional culture. It has united and led the Chinese people to confidently and steadfastly innovate while upholding fundamental principles. By adhering to and improving the system of socialism with Chinese characteristics, advancing the modernization of the country's governance system and capacity, governing the Party with established regulations, and forming comprehensive intra-Party regulations, the Central Committee has overcome a series of major risks and challenges. It has achieved the First Centenary Goal, outlined the strategy for the Second Centenary Goal, and attained historic accomplishments and transformations in the Party and national endeavors. These efforts have provided a more robust institutional guarantee, a firmer material foundation, and a more proactive spiritual force for the realization of the rejuvenation of the Chinese nation. The Chinese nation has witnessed a remarkable transformation from standing up and growing rich to becoming strong. This irreversible historical process has brought the Chinese people into an exceptionally bright future, achieved great successes in building socialism with Chinese characteristics in the New Era, and accumulated valuable experience for realizing the rejuvenation of the Chinese nation.

The New Era has given rise to new ideas. Since the 18th CPC National Congress, the Central Committee, with General Secretary Xi Jinping at its core, has consistently upheld the progressive theoretical qualities of Marxism, courageously advancing theoretical innovation based on practical experience. It has established Xi Jinping Thought on Socialism with Chinese Characteristics for a New Era. This important thought is both a continuation of and an advancement from previous theories. It adheres to the fundamental tenets of Marxism while providing scientific answers to a series of significant theoretical and practical questions about upholding and developing socialism with Chinese characteristics in the New Era. With an immensely profound practical foundation, theoretical content, historical background, and cultural significance, it represents the latest achievement in the adaptation of Marxism to the Chinese context. It offers an effective guide for the continuous development of the Party and the country in the New Era and provides clear directions for embarking on a new journey toward building a modern socialist country in all respects.

The progressive nature of Marxism is realized through its adaptation to the Chinese context. The process of adapting Marxism to the Chinese context involves integrating its fundamental tenets with China's actual conditions. China's reality consists of two primary components: first, the contemporary reality of China, referring to its current conditions; and second, the reality of the best elements of traditional Chinese culture, which encompasses both the material progress created by the Chinese people throughout history and the cultural-ethical progress that is largely defined by these best elements of traditional Chinese culture. The process of advancing the adaptation of Marxism to the Chinese context is not only about integrating Marxism with China's specific reality but also about merging it with the best elements of traditional Chinese culture. Xi Jinping Thought on Socialism with Chinese Characteristics for a New

Era integrates Marxism with both China's current conditions and the best elements of its traditional culture, making the adaptation of Marxism to the Chinese context more comprehensive, profound, and thorough, thus significantly broadening the dimensions and connotations of the adaptation.

The practical experience of China's revolution, development, and reform has powerfully demonstrated that Marxism is the essence of the spirit of the times. It evolves with the progress of time, practice, and science, embodying the quality of adapting to the times.

3. Solid class support and broad popular support

For a political party to achieve and maintain long-term governance, it must secure extensive social support. Political parties worldwide strive to secure political and social spaces for survival and development, though their specific approaches may vary. Adapting to the development of the times and changes in the economic and social landscape, continuously adjusting strategies and tactics to expand the party's social base, and seeking to maximize social support and space for survival and development are key to the CPC's success.

Our Party insists on and openly declares its class nature to maintain its vanguard character. Its Constitution states that the Communist Party of China is the vanguard both of the Chinese working class and of the Chinese people and the Chinese nation. A political party is an organization of a class, and class nature is the essential attribute of a political party. The crucial distinction between the Communist Party and other parties is that it does not conceal, but openly declares, its class nature, which is being the vanguard of the working class. Mao Zedong once pointed out, "To unite the entire Party and the entire people, it does not mean that we have no inclinations. Some people say the Communist Party is a 'party of the whole people,' but we do not see it that way. Our Party is a proletarian party, an advanced detachment of the proletariat, an armed fighting force with Marxism-Leninism."[1]

History and practice have proven that for a Marxist party, openly declaring its class nature not only does no harm but actually helps gain social support and solid public support. The class foundation and public support of the Party are intertwined and inseparable. In many Western countries, political parties, operating in an environment of rotating governance, aim to come to power through elections. They strive to increase the number of voters and their social support by deliberately portraying themselves as "class-transcending parties," thereby separating and opposing the relationship between class nature and mass nature.

The CPC strives to maintain its advanced nature and long-term governance by continuously consolidating its class support and expanding its public support. It openly declares its class nature, always playing the role of a "vanguard" and a "leading party," while correctly handling the relationship between class nature and mass nature.

Our Party emphasizes the organic integration of consolidating class support and expanding public support. General Secretary Xi Jinping pointed out that the Chinese working class is the most solid and reliable class foundation of our Party. Class support is the foundation for the Party's establishment, while public support is the source of its strength. The two are organically unified and neither is dispensable. As Xi Jinping has stated: "We must focus on maintaining the Party's close bond with the people, keep them firmly in mind, develop a closer affinity with them, and keep working to foster stronger public support for the Party's governance."[2]

On one hand, there should be new efforts to consolidate class support

1 Mao Zedong, *Collected Works of Mao Zedong*, Beijing: People's Publishing House, 1999, vol. VIII, p. 307.
2 *Documents of the 19th CPC National Congress*, Beijing: People's Publishing House, 2017, p. 53.

by always relying wholeheartedly on the working class and ensuring and enhancing its role as the master. On the other hand, there should be new initiatives to expand public support by believing that socialism is the cause of hundreds of millions of people, fully utilizing the Party's political advantage of maintaining close ties with the people, and uniting all forces that can be united to build socialism with Chinese characteristics. This continually enhances the Party's representativeness, inclusiveness, and openness.

General Secretary Xi Jinping emphasizes: "The people are the creators of history, the fundamental force determining the future of the Party and the country." Historical materialism asserts that the people are both the agents of historical activity and the decisive force in history. The grand narrative of the Chinese nation's development has been written by the Chinese people. Since our Party came into power, especially during the past 40 years of reform and opening up, it has led the Chinese people in creating miracles that have astonished the world. From the villagers of Xiaogang signing household responsibility contracts that marked the beginning of reform, to the people of Yiwu transforming small commodities into a large market by trading sugar for chicken feathers, and to technological innovations evolving from "followers" to "peers" and "leaders" in certain fields, the innovation and creativity of the Chinese people have shone brightly. The wisdom and strength of over 1.4 billion people serve as the fundamental guarantee for overcoming all challenges and the solid foundation for the rejuvenation of the Chinese nation.

4. Governance philosophy centered on the people
"For a party or a government, their future and fate are determined by whether they enjoy popular support. If we detach ourselves from the

people and lose the people's support, we will inevitably fail."[1] The CPC has been able to grow and thrive, and socialism with Chinese characteristics has been able to advance continuously because the Party has always adhered to a people-centered governance philosophy, always relying on the people. From its inception, the CPC adopted the principle that "the proletariat can only liberate itself by liberating all of humanity" as its eternal creed, with the ultimate goal of realizing communism. Guided by the belief that "[t]he people, and the people alone, are the motive force of world history,"[2] Mao Zedong dedicated himself to the liberation of the people and the pursuit of national independence. He articulated the fundamental purpose of "serving the people wholeheartedly" and established the mass line of "everything for the people, everything depends on the people, from the people, to the people," which led to the great victories of the new-democratic revolution and the socialist revolution. Throughout its century-long struggle, the CPC has consistently placed its faith in the people, worked for them, and relied on them, forging an inseparable bond with them. The Party has always been breathing the same breath, sharing the same future, and staying truly connected with the people. It has continually relied on the people to drive historical progress. By addressing the practical problems of most concern to the people that affect their immediate interests, focusing on what matters most to them, and doing what brings them satisfaction, the CPC has maintained its progressiveness and purity, strengthened its governance foundation and status, and united and led the people in creating historic achievements.

Since the 18th National Congress, under the leadership of the CPC Central Committee with General Secretary Xi Jinping at its core, the Party has comprehensively deepened reform with the determination to

---

1 *Documents Produced since the 18th CPC National Congress*, Beijing: Central Party Literature Publishing House, 2014, vol. I, p. 81.
2 Mao Zedong, *Selected Works of Mao Tse-tung*, Beijing: Foreign Languages Press, 1967, vol. III, p. 207.

"dare to enter uncharted waters and tackle tough issues," establishing the framework for modernizing the national governance system and capacity. This has written a new chapter of reforms responding to "the people's calls." With the conviction to "leave no one behind" and the resolve that "we will not stop until the victory is won," the Party has launched a decisive battle against poverty, creating a miracle in the history of human poverty alleviation. With a vision for "the benefit of future generations," it has promoted eco-civilization to "leave a blue sky, green land, and clear waters for future generations." With the courage to "offend thousands but not fail the 1.3 billion," the Central Committee has promoted full and strict self-governance of the Party, forging a strong and resilient party. With the concept that "all countries are members of one and the same family," it has sought peace and development for all humankind, promoting the building of human community with a shared future. With the commitment that "the people and their lives are paramount, and protecting people's lives and health can come at any cost," Xi Jinping has personally directed and deployed efforts to achieve significant strategic results in the battle against the COVID-19 pandemic in the shortest possible time. With the great commitment that "I will fully commit to the people and never fail them," he vividly embodies the essence of the Party's original aspirations and founding mission and inscribes the happiness of the people on the milestone leading to the Chinese Dream of national rejuvenation.

Since we entered the New Era, our Party has embarked on a new journey to create a better life for the people and gradually achieved common prosperity for all. In the practice of governance in the New Era, we always adhere to a people-centered approach, taking realizing, upholding, and developing the fundamental interests of the overwhelming majority of the people as the starting and ending points of all our work. This ensures that the fruits of reform and development benefit all people more equitably, steadily moving toward the goal of common prosperity for all. The development we pursue aims to benefit the people, and the prosperity we seek is the common prosperity of all people. "Let the achievements of development benefit all people more equitably, constantly promote the well-rounded development of individuals, and move steadily toward achieving common prosperity for all."[1] "The Chinese people who live in our great motherland in this great age all share the opportunity to accomplish something great in their lives, share the opportunity to make their dreams come true, and share the opportunity to grow and progress along with the motherland and the times."[2] "History has made it clear to us that the country is the people and the people are the country. Winning public support is vital to our Party's survival."[3] These important statements fully reflect General Secretary Xi Jinping's clear stance and sincere affection for the people, tirelessly working for their fundamental interests and the realization of common prosperity. In 2020, a trust survey released by an American company showed that the trust of the Chinese people in their government reached 95%, the highest among all surveyed countries. This is the result of our "people-centered" approach winning public support.

General Secretary Xi Jinping's genuine compassion and concern for the people has established a banner of inspiration and a shining example for Communists in the New Era. Placing the people in the highest place of his mind, he skillfully balances personal interests with the common good, and the individual with the collective, dedicating himself to great causes with the mindset of "I will fully commit to the people." The broad perspective

---

1   "Speech Delivered by Xi Jinping at a Ceremony Marking the Bicentennial of Marx's Birth" (May 4, 2018), *People's Daily*, May 5, 2018.
2   *Series of Speeches by General Secretary Xi Jinping (2016 Edition)*, Beijing: Xuexi Press and People's Publishing House, 2016, p. 12.
3   "At the Preparatory Meeting for the Education Campaign on CPC History, Xi Jinping Stresses That It Is Essential to Study Party History to Better Understand the Theories It Espouses, Work Effectively, and Achieve New Successes and to Strive for Outstanding Achievements to Celebrate the Centenary of the CPC," *People's Daily*, February 21, 2021.

of "not claiming credit for success" reflects a new people-centered concept of political achievement. This concept stresses that self-worth should ultimately be judged by history and the people, with the people serving as the highest arbiters. It reinforces the principle that "We are like examinees sitting the tests posed by this era, and the people will review our results." The commitment to "Success must include my efforts" embodies the original aspirations and founding mission of Chinese Communists. It is this dedication that enables them to shoulder heavy responsibilities for the benefit of the people, thus achieving accomplishments that stand the test of history, the times, and the people.

5. Distinctive character and spirit of self-reform

The CPC is a Marxist party shaped by progressive thought and strengthened by a well-defined theory. It possesses lofty political ideals, noble political pursuits, pure political qualities, and strict political discipline, reflecting its political advancement. One crucial reason for the Party's resilience and vitality through numerous trials is its distinctive character and spirit of self-reform. The CPC has always adhered to the principle that the Party must supervise itself and pursue full and strict self-governance. This approach has enabled the Party to continuously address the risks and challenges it faces in various historical periods, ensuring that it remains at the forefront of global changes and continues to be the backbone of the nation in tackling domestic and international challenges.

Since its founding, the Party has tirelessly explored ways to strengthen itself. Mao Zedong referred to strengthening the Party as a "great project," indicating a more conscious and profound recognition of the importance of strengthening the Party. During the Yan'an period, in response to issues such as subjectivism, sectarianism, and bureaucratism within the Party, we launched the Rectification Movement across the entire Party. This movement required members to engage in criticism and self-criticism in light of their thoughts and practical work. Through the Rectification Movement, the Party achieved new unity and cohesion under the leadership of the Central Committee with Mao Zedong at its core.

After the founding of the People's Republic of China, the Party became the ruling party nationwide, bearing the heavy responsibilities of socialist revolution and development. It faced new tests on how to maintain close ties with the people and uphold a strong revolutionary spirit. In November 1949, the Central Committee decided to establish the Party's central and local commissions for discipline inspection to oversee the behavior of Party organizations and members violating Party discipline. In December 1951, in response to corruption, waste, and bureaucratism in Party and government organs, the Central Committee launched the Campaign against the Three Evils, enduring the new test of governance. Following the Eighth CPC National Congress, we conducted extensive and in-depth rectification movements against bureaucratism, sectarianism, and subjectivism throughout the Party. After the Third Plenary Session of the 11th Central Committee, the Party demonstrated immense political courage to correct mistakes and reestablish the guiding principle of seeking truth from facts. These practices have accumulated valuable experience for the Party in solving its own problems.

Entering the new period of reform and opening up, the Party embarked on new explorations on how to strengthen its development under new historical conditions.

With the deepening of reform and opening up, and in the face of new situations and tasks, our Party has successively carried out activities such as the campaigns to help officials to stress study, politics and integrity, ensure Party members maintain their advanced nature, and carry out in-depth study and implementation of the Scientific Outlook on Development.

The Party has focused on enhancing the Party's governance capacity and advancing its progressive nature. The exploration of strengthening the Party and addressing its own issues has been a persistent pursuit and continuous struggle spanning several generations of Chinese Communists. The Party has continuously enhanced its ability to cleanse, improve and reform itself, ensuring that it remains a strong leadership core for the cause of socialism with Chinese characteristics.

Since the 18th National Congress, the Party has continuously promoted self-reform with unprecedented courage and determination to enforce full and strict self-governance. By guiding the great social revolution with the great self-reform, the Party has improved its leadership system, deepened the reform of the system for strengthening itself, improved the system of its full and strict self-governance, and adhered to regulations-based Party self-governance, forming a relatively complete system of Party regulations. This has resolutely reversed the weakening of Party leadership, the lack of efforts to strengthen the Party, and ineffective Party self-supervision and self-governance in some areas, ensuring that the Party remains the strong leadership core for the cause of socialism with Chinese characteristics.

The Party has firmly upheld the principle of guiding its entire membership with scientific theory to reinforce ideals and convictions. It has established a system dedicated to staying true to the original aspirations and founding mission of the Party. Consistently, the Party has employed Xi Jinping Thought on Socialism with Chinese Characteristics for a New Era to educate and guide its members, instruct the people, and steer its work. Efforts to institutionalize and normalize learning and education have been actively promoted, ranging from the campaign to heighten awareness of and implement the mass line to the special campaign on the Three Stricts and Three Honests," from the "Two Studies, One Action" education campaign to the education campaigns to increase awareness of honoring the Party's original aspiration and founding mission. Through these concentrated educational efforts, Party members and officials have continuously honed their political qualities, upheld their integrity, and deepened their commitment to working together to realize the Chinese Dream.

The Party has strengthened the unity and cohesion of its entire membership through the principle of the Two Upholds, enhancing various systems that firmly uphold the authority and centralized, unified leadership of its Central Committee. It has refined the leadership system of its Central Committee over major initiatives, ensuring its unity in both will and action. This has continuously bolstered the Party's political leadership, theoretical guidance, mass organization, and social influence. By promoting a clean and honest Party style and relentlessly fighting corruption, the Party has won the support of the people, resolutely punishing corruption, correcting misconduct, and removing negative factors that undermine its progress and purity.

The Party has also improved various systems for governance by and for the people, ensuring that the people remain the powerful force behind the CPC's leadership and the development of socialism with Chinese characteristics. These efforts have achieved historic and pioneering results in the full and rigorous self-governance of the Party in the New Era, leaving far-reaching and profound impacts. Comprehensive and strict governance of the Party has become a distinctive feature of the Party's leadership in the New Era, and guiding the great social revolution through great self-reform has become a defining characteristic of the great practice of socialism with Chinese characteristics in the New Era.

The distinctive character and spirit of self-reform have determined that our Party, while carrying out social revolution, continuously engages in self-reform. This is the most remarkable trait that sets our Party apart from others and is key to its ability to continuously move from one victory to the next. General Secretary Xi Jinping pointed out, "It is difficult for a Marxist party to seize power, but it is even more difficult to consolidate it. As long as the ruling Marxist party remains unblemished, the socialist state will not encounter significant problems, allowing us to avoid history's cycle of rise and fall.[1]

How can we ensure our own robustness? General Secretary Xi Jinping emphasizes, "We must dare to engage in self-reform, be strict with ourselves, and remove all irregularities regardless of the pain, becoming resolute in preventing internal strife from arising." Self-reform is a continuous process of upholding the truth and correcting mistakes. By effectively eliminating all factors that undermine the Party's advancement and purity, the Party consistently cleansed, improved and reformed itself. This process has become an invaluable experience for the Party's ongoing growth and development. Through relentless self-reform, the Party effectively prevents the deterioration and loss of its Marxist principles, greatly enriching the theory and practice of building a Marxist party. This also highlights the significant advantages of the CPC's leadership and our socialist system, making important contributions to human political advancement.

The distinctive character and spirit of self-reform have ensured that our Party consistently stays true to its original aspirations and founding mission with a commitment to self-reform. General Secretary Xi Jinping stated, "The longer we stay in power, the more we must stay true to its original aspirations and founding mission and the more we must maintain the spirit of self-reform."[2] Since the 18th National Congress, the Central

---

1   Xi Jinping, *Stay True to the Original Aspirations and Founding Mission of the Party,* Beijing: Party Building Books Publishing House and Central Party Literature Publishing House, 2019, pp. 303–304.
2   *Ibid.,* p. 179.

Committee, with General Secretary Xi Jinping at its core, has brought full and rigorous self-governance of the Party to new depths with an unwavering spirit of self-reform. It has persistently implemented the central leadership's eight-point decision on improving Party and government conduct, leading the people with integrity and a positive image, thus opening a new chapter in China's effective governance.

For the Party to resolve its own issues and achieve long-term governance, it is crucial to maintain the spirit of self-reform. Whether the Party possesses a strong spirit of self-reform, embodies the solid characteristics of self-purification, and persists in addressing its own problems are critical factors determining the Party's success or failure. Only by upholding the spirit of self-reform can the Party achieve self-transcendence, continuously resolving its internal challenges, maintaining its original mission to serve the people, and preserving its advancement and purity.

The distinctive character and spirit of self-reform determine that our Party can firmly combat and prevent corruption. General Secretary Xi Jinping stated, "Only by intensifying efforts to address both the symptoms and root causes of corruption—by making sure that officials are honest, government is clean, and political affairs are handled with integrity—can we avoid history's cycle of rise and fall."[1] Advancing self-reform must be based on the overall work of the Party and the state, addressing prominent issues in the full and strict self-governance of the Party, and striving to achieve both temporary and permanent solutions.

Since the 18th National Congress, from the phase where "corruption and anti-corruption were in a stalemate" to achieving a decisive victory in the anti-corruption struggle and consolidating it comprehensively, the fight against corruption and the punishment of wrongdoing have profoundly

---

1   *Documents of the 19th CPC National Congress*, Beijing: People's Publishing House, 2017, p. 53.

changed the political ecology and greatly inspired the morale of both the Party and the people. On our new journey, we must continue to adhere to the principles of no restricted zones, full coverage, and zero tolerance in the fight against corruption, maintaining strong deterrence, and sustained pressure. We must advance the integrated strategy of ensuring that officials do not dare to be, are not able to be, and have no desire to be corrupt, with the courage to cut off the poison to provide strong support for the development of the Party and state's cause.

The distinctive character and spirit of self-reform ensure that our Party can persist in combining internal Party supervision with external supervision. General Secretary Xi Jinping pointed out, "For some prominent issues within the Party, the people often have a clear view. Whether Party members and officials have remained true to their original aspirations and mission should be evaluated by the people and tested through practice. We cannot carry out self-reform behind closed doors but must listen to the opinions of the people and consciously accept their supervision."[1] Since the 18th National Congress, by improving the supervision system of the Party and the state, leveraging the driving role of internal Party supervision, and promoting the integration and coordination of supervision by the National People's Congress, democratic supervision, administrative supervision, judicial supervision, audit supervision, financial supervision, statistical supervision, mass supervision, and public opinion supervision, we have established an effective system of power supervision and discipline and law enforcement. This system combines internal Party supervision with external supervision, laying a solid institutional foundation for full and strict self-governance of the Party and self-reform.

In striving in the New Era and advancing on the new journey, we

---

1   Xi Jinping, *Stay True to the Original Aspirations and Founding Mission of the Party*, Beijing: Party Building Books Publishing House and Central Party Literature Publishing House, 2019, p. 1781.

must continue to promote the organic integration and mutual coordination of various supervision systems. By driving and promoting other forms of supervision through internal Party supervision, we can further eliminate the vacuum zones in power supervision, ensuring that full and strict self-governance of the Party keeps pace with the times and endures over the long term. This will ensure that the power entrusted to us by the Party and the people is always used to seek happiness for the people.

II. Why Does Marxism Always Work?

Why does Marxism always work? This question is both a fundamental theoretical issue and an important practical concern. General Secretary Xi Jinping pointed out, "Practice has proven that the fate of Marxism has long been closely tied with that of the CPC, the Chinese people, and the Chinese nation. Its scientific nature and truth have been fully tested in China, its people-oriented nature and practicality have been fully implemented in China, and its openness and contemporary relevance have been fully demonstrated in China."[1] This requires us to deeply understand the scientific, people-oriented, practical, and contemporary nature of Marxism by integrating theory with practice, and history with reality. We must comprehend this through the great historical journey in which the CPC, guided by Marxism, has led the Chinese people through revolution, development, and reform over the past century. Additionally, it is crucial to recognize that Xi Jinping Thought on Socialism with Chinese Characteristics for a New Era represents contemporary Chinese Marxism and 21st-century Marxism, which must be consistently adhered to and further developed.

1　*Documents Produced since the 19th CPC National Congress*, Beijing: Central Party Literature Publishing House, 2017,

1. Occupy the high ground of truth: scientifically answer the question of history

Marxism occupies the high ground of truth, surpassing all previous forms of idealism and old materialism, primarily because it reveals the general laws governing the development of the natural world, human society, and human thought. It consists of three fundamental components: Marxist philosophy, Marxist political economy, and scientific socialism. Together, these form a highly systematic, extensive, and profound theoretical framework. Marxism's greatest contributions to humanity are two major discoveries: historical materialism, which uncovers the underlying dynamics of historical development, and the theory of surplus value, which reveals the inner workings of capitalism. These groundbreaking discoveries creatively elucidate the general laws governing the development of human society and the specific laws governing capitalist evolution, thereby pointing the way for humanity's transition from the realm of necessity to the realm of freedom, and showing people the path to achieve true freedom and liberation.

Marxist philosophy, comprising dialectical materialism and historical materialism, deeply explores the general laws governing the development of the objective world. Dialectical materialism upholds the unity of matter, insisting on objective material existence as the foundation. It seeks to understand and grasp the essence and laws of phenomena within the dialectical interplay of specific time and space, movement and stillness. This approach begins with objective reality, follows inherent laws, and utilizes these laws effectively, rather than starting from subjective assumptions or dogmatic beliefs.

Historical materialism, as a critical component of Marxist philosophy, unveils the general laws governing the development of human society. It provides a scientific worldview and methodology for correctly understanding the essence of human society and grasping the laws governing social development amidst the complex and ever-changing human history. The thinking and working methods based on the fundamental principles of dialectical materialism and historical materialism, particularly dialectical materialism, advocate for analyzing and solving problems objectively, holistically, developmentally, and comprehensively. This method is an objective dialectic, independent of human will, reflecting the essence and laws of the interconnections and development of things. It serves both as a "telescope" for discerning direction and understanding objective laws and as a "microscope" for deeply recognizing and grasping the essence of things.

Marxist political economy reveals the general laws governing social and economic development. Using the basic principles of historical materialism, Marxist political economy takes the contradictory movements of the forces and relations of production, and the economic base and superstructure, as its main lines. It profoundly elucidates the general laws governing commodity economy development, the basic contradictions of commodity economy based on private ownership, and the labor theory of value, thereby discovering the Marxist theory of surplus value. Focusing on the creation and valorization of surplus value, it further analyzes the theory of capitalist accumulation and the circulation and reproduction of capital, revealing the inherent contradiction between socialized mass production and the capitalist private ownership of production means. This, in turn, unveils the fundamental laws governing the periodic outbreak of capitalist economic crises. Moreover, it deeply analyzes the occurrence of economic crises and the methods capitalism employs to alleviate these crises, thereby driving the adjustment and transformation of capitalist relations of production. It comprehensively elucidates the development of capitalism from free competition to monopoly, the new changes in contemporary capitalism, and the historical process of capitalism, ultimately revealing the fundamental trend and law that capitalism will be inevitably replaced by socialism.

Scientific socialism reveals the essence and development laws of socialism and communism. By employing the fundamental principles of historical materialism and focusing on the evolving contradictions within human society, scientific socialism profoundly elucidates several key ideas: the inevitability of socialism replacing capitalism, the historical mission of the proletariat, the necessity of socialist revolution and proletarian dictatorship, the essential characteristics and developmental laws of socialist society, the development of proletarian parties, and the fundamental traits and historical inevitability of communist society. It clarifies the basic characteristics and development laws of socialist and communist societies. Socialism with Chinese characteristics is the theoretical and practical outcome of integrating the fundamental tenets of scientific socialism with China's specific realities: "The fundamental tenets of scientific socialism cannot be discarded; once discarded it would cease to be socialism."[1]

Overall, Marxism fundamentally reveals the essence and development laws of the world; it discloses the essence and laws of human cognition; it clarifies the essence and laws of human society, especially the nature and developmental laws of capitalist, socialist, and communist societies. Marxism serves as the fundamental basis for understanding the complex social phenomena and various social thoughts and is the foundational methodological basis for recognizing, analyzing, and solving problems. As General Secretary Xi Jinping pointed out, "No theory in history can match Marxism in terms of rationale, truth, and spread, and no theory has exerted

---

1   *Documents Produced since the 18th CPC National Congress*, Beijing: Central Party Literature Publishing House, 2014, vol. I, p. 109.

such a huge influence on the world as Marxism. This proves the truth and vigor in Marxism."[1] This is our scientific basis for steadfastly upholding our ideals and convictions and our aspirations and mission in the New Era and for continuing to adapt Marxism to the Chinese context in keeping with the times, and increase its appeal to the people.

Marxism always works because its scientific theories and fundamental tenets are effectively combined with the realities of each country, adapting to the specific needs of different nations and peoples. This process enables Marxism to play a guiding role in the nationalization and localization of its ideas. Marxism provides concrete solutions tailored to the distinct political, economic, and cultural needs of various countries at different historical periods. It is through this integration with the realities of different nations and their stages of development that Marxism achieves its effectiveness.

Marx stated, "Theory is fulfilled in a people only insofar as it is the fulfilment of the needs of that people."[2] Lenin also emphasized that for Marxism to be effective, it is crucial to "correctly modify these principles in certain particulars, correctly adapt and apply them to national and national-state distinctions."[3] CPC leaders have profoundly grasped the essence of Marxism and the paths to its implementation, continuously advancing its adaptation to the Chinese context over the past century. Mao Zedong asserted that Marxism must be integrated with the concrete realities of the Chinese revolution and harmonized with national characteristics and that this integration must "acquire a definite national form if it is to be useful."[4] Deng Xiaoping also emphasized, "Only Marxism that is integrated with Chinese realities is the genuine Marxism we need."[5] General Secretary Xi Jinping stressed the importance of a scientific attitude toward scientific

1 Xi Jinping, *The Governance of China*, Beijing: Foreign Languages Press, 2017, vol. II, p. 68.
2 https://www.marxists.org/archive/marx/works/1843/critique-hpr/intro.htm.
3 https://www.marxists.org/archive/lenin/works/1920/lwc/ch10.htm.
4 Mao Zedong, *Selected Works of Mao Tse-tung*, Beijing: Foreign Languages Press, 1967, vol. II, p. 381.
5 Deng Xiaoping, *Selected Works of Deng Xiaoping*, Beijing: Foreign Languages Press, 1994, vol. III, p. 213.

theory: "We must not approach Marxism dogmatically or pragmatically."[1]

In the New Era, the Chinese Communists have integrated the fundamental tenets of Marxism with the specific realities of contemporary China, leading the people in waging the great struggle, building the great project, promoting the great cause, and realizing the great dream. This has propelled the Party and the nation's cause to achieve comprehensive, pioneering historical accomplishments and deep-seated, fundamental historical transformations. The Chinese nation has thus made a tremendous transformation from standing up, to growing rich prosperous, and to becoming strong. This profound transformation not only reaffirms the validity of Marxism but also highlights the effectiveness of Chinese Marxism, which combines the fundamental tenets of Marxism with China's unique realities. Additionally, it underscores the success of Xi Jinping Thought on Socialism with Chinese Characteristics for a New Era, representing the latest development in contemporary Marxism.

The enduring relevance of Marxism lies in the Chinese Communists' ongoing theoretical innovation rooted in practical experience, which continuously advances contemporary Chinese Marxism and 21st-century Marxism. Xi Jinping Thought on Socialism with Chinese Characteristics for a New Era embodies the Marxist worldview and methodology, consistently upholding Marxist positions, perspectives, and methods. It not only reflects the truth of Marxism but also introduces original, timely, and systematic innovations in the core principles of Marxist philosophy, political economy, and scientific socialism. Through a series of pioneering viewpoints, it clarifies the essential characteristics, core essence, scientific system, historical contributions, contemporary significance, practical value, and developmental trajectory of Marxism, marking a new leap in adapting Marxism to the Chinese context. As a result, it stands as both

---

1   Xi Jinping, *Promote Socialist Cultural Development*, Beijing: People's Publishing House, 2017, p. 79.

contemporary Chinese Marxism and 21st-century Marxism. Its scientific and truthful nature has been thoroughly demonstrated in the practices of the four greats of the New Era, in the coordinated implementation of the Five-Sphere Integrated Plan and the Four-Pronged Comprehensive Strategy, and in the historical creations of continuing the great social revolution and the great self-reform. It will undoubtedly continue to be proven in guiding the Chinese nation's great transformation from standing up, growing rich, and becoming strong, and in leading China's new journey toward building a great modern socialist country in all respects. In contemporary China, upholding Xi Jinping Thought on Socialism with Chinese Characteristics for a New Era is genuinely adhering to Marxism. Under the guidance of this great thought, we must continually promote theoretical innovation based on practice, making new contributions to the development of contemporary Chinese Marxism and 21st-century Marxism.

2. Occupy the moral high ground: scientifically answer the people's question

The effectiveness of Marxism also lies in its position as a scientific theory that not only stands at the pinnacle of scientific truth but also represents the interests of the overwhelming majority of the people in terms of value stance. The people-oriented nature of Marxism is its distinctive characteristic; its ethical pursuit is to seek benefits for the vast majority of the people, and its power source is the reliance on the overwhelming majority of the people to transform the world. Marxism's role as the fundamental theoretical guide for the Communist Party is due not only to its scientific nature, which reveals the essence and laws of the world and answers the fundamental question of "how to understand and transform the world," but also because it occupies the moral high ground, profoundly answering the fundamental question of "for whom Communists serve."

General Secretary Xi Jinping stated, "Marxism is broad and profound, but it boils down to one sentence: it seeks liberation for humanity."[1] For the first time, Marxism, rooted in the perspective of the people, seeks to explore the path toward human freedom and liberation, guiding the way toward the ultimate establishment of an ideal society—one without oppression or exploitation, where equality and freedom prevail for all.

The scientific nature and people-oriented nature, purposefulness, and value-orientation of Marxism are highly unified. As Engels said, "The more ruthlessly and disinterestedly science proceeds, the more it finds itself in harmony with the interests and aspirations of the workers."[2] Therefore, the more impartial the theory is, the more it aligns with the interests of the overwhelming majority of the people. Hence, Marxism is the theory of communism for the complete liberation of all humanity. Compared to other classes, the proletariat possesses no means of production, and their liberation is predicated on the liberation of all humanity. Only by eliminating exploitation and oppression, and eradicating class rule, class struggle, and class differences, can they ultimately achieve liberation. Engels also pointed out: "[T]he exploited and oppressed class (the proletariat) can no longer emancipate itself from the class which exploits and oppresses it (the bourgeoisie), without at the same time forever freeing the whole of society from exploitation, oppression, class struggles."[3] The liberation of the proletariat aligns with that of all humanity, and their fundamental interests are consistent with those of the people. To achieve the liberation of all humanity is to ultimately liberate themselves.

Marxism holds that the people are the true creators of history. "Together with the thoroughness of the historical action, the size of the

---

1   *Documents Produced since the 19th CPC National Congress,* Beijing: Central Party Literature Publishing House, 2019, p. 424.
2   Engels, *Ludwig Feuerbach,* MEW 21, p. 307; SW III, p. 376.
3   file:///C:/Users/tong1/Downloads/1603981456-0130-marx-and-engels-communist-manifesto.pdf.

mass whose action it is will therefore increase."[1] The collective power formed by the broad people in their struggle for self-liberation determines the forward direction of human social history. Marxism not only recognized the living conditions of the proletariat but also further emphasized that the people are the true heroes, the decisive force behind historical progress and social change. This provided the direction for the proletariat to achieve revolutionary victory, liberate all humanity, and ultimately liberate themselves. "As philosophy finds its material weapon in the proletariat, so the proletariat finds its spiritual weapon in philosophy."[2] The people are the decisive force in social transformation, which is a fundamental viewpoint of historical materialism. General Secretary Xi Jinping stated that whether or not one respects the people's principal status and acknowledges the people's role in creating history is the fundamental distinction between historical materialism and historical idealism. Only by unifying respect for the laws governing social development with respect for the people's historical principal status can we gather the strong force needed to achieve the rejuvenation of the Chinese nation.

The unity of Marxism's scientific and value-based nature, and the combination of Marxism's power of truth and moral power, ultimately manifest in the nature, purpose, and value pursuit of the Marxist political party. Without the theory and action of a Marxist political party, without Marxism guiding new practice with its scientific theory, Marxism's effectiveness would remain theoretical and confined to books, unable to truly guide people in transforming the world.

All theoretical viewpoints of Marxism are rooted in and culminate in the fundamental interests of the overwhelming majority of the people, aiming to realize, safeguard, and advance these interests. Marx and Engels

---

1   Marx & Engels, Collected Works, Lawrence & Wishart, 2010, vol. 4, p. 82.
2   https://www.marxists.org/archive/marx/works/1843/critique-hpr/intro.htm.

explicitly pointed out: "All previous historical movements were movements of minorities, or in the interest of minorities. The proletarian movement is the self-conscious, independent movement of the immense majority, in the interest of the immense majority."[1] Mao Zedong, when discussing the mission of Communists, stated: "[E]very comrade must be brought to understand that the supreme test of the words and deeds of a Communist is whether they conform with the highest interests and enjoy the support of the overwhelming majority of the people."[2] Always standing on the side of the people, adhering to the principle of people-first, and wholeheartedly serving the people is the mass foundation and source of strength for Marxist parties, as well as their moral basis and goal. General Secretary Xi Jinping emphasized: "When we talk about our mission, we say many things, but ultimately it comes down to serving the people."[3] The CPC has no special interests of its own apart from the interests of the state, the nation, and the people. Only by not seeking personal gains can we pursue fundamental and great interests. "The CPC has in the people its roots, its lifeblood, and its source of strength. The Party has always represented the fundamental interests of all Chinese people; it stands with them through thick and thin and shares a common fate with them. The Party has no special interests of its own—it has never represented any individual interest group, power group, or privileged stratum."[4]

The people-centered nature of Marxism finds its latest expression in Xi Jinping Thought on Socialism with Chinese Characteristics for a New Era and its best practice in the continuous development of socialism with Chinese characteristics in the New Era. The following theoretical

---

1   https://www.marxists.org/archive/marx/works/1848/communist-manifesto/ch01.htm.
2   Mao Zedong, *Selected Works of Mao Tse-tung*, Beijing: Foreign Languages Press, 1967, vol. III, p. 266.
3   Xi Jinping, *Stay True to the Original Aspirations and Founding Mission of the Party*, Beijing: Party Building Books Publishing House and Central Party Literature Publishing House, 2019, p. 127.
4   Xi Jinping, *Speech at a Ceremony Marking the Centenary of the Communist Party of China*, Beijing: People's Publishing House, 2021, pp. 11–12.

innovations and practical endeavors are the best embodiments of the people-centered nature of Marxism by contemporary Chinese Communists:

- Adhering to the original aspirations of seeking happiness for the people, upholding the fundamental stance of putting people at the center, and taking the people's aspiration for a better life as the goal of our efforts

- Always placing the interests of the people in the highest position, maintaining a heartfelt connection with the people, embracing the selfless spirit of "I will fully commit to the people and never fail them"

- Ensuring that the fruits of development benefit all people more equitably and striving for the common prosperity of all

- Adhering to the principle that "We are like examinees sitting the tests posed by this era, and the people will review our results" and ensure ensuring that the fundamental criterion of our work is whether we have the people's support, acceptance, satisfaction and approval

- Acknowledging that the people are the main force of historical development and social progress, fully harnessing the enthusiasm and creativity of the people, and relying closely on the people to create historic achievements

The most distinctive feature of the governance in the New Era under the leadership of the Central Committee with General Secretary Xi Jinping at its core is "always placing the people in the highest position in our minds," making "people-centeredness" the fundamental governing philosophy. Since the 18th CPC National Congress, the Party has led the people in winning the battle against poverty, historically resolving the issue of absolute poverty; achieving the goal of building a moderately prosperous society in all respects, greatly improving the living standards of the people; ensuring that the benefits of development are shared more equitably among all people, significantly enhancing the people's sense of fulfillment, happiness, and security; making common prosperity a fundamental requirement of the socialist system and a distinctive feature of Chinese modernization, achieving more substantial progress toward common prosperity for all—these practical achievements fully demonstrate the Party's commitment to the people-centered philosophy and highlight the people-centered nature of contemporary Chinese Marxism, allowing the people to genuinely feel the goodness of the CPC and the effectiveness of Marxism. General Secretary Xi Jinping pointed out: "On the journey ahead, we must rely closely on the people to create history. Upholding the Party's fundamental purpose of wholeheartedly serving the people, we will stand firmly with the people, implement the Party's mass line, respect the people's creativity, and practice a people-centered philosophy of development."[1]

3. Occupy the high ground of practice: scientifically answer the question of practice

The viewpoint of practice is the primary and fundamental viewpoint of Marxism. Marx believed that the truth and reality of theory can only be tested and realized in practice. "The question whether objective truth can be attributed to human thinking is not a question of theory but is a practical question. Man must prove the truth, i.e. the reality and power, the this-worldliness of his thinking in practice."[2] Lenin also said: "All theories are good if they correspond to objective reality."[3] Marxism is not a dogma but a guide to action; it is not a scholarly subject but a theory of practice. Its transcendence over past and contemporary theories lies in its provision of a powerful theoretical weapon for people to transform the world. The practicality of Marxism is concentrated in the guiding principle of Chinese Communists, which includes starting from reality in everything,

---

1   *Ibid.* p. 12.
2   https://www.marxists.org/archive/marx/works/1845/theses/engels.htm.
3   https://www.marxists.org/archive/lenin/works/1918/sep/00.htm.

integrating theory with practice, seeking truth from facts, and testing and developing truth in practice.

The reason why Marxism always works lies not only in its truth in understanding the world but more importantly in its practical function, i.e., its mission and ability to transform the world. "The philosophers have only interpreted the world in various ways; the point, however, is to change it." Practicality is a distinctive feature that sets Marxism apart from other theories. As General Secretary Xi Jinping pointed out: "Marxism is not a study confined to libraries but was founded to change the destiny of the people, formed in the practice of the people's quest for liberation, enriched and developed in this practice, providing a powerful source of inspiration for the people to understand and transform the world."[1] Marxism has not only profoundly changed the world but also deeply transformed China. It has guided the Chinese nation to achieve the great transformation from standing up, to growing rich, and to becoming strong. It has led China onto the broad path of building a great modern socialist country in all respects and ushered in a bright future for the realization of the rejuvenation of the Chinese nation. This fully demonstrates the practical power of Marxism and is the most convincing evidence of why Marxism always works.

Xi Jinping Thought on Socialism with Chinese Characteristics for a New Era adheres to and promotes the practical character of Marxism. It is rooted in the great practice of upholding and developing socialism with Chinese characteristics. By guiding and advancing practice, it demonstrates powerful truth, fully embodying the practical potency of Marxism. Upholding the viewpoint of "practice first," it is based on the great practice of the New Era, overseeing the great struggle, the great project, the great cause, and the great dream and guiding the Chinese people to achieve great

---

1   Xi Jinping, *Speech at a Ceremony Marking the Bicentennial of Marx's Birth*, People's Publishing House, 2018, p. 9.

accomplishments in socialism with Chinese characteristics in the New Era. The great practice of the New Era is magnificent.

By adhering to and strengthening the overall leadership of the Party, promoting the overall layout of the "Five-in-One" and the coordinated promotion of the "Four Comprehensives" strategy, upholding and improving the socialist system with Chinese characteristics, advancing the modernization of the national governance system and capacity, adhering to the rule of the Party by regulations, and forming a relatively complete system of intra-Party regulations, it has overcome a series of major risks and challenges, achieved the First Centenary Goal, and clarified the strategic arrangements for achieving the Second Centenary Goal. The Party and the country's undertakings have achieved historic accomplishments and undergone historic changes, providing a more perfect institutional guarantee, a more solid material foundation, and a more proactive spiritual force for realizing the rejuvenation of the Chinese nation. The realization of the rejuvenation of the Chinese nation has entered an irreversible historical process, reaching unprecedented heights in both practical and theoretical innovations. This is the great victory of socialism with Chinese characteristics and the great victory of Marxism, showcasing the most powerful and convincing truth and practical power of Marxism in 21st-century China.

4. Occupy the high ground of the era: scientifically answer the questions of the times

Zeitgeist is a distinct characteristic of Marxism, and keeping pace with the times is its theoretical quality, which is the fundamental way it retains its vitality. Marxism, unlike previous historical social theories, possesses an inherent mechanism for innovation as times evolve. It inherently stands at the forefront of its era, leading the times with its essential characteristic of advancing with the times.

Unlike other historical social theories, Marxism has a mechanism for innovation with the development of the times, possessing the essential feature of leading the era from the forefront and the quality of keeping pace with the times. Only Marxism can continuously adapt to the trend of the times, consistently researching new situations and solving new problems. Each historical era or development stage it experiences proves and advances its development. Although Marxism was born more than 170 years ago, it has not become obsolete and still maintains strong vitality. The important reason lies in Marxism's ability to stand at the high ground of the era, conform to the development trends of the era, answer the questions of the times, and promote theoretical innovation. Representative figures of Marxism in different times, conforming to the development of the era and answering the questions of the times, have formed a scientific theoretical system that is both consistent and advancing with the times. In continuously answering and solving the practical questions of the times, they have enriched and developed Marxism.

Marxism, because it occupies the high ground of the era, provides people with fundamental directions and paths for scientifically solving the problems of the times. However, due to the changes and developments in various historical periods, Marxism cannot offer ready-made answers to specific problems of each era. It is necessary to combine the fundamental tenets of Marxism with the characteristics of the times, promoting the modernization of Marxism and continuously enriching and developing it. This is the theoretical quality of Marxism's ability to keep pace with the times, which determines that Marxism is a practical, open, and developing theory. One must unify revolutionary and scientific nature, inheritance and creativity, particularity and universality, and continuously innovate theoretically according to practical requirements, consciously accepting the test of practice to maintain vitality in new practices. Marx and Engels repeatedly emphasized that their theory is not a rigid dogma but a "developing theory," a "guide to action," and a "method of research." Therefore, Deng Xiaoping said, "We cannot expect Marx to provide ready answers to questions that arise a hundred or several hundred years after his death, nor can we ask Lenin to give answers to questions that arise fifty or a hundred years after his death. A true Marxist-Leninist must understand, carry on and develop Marxism-Leninism in light of the current situation."[1] It can be said that Marxism was born out of the needs of the times and has been enriched and developed through the progress of the times, which is also the source of Marxism's lasting vitality and vigor.

The history of the development of Marxism is the history of Marx, Engels, and their successors continuously evolving according to the development of the times, practice, and cognition. It is a history of them continuously absorbing all the excellent theoretical and cultural achievements in human history to enrich themselves. Reviewing the more than 170 years of Marxism's development history, one can clearly see that the representative figures of Marxism in different historical periods, adapting to the development of the times and answering the questions of the times, have formed a theoretical system that is both consistent and uniquely characteristic. Marx and Engels scientifically answered the era's questions about the direction of capitalism and human society during the era of free capitalism, forming Marxism. Lenin scientifically answered the era's questions about the direction of imperialism and the proletarian revolution during the era of monopoly capitalism, forming Leninism. The Chinese Communists, with Mao Zedong as the main representative, scientifically answered the era's questions about the direction of China and the Chinese revolution in semi-colonial and semi-feudal China, forming

---

1 Deng Xiaoping, *Selected Works of Deng Xiaoping*, Beijing: Foreign Languages Press, 1994, vol. III, p. 284.

Mao Zedong Thought.

Since the introduction of the reform and opening up policy, successive generations of Chinese Communists have continuously addressed a series of era-defining questions, such as what kind of socialism to build, how to go about it, what kind of party to build, how to go about it, what kind of development to achieve, and how to go about it, forming the theoretical system of socialism with Chinese characteristics.

Great eras give rise to great theories. Marx once said, "Each principle has had its own century in which to manifest itself."[1] Any scientific theory is a condensation of the spirit of its era and an answer to the problems of its time. Every historically significant era has a great thought that marks and leads the era. This thought is itself a product of the era, expressing the objective needs of the time, guiding the people, and thus becoming a material force that transforms the world. Since the 18th CPC National Congress, socialism with Chinese characteristics has entered the New Era. The development of contemporary China, the changes in the contemporary world, and the development of human society all face new questions that define the era, urgently calling for new theories that embody the spirit of the times, answer the questions of the times, and become the hallmark of the era. This is an era that needs theories and will undoubtedly produce theories. It is an era that needs ideas and will undoubtedly produce ideas. The great theory and great thought that condenses the essence of the era and answers the questions of the times, thereby becoming the coordinate of the era, is the new leap in the adaptation of Marxism to the Chinese context, namely, Xi Jinping Thought on Socialism with Chinese Characteristics for a New Era. This is contemporary Chinese Marxism and 21st-century Marxism, rooted in China and leading the world.

Represented by Xi Jinping, Chinese Communists have responded

---

1   https://www.marxists.org/archive/marx/works/1847/poverty-philosophy/ch02.htm.

to the changes of the times, stood at the forefront of the era, and voiced the pioneering ideas of the times. From the combination of theory and practice, they have systematically addressed major contemporary issues such as what kind of socialism with Chinese characteristics to uphold and develop, how to go about it, what kind of socialist modernized country to build, how to go about it, what kind of long-term ruling Marxist party to build, and how to go about it. This has formed Xi Jinping Thought on Socialism with Chinese Characteristics for a New Era, scientifically constructing the latest theoretical form of contemporary Chinese Marxism and 21st-century Marxism. This great thought is both Chinese and global. It guides the Chinese people to stride confidently into the New Era of building a great modern socialist country and achieving the rejuvenation of the Chinese nation. It also guides contemporary China to approach the center stage of the world and continuously make greater contributions to humanity. Furthermore, it guides the CPC in responding to the unprecedented changes in a century and promoting the building a human community with a shared future. This is a successful practice of using Marxism to observe, interpret, and lead the era. It is the best answer to why Marxism always works and the best proof of Marxism's enduring vitality and powerful force.

Xi Jinping Thought on Socialism with Chinese Characteristics for a New Era is grounded in the foundation of its time, answering the questions of the times, and leading the changes of the era. By doing so, it grasps historical laws, maintains historical initiative, and promotes historical progress. The era-defining questions that this great thought answers are the issues raised in the intertwined domestic and international situations: the direction of contemporary China and the direction of the contemporary world. General Secretary Xi Jinping pointed out, "While today's world is undergoing changes of a scale unseen in a century, China is at the critical stage of national rejuvenation, and the CPC is leading the people in a great historic struggle with many new features. These changes that come at a staggering pace, the need to strike a balance between reform, development and stability, and the problems, risks and challenges we face—all present unprecedented tests to our Party's governance."[1] "Even if one has wisdom, it is better to seize the momentum." We must embrace the overall strategy of the rejuvenation of the Chinese nation and the unprecedented changes in a century, adopt a grand historical perspective, analyze the mechanisms of evolution and explore historical laws from the long river of history, the great tide of the times, and the global situation, propose corresponding strategies, and enhance the systematicness, foresight, and creativity of our work. Under the guidance of Xi Jinping Thought on Socialism with Chinese Characteristics for a New Era, the rejuvenation of the Chinese nation has entered an irreversible historical process, ushering in a bright future. Today, we are closer than ever in history to achieving the goal of national rejuvenation, and we are more confident and capable than ever in achieving this goal. The Chinese nation is showing a thriving scene to the world, advancing toward rejuvenation with unstoppable momentum.

Xi Jinping Thought on Socialism with Chinese Characteristics for a New Era was established and continues to develop under new historical conditions and practical contexts. It is precisely due to the full display of the practical power of this thought that it leads socialism with Chinese characteristics to achieve new developments and propels the rejuvenation of the Chinese nation to make great strides. As contemporary China and the world change and develop, this great thought continuously answers the questions of the times and the world, demonstrating the stronger and more persuasive truth power of 21st-century Marxism. In guiding China and

---

1   Xi Jinping, *Speech at the Preparatory Meeting for the Education Campaign on CPC History,* Beijing: People's Publishing House, 2021, p. 10.

leading the world, it further proves the effectiveness of Marxism.

III. Why Does Chinese Socialism Always Shine?

The questions of why the CPC always delivers and why Marxism always works manifest in the remarkable achievements of socialism with Chinese characteristics, which is reflected in its effectiveness. In the 100 years since its founding, especially in the more than 70 years since the establishment of the People's Republic of China, the CPC has led the Chinese people, consistently guided by Marxism, through continuous struggles in revolution, development, and reform, forging a correct path for achieving socialist modernization and the rejuvenation of the Chinese nation—this is the path of socialism with Chinese characteristics.

The path of socialism with Chinese characteristics is a path where the people run the country, a path for the people to achieve a better life, and a path for the rejuvenation of the Chinese nation. This path embodies the original aspirations and mission of the Chinese Communists, the relentless pursuit and expectations of the Chinese people, the blood and sweat of countless heroes and martyrs, and the hard work and dedication of generations of Chinese sons and daughters. It continues the glorious and profound civilization of 5,000 years and carries the dreams and hopes of the rejuvenation of the Chinese nation. This broad, necessary, happy, and rejuvenating road encapsulates a profound truth that has led to the earth-shaking historical changes in new China: Only the CPC can lead China, only socialism can save China, only socialism with Chinese characteristics can develop China, and only socialism with Chinese characteristics in the New Era can rejuvenate China.

Socialism with Chinese characteristics has been gradually explored and pioneered since the founding of the People's Republic of China. Over the past 70-plus years, the CPC has led the Chinese people to advance with determination on the path of socialism with Chinese characteristics, writing a magnificent epic in the history of both the Chinese nation and the world. Socialism with Chinese characteristics has experienced a great transformation from its establishment, development, to perfection. In the historical journey from standing up to growing rich and to becoming strong, the CPC has opened up the path of socialism with Chinese characteristics, formed the theoretical system of socialism with Chinese characteristics, established the system of socialism with Chinese characteristics, and developed the culture of socialism with Chinese characteristics.

Socialism with Chinese characteristics is the fundamental achievement obtained by the Party and the people through immense hardships and significant costs. It is the dialectical unity of the theoretical logic of scientific socialism and the historical logic of China's social development. It is scientific socialism rooted in Chinese soil, reflecting the will of the Chinese people, and meeting the requirements of China's and the era's development and progress. The great success of socialism with Chinese characteristics has revitalized the 170-plus-year-old scientific socialism in the ancient, populous country of over 1.4 billion people, while also holding high the great banner of socialism with Chinese characteristics on the world stage.

Both history and reality have proven this simple yet profound truth: socialism with Chinese characteristics always shines. Fully and profoundly answering why socialism with Chinese characteristics always shines reveals the fundamental logic behind China's historic achievements and captures the compelling theme running through the Chinese story.

1. It shines because of the truth of its doctrine

This doctrine is Marxism, or specifically, scientific socialism. Engels once said, "It [Our party] had the great advantage that its theoretical foundation was a new scientific conception the elaboration of which provided adequate work."[1] This "new scientific viewpoint" is the perspective of Marxism, the viewpoint of scientific socialism. Mao Zedong once pointed out: "A doctrine is like a flag; only when the flag is raised do people have something to aspire to and a direction to follow."[2] From the moment the CPC was founded, it inscribed Marxism, communism, and socialism on its banner, leading the Chinese people through the new-democratic revolution, the socialist revolution and development, and the great revolution of reform and opening up. The victories and brilliant achievements of these great undertakings profoundly interpret the "truth of the doctrine" and vividly demonstrate that "the doctrine works." Socialism with Chinese characteristics is a precious result achieved by the Party and the people through immense hardships and various sacrifices. It carries the ideals and explorations of several generations of Chinese Communists, embodies the wishes and expectations of countless patriots, and condenses the struggles and sacrifices of hundreds of millions of people. It is the inevitable choice for the development of Chinese society in modern times.

Socialism shines because of the truth of its doctrine. This is because this doctrine can address the historical issues that China faces. During the times when the Chinese nation was impoverished and weak, subject to domination by others, various doctrines and thoughts were tried—capitalism failed, and so did reformism, liberalism, social Darwinism, and anarchism. Various rescue plans were proposed one after another, but all ended in failure. China urgently needed new thoughts to guide

---

1   https://www.marxists.org/archive/marx/works/1859/critique-pol-economy/appx2.htm.
2   *A Chronicle of Mao Zedong (1893–1949)* (Revised Edition), Beijing: Central Party Literature Publishing House, 2013, p. 70.

the salvation movement and new organizations to unite revolutionary forces. Facts have proven that only socialism can save China, addressing the historical issue of the Chinese people "standing up." During the historical period of reform and opening up, the CPC integrated Marxism with China's reality, taking its own path, and building socialism with Chinese characteristics. Over more than 40 years, it has created the greatest development miracle in human history. Facts have proven that only socialism with Chinese characteristics can develop China, addressing the historical issue of the Chinese people "growing rich." Today, socialism with Chinese characteristics has entered the New Era. The CPC is leading the Chinese people in building a great modern socialist country. China is increasingly approaching the center stage of the world. Facts have proven that only by adhering to and developing socialism with Chinese characteristics can the rejuvenation of the Chinese nation be realized, thereby truly addressing the historical issue of the Chinese nation "becoming strong."

Socialism shines because of the truth of its doctrine. This is also because this doctrine can be closely integrated with China's reality and the characteristics of the times. General Secretary Xi Jinping pointed out, "Socialism with Chinese characteristics not only adheres to the fundamental tenets of scientific socialism but also endows them with distinctive Chinese characteristics according to the conditions of the times. This means that socialism with Chinese characteristics is socialism, not any other doctrine."[1] Socialism with Chinese characteristics is the dialectical unity of the theoretical logic of scientific socialism and the historical logic of China's social development. It is scientific socialism rooted in Chinese soil, reflecting the will of the Chinese people, and meeting the requirements

---

1   *Documents Produced since the 18th CPC National Congress*, Beijing: Central Party Literature Publishing House, 2014, vol. I, p. 109.

of China's and the era's development and progress. The views that claim China practices "state capitalism," "new bureaucratic capitalism," "capital socialism," or "authoritarian socialism" are all completely erroneous, subjective conjunctures seen through a distorted lens. The bright essence of socialism with Chinese characteristics is scientific socialism, and the brilliant achievements of socialism with Chinese characteristics are essentially a great victory for scientific socialism. In contemporary China, adhering to Xi Jinping Thought on Socialism with Chinese Characteristics for a New Era is truly adhering to Marxism and genuinely upholding scientific socialism.

2. It shines because of its new path

The reason why the development of the People's Republic of China over the past 70-plus years has successfully solved the historic challenge of "What is socialism, and how to go about it" is fundamentally because it has found a correct path—namely, the path of socialism with Chinese characteristics. This path was pioneered through the arduous efforts and hard work of several generations of Chinese Communists leading the Chinese people. It is a successful path forged according to the national conditions through long-term exploration and is a broad road for the Chinese nation to stride forward and lead the development of the times.

The path of socialism with Chinese characteristics is a road of innovation. Independence and self-reliance are fine traditions of the Chinese Communists and crucial tools for strengthening the Party and the country. In a country with a civilization of over 5,000 years and a population of over 1.4 billion, the revolution, development, and reform determined that we could only take our own path.

In the past, we emulated others' models and followed in their footsteps, only to encounter repeated setbacks. After numerous awakenings, practices, and breakthroughs, we finally discovered a successful path. Both history and reality have shown that no nation or country has ever achieved strength and rejuvenation by relying on external forces or by imitating others step by step. Only the path of socialism with Chinese characteristics, and none other, can lead China to progress and ensure the wellbeing of its people. As General Secretary Xi Jinping has emphasized, "The sweeping social changes that China is undergoing are not simply the extension of China's historical and cultural experiences, the repetition of socialist practices by other countries, or the duplication of modernization endeavors elsewhere."[1]

The path of socialism with Chinese characteristics is a unique creation of the CPC. We should neither retrace our steps to the rigidity and isolation of the past, nor take the wrong turn by changing our nature and abandoning our system. We must resolutely adhere to the path of socialism with Chinese characteristics. Following our own path is the bedrock of all the Party's theories and practices and the historical conclusion drawn from a century of struggle.

This path is one of well-rounded development. Marxism, with its commitment to the people, aims for the free and well-rounded development of individuals and the liberation of all humanity. Marxist thinkers have long held that the essential requirement of a new society is the free and well-rounded development of individuals. Marx envisioned a future society as "a higher form of society, a society in which the full and free development of every individual forms the ruling principle."[2] Socialism with Chinese characteristics embodies this principle, striving to achieve well-rounded development of individuals and all-around progress of society. Following the path of socialism with Chinese characteristics means,

---

1   Xi Jinping, *Speech at a Seminar on Philosophy and Social Sciences*, Beijing: People's Publishing House, 2016, p. 21.

2   https://www.marxists.org/archive/marx/works/1867-c1/ch24.htm.

under the leadership of the CPC, grounding ourselves in the basic national conditions, adhering to a people-centered approach, focusing on economic development, upholding the Four Cardinal Principles, and continuing reform and opening up. This path promotes well-rounded development of individuals, always taking the people's aspiration for a better life as its ultimate goal. It ensures coordinated implementation of the Five-Sphere Integrated Plan and the Four-Pronged Comprehensive Strategy, continuously liberating and developing social productive forces. This allows the people to share in the benefits of development across economic, political, cultural, social, and ecological domains, providing them with a stronger sense of fulfilment, happiness, and security. It consistently advances well-rounded development of individuals and common prosperity for all.

The path of socialism with Chinese characteristics is the only way to achieve national rejuvenation. General Secretary Xi Jinping pointed out, "Since the introduction of the reform and opening up policy, we have reviewed our historical experience and constantly made difficult explorations, and we have finally found the right path to achieve the great rejuvenation of the Chinese nation and our achievements have attracted the world's attention. This path is socialism with Chinese characteristics."[1]

Walking on this path, we are closer to the goal of the rejuvenation of the Chinese nation than at any time in history, and we are more confident than ever in achieving this goal. On this path, we have a clear timetable and roadmap, which is the strategic arrangement planned by the 19th CPC National Congress: to build a moderately prosperous society in all respects by 2020, basically achieve socialist modernization by 2035, and build China into a great modern socialist country that is prosperous, strong,

---

1 *Documents Produced since the 18th CPC National Congress*, Beijing: Central Party Literature Publishing House, 2014, vol. I, p. 83.

democratic, culturally advanced, harmonious, and beautiful by the middle of this century, 2050. By then, the Chinese nation will stand taller and prouder among the nations of the world. The Fifth Plenary Session of the 19th CPC Central Committee also proposed the long-term goals for 2035 and formulated specific steps and tasks to achieve medium- and long-term goals. In the new stage in the New Era, the path of socialism with Chinese characteristics is becoming wider and wider. Along this inevitable path, the rejuvenation of the Chinese nation shows an incredibly brilliant and bright future.

3. It shines because of its good system

This good system is the socialist system with Chinese characteristics. Since the founding of the People's Republic of China, the socialist system in our country has evolved from basic establishment to consolidation and development, from deepening reforms to innovation and perfection. During this process, while achieving historic accomplishments, it has continuously demonstrated the superiority and great advantages of the socialist system. General Secretary Xi Jinping pointed out, "Improving and developing the Chinese socialist system is key to China's progress. It provides a strong guarantee for unlocking and developing productivity, for releasing and enhancing social vitality, and for maintaining the vigor of the Party and the country."[1]

Entering the New Era of socialism with Chinese characteristics, our Party continues to develop a sound system of socialism with Chinese characteristics by comprehensively deepening reform, continuously enhancing its ability to effectively govern the country using this system. Specifically, our economic system effectively promotes the unity of

---

1   *Documents Produced since the 19th CPC National Congress*, Beijing: Central Party Literature Publishing House, 2019, pp. 732–733.

efficiency and fairness, our political system fully guarantees that the people run the country, our cultural system continuously advances the prosperity and development of socialist culture, our social system comprehensively ensures and improves people's livelihood, and our ecological system effectively achieves harmonious coexistence and sustainable development between humans and nature. Overall, we have formed a complete set of successful institutional systems different from other countries, demonstrating unique advantages, such as the leadership of the CPC, the ability to unite all forces that can be united, strong mobilization capabilities, the ability to concentrate resources on major tasks, and the effective promotion of social fairness and justice, among others.

The stark contrast between the effective governance of China and the disorder in the West in today's world also fully demonstrates the superiority and advantages of the socialist system with Chinese characteristics. In Western countries, the huge gap between rich and poor, the failure of social governance, continuous partisan disputes, the rise of protectionism, the prevalence of populism, and rampant terrorism all indicate the decline of Western systems and ineffective governance. Currently, many foreign theorists deeply reveal the systemic, institutional, and value crises of capitalism, which essentially highlight the structural contradictions of the capitalist system. In contrast, "the scenery here is uniquely good" in China. By promoting the further maturity and definition of the socialist system with Chinese characteristics through comprehensive deepening reforms, we provide a more complete, stable, and effective system for the development of the Party and the country, for the happiness and wellbeing of the people, for social harmony and stability, and for the long-term peace and stability of the nation. Its superiority is recognized and approved by many insightful individuals around the world. The remarkable achievements of socialism with Chinese characteristics that have garnered global attention are convincingly proven by the superior socialist system in the great practice of national prosperity, people's happiness, and national rejuvenation.

At the beginning of the reform and opening up, Deng Xiaoping confidently foresaw: "Our system will improve day by day, absorb the progressive elements we can learn from all countries in the world, and become the best system in the world."[1] Today, the system of socialism with Chinese characteristics demonstrates strong vitality and continuous development and improvement. The dual miracles of rapid economic development and long-term social stability since China's reform and opening up are complementary and mutually reinforcing, showcasing the power of the socialist system with Chinese characteristics and jointly creating a monument to the effective governance of China. The Fourth Plenary Session of the 19th CPC Central Committee, from the overall and strategic perspective of the Party and the country's undertakings, focused on the present and looked to the long-term. It specially studied and deliberated on the major issues of upholding and improving the socialist system with Chinese characteristics, and modernizing the national governance system and capacity. It systematically answered the significant political question of "what to uphold and consolidate, what to improve and develop" from the combination of strengthening institutional confidence and promoting institutional innovation. For the first time, it comprehensively summarized the interconnected, complementary, and holistic significant advantages of the socialist system with Chinese characteristics. It systematically expounded a clear, comprehensive, and scientific system composed of fundamental institutions, basic institutions, and important institutions. It explicitly proposed the guiding thought, overall requirements, overall goals, strategic approaches, and major measures for advancing our

1 *Documents Produced since the Third Plenary Session of the 11th CPC Central Committee*, Beijing: People's Publishing House, 1982, vol. I, p. 550.

institutional development and national governance, fully reflecting the superiority, resilience, vitality, and potential of the socialist system with Chinese characteristics. This formed a "cluster of institutional advantages" led by the greatest advantage of the leadership of the CPC, with various advantages playing their roles and the overall advantages collectively highlighted, indicating that our Party's understanding of the three major laws has reached an unprecedented height.

As General Secretary Xi Jinping pointed out: "This relies on continuous reform and innovation, making socialism with Chinese characteristics more efficient than the capitalist system in liberating and developing social productive forces, liberating and enhancing social vitality, and promoting the well-rounded development of individuals. It can better stimulate the enthusiasm, initiative, and creativity of all people, provide more favorable conditions for social development, and gain a comparative advantage in competition, fully demonstrating the superiority of the socialist system with Chinese characteristics."[1]

4. It shines because of the development of culture

This culture refers to the culture of socialism with Chinese characteristics. This culture stems from the elements of traditional Chinese culture, which has been nurtured over more than 5,000 years of civilization. It is forged in the revolutionary culture and advanced socialist culture created during the revolution, development, and reform under the leadership of the Party and is rooted in the great practice of socialism with Chinese characteristics. The political report of the 19th CPC National Congress stated: "Our country will thrive only if our culture thrives, and our nation will be strong only if our culture is strong. Without full

---

1 *Documents Produced since the 18th CPC National Congress*, Beijing: Central Party Literature Publishing House, 2014, vol. I, p. 550.

confidence in our culture, without a rich and prosperous culture, the Chinese nation will not be able to rejuvenate itself." Our ability to be confident in our culture and promote cultural prosperity and flourishing precisely stems from the best elements of traditional Chinese culture, revolutionary culture, and advanced socialist culture. As General Secretary Xi Jinping pointed out: "It derives from our splendid 5,000-year history and is embedded in decades of a revolutionary struggle that embodies the deep-rooted spiritual pursuits of the Chinese nation, and represents the unique cultural identity of the Chinese people."[1]

Socialism shines because of the development of culture. This is due to the profound and extensive best elements of traditional Chinese culture. "Only by advancing from history to the future and by opening up from the continuation of the national cultural lineage, can we accomplish our tasks today."[2] The great Chinese nation has forged outstanding Chinese culture, and the genes of the best elements of traditional Chinese culture have nourished the long history of the Chinese nation for thousands of years.

The best elements of traditional Chinese culture is deeply ingrained in the hearts of the Chinese people, subtly influencing their thinking habits and behaviors. It has been tested and validated over millennia by generations of Chinese, serving as the lifeline and soul of the longstanding heritage of the Chinese nation. This culture proudly stands among the collective cultures of humanity and will continue to be celebrated and recorded in history for millennia to come. Through its long history and civilization, China has developed an extensive and profound traditional culture. This outstanding traditional culture embodies the spiritual pursuit and core values recognized by generations of Chinese, reflecting the social

---

1 Xi Jinping, *The Governance of China*, Beijing: Foreign Languages Press, 2017, vol. II, p. 36.
2 Xi Jinping, *Speech at the Opening Ceremony of the Joint Session of the International Conference Commemorating the 2565th Anniversary of Confucius' Birth and the Fifth Congress of the International Confucian Association*, Beijing: People's Publishing House, 2014, p. 14.

judgment standards of right and wrong that have been inherent in the Chinese nation since ancient times, and encapsulating the essence and soul of Chinese culture. It can be said that the outstanding traditional Chinese culture, as the historical accumulation of the Chinese national spirit, is the spiritual force that ensures the continuous development and growth of the Chinese nation. It carries the distinct national characteristics and intrinsic genes of the Chinese nation, which cannot be severed or obliterated in any historical period. This cultural lineage should be inherited and carried forward in the New Era.

The 19th CPC National Congress explicitly stated the need to adhere to the principle of "the creative evolution and development" of the best elements of traditional Chinese culture, endowing these elements with new contemporary connotations. The practice since the 18th CPC National Congress has fully demonstrated that the outstanding traditional Chinese culture, with its history spanning over 5,000 years, has become an important theoretical and cultural foundation for the Party's governance and an essential historical resource for socialism with Chinese characteristics. During the ceremony marking the centenary of the CPC, General Secretary Xi Jinping stated: "We must continue to adapt the fundamental tenets of Marxism to China's specific realities and its traditional culture. We will use Marxism to observe, understand and steer the trends of our times, and continue to develop the Marxism of contemporary China and in the 21st century."[1] Over the past century, generations of Chinese Communists have, in the process of promoting the adaptation of Marxism to the Chinese context, activated the great civilization created by the Chinese nation over millennia with the power of Marxist truth. This process has enabled the mutual interaction and

---

1   Xi Jinping, *Speech at a Ceremony Marking the Centenary of the Communist Party of China*, Beijing: People's Publishing House, 2021, p. 13.

integration of Marxism and Chinese civilization, transforming traditional Chinese civilization into a modern form, unleashing powerful intellectual forces once again, forming a new pattern of Chinese civilization, and creating a new form of human advancement.

Socialism shines because of the development of culture. This is due to our uplifting and inspiring revolutionary culture. During the great struggles of the new-democratic revolution and the socialist revolution, and the arduous years of socialist development, an uplifting and inspiring revolutionary culture was formed and nurtured. From the great founding spirit of the Party, the Jinggangshan Spirit, the Long March Spirit, the Gutian Meeting Spirit, the Yan'an Spirit, and the Xibaipo Spirit of the revolutionary period, to the Lei Feng Spirit, the Daqing Spirit, the Jiao Yulu Spirit, and the Atomic and Hydrogen Bombs, Missile, and Man-Made Satellite Development Spirit of the socialist development period, to the contemporary Manned Spaceflight Development Spirit, the Poverty Alleviation Spirit, and the Earthquake Relief Spirit, these timeless revolutionary ideals and the spirit of struggle are invaluable treasures of Chinese culture. They crystallize and sublimate the hardworking, brave, and tenacious spirit of the Chinese nation, infusing the culture of socialism with Chinese characteristics with an indomitable and enterprising spirit.

Mao Zedong clearly articulated: "Revolutionary culture is a powerful revolutionary weapon for the broad masses of the people."[1] General Secretary Xi Jinping also places great importance on the education, inheritance, and promotion of revolutionary spirit and culture. In 2002, after arriving in Zhejiang, he made a special trip to Nanhu to visit the Red Boat. After the 19th CPC National Congress, Xi Jinping led the new members of the Standing Committee of the Political Bureau of the CPC Central Committee to visit the site of the First CPC National Congress and

---

1   Mao Zedong, *Selected Works of Mao Tse-tung*, Beijing: Foreign Languages Press, 1967, vol. II, p. 382

the Red Boat in Jiaxing, reaffirming the Red Boat Spirit and promoting it in the context of the New Era. At the ceremony marking the centenary of the CPC, General Secretary Xi Jinping proposed and elaborated on the great founding spirit, which is the source of the CPC's spirit. "Over the past hundred years, the Party has carried forward this great founding spirit. Through its protracted struggles, it has developed a long line of inspiring principles for Chinese Communists and tempered a distinct political character."[1] It can be said that revolutionary culture is rooted in the best elements of traditional Chinese culture and is also an important gene and direct source of the culture of socialism with Chinese characteristics. It is a crucial pillar for our confidence in the culture of socialism with Chinese characteristics.

Socialism shines because of the development of culture. This is due to advanced socialist culture inherits the past and ushers in the future. Socialist advanced culture, guided by Marxism, is oriented toward modernization, the world, and the future, embodying a scientific, popular, and national socialist culture. General Secretary Xi Jinping emphasizes that enhancing national cultural soft power is related to the realization of the Two Centenary Goals and the Chinese Dream of National Rejuvenation. He stresses the need to promote socialist advanced culture and to and reach the goal of building China into a socialist cultural power.[2]

Socialist advanced culture is richly nourished by the profound traditional Chinese culture and intellectually supported by the uplifting revolutionary culture. It represents a great cultural creation of the CPC and the Chinese nation in the New Era. This culture encompasses the shared belief in socialism with Chinese characteristics and the lofty ideal of communism, the national spirit centered on patriotism, the great spirit of

1 . Xi Jinping, *Speech at a Ceremony Marking the Centenary of the Communist Party of China,* Beijing: People's Publishing House, 2021, p. 8.
2 Xi Jinping: *The Governance of China,* Beijing: Foreign Languages Press, 2018, vol. I, p. 178.

the times centered on reform and innovation, and the core socialist values. It is the cultural gene of the Chinese path, Chinese experience, and Chinese wisdom, aligning with the laws governing the development of human society, socialist development, and CPC self-governance, representing the direction of progress for human advancement.

Since its founding, the CPC has been an active leader and practitioner of advanced Chinese culture, as well as a faithful inheritor and promoter of the best elements of traditional Chinese culture. These elements, revolutionary culture, and advanced socialist culture are interconnected and mutually reinforcing, together constructing the grand edifice of socialism with Chinese characteristics, unified in the great historical process of developing socialist culture with Chinese characteristics. It is by inheriting and promoting the longstanding and profound traditional Chinese culture, the uplifting and inspiring revolutionary culture, and the forward-looking and innovative advanced socialist culture that the Party Central Committee, with General Secretary Xi Jinping at its core since the 18th National Congress, has been empowered to pursue the goal of building a culturally strong nation, thereby promoting the prosperity of socialist culture with Chinese characteristics and further solidifying cultural confidence in socialism with Chinese characteristics.

To deeply understand why socialism with Chinese characteristics is effective, one must have a historical perspective and establish a grand historical view. Socialism with Chinese characteristics has been achieved through over 40 years of great practice in reform and opening up, over 70 years of continuous exploration since the founding of the People's Republic of China, 100 years of great social revolution led by the CPC, more than 180 years of historical progress from decline to prosperity of the Chinese nation since modern times, 500 years of tumultuous development of world socialism, and over 5,000 years of inheritance and development of Chinese civilization. We must cherish this path, unwaveringly adhere to it, and advance it with the times.

In summary, the path of socialism with Chinese characteristics is the only way to achieve socialist modernization and create a better life for the people. It is the only path to the rejuvenation of the Chinese nation. This path not only insists on economic development as the central task but also comprehensively promotes economic, political, cultural, social, and ecological advancement as well as advancement of other aspects. It adheres to the Four Cardinal Principles while also embracing reform and opening up. It continuously liberates and develops productive forces while gradually realizing common prosperity for all and promoting the well-rounded development of individuals.

The system of theories of socialism with Chinese characteristics is the correct system that guides the Party and the people in realizing the rejuvenation of the Chinese nation. It is a scientific system that stands at the forefront of the times and advances with the times. This system includes Deng Xiaoping Theory, the Theory of Three Represents, the Scientific Outlook on Development, and Xi Jinping Thought on Socialism with Chinese Characteristics for a New Era. This system closely integrates with the realities of China's reform and development, and with the conditions of the New Era. It vividly and concretely adheres to and develops Marxism-Leninism and Mao Zedong Thought, endowing Marxism with new vitality and writing the new version of the China chapter of scientific socialism.

The system of socialism with Chinese characteristics is the fundamental guarantee for the development and progress of contemporary China. It is an advanced system with significant institutional advantages and a strong capacity for self-improvement. This system ensures the organic unity of the Party's leadership, the people running the country, and the rule of law. It connects fundamental, basic, and important institutions, emphasizing the establishment of a complete, scientific, and effective institutional system. This system not only adheres to the fundamental nature of socialism but also draws upon useful results from the institution-building efforts of both ancient and modern, domestic and foreign sources. It conforms to China's national conditions and embodies the characteristics and advantages of socialism with Chinese characteristics.

The culture of socialism with Chinese characteristics embodies the deepest cultural pursuit of the Chinese nation, represents the unique cultural identity of the Chinese nation, and serves as a powerful cultural force that motivates the entire Party and the Chinese people to forge ahead. This culture originates from the best elements of traditional Chinese culture nurtured by over 5,000 years of Chinese civilization history, is forged in the revolutionary culture and advanced socialist culture created by the Party leading the people in revolution, development, and reform, and is rooted in the great practice of socialism with Chinese characteristics.

Socialism with Chinese characteristics in the New Era is the result of the great social revolution led by the CPC and the continuation of this great social revolution. It must be carried out consistently. The tremendous success of socialism with Chinese characteristics in the New Era has significant implications for the Chinese nation and people, for Marxism and scientific socialism, and for world socialism. History and practice have proven and will continue to prove that socialism with Chinese characteristics shines.

Part Four

Make Original Contributions to the Development of 21st-Century Marxism

General Secretary Xi Jinping pointed out, "The success of scientific socialism in China is of great significance for Marxism, scientific socialism, and socialism across the world."[1] As socialism with Chinese characteristics enters the New Era, both practical and theoretical innovations have reached unprecedented heights, marking new leaps in the adaptation of Marxism to the Chinese context. Xi Jinping Thought on Socialism with Chinese Characteristics for a New Era revitalizes scientific socialism in the 21st century, allowing Marxism to shine more brilliantly with the light of truth and opening up new realms for its development.

Since the founding of the People's Republic of China, especially since the implementation of the reform and opening up policy, China has undergone profound transformations. The Chinese people, situated in the midst of these historical changes, are more qualified and capable of revealing the historical experiences and developmental laws embedded

---

1   Xi Jinping, *Stay True to the Original Aspirations and Founding Mission of the Party,* Beijing: Party Building Books Publishing House and Central Party Literature Publishing House, 2019, p. 298.

within, thereby making original contributions to the development of Marxism.

The vitality of theory lies in continuous innovation, and promoting the continuous development of Marxism is the sacred duty of Chinese Communists. General Secretary Xi Jinping profoundly stated, "The secret of Marxism's perpetual vitality lies in the continuous creation of new theories by integrating adherence to Marxism with its development, based on new practices."[1] Xi Jinping Thought on Socialism with Chinese Characteristics for a New Era is the most concentrated, richest, and most practical manifestation of 21st-century Marxist theoretical innovation and creation, making significant original contributions to the development of 21st-century Marxism.

I. Innovating and Developing Marxism Based on the Two Integrations

The history of the development of Marxism has provided humanity with an inexhaustible theoretical wealth. In the history of human thought, various theories have either sooner or later exited the historical stage. However, only Marxism remains eternally youthful, continuously guiding the proletariat and its parties in advancing the cause of revolution and development.

The history of the development of Marxism is a history of the integration of the fundamental tenets of Marxism with the characteristics of the times and their continuous innovative development. It is a history of continually enriching itself by absorbing all outstanding ideological and cultural achievements in human history. Looking back at the more

---

1   Xi Jinping, *Speech at the Seminar on Philosophy and Social Sciences,* Beijing: People's Publishing House, 2016, p. 13.

than 170 years of Marxism's development, we can clearly see that the outstanding representatives of Marxism in different historical periods have, in line with the development of the times, embodied the spirit of the times, and responded to the questions of the times. They have continuously absorbed all outstanding theoretical and cultural achievements in human history, thereby promoting the rich development of Marxism and scientific socialism. This has led to the formation of theoretical forms that are both consistent and uniquely characteristic, that both conform to and lead the trends of the times in different historical periods.

In the New Era, the innovative development of Marxism faces new requirements. General Secretary Xi Jinping pointed out, "On the journey ahead, we must continue to uphold Marxism-Leninism, Mao Zedong Thought, Deng Xiaoping Theory, the Theory of Three Represents, and the Scientific Outlook on Development, and fully implement the Thought on Socialism with Chinese Characteristics for a New Era. We must continue to adapt the basic tenets of Marxism to China's specific realities and its traditional culture. We will use Marxism to observe, understand and steer the trends of our times, and continue to develop the Marxism of contemporary China and in the 21st century."[1]

This important statement adheres to the organic unity of inheritance and development, and of upholding and innovating. It represents the scientific attitude and correct stance of the CPC toward Marxism in the New Era. The major assertion of the two integrations expands the connotation and pathways of the adaptation of Marxism to the Chinese context, proposing new requirements for combining Marxism with China's realities. That is, Marxism must be integrated not only with China's contemporary realities (China's current national conditions and practical

---

1   Xi Jinping, *Speech at a Ceremony Marking the Centenary of the Communist Party of China*, Beijing: People's Publishing House, 2021, p. 13.

situations), but also with China's historical realities, meaning it must be combined with the 5,000-year-old Chinese civilization and the best of traditional Chinese culture. Only in this way can Marxism take deep root in the fertile soil of Chinese civilization, innovate and develop within the great practice of Chinese socialism, elevate the adaptation of Marxism to the Chinese context to unprecedented heights, and create a new form of Chinese civilization in the 21st century, thereby also creating a new form of human advancement.

Xi Jinping Thought on Socialism with Chinese Characteristics for a New Era is the latest achievement of the two integrations. It has made significant contributions to the enrichment and development of civilization, representing both the latest outcome of the adaptation of Marxism to the Chinese context and the latest theoretical form of 21st-century Marxism.

1. Continuously adapt Marxism to the Chinese context and the needs of our times

The tide of human history flows irresistibly forward. A theory that keenly grasps the issues of its time must advance with the times, while a theory that fails to correctly address these issues will inevitably be discarded. Marx once said the questions are the mottoes of the time and "the supremely practical utterances proclaiming the state of its soul."[1] The reason Marxism remains perpetually youthful is that it continually explores and accurately grasps new issues arising from the development of the times, responding to new challenges faced by human society. Continuously providing correct answers to the questions of the times has thus become a distinctive feature of Marxism. The history of Marxism's development shows that it is not a closed system but an theoretical system

---

1   https://libcom.org/library/question-centralisation.

that continuously innovates and develops in practice. It never rests on its laurels but advocates critically absorbing all outstanding achievements of human advancement, continuously developing sound theories based on the progress of practice. As General Secretary Xi Jinping pointed out, "The development history of Marxism and the development history of the adaptation of Marxism to the Chinese context both tell us: Social practice is constantly developing, and our understanding must continue to advance and innovate in accordance with the requirements of practice."[1]

Marxism emerged in the 1840s amidst the fervent proletarian revolutionary movement in Europe. By profoundly summarizing the experiences of revolutionary struggles, it revealed the objective law that socialism would inevitably replace capitalism and clarified the correct path for the proletariat to undertake revolution and seek liberation, thus becoming the guiding program for proletarian revolution. Throughout the development of Marxism, its founders never rigidly adhered to established conclusions but continuously revised and innovated their theories based on specific historical conditions and the development and changes of real society, improving and developing them in practice. Engels openly declared, "Marx's whole way of thinking [Auffassungsweise] is not so much a doctrine as a method. It provides, not so much ready-made dogmas, as aids to further investigation and the method for such investigation."[2] He further emphasized, "In every epoch, and therefore also in ours, theoretical thought is a historical product, which at different times assumes very different forms and, therewith, very different contents. ents."[3] The 170-year history since the publication of the *Communist Manifesto* has demonstrated that Marxism can only unleash its powerful vitality, creativity, and appeal

---

1   *Documents Produced since the 18th CPC National Congress*, Beijing: Central Party Literature Publishing House, 2014, vol. I, p. 389.
2   Karl Marx and Frederick Engels, *Collected Works*, New York: International Publishers, 1996, vol. 50, p. 461.
3   Marx & Engels, *Collected Works*, Lawrence & Wishart, 2010, vol. 25, p. 338.

when combined with the national conditions of its country, progresses with the development of the times, and shares a common destiny with the people.

In the New Era, adhering to and developing Marxism requires focusing on the real issues arising from China's reform, opening up, and socialist modernization. It should be centered on what we are currently doing, emphasizing the application of Marxist theory and continually endowing contemporary Chinese Marxism with distinct practical, national, and temporal characteristics.

General Secretary Xi Jinping pointed out, "The adaptation of Marxism to the Chinese context has achieved significant results, but it is far from over."[1] Continuing to adapt Marxism to the Chinese context in keeping with the times, and increase its appeal to the people and to enrich and develop the Party's innovative theory is an inevitable requirement of the times and practical development. In the New Era, we must base ourselves on China's realities and continue to adapt Marxism to the Chinese context in keeping with the times, and increase its appeal to the people. By centering on what we are currently doing and basing ourselves on the great practice of socialism with Chinese characteristics, we should summarize the fresh experiences created by the Party leading the people in a timely manner, and continuously achieve new leaps in the adaptation of Marxism to the Chinese context. Based on the characteristics of the times, we should continue to advance the modernization of Marxism. We must coordinate the overall strategic situation of the rejuvenation of the Chinese nation and the momentous changes of a kind unseen in the world in a century, use Marxism to observe, grasp, and lead the times, and examine the real foundation and practical needs for the development of Marxism in

---

1   Xi Jinping, *The Party's Public Communication Work*, Beijing: Central Party Literature Publishing House, 2020, p. 220.

contemporary times with a broader vision, continually advancing Marxism.

Xi Jinping has clearly articulated, "The issues of the times are the driving force of theoretical innovation. Marx, Engels, Lenin, and others advanced theoretical innovation by thinking about and answering the issues of their times."[1] Solving the issues of the times and highlighting their characteristics is crucial. Each era has its own unique issues. Only by accurately grasping and addressing the issues posed by the times can we continuously promote the progress and development of human society. Great theories such as Marxism-Leninism, Mao Zedong Thought, Deng Xiaoping Theory, the Theory of Three Represents, the Scientific Outlook on Development, and Xi Jinping Thought on Socialism with Chinese Characteristics for a New Era were formed and developed through answering and solving the historical issues faced by their respective times.

Marx and Engels lived in the era of free capitalism. They provided scientific answers to the questions of "where is capitalism headed?" and "what is the future of human society?" By doing so, they founded Marxism, transforming socialism from a utopian ideal into a scientific theory. Lenin, living in the era of monopoly capitalism, addressed the questions of "what is the future of imperialism?" and "where is the proletarian revolution headed?" His work established Leninism, which guided the October Revolution to a historic victory, turning socialism from a theoretical concept into a real-world system. In semi-feudal, semi-colonial China, Mao Zedong scientifically addressed the questions of "what is China's path?" and "where is the Chinese revolution headed?" This led to the formation of Mao Zedong Thought, under which he led the people in completing the new-democratic revolution and establishing the People's Republic of China.

---

1   "Xi Jinping, *Understanding the New Development Stage, Implementing the New Development Philosophy, and Creating a New Development Dynamic*, Beijing: Central Party Literature Publishing House, 2021, p. 377.

Since the onset of reform and opening up, successive generations of Chinese Communists have addressed a series of era-specific questions, such as "what kind of socialism should we build and how should we go about it?" "what kind of party should we build and how should we go about it?" and "what kind of development should we pursue and how should we achieve it?" This led to the development of Deng Xiaoping Theory, the Theory of the Three Represents, and the Scientific Outlook on Development, furthering the evolution of socialism with Chinese characteristics.

As socialism with Chinese characteristics enters the New Era, General Secretary Xi Jinping has emphasized the importance of adapting Marxism to the Chinese context in keeping with the times, and increase its appeal to the people, and developing contemporary Chinese Marxism and 21st-century Marxism. Under the leadership of the Party Central Committee, with General Secretary Xi Jinping at its core, the fundamental tenets of Marxism have been integrated with the specific realities of China in the New Era. Through leading the people in the great struggle, building the great project, advancing the great cause, and pursuing the great dream, the Party and the country have achieved remarkable successes. This has led to the formation of Xi Jinping Thought on Socialism with Chinese Characteristics for a New Era, providing a solid theoretical and political foundation for realizing the rejuvenation of the Chinese nation.

Since the 18th CPC National Congress, "Changes both in and outside China, and the progress made in all areas of China's endeavors, have presented us with a profound question—the question of an era. Our answer must be a systematic combination of theory and practice and must address what kind of socialism with Chinese characteristics the New Era requires us to uphold and develop, and how we should go about doing it." The Sixth Plenary Session of the 19th CPC Central Committee pointed out that

General Secretary Xi Jinping conducted profound thinking and scientific judgment on a series of major theoretical and practical issues related to the development of the Party and the country in the New Era. He has deeply summarized and made full use of the historical experience of the Party's century-long journey, and has raised a series of original new concepts, thoughts, and strategies for governance around significant contemporary issues such as "what kind of socialism with Chinese characteristics to uphold and develop in the New Era, how to go about it, what kind of great modern great modern socialist country to build, how to go about it, what kind of long-term ruling Marxist party to build, and how to go about it." Xi Jinping is the principal founder of Xi Jinping Thought on Socialism with Chinese Characteristics for a New Era." This demonstrates that our Party adheres to emancipating the mind, seeking truth from facts, keeping pace with the times, pursuing truth and pragmatism, maintaining integrity, and innovating. The Party persistently explores and consciously grasps contemporary issues, promptly answers the questions of the times and the people, and continuously adapts Marxism to the Chinese context and the needs of our times.

From the 19th CPC National Congress to the Sixth Plenary Session of the 19th Central Committee, the explanations and statements have been consistent yet progressive. Initially, a single contemporary issue was raised, but it has evolved into a comprehensive proposal of a series of significant contemporary issues, with an emphasis on three major contemporary issues. This reflects a more comprehensive understanding, deeper mastery, and more complete expression of the era's needs for the formation and establishment of scientific theories and practical requirements. Xi Jinping Thought on Socialism with Chinese Characteristics for a New Era scientifically answers a series of major contemporary issues of the New Era, thereby greatly enriching and developing the theory of socialism with

Chinese characteristics and pushing the development of Marxism in the 21st century and scientific socialism to a new stage.

Xi Jinping Thought on Socialism with Chinese Characteristics for a New Era adheres to the unity of the contemporaneity and realism of Marxism, as well as its universality and nationality. It is based on the actual conditions of China in the New Era and has achieved a new leap in the adaptation of Marxism to the Chinese context. Furthermore, facing the profound changes in today's world, it deeply considers the major issues and tasks of the 21st century, examining the theoretical and practical needs of the development of Marxism and socialism in the 21st century with profound and broad perspectives on the era and the world. It has profoundly grasped the trends of contemporary development and global development directions, and has scientifically constructed the latest theoretical form of 21st-century Marxism and scientific socialism.

2. Integrate Marxism with China's specific realities

Marxism's response to the issues of the times is based on the revolutionary and development practices of various countries and nations. Different types of countries in the same era, or countries of the same type but at different levels of development, have varying historical traditions and specific national conditions. Therefore, the content and methods of their practices, as well as the manifestation and forms of their contemporary issues, differ. As Marx stated, "Theory is fulfilled in a people only insofar as it is the fulfilment of the needs of that people."[1] Marxism provides specific means of "fulfillment" tailored to the differing political, economic, and cultural needs of various countries at different times. The advancement of Marxism is achieved through its organic integration with the specific

---

1 https://www.marxists.org/archive/marx/works/download/Marx_Critique_of_Hegels_Philosophy_of_Right.pdf.

conditions at different development stages of various countries and nations.

The fundamental tenets of Marxism can only be transformed into a powerful force for promoting socialist revolution, development, and undertakings when they are specifically adapted to the differing national conditions of each country and period. The founders of Marxism and revolutionary leaders have repeatedly interpreted this principle throughout different historical periods. Engels, for example, often criticized German "Marxists" living in the United States for their complete lack of understanding of American conditions. They did not study the American labor movement and specific needs, nor did they grasp the key points, content, and forms of the issues posed by practice and the times, which differ in European countries and the United States. He pointed out that they "have not understood how to use their theory as a lever which could set the American masses in motion."[1] He advised these individuals not to dogmatically impose their theoretical framework, often not fully understood by themselves, from their homeland onto American workers. Instead, they should point out the specific ways in which theory can be applied to American conditions. Lenin lived in a time when Marxist theory was widely disseminated and rapidly transformed into practice. However, he believed that the "application of the *fundamental* principles of Communism ... as will *correctly modify* these principles in certain *particulars*, correctly adapt and apply them to national and national-state differences."[2] He frequently emphasized that each country should independently explore Marxist theory, as the concrete application of these theories would differ in Britain, France, Germany, and Russia. Engels' admonitions to some German "Marxists" and Lenin's teachings to Russian revolutionaries undoubtedly remain profoundly instructive for today's

---

1   https://www.marxists.org/archive/marx/works/1886/letters/86_11_29.htm.
2   http://www.marx2mao.com/Lenin/LWC20.html.

socialist revolutionaries and builders.

Mao Zedong and Deng Xiaoping are shining examples of adhering to the principle of seeking truth from facts and organically combining Marxism with China's national conditions and specific practices. During the new-democratic revolution, Mao Zedong emphatically stressed the necessity of completely and appropriately unifying the universal truths of Marxism with the specific practices of the Chinese revolution, integrating them with the characteristics of the Chinese nation. This integration "acquire a definite national form if it is to be useful, and in no circumstances can it be applied subjectively as a mere formula. Marxists who make a fetish of formulas are simply playing the fool with Marxism and the Chinese revolution, and there is no room for them in the ranks of the Chinese revolution."[1] The Chinese Communists, represented by Mao Zedong, established theories suitable for China's national conditions during the dual movement of adapting Marxism to the Chinese context and rendering China Marxist for the new-democratic revolution and the Socialist Revolution. In the new period of reform and opening up, the second-generation central collective leadership of the Party, with Deng Xiaoping at its core, once again creatively combined Marxism with China's national conditions, pioneering a path of modernization for building socialism with Chinese characteristics.

Correctly combining the fundamental tenets of Marxism with the national conditions of various countries is by no means an easy, one-step process. It requires the arduous efforts of communist parties in each country to scientifically approach the universality of principles and accurately grasp the particularities of their national conditions. Historical experience shows that a correct understanding of this "integration" itself is achieved at the cost of many mistakes and failures. For example, in the

---

1 Mao Zedong, *Selected Works of Mao Tse-tung*, Beijing: Foreign Languages Press, 1967, vol. II, p. 381.

history of the international communist movement, the Soviet Union once imposed its theories and models as universal truths of socialist revolution and development on the communist parties and peoples of other countries. Many countries engaged in socialist revolution and development have, to varying degrees, made the mistake of blindly copying the Soviet model. Deng Xiaoping pointed out that integrating the fundamental tenets of Marxism-Leninism with China's actual conditions and following our own path was "[t]he lesson we have learned from our setbacks."[1]

3. Integrate Marxism with the best elements of traditional Chinese culture

The process of adapting Marxism to the Chinese context is not only about promoting its integration with China's specific realities but also about fostering its integration with the best elements of traditional Chinese culture.

In the mid-19th century, Marxism was born in Europe. After it was introduced to China, it was accepted by Chinese progressives and the Chinese people and creatively applied and developed within China. This was mainly because the CPC consistently integrated this scientific theory with the national reality and historical traditions of China across different historical periods, leading to its continuous nationalization and localization. This is the process of the internalization of scientific theory. As Mao Zedong explicitly pointed out that integrating Marxism with the specific characteristics of China "acquires a definite national form" "to apply Marxism concretely in China so that its every manifestation has an indubitably Chinese character."[2] In this process of theoretical internalization, the integration of Marxism with Chinese civilization and the best elements of traditional Chinese culture holds fundamentally

---

1 Deng Xiaoping, *Selected Works of Deng Xiaoping*, Beijing: Foreign Languages Press, 1994, vol. III, p. 101.
2 *Op. cit.*, p. 209.

important significance.

The integration of Marxism with fine traditional Chinese culture and Chinese civilization is possible because of their inherent compatibility. Both possess characteristics of openness, dialectics, and progressiveness, with intrinsic genes that align and merge with the best elements of traditional Chinese culture. For instance, these best elements have a longstanding tradition of materialism, dialectics, and atheism, a profound tradition of people-oriented thought, and many elements of historical materialism, and pursue the ideal of a harmonious society. This intrinsic compatibility, combined with the inherent continuity, inclusiveness, and openness of the best elements of traditional Chinese culture, determines that despite differences in time, space, and intent, the shared cognitive traits and potential compatibility between the two allow for the deep integration of Marxism with the best elements of traditional Chinese culture and Chinese civilization. This makes it feasible and practical for Marxism to take root in Chinese soil and, under the combined influence of various subjective and objective factors, achieve nationalization and localization, continually evolving into a consistent theoretical form across different periods.

The best elements of traditional Chinese culture have a long history, embodying the deepest cultural pursuits of the Chinese nation and representing its unique cultural symbols. They have provided strong support for the continuous vitality of the Chinese nation. Like Marxism, these best elements possess an open spirit of inclusiveness and have played a significant role in China's revolution, development, and reform. As early as the Chinese People's War of Resistance against Japanese Aggression, Mao Zedong proposed using Marxist methods to critically summarize China's historical heritage. He pointed out, "Contemporary China has grown out of the China of the past; we are Marxist in our historical approach and must not lop off our history. We should sum up our history from Confucius to Sun Yat-sen and take over this valuable legacy. This is important for guiding the great movement of today."[1]

During the new-democratic revolution, Mao Zedong succinctly expressed the Marxist idea of basing everything on reality using the Chinese idiom "seeking truth from facts," a phrase well-received by the Chinese people. At the beginning of the reform and opening up period, Deng Xiaoping used the term "moderately prosperous society," which originally appeared in the *Book of Songs,* to explain the development goal of achieving Chinese modernization. Historical practice has shown that the best elements of traditional Chinese culture possesses strong cohesion and appeal. Since the 18th CPC National Congress, the Central Committee, with General Secretary Xi Jinping at its core, has extracted many new viewpoints and assertions from the best elements of traditional Chinese culture, forming a series of new concepts, thoughts, and strategies for governance. Many of these theoretical innovations not only have deep historical and cultural roots but also resonate with contemporary times, endowing Marxism with contemporary significance and shaping the unique Chinese style and characteristics of contemporary Chinese Marxism and 21st-century Marxism. During an inspection in Fujian in March 2021, General Secretary Xi Jinping stated, "If there were no 5,000-year Chinese civilization, how could we build anything with what we describe today as "Chinese characteristics"? And if it were not for these characteristics, how could we have successfully embarked on the path to "socialism with Chinese characteristics"? That is why we should value the cream of our civilization, and explore its depths. We should carry forward the best of traditional Chinese culture from a Marxist standpoint and with a Marxist viewpoint and methodology, and stick to the path of Chinese

---

1   *Ibid.*

socialism."[1] This important assertion fully acknowledges the historical role of the best elements of traditional Chinese culture and reveals that Chinese civilization and culture have provided rich resources for the success of the path of socialism with Chinese characteristics and a fertile historical and intellectual soil for the adaptation of Marxism to the Chinese context.

Over the century since the founding of the CPC, Marxism and Chinese civilization, along with the best elements of traditional Chinese culture, have gradually merged and organically unified in the process of the adaptation of Marxism to the Chinese context. The century-long history of the CPC also fully demonstrates that the Chinese Communists are faithful inheritors and successful practitioners of Marxism, as well as faithful inheritors and promoters of the best elements of traditional Chinese culture. Marxism, as the guiding thought of the Party and the state, holds a leading and dominant position, while Chinese civilization, as the main body of Chinese national civilization, holds the principal position of civilization. Marxism and Chinese civilization are integrated and unified in the practice of socialism with Chinese characteristics.

The Marxist worldview and methodology have become the soul of Chinese civilization. In the 21st century, Marxism possesses comprehensive Chinese characteristics, and Chinese civilization manifests distinct Marxist features. In this sense, the integration of Marxism with the best elements of traditional Chinese culture and Chinese civilization has undergone a process of "difference—convergence—fusion." Since the 18th CPC National Congress, General Secretary Xi Jinping clearly advocated for cultural confidence, which he regards as the foundation and essence of the four-sphere confidence. To be confident in the path, theory, and system of socialism with Chinese characteristics ultimately requires confidence

---

1   Xi Jinping, "I Am Deeply Attached to the Mountains, Rivers, and Every Blade of Grass Here," *People's Daily*, March 27, 2021.

in our culture: "Without full confidence in our culture, without a rich and prosperous culture, the Chinese nation will not be able to rejuvenate itself."[1] Xi Jinping has elucidated the profound logic that Marxism must combine with the characteristics of the era, the national reality, and historical culture: "The core values of a nation and a country must align with the historical culture of that nation and country, integrate with the ongoing struggle of its people, and adapt to the issues of the era that need to be addressed."[2] Xi Jinping places great importance on the best elements of traditional Chinese culture, considering them a crucial intellectual and cultural resource for governance, emphasizing that these best elements are a prominent advantage of the Chinese nation and the foundation for standing firm amidst global cultural exchanges. To achieve the rejuvenation of the Chinese nation, it is essential to inherit and promote the best elements of traditional Chinese culture in line with the conditions of the New Era. The practical pathway for this inheritance and promotion is through creative transformation and innovative development.

Promoting traditional Chinese governance experience is a key aspect of achieving creative transformation and innovative development. Xi Jinping has proposed to deeply explore and elucidate the contemporary values of the best elements of traditional Chinese culture, emphasizing benevolence, people-orientation, integrity, harmony, and the pursuit of a common good, making it an "important source for nurturing core socialist values."[3] For example, the traditional people-oriented thought of "valuing people over rulers and governance for the people" has been critically inherited and adapted. This thought has a long history and holds significant importance and far-reaching implications within the treasure

---

1   Documents of the 19th CPC National Congress, Beijing: People's Publishing House, 2017, p. 33.
2   *Documents Produced since the 18th CPC National Congress*, Beijing: Central Party Literature Publishing House, 2014, vol. I, p. 5.
3   *Ibid.*, p. 135.

trove of Chinese civilization. The contemporary principle of "people-centered development" always puts people at the highest priority, serving the people wholeheartedly, striving for their interests and happiness, and continually advancing toward the goal of common prosperity for all. It maintains the principal position of the people, relies on them to create historical achievements, adheres to the mass line and maintains close ties with them. This not only encapsulates the essence of traditional Chinese people-oriented philosophy but also represents its critical inheritance, refinement, and transcendence.

General Secretary Xi Jinping emphasized: "Inheriting Chinese culture is not about simply reviving ancient traditions or blindly rejecting foreign influences. Instead, it involves using the past to serve the present, using foreign ideas for our purposes, making dialectical choices, discarding negative elements, and inheriting positive thoughts. We should apply the fundamental principles and guidelines distilled by the ancients over centuries to forge a new path in our creative endeavors and achieve the creative transformation and innovative development of Chinese culture."[1] To promote the creative transformation and innovative development of the best elements of traditional Chinese culture, we must adhere to the Marxist stance, viewpoint and method, inheriting and promoting the best elements of traditional Chinese culture in line with New Era conditions, and revitalizing its vitality with the spirit of the times. Over the past 100 years, generations of Chinese Communists have activated the great civilization created by the Chinese nation over millennia through the power of Marxist truth, realizing the mutual interaction and integration of Marxism and Chinese civilization. This has elevated Chinese civilization from its traditional forms to modern forms, unleashing a powerful source of inspiration once again, creating a new form of Chinese civilization, and

---

1 *Ibid.*, p. 136.

contributing a new model of human advancement.

Xi Jinping Thought on Socialism with Chinese Characteristics for a New Era is the product of integrating the fundamental tenets of Marxism with the conditions of contemporary China, the best elements of traditional Chinese culture, and the characteristics of the times. It exemplifies and is the latest achievement of the two integrations. It not only integrates Marxism with China's current realities but also integrates it with the best elements of traditional Chinese culture, making the adaptation of Marxism to the Chinese context more comprehensive, profound, and thorough, significantly expanding the dimensions and connotations of this adaptation.

Xi Jinping Thought on Socialism with Chinese Characteristics for a New Era adheres to the fundamental tenets of Marxism, consistently embodying the soul of the Marxist worldview and methodology. It also extensively absorbs outstanding achievements of human advancement, carrying the unique national characteristics of Chinese civilization. It represents the latest achievement of the deep integration and organic unity of both, showcasing a new synthesis of these traditions.

In advancing the integration of Marxism with the best elements of traditional Chinese culture, Xi Jinping Thought on Socialism with Chinese Characteristics for a New Era examines the vitality of these best elements from the high ground of truth and morality. It continues the Chinese cultural lineage from a modern perspective, breaking new ground while upholding fundamental principles. This approach has achieved a deep integration of Marxism with the best elements of traditional Chinese culture in terms of institutions, culture, and values, while also promoting the creative transformation and innovative development of these best elements. For example, from the perspective of combining history and reality, theory and practice, and based on the needs of the times, it transforms the institutional achievements of Chinese civilization into important supports for the modernization of the national governance system and capacity. It creatively transforms the cultural achievements of Chinese civilization into the foundation of cultural confidence, the value achievements into the core values of socialism with Chinese characteristics, the historical achievements into the historical foundation of the Chinese path, and the Chinese humanistic theoretical achievements into the Chinese spirit. By enriching Chinese civilization with New Era connotations and illuminating the path of rejuvenation with the light of civilization, it showcases new paths and forms for the development of human advancement.

Xi Jinping Thought on Socialism with Chinese Characteristics for a New Era scientifically addresses the historical task of organically integrating Marxism with the best elements of traditional Chinese culture and Chinese civilization, which have over 5,000 years of history. It has achieved a new leap in the adaptation of Marxism to the Chinese context, invigorated Chinese civilization with new powerful vitality, accelerated the modernization process of Chinese civilization, and greatly advanced the historical process of the Chinese nation's march toward rejuvenation.

II. Creatively Applying Marxism to Address China's Issues

1. Uphold and promote Marxist stance, viewpoint and method

Marxism is the fundamental guiding thought for the founding and governance of our Party and country. Deviating from or abandoning Marxism would lead us to lose our soul and direction. The Marxist stance, viewpoint, and method are embedded in Marxism-Leninism, Mao Zedong Thought, and the theoretical system of socialism with Chinese characteristics. They form the essence of the scientific system of Marxist thought. Mastering and applying the Marxist stance, viewpoint, and method to study and solve China's practical problems have been the secret for the continuous victories of the Chinese Communists. Our Party has always maintained sobriety and determination, a strong sense of forward direction, and has neither retrace our steps to the rigidity and isolation of the past, nor take the wrong turn by changing our nature and abandoning our system. Instead, it has steadfastly followed the path of socialism with Chinese characteristics, while also adhering to emancipating the mind, seeking truth from facts, keeping up with the times, and pursuing truth and pragmatism, courageously advancing theoretical innovation. Xi Jinping Thought on Socialism with Chinese Characteristics for a New Era not only adheres to and applies the Marxist worldview and methodology but also enriches and develops them in guiding the great practice of the New Era.

Seek truth from facts and reflect an accurate grasp of development laws

As socialism with Chinese characteristics enters the New Era, we aim to build a great modern socialist country in all respects and realize the Chinese Dream of National Rejuvenation. This is an era that requires theory and will undoubtedly generate theory, an era that needs thought and will inevitably produce thought. Xi Jinping Thought on Socialism with Chinese Characteristics for a New Era emerged and developed based on this new historical juncture in our country's development, in response to the new changes in the principal contradiction of our society, in line with the new conditions and practical requirements of the era, and to meet the historical mission of our Party in the New Era. This thought employs the Marxist stance, viewpoint, and method, focusing on what we are doing and what we will do, adhering to problem awareness and problem orientation, distilling the essence of the times, summarizing practical experiences, and proposing many important ideas, viewpoints, and conclusions in areas such as reform, development, stability, domestic and foreign affairs, national defense, Party self-supervision and self-governance, state governance, and military governance. It systematically addresses major contemporary issues from the integration of theory and practice, such as what kind of socialism with Chinese characteristics to uphold and develop in the New Era, how to go about it, what kind of modern socialist country to build, how to go about it, what kind of long-term governing Marxist party to build, and how to go about it. It is a scientific theoretical system established in accordance with objective laws and continuously developed based on practical progress, fully reflecting our Party's latest understanding of the laws of Communist Party self-supervision and self-governance, socialist development, and the development of human society.

Adhere to a people-centered approach and reflect the fundamental political stance of a Marxist party

Looking back at the century-long glorious history of our Party, whether during the period of revolution and development or in the new historical period of reform and opening up, our Party has always held the original mission of seeking happiness for the people, rejuvenation for the nation, and harmony for the world. General Secretary Xi Jinping, a people's leader who comes from the people and holds deep affection and a strong sense of responsibility toward them, has always kept the people in his heart, whether working at the grassroots level, in local areas, or at the central level.

From "our aim is to see the people's aspirations for a happy life fulfilled" to "we should serve the people, taking on the responsibilities we should," from "the development we pursue is development that benefits the people," to "the people are our greatest source of confidence in governance," from "our Party is from the people, for the people, and successful because of the people," to "We have a grand yet simple goal—a better life for all our people," all these statements highlight a deep affection for the people and embody the spirit of dedicating oneself to the Party and the country. Xi Jinping Thought on Socialism with Chinese Characteristics for a New Era scientifically answers the questions of whom we serve, whom we rely on, and who we are,, specifically translating everything for the people into the fundamental value orientation of governance, fully reflecting the fundamental political stance of the people.

Promote the distinctive character of Marxism's people-centeredness and thoroughly practice the fundamental purpose of wholeheartedly serving the people

General Secretary Xi Jinping pointed out, "When we talk about our purpose, we say many things, but in the end, it is about serving the people."[1] Always placing the people at the highest position in our minds and always striving for the people's interests and happiness is the main idea of Xi Jinping Thought on Socialism with Chinese Characteristics for a New Era. For example, proposing that the people's aspiration for a better life is our goal, emphasizing that "we are like examinees sitting the tests posed by this era, and the people will review our results," taking the people's judgment of the Party's governance level and effectiveness as the highest standard; pointing out that "the country is the people, and the people are the country," the greatest source of strength is the people, relying on the people to create historical achievements; and stating that the development we pursue is development that benefits the people, aiming for common prosperity for all, making significant and substantial progress in the well-rounded development of individuals and the common prosperity of all, and making people's lives better. These important ideas and viewpoints

---

1   Xi Jinping, *The Campaign to Heighten Awareness of and Implement the Mass Line*, Beijing: Central Party Literature Publishing House, 2014, p. 16.

collectively represent the adherence to and development of the Marxist mass historical view, mass stance, and mass viewpoint.

Put practice first and reflect a distinctive practical character

The viewpoint of practice is the foremost and fundamental viewpoint of Marxism. Combining the transformation of the subjective world and the objective world is the most precious character of Communists. The practical principle of uniting knowledge and action encapsulates the distinctive philosophical wisdom of Chinese civilization while also reflecting the organic integration of Marxist epistemology and methodology.

Xi Jinping Thought on Socialism with Chinese Characteristics for a New Era focuses on the great struggle, great project, great cause, and great dream. It scientifically grasps the global and Chinese development trends, confronts various contradictions, risks, and challenges on the path forward, and proposes a series of new ideas, new thoughts, and new strategies. These are the crystallization of the practical experiences and collective wisdom of the Party and the people, showcasing the distinct practical character of Marxism. "Just as there are no bounds to practice, there is no end to theoretical innovation."[1] The world is changing every moment, and so is China. Xi Jinping Thought on Socialism with Chinese Characteristics for a New Era starts from the issues raised by social practice, begins with analyzing the nature of the problems and the realistic conditions, and focuses on solving problems and achieving practical results. It highlights a clear orientation toward practice, problems, and effectiveness. Whether it is ensuring strict Party self-supervision and self-governance, winning the battle against poverty, advancing the cause of a strong military in the New Era, or building new international relations, General Secretary Xi Jinping

---

1   Xi Jinping, *The Party's Work to Improve Publicity and Guide People in Their Thinking*, Beijing: Central Party Literature Publishing House, 2020, p. 131.

advocated and personally practiced these principles. He has persistently pursued the matters he deemed important. It is precisely this tenacity in prioritizing practice that has enabled our Party to solve many longstanding problems and achieve many significant accomplishments that were previously unattainable.

Adhere to the correct holistic approach and means grasping and planning the Party and the country's cause from an overall standpoint

"Anyone who is unable to make comprehensive plans is not qualified to make plans in a limited area either." To adhere to the holistic approach is to persist in the viewpoints of universal connection and comprehensive development in practical work, coordinating and planning various endeavors. General Secretary Xi Jinping emphasized, "A holistic approach is to look beyond individual phenomena or specifics to capture the essence of developments and see the broader picture." Leading officials must "consciously think and work under the overall perspective," be mindful of the overall situation, grasp the trends, and focus on significant matters. For example, he laid out the ambitious goal of achieving the Chinese Dream of National Rejuvenation and set forth the Two Centenary Goals. He advocated for coordinated implementation of the Five-Sphere Integrated Plan and the Four-Pronged Comprehensive Strategy. He also emphasized the importance of integrating the grand strategy of national rejuvenation with the unprecedented global changes not seen in a century. Furthermore, he stressed that comprehensive deepening of reform must be systematic and holistic, requiring the interconnection and integration of reforms across various sectors. He called for the full, accurate, and comprehensive implementation of the new development philosophy, ensuring it permeates all aspects and stages of development. He also highlighted the need to bear in mind the country's most fundamental interests, to strengthen the

Four Consciousnesses, to reinforce the Four-Sphere Confidence, and to resolutely ensure the Two Upholds, among other principles. All of these initiatives clearly demonstrate the broad strategic vision and holistic perspective of contemporary Chinese Communists.

Adhere to a correct view of the times and advance theoretical and practical innovation in response to the challenges of our times

Xi Jinping Thought on Socialism with Chinese Characteristics for a New Era is a scientific theory grounded in the realities of our times, providing answers to the questions posed by the era. This thought emerged in response to the demands of a transformative era and represents the essence of its spirit, continually evolving with the development of time and practice. General Secretary Xi Jinping has emphasized the importance of grounding our efforts in the characteristics of the era, adapting Marxism to the needs of our times, and better utilizing Marxism to observe, interpret, and guide the times, fully understanding the challenges of our era. He stated, "For any country or nation to thrive, it must follow the logic of history and develop in line with the trend of the times."[1] Only by addressing the specific challenges of our times can we drive social progress. In this New Era, the Party's leadership in the great struggle, the great project, the great cause, and the great dream—collectively promoting both a great social revolution and a great self-reform—scientifically addresses the questions of our times, successfully resolving the challenges of the era, and continually opening new horizons for the development of socialism with Chinese characteristics through the interplay of theoretical and practical innovation.

Adhere to a correct view of history and better address current tasks and shape the future through deep reflection on historical

---

1   Xi Jinping, *On Building a Human Community with a Shared Future,* Beijing: Central Party Literature Publishing House, 2018, p. 521.

experiences

Understanding history allows us to see further, and comprehending history enables us to advance further. General Secretary Xi Jinping pointed out: "Our practical innovation must be grounded in the laws governing historical development and must proceed in the correct direction of history."[1] He emphasizes that the purpose of reviewing history is to summarize its lessons, grasp its laws, and enhance our courage and determination to forge ahead. History is the best textbook, and studying the history of the Party and the nation is essential for upholding and developing socialism with Chinese characteristics and advancing the Party and the country's various undertakings. To better address both foreseeable and unforeseeable risks and challenges on the path forward, we must draw insights from history and distill key strategies from historical experiences to overcome challenges. We should adopt a grand view of history, analyze its evolution and explore its laws within the broad sweep of history, the tides of the times, and the global landscape, and propose corresponding strategies to make our work more systematic, predictive, and creative.

Adhere to a scientific epistemology and methodology and reflect profound dialectical thinking

General Secretary Xi Jinping emphasized: "For our Party to unite and lead the people in achieving the Two Centenary Goals and realizing the Chinese Dream of National Rejuvenation, we must continually draw nourishment from Marxist philosophical wisdom and consciously adhere to and apply the dialectical materialist worldview and methodology."[2] For example, it is crucial to:

- Master the foundational methods of dialectical materialism.

---

1   Xi Jinping, "Building an Archaeology with Chinese Characteristics, Style, and Ethos to Better Understand the Profound and Enduring Chinese Civilization," *Qiushi,* Chin. ed., no. 23, 2020.
2   Xi Jinping, *The Party's Work to Improve Publicity and Guide People in Their Thinking,* Beijing: Central Party Literature Publishing House, 2020, p. 125.

▪ In practical work, grasp the relationships between phenomena and essence, form and content, cause and effect, chance and necessity, possibility and reality, internal and external factors, as well as universality and particularity.

▪ Continuously develop capabilities in strategic thinking, historical thinking, dialectical thinking, innovative thinking, legal thinking, and worst-case scenario planning.

▪ Maintain a systematic approach.

▪ Accurately understand and manage significant relationships.

▪ Enhance forward-looking thinking, holistic planning, strategic layout, and comprehensive analysis.

▪ Combine a domestic focus with a global perspective.

▪ Harmonize problem-oriented and goal-oriented approaches.

▪ Integrate long-term and short-term objectives.

▪ Ensure a balance between comprehensive planning and key priorities.

The proficient application of these scientific ways of thinking and working methods fully demonstrates a high level of consciousness and exceptional skill in long-term governance and state administration.

Xi Jinping Thought on Socialism with Chinese Characteristics for a New Era not only addresses the "what" and "why" but also the "how" and "what to do." It involves both assigning the tasks of "crossing the river" and guiding the access to bridges or boats, serving as a model for adhering to and applying the Marxist worldview and methodology. In terms of scientific ways of thinking, it emphasizes maintaining strategic thinking, historical thinking, dialectical thinking, innovative thinking, legal thinking, and worst-case scenario mentality planning, alongside scientifically formulating and firmly executing the Party's policies. Regarding problem investigation and research, Xi Jinping stresses the importance of "encouraging research and fact-finding in the Party," stating that "investigations and studies are the basis for planning and the path to success. If one does not investigate, one has no right to speak, let alone the power to decide. Investigation and research are our basic skills for doing our work well." In emphasizing work implementation, he advocates for the need to pursue endurance, seize opportunities, take concrete actions, and adhere to the principle of dedicating 10% to planning and 90% to execution, striving to transform strategic plans into reality.

2. Consciously apply Marxism to plan China's development

The decisions and plans since the 18th CPC National Congress profoundly illustrate that, whether it is the scientific judgment of the international and domestic situation, the significant judgment of China entering a new development stage, the guiding thought and principles of economic and social development, or the emphasis on maintaining major relationships, they are all imbued with the grand wisdom and strategies of Marxist worldview and methodology. These decisions also fully demonstrate that the century-old party has achieved an unprecedented understanding of the laws governing the Communist Party's governance and the development of socialism and human society. The CPC Central Committee, with General Secretary Xi Jinping at its core, exhibits a high degree of self-awareness, outstanding wisdom, and superb capabilities in long-term governance and state administration.

(1) Coordinating both domestic and international overarching situations and fully understanding the "changes" and "constants" in China's development environment is an outstanding result of applying dialectical materialism to understand the broader trends and manage overall situations.

The deeply complex and evolving domestic and international

environments require adhering to a correct view of history, the broader situation, and development, while overseeing both domestic and international situations. It is essential to skillfully discern the "changes" and "constants" and their dialectical relationships in an increasingly intricate domestic and international environments. Most importantly, we must better coordinate the overall strategy for the rejuvenation of the Chinese nation and the unprecedented global changes not seen in a century. By analyzing the domestic and international environments and situations, the CPC Central Committee, with General Secretary Xi Jinping at its core, made an overarching, strategic, and forward-looking judgment at the Fifth Plenary Session of the 19th CPC Central Committee: that in the current and upcoming periods, China's development remains in a important period of strategic opportunity, but both opportunities and challenges have undergone new developments and changes. This judgment, made by applying dialectical materialism to grasp the overall situation, accurately identifies the essence of the complex domestic and international phenomena, recognizes and grasps the laws of development, accurately perceives changes, responds scientifically to changes, proactively seeks changes, turns crises into opportunities, transforms challenges into opportunities, and open up new horizons.

(2) The significant judgment that China has entered a new development stage is based on the principle that social existence determines social consciousness, and the dialectical unity of productive forces and relations of production, thus establishing a new historical coordinate for China's development.

Marxism holds that the ultimate cause of all social changes and political transformations should be sought in changes in the mode of production or exchange. "Just as one does not judge an individual by what he thinks about himself, so one cannot judge such a period of transformation by its consciousness, but, on the contrary, this consciousness must be explained from the contradictions of material life, from the conflict existing between the social forces of production and the relations of production."[1] The development stage a society enters is not merely a subjective judgment, but a scientific understanding of the objective situation, major changes, and stage-specific characteristics of the economic and social development of a given period. Over the past 40-plus years of reform and opening up, the Party has consistently and scientifically grasped developmental trends and stage-specific characteristics, seizing opportunities for reform to advance China's development in response to changes in global, national, and popular conditions. The Party made the timely significant judgment that China is and will remain in the primary stage of socialism for a long time, elaborated on the theory of the primary stage of socialism, and outlined the Party's basic line in this stage, which has fundamental, overarching, and strategic significance for the development of the Party and the country. The 19th National Congress of the CPC made the major political judgment that socialism with Chinese characteristics has entered the New Era, marking a new historical position for China's development and providing a temporal coordinate and fundamental basis for the scientific formulation of the Party's policies and guidelines. From the beginning of the new period to entering the new century, from standing at a new starting point to stepping into a new era, at different stages of development, we have not only continued our efforts but also continuously written new chapters.

Currently, while emphasizing that China remains in the primary stage of socialism, we also clearly propose that China has entered a new development stage. On one hand, the primary stage of socialism is the greatest national reality of contemporary China; on the other hand, the

---

1   https://www.marxists.org/archive/marx/works/1859/critique-pol-economy/preface.htm.

14th Five-Year Plan period marks the entry into a new development stage, an important phase in the new journey of the New Era. Faced with new development environments and conditions, we must unswervingly adhere to the new development philosophy, accelerate the development of a new development dynamic that focuses on domestic circulation and features positive interplay between domestic circulation and international circulation, and promote higher quality, more efficient, more equitable, more sustainable, and safer development of the economy.

China has entered a new stage of development. This stage marks the phase of building a modern socialist country in all respects and marching toward the Second Centenary Goal. It follows the stage where China has generally achieved a moderately prosperous society and then fully established such a society. This significant strategic judgment was made by the Party Central Committee with General Secretary Xi Jinping at its core, deeply understanding the domestic and international development trends. The judgment on this new stage of development adheres to the reality that China is still in the primary stage of socialism and takes into account the new changes in the principal social contradictions in the New Era and the objective changes in economic and social development. This timely advancement of China's social development to a new historical stage has major theoretical and practical significance.

On one hand, China remains in the primary stage of socialism and is still the largest developing country in the world. Development continues to be the primary task for the Party in governing and rejuvenating the nation. We must bear the two "unchanged" situations in mind, avoiding haste which may lead to counterproductive results and ultimately harm the healthy development of the Party and the country's undertakings. On the other hand, as China's development progresses and its comprehensive national strength increases, different historical periods will inevitably have different stage-specific characteristics and primary tasks. Currently, China is experiencing profound stage-specific changes and has entered a new stage of development with the theme of achieving high-quality development. It is essential to keep pace with the times, innovate and transform under the changed circumstances and conditions. Clinging to outdated ways and rigid conservatism will inevitably result in falling behind the times.

(3) Fully grasping and managing various key relationships entails applying the fundamental principles of dialectical contradiction to creatively harness the laws of development, driving new progress while proactively resolving contradictions.

Marxism posits that contradictions exist in all processes and permeate throughout. Contradictions are the universal law of development of things, as "movement itself is a contradiction." General Secretary Xi Jinping pointed out, "Contradictions are universally present, and are the essence of the connections between things and the fundamental driving force for the development of things. Human cognitive and practical activities are fundamentally processes of continuously understanding and resolving contradictions."[1] Therefore, judgments on contradictions are crucial for observing the situation, analyzing things, and formulating major Party and national policies.

Currently, China faces profound changes in the international and domestic environments, with emerging issues and complex relationships. This necessitates the use of contradiction analysis methods to handle complex problems, grasp major relationships, and respond to severe challenges.

General Secretary Xi Jinping emphasizes the use of the worldview and methodology of dialectical materialism. By carefully analyzing various

---

1   Xi Jinping, *The Party's Work to Improve Publicity and Guide People in Their Thinking*, Beijing: Central Party Literature Publishing House, 2020, p. 127.

domestic and international issues and contradictions, whether at the level of macro principles or specific work, he stresses the importance of fully understanding the main relationships. Grasping relationships means correctly recognizing the connections between things and mastering the use of laws to solve contradictions and problems. For instance, at the level of understanding the macro situation and overall picture, he explicitly proposes coordinating the overall strategy for the rejuvenation of the Chinese nation and the profound changes unseen in a century. At the level of guiding principles for development planning, he addresses five main relationships.

The relationship between inheritance and development, ensuring the organic connection of the Two Centenary Goals.

1. The relationship between government and market, better leveraging our institutional advantages.

2. The relationship between openness and self-reliance, better coordinating the domestic and international overall situations.

3. The relationship between development and security, effectively preventing and addressing systemic risks that may impact the modernization process.

4. The relationship between strategy and tactics, formulating a forward-looking, pragmatic, and useful planning proposal.

In terms of economic development goals, the approach is to have the Party steer the overall direction and major strategies, combining qualitative and quantitative methods, with a primary focus on qualitative expressions that inherently contain quantitative aspects. In the deployment of economic and social development, the strategy is to build a new development dynamic with domestic circulation as the mainstay and domestic and international circulations reinforcing each other. This includes combining supply-side structural reform with the strategy of expanding domestic demand and coordinating comprehensive planning with emphasizing key points. All these represent the creative application of dialectical materialism in understanding and solving development issues, making strategic and scientific plans and deployments by correctly handling various major relationships.

For example, a prominent highlight and strategic deployment of the Fifth Plenary Session of the 19th CPC Central Committee is the clear proposal to coordinate development and security from the perspective of the overall development situation. Observing changes in China's external environment and internal development conditions as a whole and as a system, the proposal aims to "coordinate the domestic and international overall situations and manage both development and security well." During the period of turbulence and transformation in the great changes, it underscores the extreme importance of correctly handling the relationship between development and security. It insists that security is the premise of development, while development is the guarantee of security. The integration of the two leads to prosperity, while their separation leads to weakness. Planning security within the overall context of economic and social development to create a harmonious and mutually reinforcing relationship between development and security is crucial for constructing the new development dynamic.

In coordinating development and security, it is crucial to effectively integrate holistic thinking, a worst-case scenario mindset, and systematic analysis to ensure fundamental, strategic, and long-term planning. As General Secretary Xi Jinping emphasized, "We must ensure both development and security, be better aware of the opportunities and risks we face, and always have plans in place to respond to worst-case scenarios. We should think harder and more deeply ... and make preemptive moves to deal with various risks and challenges, so as to ensure smooth progress in our socialist modernization drive."[1]

For another example, the new development dynamic proposed at the Fifth Plenary Session of the 19th CPC Central Committee is a strategic choice that aims to adapt to and steer changes in the global political and economic environment while grasping the regular changes in China's economic development and new characteristics of the new stage in a timely manner. This approach keeps pace with the times, elevates China's economic development level, and shapes new advantages in international economic cooperation and competition.

1. Focusing on the characteristics and laws of major economies, the session constructs an economic development dynamic dominated by domestic demand and internally sustainable circulation.

2. Aiming at the stage-specific characteristics of China's economic development, it adjusts the relationship between domestic economic circulation and international economic circulation in a timely manner.

3. In light of the increasingly unstable and uncertain international situation, it mitigates the risks of external shocks and ensures development security.

It clearly advocates for the proper management of the relationship between domestic and international circulation, with domestic circulation as the primary focus. By tapping into the potential of domestic demand, it promotes a more effective use of both domestic and international markets and resources, as opposed to pursuing a closed domestic circulation. The emphasis is on ensuring that China's doors to the global economy will not close but will, in fact, open even wider.

(4) Enhancing awareness of opportunities and risks and establishing strategic thinking, holistic thinking, worst-case scenario mentality, and

---

1 *Documents from the Fifth Plenary Session of the 19th Central Committee of the Communist Party of China,* Beijing: People's Publishing House, 2020, p. 85.

dialectical thinking is a creative application of Marxist methodology for planning China's development.

The blueprint and goals have been defined, and the major policies have been determined. The key now is to diligently carry out the work, properly implement the Party's line, principles, and policies. This requires guidance from a scientific epistemological methodology, improving scientific thinking abilities, enhancing the capacity to manage complex situations, creatively conducting work, and strengthening the ability to tackle tasks and overcome difficulties. General Secretary Xi Jinping pointed out, "The deeper our cause develops, the more we need to continuously enhance our dialectical thinking ability."[1]

Currently, the domestic and international environments are undergoing complex and profound changes, requiring us to skillfully handle various contradictions and problems, properly manage various major relationships, and make beneficial strategic choices by weighing the pros and cons to avoid harm and maximize benefits.

The Fifth Plenary Session of the 19th CPC Central Committee pointed out that in the context of profound changes in the domestic and international environments, it is essential to enhance the awareness of opportunities and risks, maintain strategic resolve, understand and grasp the laws of development, adopt a worst-case scenario mentality, accurately recognize changes, respond to changes scientifically, and proactively seek changes. We must be skilled at fostering opportunities amid crises and creating new situations in the midst of changes, seizing opportunities, meeting challenges, avoiding harm, and advancing courageously.

Applying dialectical thinking to fully understand the current development issues in China requires us to bravely face contradictions and

---

1   Xi Jinping, *The Party's Work to Improve Publicity and Guide People in Their Thinking*, Beijing: Central Party Literature Publishing House, 2020, p. 129.

problems, skillfully grasp key points, identify priorities, and discern the laws governing development. We should observe things objectively rather than subjectively, dynamically rather than statically, comprehensively rather than partially, systematically rather than fragmentarily, and in terms of universal connections rather than in isolation.

The Recommendations of the CPC Central Committee for Formulating the 14th Five-Year Plan for Economic and Social Development and the Long-Range Objectives through 2035 exemplify the integration of both domestic and global perspectives, the alignment of problem-oriented and goal-oriented approaches, the linkage between medium- and long-term goals with short-term objectives, and the balance between comprehensive planning and key priorities. This reflects a deliberate and sophisticated application of dialectical thinking. For example, the Recommendations elevate "adhering to a systematic perspective" to the level of a fundamental principle for economic and social development. This marks the first time that this concept has been elevated to a principle level, thoroughly elaborated in our Party's documents, and significantly emphasized as a fundamental thought and working method.

From a philosophical standpoint, adhering to a systematic perspective means adhering to materialist dialectics, focusing on the new situations and circumstances facing China's development. It involves planning development with systematic thinking and methods, considering China's development and the entire socialist modernization as a grand system to be designed and planned. This approach emphasizes forward-looking thinking, holistic planning, strategic layout, and integrated consideration, and concerted efforts across the country to better leverage the initiative of the central, local, and various sectors.

In a situation where contradictions are complex and uncertainties are increasing, enhancing awareness of potential dangers and risks is very important. "Thinking about what could lead to danger ensures safety; thinking about what could lead t(o disorder ensures stability; thinking about what could lead to demise ensures survival." General Secretary Xi Jinping often emphasizes the continuous need to enhance awareness of potential dangers and prevent risks and challenges. The road ahead will not be smooth, with many twists and turns and challenges and difficulties. We must proceed with caution, be mindful of potential dangers even in times of safety, and avoid making strategic and subversive mistakes.

(5) Adhering to a people-centered approach and steadily advancing substantive progress toward common prosperity exemplifies applying the Marxist historical perspective on the people, standing on their side, and using their viewpoint in the pursuit of realizing a better life for the populace. Marxism asserts that the people are the true heroes, the driving force behind social development, and the creators of history. For a century, the Chinese Communists have consistently maintained a heartfelt dedication to the people, embedding the principle of doing everything for the people and relying on them throughout the entire process of revolution, development, and reform.

General Secretary Xi Jinping's series of significant statements—such as "our aim is to see the people's aspirations for a happy life fulfilled," "I will fully commit to the people and never fail them," "The people are the creators of history; they are the fundamental force that determines our Party and country's future," "Standing on the people's side represents the fundamental political stance of the CPC," "The people are the greatest source of confidence for our Party's governance, the solid foundation of our republic, and the fundamental underpinning of our Party's strength and the country's prosperity," and "Always keep the people in the highest position in our minds"—serve as exemplary expressions of adhering to and developing the Marxist historical perspective, stance, and viewpoint on the people.

In the Recommendations for Formulating the 14th Five-Year Plan for Economic and Social Development and the Long-Range Objectives through 2035, the people-centered philosophy of development is a consistent thread throughout. Among the principles that must be followed for economic and social development during the 14th Five-Year Plan period, "adhering to a people-centered approach" is identified as a fundamental stance and an important principle. It is explicitly required that China should "uphold the people's principal status, pursue common prosperity, ensure that development is for the people and by the people, and that its fruits are shared among all the people, safeguard the fundamental interests of the people, stimulate the enthusiasm, initiative, and creativity of all the people, promote social fairness, enhance people's wellbeing, and continuously realize the people's aspirations for a better life."

In the Recommendations, the statement "The people's lives will be better, and more substantive progress will be made in the well-rounded development of individuals and the common prosperity of all the people" is distinctly highlighted. This emphasis on "steadily advancing common prosperity" and the clear articulation of a series of important requirements and major initiatives marks the first time such points have been highlighted in a Party plenary document.

In the specific measures proposed in the recommendations for the 14th Five-Year Plan and the 2035 Long-Range Goals, the focus on meeting the people's growing needs for a better life is steadfastly implemented through the new development philosophy of innovation, coordination, green development, openness, and sharing. To enhance people's wellbeing, efforts are made to improve the quality of life, raise income levels, prioritize public health, improve the safety and security of products and services related to health such as food and medicine, and establish a multi-level social security system that covers everyone, integrates urban and rural areas, and is fair, unified, and sustainable. Other measures include improving the holiday system, implementing paid leave, and strengthening consumer rights protection. These actions reflect the scientific application and vivid expression of the Marxist historical perspective on the people in the Party's governance practices.

As General Secretary Xi Jinping emphasized, "Promoting the common prosperity of all the people is a long-term task. However, as we complete the building of a moderately prosperous society in all respects and embark on the new journey of building a modern socialist country in all respects, we must place greater emphasis on promoting the common prosperity of all the people, work steadily and persistently toward this goal, and strive to make more active efforts in this direction."[1]

The Fifth Plenary Session of the 19th CPC Central Committee highlighted the people's nature of socialist modernization, fully reflecting the distinctive feature that China's modernization is the modernization of common prosperity for all. Pursuing common prosperity is the essential requirement of socialism with Chinese characteristics. It involves taking effective measures and policy arrangements to consciously and proactively address regional disparities, urban-rural gaps, and income distribution disparities, persistently promoting fairness and justice, resolutely preventing polarization, and making solid progress toward the goal of achieving common prosperity for all.

---

1   *Documents from the Fifth Plenary Session of the 19th Central Committee of the Communist Party of China,* Beijing: People's Publishing House, 2020, p. 84.

III. Enrich and Develop the Fundamental Tenets
of Marxism

1. Develop Marxist philosophy

Studying and applying philosophy has always been a fine tradition of the CPC. Marxist philosophy, which "includes dialectical materialism and historical materialism, is the concentrated embodiment of Marxist stance, viewpoint, and method. It forms the ideological foundation of Marxist theory,"[1] deeply revealing the general laws of the objective world, especially the development of human society. This scientific theory, proven by history and practice, despite being born over a century ago, remains a fundamental skill of Communists. "We must continually be nourished by the wisdom of Marxist philosophy."[2]

Consciously applying dialectical materialism and historical materialism to understand and transform the world is the fundamental way in which Marxist philosophy realizes its theoretical value and demonstrates its scientific truth. It is also the practical pathway through which Marxist philosophy is enriched and developed continuously. General Secretary Xi Jinping has emphasized: "Both history and reality show that only by adhering to historical materialism can we continuously elevate our understanding of the laws governing socialism with Chinese characteristics to new levels, and constantly open up new horizons for the development of contemporary Chinese Marxism."[3]

Xi Jinping Thought on Socialism with Chinese Characteristics for a New Era creatively applies dialectical materialism and historical materialism

---

1   Xi Jinping, *The Party's Work to Improve Publicity and Guide People in Their Thinking*, Beijing: Central Party Literature Publishing House, 2020, p. 30.
2   *Ibid.,* p. 125.
3   *Ibid.,* p. 32.

to all of the Party and the country's work. It encapsulates the philosophical reflection on "what kind of socialism with Chinese characteristics should be upheld and developed in the New Era, and how to go about it," thereby endowing Marxist philosophy with new contemporary significance.

General Secretary Xi Jinping has pointed out the need to make Marxist philosophy a fundamental skill, improving the ability to apply the Marxist stand, viewpoint and method to analyze and solve problems. For instance, based on the basic principle that social existence determines social consciousness, we must formulate policies and advance work by starting from actual conditions. This approach considers both the fundamental reality of the primary stage of socialism and the new characteristics of China's economic and social development, leading to the significant judgment that China has entered a new development stage. This reflects the dialectical unity of inheritance and innovation, quantitative change and qualitative change, continuity and stages. Based on the principle of the movement of society's basic contradictions, we should promote comprehensive deepening of reform, improve and develop the socialist system with Chinese characteristics, modernize the national system and capacity for governance, and work to enhance the systemic, holistic, and coordinated nature of reforms. According to the principle of the unity of the universality and particularity of contradictions, we must strengthen problem awareness and adhere to a problem-oriented approach, actively responding to various major risks and challenges, especially focusing on preventing and resolving any major risks and challenges that could delay or interrupt the process of the rejuvenation of the Chinese nation.

Firstly, by applying the basic principles of dialectical materialism, seeking truth from facts, and starting from objective reality, we have scientifically understood the historical juncture and the most fundamental reality of contemporary China. This has led to the scientific judgment that socialism with Chinese characteristics has entered the New Era, highlighting the truth power of the basic principles of dialectical materialism.

Dialectical materialism holds that the world is unified in material substance, which inherently exists independently of human will and can be reflected in human consciousness. However, objective reality is not static; it moves, changes, and develops within specific times and spaces. This is the most basic and core viewpoint of dialectical materialism and the cornerstone of Marxist philosophy.

Adhering to the principle of material unity requires recognizing objective material existence as a premise, leveraging human subjective initiative, and understanding and grasping the essence and laws of things within the dialectical relationship between movement and stillness in specific times and spaces. It necessitates starting from objective reality, following and utilizing laws, rather than placing subjective will and bookish doctrines in a decisive position, or starting from subjective impressions or doing everything by the book

Socialism with Chinese characteristics combines the fundamental tenets of scientific socialism with the realities of China. It adheres to the general laws of socialist society while being deeply rooted in Chinese soil and reflecting the will of the Chinese people. This fundamental achievement has been obtained through long-term practice by the CPC and the people.

Currently, understanding the historical conjuncture in socialism with Chinese characteristics and identifying China's critical reality are essential prerequisites and bases for our Party to formulate the line, principles, and policies. This scientific judgment is also the solid foundation upon which Xi Jinping Thought on Socialism with Chinese Characteristics for a New Era is established.

"Dialectical materialism is the worldview and methodology of the Chinese Communists."[1] General Secretary Xi Jinping emphasized, "Learning and mastering the principle that the world is unified in material substance and that material determines consciousness, we must formulate policies and promote work starting from objective reality."[2] This principle is also the fundamental basis for our Party to scientifically judge the critical reality and historical conjuncture in contemporary China.

The political report of the 19th CPC National Congress, after comprehensively summarizing the historic changes and achievements in various aspects of Party and national development in the five why years since the 18th National Congress, clearly articulated: "With decades of hard work, socialism with Chinese characteristics has crossed the threshold into a new era. This is a new historic juncture in China's development... The principal contradiction facing Chinese society has evolved. What we now face is the contradiction between unbalanced and inadequate development and the people's ever-growing needs for a better life." That being said, "The evolution of the principal challenge facing Chinese society does not change our assessment of the present stage of socialism in China."[3] This is the current historical juncture and the critical reality facing China, and all our principles and policies must start from this largest reality.

This scientific conclusion of our Party is neither based on subjective will nor a mere replication of past or foreign experiences. It is a scientific judgment grounded in the actual conditions of China's reform and development and the global development landscape. As General Secretary Xi Jinping pointed out, "We must see that the basic national condition of the primary stage of socialism has not changed, and we must also

1   *Ibid.*, p. 124.
2   *Ibid.*, p. 125.
3   Xi Jinping, *Secure a Decisive Victory in Building a Moderately Prosperous Society in All Respects and Strive for the Great Success of Socialism with Chinese Characteristics for a New Era: Report at the 19th National Congress of the Communist Party of China*, Beijing: People's Publishing House, 2017, p. 12.

recognize the new characteristics presented by each stage of our economic and social development."[1] Since the founding of the People's Republic of China, the country has experienced a tremendous transformation from standing up to becoming rich and growing strong, ushering in a bright prospect for the rejuvenation of the Chinese nation. As China increasingly takes center stage on the world platform and people's living standards undergo dramatic changes, the connotation of our basic national condition continually evolves. The domestic and international situations we face are also constantly changing. Problems that once troubled us have disappeared or turned into advantages, while issues and challenges that were previously nonexistent have now emerged as new contradictions, many of which are unprecedented and uncharted for us. Given this situation, we must avoid rigid dogmatism and refrain from copying and pasting solutions. We should base our actions on China's specific realities, seek truth from facts, and leverage subjective initiative. While recognizing that China will remain in the primary stage of socialism for a long time as the fundamental basis for building socialism with Chinese characteristics, we must also acknowledge that China has entered the New Era, and the principal contradiction in society has changed. We should adapt to the new domestic and international situations and tasks, scientifically grasp the new changes and characteristics of our economic and social development, respect objective reality, and proactively take action.

Secondly, the tide of human social history is vast and ever-flowing, with its development being complex and changeable. Historical materialism, as a crucial component of Marxist philosophy, reveals the general laws governing the development of human society. It provides a scientific worldview and methodology for people to consciously stand at

---

1   Xi Jinping, *The Party's Work to Improve Publicity and Guide People in Their Thinking*, Beijing: Central Party Literature Publishing House, 2020, p. 126.

the forefront of the era and history, enabling them to fully understand the essence of human society and grasp its development laws amidst the complexities of human social history. "In the various historical periods of revolution, development, and reform, our Party has utilized historical materialism to systematically, concretely, and historically analyze the movement and development laws of Chinese society, continuously grasping and applying these laws in the process of understanding and transforming the world, thereby driving the Party and people's cause to one victory after another."[1]

Currently, it remains crucial to promote the study and mastery of the basic principles of historical materialism within the Party, enabling better understanding of our national conditions, the overarching trends in the development of the Party and the country, and the laws governing historical development. This will enhance our proactive efforts in advancing various initiatives.

(1) Applying the principle of the dialectical relationship between social existence and social consciousness is essential. This approach clarifies the realistic basis for our Party's formulation of policies while steadfastly guiding us with the noble ideals of communism. The fundamental view of historical materialism is that social existence determines social consciousness. This principle clearly indicates that we should understand the nature and laws of the superstructure, particularly the development of social history, from the perspective of social existence, mainly the mode of material production and economic foundation. This understanding serves as the basis for formulating the Party's line, principles, and policies. General Secretary Xi Jinping emphasized, "The interaction and mutual restriction between productive forces and relations of production, as well as the economic base and the superstructure, govern the entire process of

---

1   *Ibid.,* p. 31.

social development."[1] Simultaneously, we must highly regard the relative independence of social consciousness and its dynamic influence on social existence. By fully understanding and grasping the objective laws of social and historical development, we can fully exercise our subjective initiative to create better conditions for social and historical progress.

The political report of the 19th CPC National Congress made eight things clear,[2] which profoundly elucidates what kind of socialism with Chinese characteristics should be upheld and developed in the New Era. In making the eight things clear, the Party adopted a perspective grounded in historical materialism and the dialectical relationship between social existence and social consciousness. It makes clear the principles, lines, and policies for socialism with Chinese characteristics in the New Era. By considering both social existence, especially the principal social contradiction in China at the current stage, and the proactive influence

---

1   *Ibid.,* p. 328.
2   These are:
■ The overarching goal of upholding and developing socialism with Chinese characteristics is to realize socialist modernization and national rejuvenation, and, that on the basis of finishing the building of a moderately prosperous society in all respects, a two-step approach should be taken to build China into a great modern socialist country that is prosperous, strong, democratic, culturally advanced, harmonious, and beautiful by the middle of the century.
■ The principal contradiction facing Chinese society in the New Era is that between unbalanced and inadequate development and the people's ever-growing needs for a better life. We must therefore continue commitment to our people-centered philosophy of development, and work to promote well-rounded human development and common prosperity for everyone.
■ The overall plan for building socialism with Chinese characteristics is the five-sphere integrated plan, and the overall strategy is the four-pronged comprehensive strategy. It highlights the importance of fostering stronger confidence in the path, theory, system, and culture of socialism with Chinese characteristics.
■ The overall goal of deepening reform in every field is to improve and develop the system of socialism with Chinese characteristics and modernize China's system and capacity for governance.
■ The overall goal of comprehensively advancing law-based governance is to establish a system of socialist rule of law with Chinese characteristics and build a country of socialist rule of law.
■ The Party's goal of building a strong military in the New Era is to build the people's forces into world-class forces that obey the Party's command, can fight and win, and maintain excellent conduct.
■ Major country diplomacy with Chinese characteristics aims to foster a new type of international relations and build a community with a shared future for mankind.
■ The defining feature of socialism with Chinese characteristics is the leadership of the Communist Party of China; the greatest strength of the system of socialism with Chinese characteristics is the leadership of the Communist Party of China; the Party is the highest force for political leadership. It sets forth the general requirements for Party building in the New Era and underlines the importance of political work in Party building.

of social consciousness and the superstructure, the Party makes clear the overall and strategic layout, development methods, driving forces, and strategic steps for socialism with Chinese characteristics in the New Era. Recognizing the guiding role of social consciousness and the superstructure, the Party also makes clear the goals and tasks of socialism in the New Era. Furthermore, it makes clear the role of the superstructure in ensuring legal, military, diplomatic, and overall Party leadership. Since the 18th National Congress, our Party has placed great importance on ideological work, emphasizing the guiding role of communist ideals and convictions. General Secretary Xi Jinping stated that the lofty ideal of communism is the political soul and a source of inspiration of Communists. Achieving communism is a historical process achieved through successive stages, "with our current and future efforts, spanning many generations, all aimed at ultimately realizing this great goal."[1] Therefore, we must unify the lofty ideal of communism with the common ideal of socialism with Chinese characteristics and integrate it with our ongoing endeavors.

(2) By applying the principles and analytical methods of fundamental social contradictions, we can consistently uphold the direction of socialism while continuously refining and developing the system of socialism with Chinese characteristics. This, in turn, advances the modernization of our national governance system and capacity. Understanding the direction, future prospects, and pathways for development in the movement of socialism with Chinese characteristics in the New Era is essential not only for China's development but also for the global socialist movement. General Secretary Xi Jinping emphasized, "Only by combining the contradictory movement between productive forces and relations of production with the contradictory movement between the economic base and the

---

1   *Documents Produced since the 18th CPC National Congress,* Beijing: Central Party Literature Publishing House, 2014, vol. I, p.115.

superstructure, and by observing these fundamental social contradictions as a whole, can we fully grasp the fundamental aspects and development direction of society."[1]

The principle of fundamental social contradictions is a core tenet of historical materialism, encompassing the contradictory movements between productive forces and relations of production, as well as between the economic base and the superstructure. The interactions and movements of these two sets of contradictions form the basic laws of societal motion, scientifically elucidating the two inevitables[2] and the two nevers[3] of the development of human society and providing a theoretical basis for understanding the direction, path, and laws of social history. This understanding substantiates the scientific argument that socialism is superior to and will inevitably replace capitalism.

Since the 18th CPC National Congress, General Secretary Xi Jinping repeatedly underscored from the perspective of historical materialism that socialism with Chinese characteristics is socialism, not any other doctrine. In making the eight things clear, the political report of the 19th National Congress is centered on the fundamental attributes of the socialist system, deeply elucidating the profound connotations of socialism with Chinese characteristics in the New Era and clearly defining its nature and forward direction.

Nevertheless, adhering to socialism does not mean clinging to dogma or remaining stagnant; it requires adapting to changes in the movement of fundamental social contradictions to drive social development and comprehensively advance reform and opening up. Xi Jinping pointed

---

1 Xi Jinping, *The Party's Work to Improve Publicity and Guide People in Their Thinking*, Beijing: Central Party Literature Publishing House, 2020, p. 34.
2 The inevitable. fall of the bourgeoisie and the inevitable victory of the proletariat.
3 No social order is ever destroyed before all the productive forces for which it is sufficient have been developed, and new superior relations of production never replace older ones before the material conditions for their existence have matured within the framework of the old society.

out, "To uphold and develop socialism with Chinese characteristics, we must continually adapt the relations of production to the development of productive forces and continually improve the superstructure in line with the development of the economic base."[1] These fundamental social contradictions are dynamic and evolving, and the process of reform and opening up is ongoing, never complete. The 19th CPC National Congress set the overarching goal of reform as improving and developing the system of socialism with Chinese characteristics and modernizing the national governance system and capacity.

The Fourth Plenary Session of the 19th Central Committee specifically addressed this issue, issuing the Resolution of the CPC Central Committee on Upholding and Improving the System of Socialism with Chinese Characteristics and Modernizing the National Governance System and Capacity. This established, for the first time in human history, a system fundamentally different from those of Western countries, prominently raising the banner of the socialist system with Chinese characteristics and showcasing the superiority of socialism. This successful application of historical materialism to address the challenges of the global socialist movement exemplifies our Party's capacity for scientific analysis and adaptation.

(3) By applying the fundamental principle that the people create history, we can maintain the people's principal position and commit to a people-centered approach, while also upholding the overall leadership of the Party and resolutely ensuring the Two Upholds. This ensures the intrinsic unity between the people's will and the Party's directives. The viewpoint that the people are the creators of history is a fundamental tenet of historical materialism, and the stance of siding with the people

---

1 Xi Jinping, *The Party's Work to Improve Publicity and Guide People in Their Thinking*, Beijing: Central Party Literature Publishing House, 2020, p. 34.

is our Party's fundamental political stance. The mass line is the Party's fundamental working method. "The people are the creators of history; they are the fundamental force that determines our Party and country's future. We must ensure the principal status of the people, and adhere to the Party's commitment to serving the public good and exercising power in the interests of the people. We must observe the Party's fundamental purpose of wholeheartedly serving the people, and put into practice the Party's mass line in all aspects of governance. We must regard as our goal the people's aspirations to live a better life, and rely on the people to move history forward."[1]

General Secretary Xi Jinping, recognizing the people as the creators of history, has proposed the people-centered philosophy of development, which forms the fundamental stance and value pursuit of Xi Jinping Thought on Socialism with Chinese Characteristics for a New Era. "Seeking happiness for the people, rejuvenation for the nation, and harmony for the world are the keys to deeply understanding and comprehensively grasping Xi Jinping Thought on Socialism with Chinese Characteristics for a New Era."[2] This philosophy adheres to the original aspirations of the CPC to seek happiness for the people, emphasizes the principal position of the people, and upholds the principles of everything for the people and everything relying on the people, highlighting the materialist historical view that the people are the creators of history and the true heroes.

Furthermore, historical materialism posits that the people are not a supra-class entity or a mere aggregation of individuals, but rather their unity with the advanced class and the Party's class character is essential. The vast majority of the people can consciously create history and drive

---

1   Xi Jinping, *Secure a Decisive Victory in Building a Moderately Prosperous Society in All Respects and Strive for the Great Success of Socialism with Chinese Characteristics for a New Era: Report at the 19th National Congress of the Communist Party of China*, Beijing: People's Publishing House, 2017, p. 21.

2   *Series of Speeches by General Secretary Xi Jinping (2016 Edition)*, Beijing: Xuexi Press and People's Publishing House, 2019, p. 12.

the progress of human society only under the leadership of the advanced class and party, with the exemplary roles of outstanding figures and heroes among the people, and by supporting the Party's core leadership position.

Since the 18th CPC National Congress, significant historical achievements have been made in Party self-supervision and self-governance, fundamentally improving the development situation of the Party and the country. The Party's progressive and wholesome nature have been further enhanced, and its core leadership position has been further consolidated. It has been clearly articulated that the Party's leadership is the most essential characteristic of socialism with Chinese characteristics and the greatest advantage of the socialist system with Chinese characteristics. Emphasizing political development as the Party's fundamental development, enhancing the Four Consciousnesses, strengthening the Four-Sphere Confidence, and resolutely ensuring the Two Upholds, the overall leadership of the Party is integrated into the basic strategy of the cause of socialism with Chinese characteristics in the New Era. This provides a strong political guarantee for uniting and leading the people to create great historical achievements together.

Thirdly, by employing the thought and working methods rooted in the fundamental tenets of dialectical materialism and historical materialism, we have taken a principled, holistic, forward-looking and innovative approach to work, adopted a series of major initiatives and a scientific explanation of how to uphold and develop socialism with Chinese characteristics in the New Era. We have enriched and developed Marxist methodology, particularly dialectical materialism. This methodology advocates for analyzing and solving problems in an objective, connected, developmental, comprehensive, and balanced manner, rather than subjectively, in isolation, statically, one-sidedly, or absolutely.

Dialectical materialism is essentially an objective dialectic, independent of human will. It reflects the essence and laws of the connections and development of things, embodying the method and working approach of "harmony between humanity and nature." This method is profound and encompassing, containing powerful transformative capabilities. It serves as a "telescope" for understanding direction and laws and as a "microscope" for deeply comprehending the essence of things. It is a potent intellectual tool for our Party to overcome difficulties, maintain advancement, lead the times, and fully understand and transform the world.

General Secretary Xi Jinping emphasized: "Learning and mastering the fundamental method of dialectical materialism enhances our ability to think dialectically and improves our capability to navigate complex situations and handle complex problems."[1] Currently, the various interest relationships in our society are extremely complex, requiring us to adeptly use the perspective of connection and development in dialectical materialism. We must skillfully apply the five major categories and three major laws of dialectical materialism, continually strengthening problem awareness to better handle the relationships between parts and the whole, the present and the future, and major and minor issues. In weighing pros and cons, we should strive to avoid harm and make the most beneficial strategic decisions, actively facing and resolving contradictions encountered in our progress.

During his long-term leadership roles in local governance, General Secretary Xi Jinping skillfully applied dialectical materialism, laying a solid practical and theoretical foundation for the establishment of Xi Jinping Thought on Socialism with Chinese Characteristics for a New Era. For example, while serving as the Party Secretary of Ningde Prefecture in

---

1   Xi Jinping, *The Party's Work to Improve Publicity and Guide People in Their Thinking*, Beijing: Central Party Literature Publishing House, 2020, p. 129.

Fujian, facing fiscal difficulties, he effectively used dialectical analysis to study and resolve various contradictions. Recognizing the universal connections of things, he fully understood the relationship between Ningde and the province, as well as the nation, asserting that "the overall situation of eastern Fujian must submit to that of the province and the nation." From a developmental viewpoint, he identified that the key to solving Ningde's fiscal difficulties lay in internal contradictions. He fostered a spirit of self-reliance and determination to overcome difficulties, ensuring that, even when both national and local finances were strained, they would "not reach out for help unless absolutely necessary, and minimize requests for assistance as much as possible."[1]

During his tenure in Zhejiang, Xi Jinping clearly articulated, "Dialectical materialism tells us that all things are interconnected and inseparable. If we view issues in isolation, one-sidedly, or simplistically while promoting reform, opening up, and modernization, we will fall into the error of metaphysical thinking."[2] He emphasized using a connected, developmental, and dialectical perspective to maintain stability, advocating for efforts in "understanding higher-level directives, grasping local realities, comprehending internal conditions, and being aware of external situations ... and achieving alignment between being accountable both to higher authorities and to the public."[3]

Xi Jinping skillfully integrated dialectical materialism into his governance philosophy, infusing profound dialectical thinking into his accessible and important speeches. For example, he highlighted that deepening reform requires both courage and careful, deliberate steps— strategically advancing boldly while tactically proceeding with caution.

---

1   Xi Jinping, *Up and Out of Poverty,* Fuzhou, Fujian People's Publishing House, 1992, p. 103.
2   Xi Jinping, *Zhejiang, China: A New Vision for Development*, Hangzhou: Zhejiang People's Publishing House, 2007, p. 62.
3   Xi Jinping, *Striving for Practical Results and Leading the Way: Thoughts and Practices on Advancing Zhejiang's New Development, "* Central Party School Press, 2006, p. 543.

He advised "crossing the river by feeling the stones" while simultaneously enhancing top-level design. Using vivid metaphors, he spoke of "nourishing the blood to eliminate dryness, promoting circulation to remove stasis, and strengthening both the body's core and its muscles and bones." In social governance, he warned against over-regulation, which can stifle progress, and under-regulation, which can lead to chaos. Addressing the dialectical relationship between the commonality and individuality of contradictions, he emphasized the importance of "finding the root cause and applying targeted solutions," "hitting the target with pinpoint accuracy," and "answering questions from above and below while collaboratively addressing shared issues." He advocated for a concrete analysis of specific problems, advising that "one must ask the woodcutter about the mountain and the fisherman about the water." In promoting economic and social development, he advocated for "seeking progress while maintaining stability," ensuring "swift but steady steps." Confronted with the complexities of governance, he likened it to "cooking a small fish," requiring precise handling, and stressed the importance of grasping the "key link" and focusing on the "critical few." General Secretary Xi Jinping's classic remarks, though straightforward, deeply embody the essence of dialectical materialism. They are rooted in objective reality, clearly problem-oriented, and highly relevant, addressing specific issues with outstanding governance philosophy and leadership artistry.

Xi Jinping Thought on Socialism with Chinese Characteristics for a New Era consistently applies the scientific methods of dialectical materialism, proposing a series of governance strategies to lead the New Era. The 14 principles to uphold outline the fundamental strategies for adhering to and developing socialism with Chinese characteristics in the New Era. These principles reflect the viewpoint of universal interconnection, covering areas such as the economy, politics, law, science and technology, culture, education, livelihood, ethnicity, religion, society, eco-civilization, national security, defense and military affairs, One Country, Two Systems and national reunification, the united front, diplomacy, and strengthening the Party. Together, they form an organically unified whole of governance strategies for socialism with Chinese characteristics in the New Era. These principles embody the viewpoint of development, rooted in the realities of the New Era, clarifying the overarching goals, fundamental tasks, and general direction. They deepen the understanding of the laws governing socialist development in China, review the valuable experiences of the Party in adhering to and developing socialism with Chinese characteristics, and propose a series of development policies and measures, using development to guide and explain the New Era.

The 14 principles also embody a dialectical and balanced perspective. For instance, they stress both the leadership of the Party over all work and the principle of being people-centered, maintaining this balance throughout the fundamental strategies of the New Era. The unity of Party leadership and the people's interests is consistently upheld. Each specific strategy reflects a dialectical approach, such as the initiatives to maintain harmony between humanity and nature, as well as the measures to implement One Country, Two Systems while promoting national reunification.

In practical terms, the principles encompass:

- Unwavering support for the consolidation and development of the public sector while also encouraging, supporting, and guiding the non-public sector.

- Improving the distribution system with labor-based distribution as the mainstay, alongside multiple distribution methods.

- Focusing on economic development while giving due importance to ideological work.

- Emphasizing the decisive role of the market in resource allocation while also enhancing the role of the government.

These approaches inherently embody the thought and methods of dialectical materialism.

Xi Jinping has enriched and developed Marxist methodology through his adept application of fundamental dialectical methods. He concretized and applied these methods to practical thinking and work processes, enhancing cognitive abilities and infusing new content into Marxist methodology. "We must continually nourish ourselves with the wisdom of Marxist philosophy, more consciously adhere to and apply the worldview and methodology of dialectical materialism, enhance our capacity for dialectical thinking and strategic thinking, and better guide our practice."[1] At the First Plenary Session of the 19th Central Committee, Xi Jinping reiterated to all Party members that on the new journey of the New Era, it is essential to meet the development requirements of socialism with Chinese characteristics, improve strategic thinking, historical thinking, dialectical thinking, innovative thinking, rule-of-law thinking, and worst-case scenario mentality, and enhance the principle-based, systematic, foresighted, and creative nature of their work. Among these cognitive approaches, dialectical thinking is the core essence, integrating strategic, historical, innovative, rule-of-law, and worst-case scenario mentality, all fundamentally rooted in materialistic and dialectical perspectives.

2. Develop Marxist political economy

Marxist political economy reveals the general laws of social and economic development. Applying the principles of the dialectical movement between productive forces and production relations, it explores fundamental aspects such as the general laws of commodity economy,

---

1   *Series of Speeches by General Secretary Xi Jinping (2016 Edition),* Beijing: Xuexi Press and People's Publishing House, 2016, p. 279.

the basic contradictions within a commodity economy based on private ownership, the labor theory of value, the theory of surplus value, the theory of capitalist accumulation, the circulation and reproduction of capital, and the theory of economic crises. Through these analyses, it reveals the insurmountable contradiction within capitalism between the socialized nature of large-scale production and the capitalist private ownership of the means of production.

Using the principles of the dialectical movement between the economic base and the superstructure, Marxist political economy examines the evolution from free-market capitalism to monopoly capitalism, the new changes in contemporary capitalism, and the historical progression of capitalism, ultimately revealing the inevitable trend that capitalism will be replaced by socialism. While Marxist political economy cannot provide specific answers for future developments, it paves the correct path for the continuous pursuit of truth and offers guidance and direction for the formulation of economic policies, strategies, and guidelines.

General Secretary Xi Jinping has emphasized: "In the face of an extremely complex domestic and international economic environment and a wide range of economic phenomena, studying the fundamental principles and methodology of Marxist political economy helps us master scientific economic analysis methods, understand the processes of economic movement, grasp the laws of social and economic development, enhance our ability to navigate the socialist market economy, and better address the theoretical and practical issues in China's economic development."[1]

By distilling and summarizing the regular achievements of China's economic development practices, General Secretary Xi Jinping has formed

---

1   Xi Jinping, *Comprehensively Deepen Reform*, Beijing: Central Party Literature Publishing House, 2018, p. 187.

Xi Jinping Thought on Socialist Economy with Chinese Characteristics for a New Era.

Since the 18th CPC National Congress, General Secretary Xi Jinping, focusing on the principal contradiction and the critical realities of Chinese society, has conducted an in-depth analysis of the new situations and challenges faced by both the global and Chinese economies. He has effectively integrated the fundamental principles of Marxist political economy with the practical development of China's economy and society in the New Era, identifying the underlying patterns of China's economic development. Xi has successfully coordinated the relationships between productive forces and production relations, government and market, supply and demand, urban and rural areas, and international and domestic spheres, transforming China's economic development experiences into a coherent economic theory.

Xi has introduced numerous new concepts, ideas, and strategies that encompass various aspects of development, including guarantees, goals, concepts, main threads, tasks, strategies, and methods. These strategies address all stages of social production, including production, distribution, exchange, and consumption, thereby shaping Xi Jinping's economic thinking of socialism with Chinese characteristics for the New Era. This framework was first articulated at the Central Economic Work Conference held from December 18 to 20, 2017, marking a significant advancement in the political economy of socialism with Chinese characteristics and making an original contribution to the development of 21st-century Marxist political economy.

The core contents of this thinking mainly include the following seven aspects:

First, maintaining the centralized, unified leadership of the Party over economic work is a unique contribution of the CPC to Marxist political economy. The leadership of the CPC is the defining feature of socialism with Chinese characteristics and constitutes the greatest strength of this system. It is the fundamental guarantee for the historic achievements in China's economic development since the 18th National Congress of the Party. Economic development as the central task is a fundamental national policy and the core work of the Party in governing the country. Therefore, the Party's leadership must be fully reflected in economic work. By upholding and strengthening the centralized, unified leadership of the Party over economic work, and allowing the Central Committee to play its core role in steering the course, making overall plans, devising policies, and promoting reform and in exercising overall leadership and coordinating the efforts of all sides, we can ensure that the "one central task" and the "two basic points" are unified, continuously improving the economic system and structure, leveraging the advantages of the socialist economy, mitigating economic risks, and ensuring that China's economic development always follows the correct direction. This new requirement proposed by the Central Committee with General Secretary Xi Jinping at its core, grounded in the New Era, has written a new chapter in the development of the socialist economy under the Party's leadership. It is the foremost, overarching, and fundamental content of Xi Jinping's economic thinking of socialism with Chinese characteristics for the New Era.

Second, adhering to a people-centered philosophy of development advances the Marxist theory regarding the nature and purpose of socialist production. The contradiction between unbalanced and inadequate development and the people's ever-growing needs for a better life is not only the principal contradiction in our society today but also serves as a clear definition of the goal of our economic development. All economic efforts must address the immediate material needs of the people, as well as their higher aspirations for quality, safety, healthy living, environmental sustainability, culture, and the free development of individuals. Development should be for the people and by the people. Development should be for the people and by the people, and unwaveringly follow the path of common prosperity. This involves promoting shared prosperity where everyone participates, everyone benefits, everyone contributes, and progress is made gradually. The ultimate goal is to achieve prosperity for all. This is the logical starting point and ultimate destination of Xi Jinping's economic thinking of socialism with Chinese characteristics for the New Era.

Third, adapting to, grasping, and leading the new normal of economic development innovates the Marxist view of development. China's entry into a new stage of development, characterized by a new normal in economic development, is a major strategic judgment made by the Central Committee with General Secretary Xi Jinping at its core, based on a comprehensive analysis of the changes in international economic cycles, the current phase-specific characteristics of China's economic development, and the country's continued important period of strategic opportunity. This judgment deeply reflects the important characteristic of China's economy transitioning from a phase of rapid growth to a stage of high-quality development.

Creatively proposing and implementing new development philosophy of innovative, coordinated, green, open and inclusive development, and constructing a new development dynamic not only finds the balance between reform, development, and stability and between steady growth, promoting reform, adjusting the structure, benefiting people's livelihoods, and preventing risks, but also form a comprehensive approach to addressing the issues of unbalanced, uncoordinated, and unsustainable development in China, guiding the economy toward higher quality, greater efficiency, increased fairness, and enhanced sustainability. They reflect the Party's deepening understanding of the patterns underlying China's economic and social development.

Fourth, the innovative proposal to ensure that the market plays a decisive role in resource allocation, while the government assumes a more effective role, has enhanced the socialist market economy and further developed the theory underlying it. Proposing the improvement of the socialist market economy system ensures that the market plays a decisive role in resource allocation and that the government can function more effectively. By respecting the general rule of market economies where market forces determine resource allocation, resources can be allocated to maximize efficiency and optimize benefits according to market rules, prices, and competition. The government's role is to manage what the market cannot handle well, maintain macroeconomic stability, enhance and optimize public services, ensure fair competition, strengthen market regulation, maintain market order, and address market deficiencies. This approach highlights the advantages of the socialist economy, marking a new breakthrough in our Party's understanding of the development laws of socialism with Chinese characteristics and indicating that the development of China's socialist market economy has entered a new stage.

Fifth, adapting to changes in the principal contradiction of China's economic development and improving macroeconomic regulation has developed the Marxist theory of socialist economic development. Recognizing the significant shift from high-speed growth to high-quality development, the strategy is to actively adapt to, grasp, and lead the new normal of economic development. Emphasizing quality first and efficiency foremost, with supply-side structural reform as the main thread, focuses on addressing production issues, effectively resolving overcapacity, optimizing and restructuring industries, reducing enterprise costs, developing strategic emerging industries and modern service industries, and increasing the supply of public goods and services. By reducing excess capacity, inventory, and leverage, lowering costs, and addressing areas of weakness, this approach promotes transformations in the quality, efficiency, and driving forces of economic development, thereby building a modern economic system.

Sixth, adhering to a problem-oriented approach in deploying new economic development strategies has developed the Marxist economic development strategy and theory. To address prominent issues in economic development, a problem-oriented approach must be maintained, focusing on the principal contradiction and their main aspects, identifying problems accurately, and deploying new economic development strategies. The Party Central Committee, with General Secretary Xi Jinping at its core, has identified weaknesses and key entry points in China's economic development, basing its understanding on practice. It has deepened the recognition of essential issues in both the global and domestic economies, acknowledging imbalances in regional and urban-rural development, lack of coordination between economic growth and ecological protection, insufficient technological innovation, and limited openness. Addressing these issues, the strategies include regional coordinated development, rural revitalization, sustainable development, innovation-driven development, and the BRI. These are new requirements, measures, and strategies for economic, social, and temporal development and for building a human community with a shared future.

Seventh, adhering to sound strategies and methods has deepened the practice of socialist economic development, both strategically and methodologically. It is essential to remember that "Smart work can capture a lion, but unsmart use of force may fail to catch even a cricket." To translate a full understanding of economic laws into effective economic activities, appropriate strategies and methods are crucial. Successful economic work requires both the entrepreneurial drive—symbolized by "rolling up one's sleeves" and "taking bold action"—and the application of thoughtful strategies and methods, represented by "using one's brain" and "thinking creatively."

The Central Committee, with General Secretary Xi Jinping at its core, advocates for adhering to sound tactics and approaches, maintaining stability while making progress in our work, staying steadfast, and upholding a worst-case scenario mentality, advancing step by step. The approach of maintaining stability while making progress in our work, with "stability" as the foundation and "progress" as the goal, clearly outlines the underlying principle for achieving rapid yet stable and orderly economic development. Maintaining strategic resolve and upholding a worst-case scenario mentality firmly articulate the overarching principles of economic development. In addressing specific issues, it is vital to maintain a persistent spirit, striving relentlessly pushing for high-quality economic development. This series of methodologies encompasses the practical requirements for implementing various economic policies and measures, as well as the practical strategies and methods necessary for their success.

Additionally, Xi Jinping's economic thinking of socialism with Chinese characteristics for a new era emphasizes the path to common prosperity, gradually achieving shared prosperity for all people, which develops the Marxist theory on the essence and purpose of socialist production. It creatively proposed the new development philosophy of innovative, coordinated, green, open and inclusive development. Grounded in a new stage of development, it constructed a new development dynamic, innovating the Marxist view of development. It also creatively proposed the BRI, deepening the socialist theory of opening up to the outside world, among other contributions.

These contributions have enriched and developed Marxist political economy, creatively adhering to and advancing its fundamental principles and methodology. This has resulted in the innovative development of the academic, discourse, and methodological systems of the political economy of socialism with Chinese characteristics, thereby opening new horizons for it.

3. Developing scientific socialism

(1) Clarify the distinctive theme and core content, enrich and develop the overall nature and creativity of socialism with Chinese characteristics

Reviewing the development of scientific socialism and the century-long struggle of our Party, each theoretical innovation has emerged from answering major theoretical questions of the times and has been proposed to solve our practical issues. Since the 18th CPC National Congress, Chinese Communists, with Xi Jinping as their principal representative, have responded to the issues of the times by scientifically addressing a series of fundamental questions about what kind of socialism with Chinese characteristics to uphold and develop in the New Era and how to go about it. This has formed the core content and practical requirements of Xi Jinping Thought on Socialism with Chinese Characteristics for a New Era.

From the 19th CPC National Congress to the Sixth Plenary Session of the 19th Central Committee, the Party has maintained a consistent yet evolving approach. It has moved from proposing one major question of the era to comprehensively addressing a series of major questions of the times, highlighting three specific questions of the times. The core content of the scientific theory has evolved from the eight things to make clear to the ten principles to make clear, which is a necessary requirement for the innovative development of the scientific theory. This evolution is also a crucial theoretical support for the new leap in Marxism represented by this thought, constructing the major principles of socialism with Chinese characteristics in the New Era. It clearly outlines the explicit content and requirements of socialism with Chinese characteristics in the New Era.

The ten things to make clear for the core content of the scientific theory are:

- The leadership of the Communist Party of China is the defining feature of socialism with Chinese characteristics and the greatest strength of the system of socialism with Chinese characteristics, and that the Party is the highest force for political leadership. Therefore, all Party members must strengthen their consciousness of the need to maintain political integrity, think in big-picture terms, follow the leadership core, and keep in alignment with the central Party leadership; stay confident in the path, theory, system, and culture of socialism with Chinese characteristics; and uphold Comrade Xi Jinping's core position on the Party Central Committee and in the Party as a whole, and uphold the Central Committee's authority and its centralized, unified leadership.

- The overarching task of upholding and developing socialism with Chinese characteristics is to realize socialist modernization and national rejuvenation, and that on the basis of completing the goal of building a moderately prosperous society in all respects, a two-step approach should be taken to build China into a great modern socialist country that is prosperous, strong, democratic, culturally advanced, harmonious, and beautiful by the middle of the 21st century, and to promote national rejuvenation through a Chinese path to modernization.

- The principal contradiction facing Chinese society in the New Era is that between unbalanced and inadequate development and the people's ever-growing needs for a better life, and the Party must therefore remain committed to a people-centered philosophy of development, develop whole-process people's democracy, and make more notable and substantive progress toward achieving well-rounded human development and common prosperity for all.

- The integrated plan for building socialism with Chinese characteristics covers five spheres, namely economic, political, cultural, social, and ecological advancement, and that the comprehensive strategy in this regard includes four prongs, namely building a modern socialist country, deepening reform, advancing law-based governance, and strengthening Party self-governance.

- The overall objectives of comprehensively deepening reform are to develop and improve the system of socialism with Chinese characteristics and to modernize China's system and capacity for governance.

- The overall goal of comprehensively advancing law-based governance is to establish a system of socialist rule of law with Chinese characteristics and to build a socialist rule of law country.

- China must uphold and improve its basic socialist economic system, see that the market plays the decisive role in resource allocation and the government plays its role better, have an accurate understanding of this new stage of development, apply a new philosophy of innovative, coordinated, green, open, and shared development, accelerate efforts to foster a new pattern of development that is focused on the domestic economy but features positive interplay between domestic and international economic flows, promote high-quality development, and balance development and security imperatives.

- The Party's goal for military development in the New Era is to build the people's armed forces into world-class forces that obey the Party's command, that are able to fight and to win, and that maintain excellent conduct.

- Major-country diplomacy with Chinese characteristics aims to serve national rejuvenation, promote human progress, and facilitate efforts to foster a new type of international relations and build a human community with a shared future.

- Full and rigorous self-governance is a policy of strategic importance for the Party, and the general requirements for Party building in the New Era include making all-around efforts to strengthen the Party in political, ideological, and organizational terms and in terms of conduct and discipline, with institution building incorporated into every aspect of this process, continuing the fight against corruption, and ensuring that the political responsibility for governance over the Party is fulfilled. By engaging in great self-transformation, the Party can steer great social transformation.

These strategic concepts and innovative ideas are the important outcomes of the Party's theoretical development based on a deeper understanding of the underlying laws of socialism with Chinese characteristics. They has enriched and expanded the core content of scientific theory, providing more comprehensive, systematic, and profound answers to fundamental questions in the New Era of upholding and developing socialism with Chinese characteristics. These questions include the overall goals, tasks, overall and strategic layout, development direction, methods, driving forces, strategic steps, external conditions, and political guarantees. This has deepened the understanding of the governing laws of the Communist Party, the laws of socialist development, and the laws of human social development from a new perspective.

The Resolution of the Central Committee of the Communist Party of China on Further Deepening Reform Comprehensively to Advance Chinese Modernization highlights the original ideas and thoughts that have emerged from this period. For example, it emphasizes the necessity of upholding the Party's overall leadership, which is fundamental to the Party and the country's core interests and vital to the welfare and destiny of the Chinese people. It stresses that it takes a good blacksmith to make good steel and that China's success hinges on the Party, especially on the Party's efforts to exercise effective self-supervision and full and rigorous self-governance. The resolution underscores that implementing the new development philosophy represents a profound transformation that affects the entire landscape of China's development, driving changes in the quality, efficiency, and dynamics of economic growth. It highlights that comprehensive deepening of reforms will make the socialist system with Chinese characteristics more mature and well-defined, thereby continuously enhancing the modernization of the national governance system and capacity.

The resolution insists on the organic unity of the Party's leadership, the people's role as masters of the country, and the rule of law. It advocates for the active development of whole-process people's democracy and the building of a strong socialist culture that inspires nationwide cultural innovation and creativity. It aims to better cultivate Chinese spirit, Chinese values, and Chinese strength, maintaining the fundamental guiding role of Marxism in the ideological sphere. It promotes leading cultural development with core socialist values and encourages the creative transformation and innovative development of the best elements of traditional Chinese culture.

The resolution also emphasizes that social development must prioritize ensuring and improving people's livelihoods, thereby enhancing the people's sense of fulfilment, happiness, and security in a more substantial, assured, and sustainable manner. It insists on the concept that "lucid waters and lush mountains are invaluable assets" and on pursuing a model of sustainable development featuring increased production, higher living standards, and healthy ecosystems. Moreover, it advocates for the building of a human community with a shared future, championing the common values of peace, development, fairness, justice, democracy, and freedom, thereby leading the trend of human progress.

These new ideas, strategies, and valuable experiences that have emerged from the great practice of the New Era have significantly enriched and developed Xi Jinping Thought on Socialism with Chinese Characteristics for a New Era. This thought continues to develop, becoming more enriched and refined as the great practice of the New Era progresses.

Xi Jinping Thought on Socialism with Chinese Characteristics for a New Era is both the theoretical framework of our current era—the New Era of socialism with Chinese characteristics—and the historical product of the major achievements and historical experiences of the CPC's centennial struggle. This thought organically combines history with reality, forming innovative theoretical content and a novel theoretical structure of contemporary Chinese Marxism and 21st-century Marxism. It embodies the original ideas, transformative practices, breakthrough progress, and landmark achievements of the New Era.

The resolution states: "The Party's endeavors over the past century have demonstrated the strong vitality of Marxism.... In China, Marxism has been fully tested as a scientific truth, its people-centered and practical nature has been brought into full play, and its open-ended nature and contemporary relevance have been fully demonstrated."[1] The thorough testing, implementation, and manifestation of Marxism's truth, practical power, and powerful vitality in contemporary China are concentrated in the historical achievements and transformations of the New Era, embodied in the new leap in the adaptation of Marxism to the Chinese context realized by Xi Jinping Thought on Socialism with Chinese Characteristics for a New Era, and reflected in the irreversible new journey of the

---

1   *The Resolution of the Central Committee of the Communist Party of China on the Major Achievements and Historical Experience of the Party over the Past Century,* Beijing: People's Publishing House, 2021, p. 63.

rejuvenation of the Chinese nation under this great thought.

Since the 18th CPC National Congress, under the leadership of the Central Committee with General Secretary Xi Jinping at its core, the Party has given full consideration to both domestic and international imperatives, kept to the Two Centenary Goals, advanced the great struggle for national development, the great project to strengthen the Party, the great cause of Chinese socialism, and the great dream of national rejuvenation, and carried out the great social revolution and the great self-reform. This has led to the writing of a new chapter in socialism with Chinese characteristics for the New Era. Practice innovation and theoretical innovation have reached unprecedented heights, significantly enriching and developing the Party's innovative theory. A comprehensive, logically rigorous, richly connoted, and profound scientific theoretical system has been formed, integrating Marxist philosophy, political economy, and scientific socialism, and connecting history, reality, and the future. It spans various fields, including reform, development, stability, domestic and foreign affairs, national defense, and Party, state, and military governance.

Xi Jinping Thought on Socialism with Chinese Characteristics for a New Era represents a profound and dynamic theoretical framework, continuously evolving through the accumulation of experience and theoretical advancement.

The Resolution of the Central Committee of the Communist Party of China on the Major Achievements and Historical Experience of the Party over the Past Century concisely summarizes the invaluable historical experience accumulated over a century of leading the people in great struggles: upholding Party leadership, prioritizing the people, persisting in theoretical innovation, maintaining independence, adhering to the Chinese path, keeping a global perspective, fostering innovation, daring to struggle, upholding the united front, and committing to self-reform. These ten aspects are invaluable experiences accumulated through long-term practice and are integral components of Xi Jinping Thought on Socialism with Chinese Characteristics for a New Era. They represent a systematic understanding and fundamental principles for achieving a new leap in the adaptation of Marxism to the Chinese context and will continue to be enriched and developed through practice in the New Era.

(2) Propose the organic unity of the path, theory, system, and culture to expand the scientific framework of socialism with Chinese characteristics

On the grand journey of continuing the great cause of socialism with Chinese characteristics, the Chinese Communists, with General Secretary Xi Jinping as the principal representative, have adhered to the basic principles of scientific socialism and combined them with China's reality and contemporary characteristics. This approach has "successfully opened a viable and practical path in the world's most populous country, making the socialist proposition, which has a history of five hundred years, radiate with new vitality in the 21st century."[1] Since the 18th CPC National Congress, General Secretary Xi Jinping focused on the theme of adhering to and developing socialism with Chinese characteristics, further expanding this "correct path," and emphasizing the need to "enhance cultural confidence" and fully leverage culture's role in building a great modern socialist country and achieving the rejuvenation of the Chinese nation, thus pioneering a new realm of cultural consciousness and confidence.

At the Seminar on Philosophy and Social Sciences on May 17, 2016, he pointed out, "Our confidence in the path, theory, system and culture of socialism with Chinese characteristics."[2] During the 33rd group study session of the Political Bureau of the Central Committee on June 28, 2016, he proposed, "We should remain confident in the path, theory, system and

---

1 *Documents Produced since the 18th CPC National Congress*, Beijing: People's Publishing House, 2018, vol. II, p. 343.
2 *Ibid.*, p. 323.

culture of socialism with Chinese characteristics." In various occasions, he elaborated on the significant importance of cultural confidence, stating that "cultural confidence is a more fundamental, more profound and long-lasting force that sustains a country," "cultural confidence is a more essential, broader and deeper confidence," and "the culture of socialism with Chinese characteristics is a powerful source of inspiration for the Chinese people to move forward victoriously," adding that "increasing confidence in our own culture is critical to the prospects of our country, to our cultural security, and to the independence of our national character."

The Sixth Plenary Session of the 18th CPC Central Committee explicitly proposed "upholding the path, theory, system, and culture of socialism with Chinese characteristics,"[1] and "strengthening confidence in the path, theory, system, and culture of socialism with Chinese characteristics."[2] This development from the "three-pronged" path, theory, and system of socialism with Chinese characteristics to the "four-pronged" path, theory, system, and culture, and from "three spheres of confidence" to "four spheres of confidence," reflects the Party's new understanding of the development of socialism with Chinese characteristics. It further enriches and expands the scientific connotations of socialism with Chinese characteristics.

(3) Propose a people-centered philosophy of development to deepen the theory of the essence of socialism

The principle of prioritizing the people is the core principle of the governance and administration of the CPC. As General Secretary Xi Jinping pointed out: "Standing on the people's side represents the fundamental political stance of the CPC, and it is what distinguishes a Marxist political

---

1   *Ibid.*, p. 422.
2   *Ibid.*, p. 420.

party from other political parties."[1] General Secretary Xi Jinping's profound affection for the people is vividly reflected in his practice of governance. At the Forum on Literature and Art in 2014, he urged writers and artists to "take a people-centered approach"; during the Seventh Meeting of the Central Leading Group for Deepening Reform, he emphasized the need to "firmly establish a people-centered work orientation.

Since the New Era began, the Party and the country's endeavors have achieved historic accomplishments and undergone historic transformations, fully demonstrating the theoretical and practical power of the people-centered philosophy of development. The Recommendations for Formulating the 13th Five-Year Plan for Economic and Social Development, passed by the Fifth Plenary Session of the 18th CPC Central Committee, emphasized that it is necessary to adhere to the people-centered philosophy of development. This means taking the enhancement of people's wellbeing and the promotion of well-rounded development of individuals as the starting point and ultimate goal of development. It involves developing people's democracy, maintaining social fairness and justice, ensuring people's equal rights to participate and develop, and fully mobilizing people's enthusiasm, initiative, and creativity. After the Fifth Plenary Session of the 18th CPC Central Committee, General Secretary Xi Jinping repeatedly reaffirmed this new theoretical summary in significant speeches at various key occasions, such as the New Year's tea party of the National Committee of the Chinese People's Political Consultative Conference, the 30th group study session of the Political Bureau of the CPC Central Committee, the special seminar on the guiding principles from the Fifth Plenary Session of the 18th CPC Central Committee for principal provincial and ministerial leaders, the 13th Meeting of the

---

1   Xi Jinping, *Ensure Full and Rigorous Self-Governance of the Party*, Beijing: Central Party Literature Publishing House, 2016, p. 169.

Central Leading Group for Financial and Economic Affairs, and the ceremony marking the 95th anniversary of the CPC. He profoundly pointed out that leading the people to create a happy life has always been the unyielding goal of our Party; the basic criterion of our work is whether we have the people's support, acceptance, satisfaction and approval; and it is necessary to ensure that people have a greater sense of fulfillment, making sure that development is for the people and by the people, and that its fruits are shared among all the people.

The people-centered philosophy of development is vividly embodied in practical actions, which means leading the people to create a better life. The increasing demand of the people for a better life is not abstract but is reflected in specific areas of life, where the people's sense of fulfilment is enhanced. "The issues of concern to the people, be they big or small, should be handled with utmost care and attention. We must start by addressing issues of public concern, start by delivering the outcomes that satisfy public needs, and work without rest to lead our people in pursuing a better life"[1] by keeping working year by year to tackle one issue after another. Adhering to the unity of the Party's principles and the people's interests means that our Party's fundamental starting point in its political stance is to serve the people wholeheartedly, and its purpose is to fulfill the people's aspirations for a better life. New situations, tasks, and challenges require us to thoroughly advance full and rigorous self-governance of the Party and constantly improve our capabilities in learning, political leadership, reform and innovation, scientific development, law-based governance, mass work, implementation, and risk management, always being in tune with the people's thoughts and actions, and continually addressing the people's concerns and expectations.

The 19th CPC National Congress established "continuing

---

1 *Documents from the 19th CPC National Congress*, Beijing: People's Publishing House, 2017, p. 40.

commitment to the people-centered philosophy of development" as one of the fundamental strategies for upholding and developing socialism with Chinese characteristics in the New Era. This development philosophy profoundly reveals the purpose of the development of socialism with Chinese characteristics and clearly reflects the high unity of the Communist Party's governing philosophy and the laws of socialist economic development. Proposing the commitment to a people-centered philosophy of development is the concrete application of historical materialism in contemporary China's development, adhering to and applying the principle that the people are the creators of history. It is a concentrated embodiment of the Party's purpose in its development outlook, a significant development in the Marxist development outlook, and a deepening of the theory of the essence of socialism.

(4) Propose that the principal contradiction in Chinese society has undergone a historic transformation to enrich the theory of the primary stage of socialism and develop the theory of the stages of socialist developmen.

The principal contradiction in society is fundamental and overarching. Accurately understanding the current principal contradiction in Chinese society is the basis for the Party and the state to formulate correct policies and strategies and concerns the overall development of the Party and the country's endeavors. The principal contradiction in society is also subject to change and will evolve with changes in global, national, Party, social, and popular conditions. Our understanding of the principal contradiction in society should also keep pace with the times.

In the political report of the 19th CPC National Congress, General Secretary Xi Jinping pointed out: "The principal contradiction facing Chinese society has evolved. What we now face is the contradiction between unbalanced and inadequate development and the people's ever-growing needs for a better life."[1] Previously, the principal contradiction in Chinese society was described as "the ever-growing material and cultural needs of the people are unable to be met by China's underdeveloped social production." This assertion originated from the resolutions of the Eighth CPC National Congress in 1956 and was formally summarized in the Resolution on Historical Issues and Resolution on Historical Issues of the Party since the Founding of the People's Republic of China passed at the Sixth Plenary Session of the 11th Central Committee in 1981.

Over the more than 60 years from the Eighth CPC National Congress until now, China's social productivity has seen tremendous development. The country's GDP has risen to the second highest in the world, solving the problem of providing enough food and clothing for over a billion people and basically making it possible for people to live decent lives. In some fields, such as foreign trade, foreign investment, foreign exchange reserves, high-speed rail, aerospace, bridges, and 5G communications, China has advanced to the forefront of the world. During this period, the per capita disposable income of Chinese residents increased from 98 yuan in 1956 to 32,189 yuan in 2020, and per capita consumption expenditure increased from 88.2 yuan in 1956 to 21,210 yuan in 2020. The standard of living for the people has greatly improved, with a substantial increase in the supply of living goods such as clothing, food, housing, and transportation, as well as more diverse cultural lives. A social security system covering urban and rural residents has been basically established, and the health and medical standards of the people have significantly improved.

Now, the people's aspirations for a better life are even stronger, with expectations for better education, jobs, income, social security, healthcare services, living conditions, and environment, as well as a richer cultural

---

1   Xi Jinping, *Secure a Decisive Victory in Building a Moderately Prosperous Society in All Respects and Strive for the Great Success of Socialism with Chinese Characteristics for a New Era: Report at the 19th National Congress of the Communist Party of China*, Beijing: People's Publishing House, 2017, p. 11.

and ethical life. Based on these changes, General Secretary Xi Jinping made a new judgment on the profound shift in the principal contradiction in Chinese society. This is also a profound summary of the development of socialism with Chinese characteristics reaching a certain stage.

On the premise of accurately grasping the shift in the principal contradiction in Chinese society, General Secretary Xi Jinping emphasized: "The evolution of the principal contradiction facing Chinese society does not change our assessment of the present stage of socialism in China. The basic dimension of the Chinese context—that our country is still and will long remain in the primary stage of socialism—has not changed. China's international status as the world's largest developing country has not changed."[1] This serves as the "fundamental basis" for planning the next stage of development in China. The shift from "material and cultural needs" to "needs for a better life," from addressing the "problem of backward social production" to addressing the "problem of unbalanced and inadequate development," from emphasizing the primary stage of socialism as the "general basis" for building socialism with Chinese characteristics to proposing new practical bases such as the new normal of economic development in light of new stages and circumstances, enriches the theory of the primary stage of socialism and advances the theory of the stages of socialist development. These are significant theoretical innovations and historical contributions of our Party.

(5) Comprehensively deepen reform in the New Era to advance the theory of the driving force behind socialist developmen.

Reform is the fundamental driving force for the development of socialism with Chinese characteristics. The Third Plenary Session of the 11th CPC Central Committee initiated a new historical period of reform, opening up, and socialist modernization, leading to a rapid takeoff

---

1   *Ibid.,* p. 12.

of China's economy, improvement in people's lives, and enhancement of China's international status. However, issues such as unbalanced development and challenges to government credibility emerged, alongside incomplete social public management and public services, and a relatively lagging comprehensive legal system. These all indicate that societal progress requires not only economic development but also comprehensive advancements in politics, culture, law, and society.

The essence of comprehensively deepening reform is the self-improvement and development of the socialist system with Chinese characteristics, constituting a comprehensive and profound social transformation. This is undoubtedly one of the prominent contributions of Xi Jinping Thought on Socialism with Chinese Characteristics for a New Era to scientific socialism. The Third Plenary Session of the 18th CPC Central Committee initiated a new era of comprehensively deepening reform, with systematic and holistic design promoting reform, opening up a new phase for China's reform and opening up.

On the new journey, under the leadership of the CPC Central Committee with General Secretary Xi Jinping at its core, we adhere to promoting development through reform, advancing comprehensive reforms focusing on and driven by economic structural reform, covering economic, political, cultural, social, eco-civilization systems, and the system for strengthening the Party. This involves both productive forces and relations of production, the economic base, and the superstructure. Through new reforms, we properly manage the relationship between the government and the market, enabling the market to play a decisive role in resource allocation while better leveraging the role of the government. We resolutely eliminate outdated thoughts and institutional barriers, break down the vested interests, absorb the achievements of human advancement, make the system more mature and well-defined, improve the quality of development, enhance the level of governance, and increase the sense of fulfilment for the people. This greatly enhances the theory of the driving forces of socialist development.

Effective top-level design

General Secretary Xi Jinping repeatedly emphasized, "Reform and opening up has been a crucial move in making China what it is today, and will remain crucial to achieving the Two Centenary Goals and the rejuvenation of the Chinese nation."[1] Accurately grasping the historical conjuncture in the Party and the country, he devised the strategic thought of comprehensively deepening reform. He places high importance on the top-level design and overall planning of comprehensive deepening reform, personally serving as the head of four central leading groups: the Central Leading Group for Comprehensively Deepening Reform, the Central Military Commission Leading Group for Deepening National Defense and Military Reform, the Central Leading Group for Financial and Economic Affairs, and the Central Leading Group for Cybersecurity and IT Application. Before the promulgation and implementation of related resolutions, plans, opinions, regulations, rules, and outlines, thorough consideration, special investigations, and extensive solicitation of opinions from various parties are conducted. Consequently, these theoretical achievements, proven correct through practice, become an integral part of the key policies for comprehensively deepening reform.

Ensure that institutions become more material and well-defined

The overall goal of comprehensively deepening reform is to improve and develop the socialist system with Chinese characteristics and modernize the national governance system and capacity. Reform is the self-

---

1   Xi Jinping, *How to Comprehensively Deepen Reform*, Beijing, Central Party Literature Publishing House, 2014, p. 3.

improvement and development of the socialist system. Comprehensive deepening reform is carried out under the premise of adhering to the socialist direction and, through the reform of systems and mechanisms in key areas and crucial links, provides strong support for upholding and consolidating the socialist system and modernizing the socialist system. To modernize the national governance system and capacity, "we should adapt properly to the changing times, and reform outdated systems, mechanisms, laws and regulations, while building new ones to make our institutions in all respects more appropriate and complete and the governance of Party, state and social affairs more institutionalized, standardized and procedure-based."

Continually highlight the superiority of the socialist system

"We need to rely on constant reform and innovation to ensure that socialism with Chinese characteristics is more efficient than capitalism in emancipating and developing the productive forces, emancipating and boosting social dynamism, and promoting individuals' well-rounded development. We also need to ensure that it sparks greater enthusiasm, initiative and creativity among all of our people, creates more favorable conditions for achieving social progress and gives us a competitive edge, thus giving full expression to the superiority of socialism with Chinese characteristics."[1] Since the global financial crisis, the development of capitalism has faltered, while socialism with Chinese characteristics has achieved remarkable successes. The successful practice of governance has fully demonstrated the superiority of the socialist system, further strengthening confidence in the socialist system with Chinese characteristics.

(6) Modernize the national governance system and capacity to enrich and develop socialist modernization theory

---

1   Xi Jinping, *The Governance of China*, Beijing: Foreign Languages Press, 2018, vol. I, p. 103.

Since the 18th CPC National Congress, the Central Committee, with General Secretary Xi Jinping at its core, has examined issues of national governance with a broad world-historical perspective, stating: "In fact, how to govern a socialist society, which is a completely new society, has not been well resolved in the past world socialist practices."[1] Marx and Engels did not encounter the practice of comprehensively governing a socialist country; Lenin passed away shortly after the October Revolution in Russia, and thus did not have the opportunity to deeply explore this issue. The Soviet Union conducted some exploration on this issue, gaining practical experience but also making serious mistakes, and ultimately did not solve this problem. the People's Republic of China, guided by Marxism in its founding principles, has promoted the modernization of industry, agriculture, national defense, and science and technology from the perspective of social production, while also modernizing the national governance system and capacity from an institutional perspective, providing a more mature and well-established institutional guarantee for effectively governing a socialist society.

The historical development of the People's Republic of China clearly demonstrates that how to effectively govern a socialist society has fundamental, overall, stable, and far-reaching significance. Deng Xiaoping, with a strong sense of urgency and concern, pointed out: "If even now we still don't improve the way our socialist system functions, people will ask why it cannot solve some problems which the capitalist system can. Such comparisons may be one-sided, but we must not just dismiss them on that account."[2] From the perspective of the historical continuity and development of our Party's governance, the historical practice of governing a socialist society has already gone through an extraordinary historical process. In past socialist practices, the main historical task was to establish

---

1   *Documents Produced since the 18th CPC National Congress*, Beijing: Central Party Literature Publishing House, 2014, vol. I, p. 548.
2   Deng Xiaoping, *Selected Works of Deng Xiaoping*, Beijing: Foreign Languages Press, 1995, vol. II, p. 332.

the basic socialist system and then carry out reforms on this basis. Now, we have a very good foundation.

Today, on this new historical starting point, we are further resolving the issues that past world socialist practices "have not well solved" and fully demonstrating the superiority of the socialist system through successful governance. As General Secretary Xi Jinping pointed out, "We need to rely on constant reform and innovation to ensure that socialism with Chinese characteristics is more efficient than capitalism in emancipating and developing the productive forces, emancipating and boosting social dynamism, and promoting individuals' well-rounded development. We also need to ensure that it sparks greater enthusiasm, initiative and creativity among all of our people, creates more favorable conditions for achieving social progress and gives us a competitive edge, thus giving full expression to the superiority of socialism with Chinese characteristics."[1]

Since the 18th CPC National Congress, the Central Committee, with General Secretary Xi Jinping at its core, has systematically advanced the reform and opening up as well as the modernization of socialism. It has ensured coordinated implementation of the Five-Sphere Integrated Plan and the Four-Pronged Comprehensive Strategy, establishing the improvement and development of the socialist system with Chinese characteristics and the modernization of the national governance system and capacity as the overarching goals of reform and opening up. This involves reforming outdated systems, mechanisms, and laws while continuously building new frameworks to make the socialist system more mature and well-defined. Efforts aim to create a more comprehensive, stable, and effective institutional framework to support the development of the Party and the country, enhance people's happiness, ensure social

---

1   *Documents Produced since the 18th CPC National Congress*, Beijing: Central Party Literature Publishing House, 2014, vol. I, p. 550.

harmony and stability, and maintain long-term national security. Under the guidance of Xi Jinping's Thought on Socialism with Chinese Characteristics for a New Era, the national governance system and capacity will undergo thorough transformation and improvement, driving reforms across various fields to achieve overall effects by 2035, and further modernize by the mid-21st century, thereby enhancing the governance system's efficiency and showcasing the advantages of socialism with Chinese characteristics.

The realization of the rejuvenation of the Chinese nation means achieving socialist modernization, building China into a great modern socialist country that is prosperous, strong, democratic, culturally advanced, harmonious and beautiful. General Secretary Xi Jinping's new concepts, ideas, and strategies for governance profoundly elucidate the necessary path, development blueprint, overall layout, strategic framework, development philosophy, support forces, foreign relations, leadership core, and scientific methodology for socialist modernization. This serves as a scientific guide for building a great modern socialist country, facilitating the transition from a developing socialist country to a modern socialist country under new historical conditions.

Forming a sound national governance system, possessing strong governance capabilities, and establishing a scientific, comprehensive, systematic, and effective system have a decisive impact on the fate of a country. After the founding of the People's Republic of China, our Party deeply contemplated and explored the fundamental question concerning the country's future and people's destiny: "How should state power be organized? How should the country be governed?" In this regard, we have accumulated rich experience and achieved significant results in the national governance system and capacity. Especially since the reform and opening up, China has sustained rapid development at an unprecedented speed, significantly improved people's living standards, and transformed the country's appearance, fully demonstrating that our national governance system and capacity are generally good and suitable for our national conditions and development requirements.

At the same time, we must recognize that, compared to the demands of our economic and social development, the expectations of the people, the increasingly fierce international competition, and the goal of achieving long-term peace and stability, there are still many deficiencies in our national governance system and capacity that need urgent improvement.

Deng Xiaoping once pointed out during his 1992 Southern Tour that it might take another 30 years for us to form a more mature and well-defined system in all aspects. Since the 18th CPC National Congress, our Party has sized up the situation, creatively advancing the cause of governance by focusing on the main line of "What is the governance of a socialist society, and how should a socialist society be governed?" Based on our traditions, current national conditions, and long-term governance experience, and on the strategic goals proposed by Deng Xiaoping, we have decided to modernize the national governance system and capacity. The aim is to make the system of socialism with Chinese characteristics more mature and well-defined through continuous reform and innovation.

In recent years, our country's practice of modernizing the national governance system and capacity has created a governance model that is different from other historical socialist countries and from Western capitalism. This has formed a unique advantage compared to Western social governance and provided successful experience on how to govern a socialist society. This represents a fundamental characteristic and significant innovation of our Party's governance in a new historical period. The current world contrasts the "China's effective governance" with the "Western chaos," which also reflects our Party's deeper understanding of the laws of governance and the effectiveness and superiority of using the system of socialism with Chinese characteristics to govern the country. The proposal and promotion of the modernization of the national governance system and capacity are extremely significant contributions made by the Central Committee with General Secretary Xi Jinping at its core to socialism with Chinese characteristics.

(7) Ensure coordinated implementation of the Five-Sphere Integrated Plan and the Four-Pronged Comprehensive Strategy to enhance the theory of comprehensive socialist development

How to handle the relationship between economic, political, cultural, social, and ecological advancement is a major issue that tests the governance level of all countries and ruling parties. Countries that successfully solve this problem can often achieve mutual promotion and progress in these areas, leading to long-term stability and sustainable development. With the deepening of economic and social development and practical exploration, and with our Party's continuous understanding of the overall layout of socialism with Chinese characteristics, the 18th CPC National Congress incorporated ecological advancement into the overall layout of socialism with Chinese characteristics. Our Party has formed and coordinated the promotion of the Five-Sphere Integrated Plan for economic, political, cultural, social, and ecological advancement.

Since the 18th CPC National Congress, to achieve the Two Centenary Goals and realize the Chinese Dream of National Rejuvenation, our Party, based on the Five-Sphere Integrated Plan and the actual development of China, has formed and coordinated the promotion of the Four-Pronged Comprehensive Strategy for making comprehensive moves to finish building a moderately prosperous society in all respects (later updated to building a modern socialist country in all respects), deepen reform, advance law-based governance, and strengthen Party self-governance. This represents the comprehensive implementation and specific deepening of the coordinated promotion of the Five-Sphere Integrated Plan. General Secretary Xi Jinping emphasized, "The five-point strategy and the four-pronged strategy promote each other and develop together. We should carry them forward in an integrated way."[1]

The Five-Sphere Integrated Plan encompasses the objectives of coordinating economic, political, cultural, social, and ecological advancement. The Four-Pronged Comprehensive Strategy represents the methods and paths for coordination, which include making comprehensive moves to finish building a moderately prosperous society in all respects (building a modern socialist country in all respects), deepen reform, advance law-based governance, and strengthen Party self-governance. Each goal within the Five-Sphere Integrated Plan should be advanced using the coordinated methods of the Four-Pronged Comprehensive Strategy. For example, in advancing economic development, it is essential to not only incorporate the goal of building a moderately prosperous society in all respects (building a modern socialist country in all respects) into the economic realm, but also to reflect the major measures of comprehensive deepening of reform, the legal regulations of comprehensive law-based governance, and the anti-corruption efforts of full and rigorous Party self-governance within the sphere of economic development. Pursuing the Five-Sphere Integrated Plan and the Four-Pronged Comprehensive Strategy is a strategic maneuver by General Secretary Xi Jinping, responding to new development requirements and standing at the forefront of the era. This approach enhances the systematic, comprehensive, and coordinated nature of development, thereby refining the theory of comprehensive socialist development. The the Five-Sphere Integrated Plan and the Four-Pronged Comprehensive Strategy complement each other, working

---

1   Xi Jinping, *Speech at the Ceremony Marking the 95th Anniversary of the Founding of the CPC*, Beijing: People's Publishing House, 2016, p. 15.

together holistically to establish the strategic framework and deployment for adhering to and developing socialism with Chinese characteristics in the New Era. This fully embodies the overall, comprehensive, and coordinated nature of China's development, reflects the Party's deepening understanding of coordinated development, and highlights the methodological significance of materialist dialectics in addressing China's development challenges.

Incorporating the Five-Sphere Integrated Plan into the scientific connotation of the path of socialism with Chinese characteristics makes the development goals in these five areas clearer and the ideas more coherent. Adhering to economic development as the center is a fundamental requirement of sticking to the Party's basic line for 100 years and is also the fundamental requirement for solving all problems in contemporary China. Since the introduction of the reform and opening up policy, our country has always focused on economic development, putting efforts into boosting the economy and improving people's lives, achieving significant results. Our Party clearly articulates that as long as there are no fundamental changes in domestic and international situations, the focus on economic development should not and cannot change. By focusing on economic development, we continuously promote healthy economic development and further expand the economic "pie." This does not mean we wait for economic development to solve political, cultural, social, and ecological issues. Each period has its own set of challenges: periods of higher economic development face the issues that come with higher development, while periods of lower economic development encounter the problems associated with lower development. Socialism with Chinese characteristics is comprehensive; while the economy develops, we also need to ensure coordinated political, cultural, social, ecological and other advancement. The advancement in these five aspects are interconnected and interact with each other, forming a comprehensive approach to open up broad prospects for the development of socialism with Chinese characteristics. According to the overall objectives of the Four-Pronged Comprehensive Strategy, we must adhere to economic development as the center, ensure coordinated economic, political, cultural, social, and ecological advancement, and align the relations of production with the productive forces, and the superstructure with the economic base, thus advancing the all-around development and progress of the cause of socialism with Chinese characteristics.

The Four-Pronged Comprehensive Strategy is a new governance strategy formulated by our Party from a new historical starting point. It is a long-term development strategy concerning the Party and the country, a strategic choice for advancing reform, opening up, and socialist modernization under New Era conditions, and for adhering to and developing socialism with Chinese characteristics. The strategy includes strategic goals and measures, with each of the four aspects having significant strategic importance.

Finishing building a moderately prosperous society in all respects (building a modern socialist country in all respects) is a crucial step toward our goal. To achieve this goal, we must make comprehensive moves to deepen reform and continuously advance the modernization of the national governance system and capacity. Making comprehensive moves to advance law-based governance plays a fundamental and safeguarding role, providing long-term and stable legal assurance for the comprehensive moves to advance the other three areas. comprehensively deepening reform and advancing law-based governance are like the two wings of a bird or the two wheels of a cart—both are essential for completing the building of a moderately prosperous society in all respects. Full and rigorous Party self-governance is not only an important component of the Four-Pronged Comprehensive Strategy but also holds a key position within it. It is the crucial guarantee for finishing building a moderately prosperous society in all respects, deepening reform comprehensively, and advancing law-based governance comprehensively. Currently, as we work to promote the sustained and healthy development of the economy and society in the New Era, we must remain firmly committed to the strategic goal of finishing building a moderately prosperous society in all respects (building a modern socialist country in all respects) without wavering. We must firmly implement the three strategic measures of comprehensively deepening reform, advancing law-based governance, and ensuring full and rigorous Party self-governance, without easing our efforts. We must also strive to ensure that the four components of the Four-Pronged Comprehensive Strategy complement and reinforce one another, fostering a harmonious and beneficial interaction.

Practice evolves, society progresses, reforms must be deepened, and theories must be innovated. The Four-Pronged Comprehensive Strategy and the Five-Sphere Integrated Plan originate from and are unified in the great practice of socialism with Chinese characteristics. In the process of promoting reform and opening up and socialist modernization, our Party has gradually enriched and improved the strategy and the plan as basic strategies. The Five-Sphere Integrated Plan and the Four-Pronged Comprehensive Strategy are mutually promoting and coordinated. We must implement them well in a coordinated manner, and on the basis of promoting economic development, build a socialist market economy, democracy, advanced culture, harmonious society, and eco-civilization. We must promote the prosperity of the people, the strength of the country, and the beauty of China in a coordinated manner. This plan and strategy are key components of Xi Jinping Thought on Socialism with Chinese Characteristics for a New Era. They represent the theoretical achievements of our Party, which adheres to the principles of emancipating the mind, seeking truth from facts, keeping up with the times, and being pragmatic and innovative. These concepts have been continually developed and refined through practice and reform. They will undoubtedly provide strong theoretical support and strategic guarantees for realizing the Chinese Dream of the rejuvenation of the Chinese nation.

(8) Adhere to the Party's overall leadership to enrich and develop the theory of strengthening a socialist ruling part.

Since the founding of the CPC, significant insights have been gained into the laws governing what kind of party to build and how to build it. Since the 18th CPC National Congress, the domestic and international landscape has evolved at an unprecedented pace. The tasks of reform, development, and maintaining stability have become more demanding than ever, while the challenges, risks, and problems faced by the Party have multiplied. Profound changes have occurred in the composition and theoretical standing of the Party membership, requiring the Party to lead the Chinese people in a great struggle marked by new historical features.

Under the leadership of the CPC Central Committee, with General Secretary Xi Jinping at its core, the Party has continuously advanced the integration of Marxist theory with the practical development of the CPC in the New Era. This effort has creatively addressed the question of "what kind of Marxist ruling party to build and how to build it," encompassing areas such as ideology, organization, work style, systems, discipline, and anti-corruption. As a result, a series of major strategic insights on strengthening the Party in the New Era have been proposed.

First, the important assertion that leadership by the CPC is the defining feature of socialism with Chinese characteristics and constitutes the greatest strength of this system was put forward. This elevates the Party's leadership to the level of social essence and national system.

Second, it was proposed that the Party's self-reform should drive the great social revolution carried out by the people under the leadership of the Party. Self-reform has served to advance the social revolution by achieving a deep unity of the Party's political courage, innovative spirit, and lofty goals. This has shaped the distinctive character of the CPC in the New Era, highlighting the Party's unique qualities and political advantages, while contributing Chinese wisdom to global party governance.

Third, General Secretary Xi Jinping has emphasized full and rigorous Party self-governance as a central theme, integrating theoretical and institutional strengthening of the Party. By incorporating full and rigorous Party self-governance into the Four-Pronged Comprehensive Strategy, he has achieved a unified approach to the Marxist ruling party's governance of the nation and its internal development, bringing together the great struggle, great project, great cause, and great dream.

Fourth, the principle of uniting Party spirit with the people's interests has been upheld. The nature of a political party and government is determined by whom they serve. Since its founding, the CPC has maintained its belief in, dedication to, and reliance on the people, forging an unbreakable bond between the Party and the people, which strengthens the foundation of its governance. As socialism with Chinese characteristics enters the New Era, the CPC Central Committee, with General Secretary Xi Jinping at its core, has innovated and developed Marxist theory of strengthening the party. It has deeply recognized the pressing internal issues and severe challenges facing efforts to strengthen the Party, upheld a people-centered philosophy of development, and remained steadfast in advancing full, rigorous and rule-based Party self-governance. By unifying Party spirit with the people's interests and embedding the people's wellbeing into the overall strategy of strengthening the Party, the CPC has created institutionalized, normalized, and systematic theoretical achievements. These outcomes fully highlight the "people-centered" characteristic of the new requirements for strengthening the Party in the New Era, shaping the Party into a Marxist political party that remains at the forefront of the times, enjoys the heartfelt support of the people, embraces self-reform, withstands all challenges, and brims with vitality. This has injected fresh theoretical content and practical depth into the theory of strengthening the Party.

Raising Party self-supervision and governance to the level of self-reform and putting it into practice marks a significant contribution to the history of Marxist party building.

General Secretary Xi Jinping repeatedly emphasized that the Party must have the courage for self-reform and adhere to a problem-oriented approach. He has stated, "With the political courage to make itself the target of reform, the entire CPC must devote major efforts to addressing pronounced problems within itself"[1] and proposed to "carry forward the spirit of revolution to the end,"[2] believing that for a long-ruling Marxist party, "how to maintain a revolutionary spirit is a very significant and essential issue to be resolved." The primary aspect of carrying forward the revolutionary spirit is self-reform. General Secretary Xi Jinping deeply summarized the historical experience of our Party's development, pointing out that the Party "has always maintained the spirit of self-reform, the courage to acknowledge and correct mistakes, and has repeatedly removed its own ailments and resolve its problems on its own."[3] This ability is both a distinctive hallmark of our Party compared to other parties worldwide and a crucial reason for its enduring prosperity. Through self-reform, the Party has found a way to avoid history's cycle of rise, effectively countering the

---

1   Xi Jinping, *Speech at the Ceremony Marking the 95th Anniversary of the Founding of the CPC,* Beijing: People's Publishing House, 2016, p. 22.

2   Documents Produced since the 18th CPC National Congress, Beijing: People's Publishing House, 2018, vol. II, p. 589.

3   *An Introduction to Xi Jinping Thought on Socialism with Chinese Characteristics for a New Era*, Beijing: Xuexi Press and People's Publishing House, 2019, p. 223.

so-called "paradox" that "a single-party rule cannot solve its own problems" and creatively addressing the significant issue of how a Marxist party can maintain its integrity, advanced nature, and purity over long-term governance. This has greatly enriched the theory and practice of building a Marxist ruling party and is a significant achievement of the Chinese Communists in the New Era.

General Secretary Xi Jinping's important statements on strengthening the Party in the New Era has further deepened the understanding of the nature, purpose, historical mission, ruling philosophy, ruling foundation, ruling pathways, and fundamental guarantees of a Marxist ruling party. They have made original contributions to the theory of strengthening the socialist party and have become a crucial theoretical basis and academic source for establishing Xi Jinping Thought on Socialism with Chinese Characteristics for a New Era as 21st-century Marxism. Under the guidance of General Secretary Xi Jinping's important statements on strengthening the Party in the New Era, the CPC has undergone unprecedented significant changes, demonstrating its strong confidence and deep sense of responsibility in the New Era. This has provided a core theoretical backbone to the cause of socialism with Chinese characteristics. In upholding the Party's overall leadership, China has pioneered new experiences, representing a major contribution of the CPC to Marxist party-building theory and political theory.

(9) Clarify the inevitable trend of human social and historical development and proposing new ideas for scientifically understanding the relationship between the two major social systems to enrich the theory of correctly handling the relationship between socialism and capitalism

How to fully understand and handle the relationship between capitalism and socialism has been a major issue for Chinese people, especially the progressive elements among them. Marx and Engels deeply analyzed the irreversible general trend of social and historical development, concluding that the development of human society follows the law where socialist and communist societies replace capitalist societies. After the outbreak of the global financial crisis in 2008, a wave of de-globalization emerged in Western countries led by the United States. This gave rise to trade protectionism, isolationism, and populism, exacerbating the challenges to world peace and development. The facts show that Marx and Engels' analysis of the fundamental contradictions of capitalist society remains relevant, and the general historical trend of socialism replacing capitalism has not changed. However, the demise of capitalism and the victory of socialism are part of a long and tortuous process.

Based on a profound analysis of the relationship between socialism and capitalism, General Secretary Xi Jinping pointed out: "We must fully understand the self-regulating ability of capitalist society, fully account for the objective reality that Western developed countries have long held economic, technological, and military advantages, and seriously prepare for long-term cooperation and struggle between the two social systems... Most importantly, we must focus on managing our own affairs well, continuously enhancing our composite national power, improving the lives of our people, and building a socialism that demonstrates its superiority over capitalism. This will lay a more solid foundation for us to gain initiative, advantage, and the future."[1] This assertion indicates that it is crucial to recognize that socialism and capitalism are two different ideologies and social systems, and their struggle is long-term. It is necessary to maintain a clear mind and correct methods of struggle to overcome the negative impacts capitalism may bring. At the same time, one should not fear capitalism due to its negative impacts on socialism; instead, it is beneficial to critically absorb

---

1   *Documents Produced since the 18th CPC National Congress*, Beijing: Central Party Literature Publishing House, 2014, vol. I, p. 117.

and inherit all the productive forces created by capitalist society to uphold and develop socialism with Chinese characteristics.

As Lenin said: "If you are unable to erect the edifice with the materials bequeathed to us by the bourgeois world, you will not be able to build it at all, and you will not be Communists, but mere phrase-mongers. For the purpose of building socialism, we must make the fullest use of the science, technology and, in general, everything that capitalist Russia bequeathed to us."[1]

General Secretary Xi Jinping's insightful discussions on the relationship between socialism and capitalism are filled with wise considerations and original ideas about significant issues, enriching the theory of correctly handling the relationship between socialism and capitalism.

(10) Propose building a human community with a shared future to enrich and develop the Marxist theory of future society

China's issues have always been global issues. When Mao Zedong spoke in 1921 about "transforming China and the world," he boldly stated: "By mentioning 'the world,' we emphasize that our vision is international; by mentioning 'China,' we clarify where we will begin our efforts." He further pointed out, "China's issues are inherently global issues. If we attempt to transform China without considering the transformation of the world, our efforts will be narrow in scope and will inevitably hinder the progress of the world."[2] A hundred years later, at a historic moment when China truly approached the center stage of the world, General Secretary Xi Jinping clearly expressed the same thought, confidently proposing to "provide a Chinese approach for humanity's exploration of a better social system." Entering the 21st century, China's development has become more

---

1   V. I. Lenin: *Collected Works,* Moscow: Progress Publishers, 1965, vol. 29, p. 24.

2   Mao Zedong, *Collected Works of Mao Zedong*, Beijing: People's Publishing House, 1993, vol. I. p. 1.

closely linked with the development of human society, and the exploration and innovation of China's development path are also providing new wisdom and experience for the development of human society. Our Party, focusing on the new stage and new situation of China moving toward the center stage of the world, is committed to providing a Chinese approach for humanity's exploration of a better social system. In terms of the trend, goals, and path of the development of human society, as well as establishing more reasonable international relations and order in the development of human society, new ideas and thoughts have been proposed, deepening the understanding of the laws governing the development of human society.

In the profound and complex major changes and turbulent dynamics of the world, many people are turning their attention to China. As a responsible major country, China has issued the powerful call of the times: "China should make greater contributions and take on greater responsibilities for human society," proposing the beautiful initiative to "let the torch of peace be passed on from generation to generation, let the driving force of development continue, and let the light of civilization shine brightly." China has also put forward the grand vision of building a human community with a shared future. General Secretary Xi Jinping emphasized that in building a human community with a shared future, countries should respect one another, embrace inclusivity, and uphold the common values shared by all humanity. Each nation should strive to contribute its best, learn from others, and work together to achieve mutual benefit and win-win outcomes.

Building a human community with a shared future is based in China but oriented toward the world. It organically combines China's development with the development of other countries, steadfastly adhering to China's development path while grasping the historical trend, following the laws governing the development of human society, and providing abundant and vibrant Chinese wisdom, experience, and approaches to human society. This aims to lead and shape a new future for the development of human society through China's path and development philosophy.

General Secretary Xi Jinping pointed out, "Only after solving national problems will we be in a better position to solve international problems. And by reviewing domestic practices we will develop a greater ability to offer suggestions and solutions for global issues."[1] Persisting in the organic unity of China's development and the development of human society, new concepts for promoting the prosperity and development of human society have been proposed. Initiatives such as promoting the Belt and Road, establishing the Asian Infrastructure Investment Bank and the BRICS Bank, promoting the development of a new international political and economic order, actively participating in global economic governance, and guiding the global economic agenda have been put forward. The advocacy of building a human community with a shared future, proposing new principles for international order and new visions for human social relations, represents our Party's creative response to the contemporary question of "what kind of world to build and how to build it." Its fundamental purpose is to make the world better and to make people happier. This reflects China's philosophy that "should each treasure what of its own and what of others is beautiful, what is different but beautiful can be shared, and all under Heaven can be at peace" in today's global context. In summary, as General Secretary Xi Jinping said, "China will do well only when the world does well, and vice versa."[2]

The concept and practice of building a human community with a

---

1   Xi Jinping, *Speech at the Seminar on Philosophy and Social Sciences,* Beijing: People's Publishing House, 2016, p. 18.
2   *An Introduction to Xi Jinping Thought on Socialism with Chinese Characteristics for a New Era,* Beijing: Xuexi Press and People's Publishing House, 2019, p. 221.

shared future are significant innovative achievements in the theory and practice of scientific socialism. They embody the Marxist value goals of human liberation and the grand ideal of achieving communism under the conditions of the New Era, further deepening the understanding of the laws governing the development of human society. As China's friendly cooperation with countries around the world continues to expand, the concept of building a human community with a shared future is gaining more support and approval. Particularly during the global spread of the COVID-19 pandemic, this concept has been practically tested and has gained increasing recognition and support from people worldwide, exerting an increasingly broad and profound influence on the international community. This will undoubtedly promote the new development of world socialism in the 21st century.

The promotion of the building of a human community with a shared future has received high praise and enthusiastic responses from the international community. International organizations, including the United Nations, have incorporated "building a human community with a shared future" into various resolutions, fully reflecting the widespread recognition of this grand concept and beautiful vision by the international community. It also demonstrates China's significant contribution to global governance and the development of human society. The 19th CPC National Congress established "Promoting the building of a human community with a shared future" as one of the basic strategies for upholding and developing socialism with Chinese characteristics in the New Era. This is another important original contribution of Xi Jinping Thought on Socialism with Chinese Characteristics for a New Era to the theory of scientific socialism.

IV. Deepen the Understanding of Laws and Make Original Contributions

As socialism with Chinese characteristics enters the New Era, the CPC Central Committee, with General Secretary Xi Jinping at its core, has given full consideration to both domestic and international imperatives, kept to the Two Centenary Goals, advanced the great struggle, great project, great cause, and great dream, and carried out the great social revolution and the great self-reform. This has led to the writing of a new chapter in socialism with Chinese characteristics for the New Era. Practical and theoretical innovation has reached unprecedented heights. The series of innovative and strategic theoretical viewpoints proposed and elaborated by General Secretary Xi Jinping have greatly enriched and developed the Party's innovative theory, further deepening the understanding of the laws governing Communist Party self-supervision and governance, socialist development, and the development of human society. These have achieved a new leap in the adaptation of Marxism to the Chinese context, making original contributions to enriching and developing Marxism. They fully demonstrate that Xi Jinping Thought on Socialism with Chinese Characteristics for a New Era is contemporary Chinese Marxism and 21st-century Marxism, rooted in China and leading the world.

The core content of scientific theory is foundational, comprehensive, and decisive, serving as the main pillars supporting the theoretical edifice. As scientific theory is enriched and developed, its answers to and solutions for the era's questions and fundamental issues expand, and the core content is correspondingly deepened or extended. This is also an important law governing the development of scientific theory. The resolution of the Sixth Plenary Session of the 19th CPC Central Committee further summarized the core content of Xi Jinping Thought on Socialism with Chinese Characteristics for a New Era into the Ten Principles on the basis of the Eight Principles specified in the political report of the 19th CPC National Congress. This is an inevitable requirement of the innovative development of scientific theory and an important theoretical support for this thought to achieve a new leap in Marxism. From the Eight Principles to the Ten Principles, what is concentrated is the practical innovations of socialism with Chinese characteristics in the New Era, the original theoretical contributions of Xi Jinping Thought on Socialism with Chinese Characteristics for a New Era, the historical achievements and transformations in the Party and the country's undertakings in the New Era, and the accumulation of new fresh experiences. Comparatively, the main differences are: placing "making clear that the defining feature of socialism with Chinese characteristics is the leadership of the CPC and the greatest strength of the system of socialism with Chinese characteristics is the leadership of the CPC" in the first position, and emphasizing that the entire Party must enhance the Four Consciousnesses, strengthen the Four-Sphere Confidence, and ensure the Two Upholds; in the clarification of the overall task of upholding and developing socialism with Chinese characteristics, emphasizing "promoting the rejuvenation of the Chinese nation through Chinese modernization"; in clarifying the principal contradiction in the New Era, emphasizing the need to adhere to the people-centered philosophy of development, develop whole-process people's democracy, and promote more significant and substantive progress in the well-rounded development of individuals and the common prosperity of all. In clarifying the strategy, a new formulation of the Four-Pronged Comprehensive Strategy is adopted: making comprehensive moves to building a modern socialist country in all respects, deepen reform, advance law-based governance, and strengthen full and rigorous Party self-governance. Additional content regarding economic development is included, emphasizing the need to uphold and improve the basic socialist economic system, allowing the market to play a decisive role in resource allocation while better leveraging the role of the government, grasping the new development stage, implementing the new development philosophy, constructing a new development dynamic, promoting high-quality development, and balancing development and security. In clarifying the characteristics of major-country diplomacy with Chinese characteristics, the statement "serving national rejuvenation and promoting human progress" is added. The strategic guidelines for full and rigorous Party self-governance are clarified, including the overall requirements for strengthening the Party in the New Era and leading the great social revolution through great self-reform. These innovative strategic thoughts and concepts provide innovative core content for achieving a new leap in the adaptation of Marxism to the Chinese context.

New achievements have been made in various fields, and original ideas have emerged from practice. The perspective of practice is the primary and fundamental viewpoint of Marxist epistemology. Xi Jinping Thought on Socialism with Chinese Characteristics for a New Era is deeply rooted in the century-long practical experience of our Party, with the great practice of the New Era serving as its direct theoretical source. This thought promotes theoretical development through the vibrant and diverse practices of contemporary China, elevating rich experience into theory, deepening the understanding of underlying principles, and achieving a new leap forward in the adaptation of Marxism through the interaction between practical and theoretical innovation.

As Marx once pointed out: "[T]heory must be perfected by accumulated experience on a large scale."[1] The Resolution of the Sixth

---

1   https://www.marxists.org/archive/marx/works/1867-c1/ch15.htm.

Plenary Session of the 19th CPC Central Committee focuses on summarizing the historic achievements and transformations of the Party and the state in the New Era, as well as the valuable new experiences accumulated. It systematically outlines the major strategies, key initiatives, and significant measures adopted by the Party across 13 areas since the 18th National Congress in governing the country. It highlights original ideas, transformative practices, breakthrough achievements, and landmark outcomes. The series of new ideas, concepts, strategies, and valuable experiences that have emerged from the great practice of the New Era have greatly enriched and developed Xi Jinping Thought on Socialism with Chinese Characteristics for a New Era. This body of thought will inevitably continue to grow, evolve, and become more refined as the great practice of the New Era deepens.

Specifically, General Secretary Xi Jinping's original theoretical contributions to the development of 21st-century Marxism can be summarized as creatively addressing six major issues, deepening the understanding of six fundamental principles.

First, focusing on the historical task of continuing to adapt Marxism to China's conditions, keep it current, and enhance its popular appeal, it creatively answers the question of "what is 21st-century Marxism and how to develop it," further deepening the understanding of the laws governing Marxist development.

Since the 18th CPC National Congress, General Secretary Xi Jinping has placed great emphasis on the study, research, and application of Marxism. He has led the Central Committee's Political Bureau in studies on historical materialism, dialectical materialism, Marxist political economy, contemporary global Marxist trends and their impacts, the *Communist Manifesto* and its significance in the current era, among other topics. During important meetings such as the ceremony marking the bicentenary of Marx's birth and the gathering to celebrate the 40th anniversary of reform and opening up, he made a series of important statements on adhering to and developing Marxism, and continuing to adapt Marxism to China's conditions, keep it current, and enhance its popular appeal, enriching and developing Marxism in the New Era.

General Secretary Xi Jinping pointed out that since the birth of Marxism, human society has undergone tremendous changes, but the general principles expounded by Marxism remain entirely correct. Marxism is a scientific theory, a theory of the people, a theory of practice, and a theory that continuously develops. It is the guiding thought of our Party and country. If we deviate from or abandon Marxism, our Party would lose its soul and direction. We must uphold the guiding position of Marxism, continuously advance theoretical innovation based on practice, and developing 21st-century Marxism and contemporary Chinese Marxism is an unshirkable historical responsibility for contemporary Chinese Communists. The vitality of theory lies in constant innovation. We must observe, interpret, and lead the times with Marxism, and promote the development of Marxism with the vivid and rich contemporary Chinese practice, constantly opening up new frontiers for Marxism. Xi Jinping Thought on Socialism with Chinese Characteristics for a New Era adheres to the fundamental tenets, viewpoints, and methods of Marxism and makes original, contemporary, and systematic innovations to the main principles of Marxist philosophy, political economy, and scientific socialism. It creatively answers the question of "what is 21st-century Marxism and how to develop it," elucidating with a series of original viewpoints the essential characteristics, core essence, scientific system, historical contributions, contemporary significance, practical value, and development paths of Marxism. This further deepens the understanding of the laws governing Marxist development, advances the overall development of Marxism, forms a scientific theoretical system of 21st-century Marxism, and achieves a new leap in the adaptation of Marxism to the Chinese context.

Second, focusing on the theme of upholding and developing socialism with Chinese characteristics, it creatively answers the question in the New Era of "what kind of socialism with Chinese characteristics to uphold and develop, and how to uphold and develop it," further deepening the understanding of the laws governing socialism with Chinese characteristics, i.e., the laws governing socialist development.

General Secretary Xi Jinping pointed out that the success of scientific socialism in China has significant implications for Marxism, scientific socialism, and world socialism. The entry of socialism with Chinese characteristics into the New Era marks a new stage in the development of the cause of socialism with Chinese characteristics. Under the leadership of the CPC Central Committee, with General Secretary Xi Jinping at its core, a new development landscape for the cause of socialism with Chinese characteristics has been created in practice. Theoretically, a series of innovative ideas have enriched and developed scientific socialism.

General Secretary Xi Jinping emphasized that socialism with Chinese characteristics in the New Era is the result of the great social revolution carried out by the people under the leadership of our Party, and it must continue as such, proceeding with the great struggle of the new historical characteristics. We must keep in mind the strategy for the rejuvenation of the Chinese nation and the profound changes of a kind unseen in the world in a century, and promote the social revolution of upholding and developing socialism with Chinese characteristics and the great self-reform of full and rigorous Party self-governance.

In terms of theoretical innovation, General Secretary Xi Jinping proposed the Eight Principles and the 14 Guidelines, forming the path, theory, system, and culture of socialism with Chinese characteristics, thereby enriching and developing the theory of the socialist social structure. He proposed the people-centered philosophy of development, deepening the theory of the essence of socialism. He pointed out the historic transformation of the principal contradiction in Chinese society, developing the theory of the stages of socialist development. He promoted comprehensive deepening of reform, enhancing the theory of the driving force of socialist development. He advanced the modernization of the national governance system and capacity, developing the theory of socialist modernization. He coordinated efforts to pursue the Five-Sphere Integrated Plan and the Four-Pronged Comprehensive Strategy, improving the theory of comprehensive socialist development. He proposed and practiced the new development philosophy, expanding the theory of the paths and objectives of socialist development. He insisted on the overall leadership of the Party, asserting that CPC leadership is the defining feature of socialism with Chinese characteristics and constitutes the greatest strength of the system of socialism with Chinese characteristics. He proposed the overall requirements for strengthening the Party in the New Era, the new strategy for strengthening the Party, and the organizational line of the Party for the New Era, enriching and developing the theory of building the Marxist ruling party, among other contributions.

These significant theoretical innovations profoundly articulate the overarching goals, tasks, holistic strategy, strategic framework, development direction, development methods, development drivers, strategic steps, external conditions, and political guarantees for adhering to and developing socialism with Chinese characteristics in the New Era. They have elevated the understanding of the laws governing socialist development to unprecedented heights. Under the guidance of these innovative theories, a new chapter has been written in the development of socialism with Chinese characteristics in the New Era, demonstrating the vibrant vitality of scientific socialism. Moreover, socialism with Chinese characteristics has become the leading banner of scientific socialism and the mainstay of world socialism development in the 21st century, propelling global socialism into a new stage of development.

Third, focusing on achieving the rejuvenation of the Chinese nation, it creatively answers the questions of "what kind of national rejuvenation to achieve and how to realize it," further deepening the understanding of the laws governing socialist modernization.

Achieving the rejuvenation of the Chinese nation has been the greatest dream of the Chinese people since modern times. From its inception, the CPC has taken the realization of the rejuvenation of the Chinese nation as its historical mission. After generations of exploration and struggle, the Chinese nation has achieved a historic leap from lagging behind to catching up with the times, and to steering current and future trends. Over the past century, the establishment of the CPC, the founding of the People's Republic of China, the promotion of reform and opening up and the cause of socialism with Chinese characteristics, the completion of a moderately prosperous society in all respects and the building of a modern socialist country are four major milestones in the process of achieving the rejuvenation of the Chinese nation. Socialism with Chinese characteristics has entered the New Era, ushering in a bright prospect for the rejuvenation of the Chinese nation.

General Secretary Xi Jinping, with a broad and profound perspective that combines history with reality, theory with practice, and domestic with international contexts, has deeply expounded on the significant question of "what kind of national rejuvenation to achieve and how to achieve it." He has clearly pointed out the following:

- Today, we are closer, more confident, and more capable than ever before of making the goal of national rejuvenation a reality;

- Achieving national rejuvenation will be no walk in the park; it will take more than drum beating and gong clanging to get there; it is imperative to be prepared to work even harder toward this goal;

- The realization of the rejuvenation of the Chinese nation should be integrated into the practice of the great struggle, great project, great cause, and great dream of the New Era and align with the pursuit of national strength, rejuvenation, and the people's happiness—collectively known as the Chinese Dream;

- To realize the rejuvenation of the Chinese nation, we must not only strengthen ourselves materially but also culturally and ethically.

- We must be vigilant and have a strong sense of crisis, avoiding strategic or subversive mistakes, and focusing on preventing systemic risks that could delay or interrupt the process of national rejuvenation;

- Now, the immense energy accumulated by the Chinese people and the Chinese nation throughout history has been fully unleashed, providing an unstoppable force for the rejuvenation of the Chinese nation; an.

- Great dreams are not achieved by waiting or through mere slogans; they are forged through hard work and dedication. There can be no room for arrogance, complacency, or stagnation, nor can there be any hesitation or wavering. We must courageously stand at the forefront and fight with determination.

These statements further deepen the understanding of the laws governing socialist modernization. They offer profound insights into the journey, historical context, scientific essence, leadership strength, sources of support, practical paths, and strategic steps for realizing national rejuvenation. These ideas are of decisive significance in the history of the Chinese nation's development and hold groundbreaking importance in the history of Marxism and global socialism.

Fourth, focusing on the main line of governance, creative answers have been provided to the questions of "what is the governance of a socialist society and how to govern a socialist society," further deepening the understanding of the laws governing governance.

Since the 18th CPC National Congress, the Party Central Committee, with General Secretary Xi Jinping at its core, has continued to adhere to and improve the system of socialism with Chinese characteristics and modernize the national governance system and capacity. The Fourth Plenary Session of the 19th CPC Central Committee, addressing the strategic significance of the Party and the country's overall situation, focused on both current and future challenges. It specifically examined and deliberated on key issues related to adhering to and improving the socialist system with Chinese characteristics, as well as modernizing the national governance system and capacity.

The session systematically addressed the major political question of "what to uphold and consolidate, and what to improve and develop," emphasizing the importance of strengthening institutional confidence and fostering institutional innovation. For the first time, it comprehensively summarized the significant advantages of the socialist system with Chinese characteristics, highlighting their organic connection, complementarity, and integration as a cohesive whole.

It clearly articulated a systematic, scientific framework of institutions, encompassing fundamental, basic, and important institutions, and proposed guiding thoughts, overall requirements, objectives, strategic paths, and key measures for advancing our country's institutional development and governance.

General Secretary Xi Jinping's series of important statements deepens the understanding of the Party's governance laws, enriches the theory and practice of scientific socialism, and provides a scientific theoretical foundation for the effective governance of China.

General Secretary Xi Jinping pointed out that modernizing the national governance system and capacity requires a complete understanding of the overall goal of comprehensively deepening reform. Our direction is the path of socialism with Chinese characteristics; our comprehensive deepening of reform is to make the socialist system with Chinese characteristics better; our insistence on institutional confidence is not to remain stagnant but to constantly eliminate institutional and mechanism drawbacks, making our system mature and enduring; a major historical task before us is to ensure the socialist system with Chinese characteristics becomes more mature and well-defined.

The primary historical task for the current and long-term future is to improve and develop the system of socialism with Chinese characteristics, achieve institutional modernization, and provide a more complete, stable, and effective system for the development of the Party and the country, the happiness and wellbeing of the people, social harmony and stability, and the long-term peace and stability of the nation.

The system of socialism with Chinese characteristics and the national governance system embody the wisdom of the Party and the people, possessing profound historical, theoretical, and practical logic. These systems have deep historical roots, multiple significant advantages, and rich practical results, having created the world's rare miracles of rapid economic development and long-term social stability. The system of socialism with Chinese characteristics is a comprehensive and complete scientific system, with fundamental, basic, and important institutions forming its main structure, among which the leadership system of the Party holds a leading position. It is essential to strengthen institutional awareness, uphold institutional authority, strictly observe and enforce institutions, and continuously improve and develop the system of socialism with Chinese characteristics and the national governance system in keeping with the times. General Secretary Xi Jinping's important statements creatively answer the questions of "what is the governance of a socialist society and how to govern a socialist society," further deepening the understanding of the laws governing governance and providing Chinese wisdom and approaches for global governance.

Fifth, focusing on the key of full and rigorous Party self-governance, creative answers have been provided to the questions of "what is self-reform and how to carry it out" and "what kind of Marxist governing party to build and how to build it," further deepening the understanding of the laws governing the Communist Party's governance.

General Secretary Xi Jinping pointed out that in the New Era, our Party must drive the great social revolution carried out by the people under the leadership of the Party through the Party's self-reform, building the Party into a Marxist governing party that is always at the forefront, sincerely supported by the people, courageous in self-reform, able to withstand various tests, and full of vitality. Since the 18th CPC National Congress, the Party Central Committee, with General Secretary Xi Jinping at its core, has promoted full and strict self-governance of the Party with the spirit of self-reform, continuously improving the Party's governance capacity and leadership level, and constantly strengthening the Party's ability to purify, improve, and reform itself. At the Fourth Plenary Session of the 19th Central Commission for Discipline Inspection, General Secretary Xi Jinping solemnly declared that we have found a successful path to solving our own problems and avoiding history's cycle of rise and fall under long-term ruling conditions, which is full and rigorous Party self-governance and continuous self-reform. From the New Road of Democracy during the Yan'an period, to the continuous strengthening of the Party's advanced development and governance capacity during the period of socialist development and reform, and to the great self-reform of full and rigorous Party self-governance in the New Era, all this embodies the relentless struggle and diligent exploration of several generations of Chinese Communists.

General Secretary Xi Jinping emphasized the following:

■ The original mission of the Party is to seek happiness for the Chinese people and rejuvenation for the Chinese nation;

■ To win constant support from the people and continue to achieve further success, our Party, with a history dating back almost 100 years, must bear in mind our original aspiration and founding mission;

■ The longer our Party is in power, the more it should stick to its nature as a Marxist party, the more it should remember its original aspiration and founding mission;

■ We should promote self-reform and combine enhancing our Party's long-term governance capacity with improving our state governance capacity;

■ We must continue to deepen self-reform, clear out whatever undermines the Party's progressive and wholesome nature, rid ourselves of any virus that erodes the Party's health, and guard against any danger that goes against our original aspiration and founding mission and has the potential to shake the foundations of the Party;

■ How will our Party, a party with a century of history, maintain its progressive nature, integrity and vigor? How will it always keep the trust and support of the people? How will our Party continue to lead the country? These are fundamental questions that we must answer and solve properly.

■ As a century-old party, maintaining our progressive and wholesome nature, youthful vitality, and continuous support and endorsement from the people, as well as achieving long-term governance, are fundamental issues we must address and resolve effectively;

▪ To avoid history's cycle of rise and fall, the Party must not lose the spirit of self-reform. By continually deepening the Party's self-reform, we can solve problems and achieve self-transcendence, maintaining the Party's progressive and wholesome nature;

▪ The great social revolution and the great self-reform of the New Era promote and reinforce each other. We should create new situations in the great social revolution and strengthen ourselves through the great self-reform. We must lead the great social revolution with a great self-reform

These important statements promote the spirit of self-reform of a Marxist party, creatively answering the significant question of "what is self-reform and how to carry it out" in the New Era. They comprehensively elaborate on the significance, guiding principles, contemporary connotations, basic strategies, main issues, important paths, and scientific methods of continuously promoting and deepening self-reform. They further deepen the understanding of the laws governing Communist Party self-supervision and -governance, enrich and develop the Marxist theory of strengthening the party, and serve as a fundamental guideline for all Party members and officials to remain true to the original aspiration and founding mission and continually push the Party's self-reform forward.

Sixth, focusing on the concept of building a human community with a shared future, creative answers have been provided to the questions of "what kind of world to build and how to build it," thereby deepening the understanding of the laws governing the development of human society.

Since the 19th CPC National Congress, facing unprecedented changes in the world in a century, increasing international uncertainties and instabilities, and the new situation of global turbulence, General Secretary Xi Jinping called for accelerating the joint development of a human community with a shared future.

The concept and practice of building a human community with

a shared future are important components of Xi Jinping Thought on Socialism with Chinese Characteristics for a New Era. This represents the CPC's scientific understanding of the future of humanity in the face of unprecedented global changes in a century. It systematically responds to the major questions of our times, "what kind of world to build and how to build it" and "what is happening to the world and where is it heading," which pertain to the future of humanity. This provides a Chinese solution for the exploration of a better social system and makes new and greater contributions to human development and the progress of civilization.

General Secretary Xi Jinping pointed out that a human community with a shared future means that the future of each and every nation and country is interlocked. We are in the same boat, and we should stick together, share weal and woe, endeavor to build this planet of ours into a single harmonious family, and turn people's longing for a better life into reality. As China's friendly cooperation with countries around the world continues to expand, the concept of a human community with a shared future gains increasing support and approval. Especially during the global spread of the COVID-19 pandemic in 2020, this concept was tested and gained broader recognition worldwide, exerting a widespread and profound influence in the international community. Striving for universal harmony highlights the CPC's global vision.

For some time now, the United States has been pursuing an "America First" policy, repeatedly acting with impropriety, injustice, and breach of trust globally. It has continuously reinforced hegemonism, power politics, unilateralism, and trade protectionism, and has even promoted nationalism and populism, seriously impacting the rule-based multilateral system. In today's historical context, the destinies of the world's countries are tightly interconnected, and no single country can tackle the various challenges facing humanity alone. The countries of the world need to work together with a responsible spirit to jointly maintain and promote world peace and development.

General Secretary Xi Jinping deeply expounded on the historical trends, contemporary currents, fundamental concepts, global transformations, evolutionary trends, and future directions of the development of human society. For the first time, he has systematically addressed the major question of where human society is heading amidst unprecedented global changes of a kind unseen in a county. He has proposed many significant concepts, important ideas, and key propositions regarding the development of human society, deepening the understanding of the laws governing the development of human society. These serve as an effective guide for leading the progress of the times and solving global problems.

In summary, Xi Jinping Thought on Socialism with Chinese Characteristics for a New Era is a scientific system rooted in China, reflecting the will of the people and meeting the needs of the times for development and progress. It is a scientific theory that leads China and influences the world, connecting China and the world, as well as history, reality, and the future. It holds profound theoretical, practical, contemporary, and historical significance. Just as there are no bounds to practice, there is no end to theoretical innovation. General Secretary Xi Jinping pointed out: "The world is changing with every second, every moment; and China, too, is changing with every second, every moment. We must ensure our theory evolves with the times, deepen our appreciation of objective laws, and advance our theoretical, practical, institutional, cultural, and other explorations." [1]

Today, the scope and depth of changes in our era and China's development far exceed the imagination of the earlier writers of Marxist

---

1   *Documents from the 19th CPC National Congress*, Beijing: People's Publishing House, 2017, p. 21.

classics of their time. This requires us to observe, interpret, and lead the times using Marxism, to advance the development of Marxism through the vivid and rich contemporary practice in China, to examine the practical foundation and needs for the development of Marxism in the present with a broader perspective, and to continue developing 21st-century Marxism. We must continuously open up new horizons for the development of Marxism, making the truth of Marxism shine even brighter.

Part Five

Promote the Development and Revitalization of World Socialism

The history of the development of world socialism is a history of Marxist parties leading the working class and laboring people in their continuous struggle for self-liberation and the liberation of all humanity. It is a history of humanity's ongoing efforts to break free from unfair and unreasonable systems of exploitation and to achieve a better social system. It is also a history of Marxist parties continuously advancing the innovation of socialist theory and practice. Throughout the development of world socialism, from the birth of scientific socialism to the present, every time the era called for it and at critical historical turning points, there have been milestone theoretical and practical leaps that have opened up new prospects for the development of the socialist cause.

Socialism with Chinese characteristics is an important part of world socialism and represents a new practical exploration for world socialism following the drastic changes in Eastern Europe, entering a new stage. Socialism with Chinese characteristics in the New Era has an even more important exemplary and leading role and world significance, becoming the guiding banner and mainstay of 21st-century socialism.

I. Bringing the Development of World Socialism into a New Stage

The entry of socialism with Chinese characteristics into the New Era holds significant historical meaning in the development history of scientific socialism, world socialism, and human society. It "means that scientific socialism is full of vitality in 21st century China, and that the banner of socialism with Chinese characteristics is now flying high and proud for all to see."[1] This confident and resolute effort to ensure the banner flies high signifies that socialism with Chinese characteristics in the New Era has become the guiding banner of 21st-century world socialism, the mainstay of world socialist development, and the dominant force driving the progress of human society. It has revived the strong vitality of scientific socialism in the 21st century, helping world socialism to gradually emerge from the overall low tide following the drastic changes in Eastern Europe and move toward revitalization.

1. Lead and shape 21st-century world socialism

Looking back at history from a broad perspective, from the birth of scientific socialism in the mid-19th century to the mid-21st century, roughly two centuries can be divided into three major historical stages, referred to as the "three 70 years." From the publication of the *Communist Manifesto* in 1848, marking the birth of scientific socialism, to the Russian October Revolution in 1917, is the first 70 years of socialist development. The historical task of this period was to promote the integration of Marxism with the workers' movement, establish workers' parties, and

---

1 Xi Jinping, *Secure a Decisive Victory in Building a Moderately Prosperous Society in All Respects and Strive for the Great Success of Socialism with Chinese Characteristics for a New Era: Report at the 19th National Congress of the Communist Party of China*, Beijing: People's Publishing House, 2017, p. 10.

carry out socialist revolutions to seize power. The development of scientific socialism during this period was characterized by the formation and enrichment of Marxism, which gained a leading position in the socialist movement.

From the October Revolution in 1917 to the drastic changes in Eastern Europe at the end of the 1980s is the second historical stage of socialist development, or the "second 70 years." The main historical tasks were to integrate Marxism with the realities of various countries, address issues related to building, consolidating, and developing socialism in countries with relatively backward economies and cultures, the national liberation movements in colonial and semi-colonial countries, the transformation from democratic revolution to socialist revolution to establish new social systems, and issues of socialist reform. The new development of scientific socialism in Russia was primarily characterized by the formation of Leninism, while in China, it was marked by the formation of Mao Zedong Thought and the initial development of the theoretical system of socialism with Chinese characteristics during the reform and opening up period.

From the late 1980s collapse of Eastern Europe to the mid-21st century marks the third stage of socialist development, or the "third 70 years." The main historical task of this period is to consolidate, develop, and improve the socialist system, fully demonstrating the superiority of the socialist system. The latest theory of the new development of scientific socialism is Xi Jinping Thought on Socialism with Chinese Characteristics for a New Era. This represents the latest achievement of contemporary Chinese Marxism and a pioneering, foundational, and exemplary theoretical achievement of 21st-century Marxism.

Examining the historical process from the downturn following the drastic changes in Eastern Europe to the quest for rejuvenation in the early 21st century, and considering the relationship between Chinese socialism and world socialism, it is evident that in the nearly 30 years since the drastic Eastern European changes, the development of socialism with Chinese characteristics has played a crucial historical role in every significant juncture for world socialism. It has become the backbone, the weather vane, and the stronghold of the world socialist movement. In summary, three critical historical junctures are particularly significant: the drastic changes in Eastern Europe, the crisis of capitalism, and the setbacks in globalization.

The first historical juncture:

In the late 1980s and early 1990s, the demise of the Soviet Union, the collapse of the Communist Party of the Soviet Union, and the drastic changes in Eastern Europe led to the temporary rise of theories such as the "failure of socialism" and the "end of history." The "China collapse theory" also gained traction internationally. The CPC withstood immense pressure and challenges, successfully upheld and developed socialism with Chinese characteristics, and through its actions, saved and defended scientific socialism. This affirmed Deng Xiaoping's assertion: "So long as socialism does not collapse in China, it will always hold its ground in the world."[1]. China defended and saved socialism.

The second historical juncture:

The early 21st century saw an entire capitalist crisis triggered by the global financial crisis. This crisis occurred less than 20 years after the drastic changes in Eastern Europe and the demise of the Soviet Union, which had sparked the so-called "crisis of socialism" and the "end of history." However, in a relatively short period, these notions transformed into a "crisis of capitalism" and the "end of capitalism." This vividly illustrates how history opens a path for inevitability through contingency.

---

1   Deng Xiaoping, *Selected Works of Deng Xiaoping*, Beijing: Foreign Languages Press, 1994, vol. III, p. 334.

The greatest surprise from the "hand of history" during this process was the "magical reversal" that opened up the "room with a view" of socialism with Chinese characteristics. This marked the beginning of a significant decline in the long cycle of world capitalism, while world socialism, although generally in a low tide since the drastic changes in Eastern Europe, started to seek rejuvenation, primarily relying on and marked by the tremendous achievements of socialism with Chinese characteristics. China developed and revitalized socialism.

The third historical juncture:

Fifteen years into the 21st century, the de-globalization trend occurring in major Western countries like the UK and the US indicated a significant decline in capitalism's ability to manage and dominate the entire world. At the same time, China has raised the banner of continuing globalization, advancing globalization in a more equitable and rational direction. As General Secretary Xi Jinping pointed out, "Twenty or even 15 years ago, the major propellants of economic globalization were the US and other Western countries. Today, China is considered the biggest driver of global trade liberalization and facilitation, resisting various forms of Western protectionisms."[1] This can be seen as a shift from a globalization long dominated by capitalism to one increasingly led by socialism. This shift holds significant transformative meaning for the development of world socialism. During this critical historical period, socialism with Chinese characteristics entered the New Era, signifying that scientific socialism in 21st-century China has radiated strong vitality. Socialism with Chinese characteristics has become the guiding banner of 21st-century world socialism and the mainstay of world socialism's revival, promising to make greater contributions to the new development of world socialism and scientific socialism. China is leading and shaping socialism.

---

1   Xi Jinping, *The Governance of China*, Beijing: Foreign Languages Press, 2017, vol. II, p. 233.

The development of world socialism is a unity of continuity and stages. In the 21st century, the development of socialism with Chinese characteristics in the New Era has not only inherited and carried forward the lessons and experiences of previous historical development, but also innovated and created under new historical conditions, advancing socialism into a new phase. It has taken on new historical tasks, new content, and new forms, making original contributions to China in this New Era.

The great strategist Deng Xiaoping, at the end of the last century, envisioned a 70-year plan: "China will take the 20 years remaining in this century, along with 50 years in the next century—a total of 70 years— to prove to the world that socialism is superior to capitalism. Through the practice of developing productive forces and advancing science and technology, and through the promotion of both cultural-ethical and material progress, we will demonstrate the superiority of the socialist system over capitalism. We aim to let the people of the developed capitalist nations realize that socialism is indeed better than capitalism."[1]

Today, more than half of the third 70-year period of socialism's development has passed. Over the next 30 years, China will enter the historical period of its two-step plan to build a great modern socialist country in all respects. The new developments of socialism with Chinese characteristics in the New Era will undoubtedly carry significant historical, epochal, and global significance for the development of world socialism. In a certain sense, socialism with Chinese characteristics represents the future of world socialism, reflecting the historical responsibility of the CPC toward the socialist cause, the development of human society, and the progress of civilization.

In the early 21st century, the development of world socialism has

---

1 *Chronology of Deng Xiaoping 1975–1997*, Beijing: Central Party Literature Publishing House, 2004, vol. II, p. 1225.

witnessed many new highlights, displayed distinct characteristics, and achieved significant advancements. Amid the major historical shifts of the "rising East and declining West," alongside a new wave of capitalist crises, world socialism finds the opportunity to rise from its low tide and rejuvenate. However, it also faces intensified and complex competition with global capitalism. Overall, the new developments in world socialism have effectively shattered the bold assertions of a "unified world under capitalism" that followed the drastic changes in Eastern Europe, undermined the long-term strategies of capitalist leaders aiming for "victory without war," and dispelled the "myth" of the "end of history," which claimed Western liberal democracy as the ultimate destination of human society. Moreover, it has powerfully reaffirmed the historical inevitability of communism replacing capitalism on a global scale, thus revitalizing the core truths of Marxism. The 21st century is indeed the century of the revival of world socialism!

2. Successfully addressing the historical question of "how to build socialism"

A crucial historical question in the development of socialism is how economically and culturally less developed countries should build socialism after a revolutionary victory. Once a Marxist party seizes power, issues of state development, reform, and governance become pressing tasks for the ruling party. The process of socialist development and reform is inherently tied to governing a socialist society.

Marx and Engels envisioned that the victory of socialist revolutions would occur simultaneously in developed countries alongside the establishment of a new society based on highly developed productive forces. They also considered the development paths for less developed countries like Russia, suggesting that these nations could leap over the Caudine Forks of capitalism. However, since they did not experience the development of socialism in their lifetimes, most of their insights were predictive, framing the historical question. After the October Revolution in Russia, Lenin explored creative solutions for building socialism in less developed countries. He proposed and implemented the New Economic Policy, pursued industrialization, fostered advanced culture, and strengthened the ruling party, achieving initial successes in practice. This laid the groundwork for practical solutions to the historical question.

Subsequently, the Soviet Union undertook several decades of large-scale socialist development, achieving significant accomplishments while also committing serious errors. Ultimately, the demise of the Soviet Union led to the failure of this exploration. It can be said that the Soviet Union conducted roughly 70 years of socialist exploration, but it ended in deviation from its original course.

Over the more than 70 years since the founding of the People's Republic of China, the country has established and continuously improved the system of socialism with Chinese characteristics. This has led to the formation and development of systems in various areas including the Party's leadership, the economy, politics, culture, society, eco-civilization, military, foreign affairs, and more. These efforts have continuously strengthened and enhanced national governance, providing robust institutional guarantees for achieving the Party's program and goals, and promoting social development and progress. This has laid a solid institutional foundation for all development and progress in contemporary China and successfully addressed the historic question of how an economically and culturally less developed country can build socialism.

After the founding of the People's Republic of China, the first generation of the Party's central leadership, with Mao Zedong at its core, adhered to the fundamental tenets of Marxism as a guide, striving to explore and solve the major issue of how an economically and culturally less developed agricultural country could adhere to and develop Marxism and establish and consolidate socialism. This enriched and developed Mao Zedong Thought.

Since the introduction of the reform and opening up policy, the CPC has played a central leadership role, combining the fundamental tenets of Marxism with the specific realities of China's reform and opening up. The Party has united and led the people in the great practice of socialism with Chinese characteristics, clearly recognizing and scientifically answering fundamental questions such as "What is socialism, and how to build it?" "What kind of Party to build, and how to build it?" "What kind of development to achieve, and how to achieve it?" "What kind of socialism with Chinese characteristics to uphold and develop, and how to uphold and develop it?" "What kind of great modern socialist country to build, and how to build it?" and "What kind of long-term ruling Marxist party to build, and how to build it?" These efforts have addressed a series of major issues on how to accelerate modernization, and consolidate and develop socialism in a large developing country with a population of more than a billion people, achieving a tremendous transformation: the Chinese nation has stood up, grown rich, and is becoming strong. This has led to the formation of Deng Xiaoping Theory, the Theory of Three Represents, the Scientific Outlook on Development, and Xi Jinping Thought on Socialism with Chinese Characteristics for a New Era. These theoretical achievements are both consistent and evolving with the times, forming an inherently unified theoretical system of socialism with Chinese characteristics, and being distinctly grounded in scientific truth, attentive to the people's interests, practical, open, and reflective of contemporary realities.

The great historical creation process of over 70 years of the People's Republic of China is divided into two historical periods: before and after the reform and opening up. General Secretary Xi Jinping pointed out: "These are two periods that are interconnected yet significantly different, but essentially both are practical explorations of socialist development led by our Party."[1]

From the founding of the People's Republic of China until the period before the reform and opening up, our Party led the people in the socialist revolution and development, arduously exploring a path of socialist development suited to China's national conditions. Although there were severe setbacks and serious mistakes, overall, the basic socialist system was fully established, achieving the greatest and most profound social transformation in Chinese history. This period produced original theoretical achievements and significant accomplishments, creating the political prerequisites and laying the institutional foundation for all progress and development in contemporary China. It also provided valuable experience, theoretical preparation, and material basis for the subsequent creation of socialism with Chinese characteristics.

Over the more than 40 years of reform and opening up, from the start of a new period to entering a new century, from stepping onto a new starting point to entering a New Era, socialism with Chinese characteristics has witnessed a great leap from its inception, development, to perfection. The continuous exploration and successful answers to the historic question of "What is socialism, and how to build socialism" have revitalized scientific socialism, which has a history of over 170 years, with immense vitality. Our Party's understanding of the laws governing socialist development has reached unprecedented heights, and the historic creation of leading the Chinese people in socialist revolution, development, and reform has reached unprecedented levels.

---

1   *Documents Produced since the 18th CPC National Congress*, Beijing: Central Party Literature Publishing House, 2014, vol. I, p. 111–112.

Over the more than 70 years since the founding of the People's Republic of China, the CPC has led the Chinese people in writing a magnificent epic on the broad avenue of socialism, with the Chinese nation achieving a tremendous transformation: it has stood up, grown rich, and is becoming strong. In this glorious historical process, socialism with Chinese characteristics has progressed from its foundation, creation, and development to perfection, finding a practical path to realization for scientific socialism, which has a history of over 170 years, in a populous country of more than 1.4 billion people in the East. This has propelled scientific socialism into a new stage of development. It can be said that Chinese socialism has made a milestone contribution by successfully addressing the historical question of socialism.

Since the 18th CPC National Congress, socialism with Chinese characteristics has entered the New Era. Our Party has creatively answered the question of "What is the governance of a socialist society, and how to govern a socialist society," further deepening the understanding of the laws governing governance.

General Secretary Xi Jinping said: "Actually, how to govern a socialist society, a completely new society, has not been clearly addressed by world socialism so far."[1] With a broad perspective on world history, he examines the development of national systems and governance issues, posing a crucial question in the history of world socialism: "How to govern a new type of socialist society?" A significant reason for the Soviet Union's demise was its failure to adequately address this issue, resulting in an ineffective national governance system and capacity. This led to the accumulation of social conflicts and problems, which became increasingly difficult to resolve, ultimately leaving a regrettable mark on the history of socialist governance.

After our Party took on nationwide governance, it actively explored

---

1   Xi Jinping, *The Governance of China*, Beijing: Foreign Languages Press, 2018, vol. I, p. 102.

the question of how to govern China and made significant progress. However, before the reform and opening up, we had yet to find a governance model that fully aligned with the realities of our country. With the launch of the reform and opening up, our Party began to address the issue of national governance from a fresh perspective, making concerted efforts to modernize systems critical to the long-term stability of the Party and the nation. Under the Party's leadership, socialism with Chinese characteristics was established, continuously refining both the socialist system and the national governance framework, injecting unprecedented vitality into contemporary China. Guided by the CPC Central Committee with General Secretary Xi Jinping at its core, the comprehensive deepening of reform, the commitment to strengthening national institutions, and the improvement of governance capacity have become seamlessly integrated, as reflected in the coordinated efforts to pursue the Five-Sphere Integrated Plan and the Four-Pronged Comprehensive Strategy. This has resulted in significant advancements in the system of socialism with Chinese characteristics and the modernization of national governance and capacity.

The Third Plenary Session of the 18th CPC Central Committee proposed that the general goal of deepening reform is to "improve and develop the system of socialism with Chinese characteristics and modernize the national governance system and capacity," and it clearly required "transforming the advantages of various systems into the effectiveness of managing the country."[1]

With a profound historical perspective, General Secretary Xi Jinping divides the process of our country's system development into the "first half" and the "second half": "From the perspective of forming an increasingly mature and more well-defined system, our country's socialist praxis has

---

1   *Documents Produced since the 18th CPC National Congress*, Beijing: Central Party Literature Publishing House, 2014, vol. I, pp. 547, 549.

already passed the halfway point. Up to this point, our main historic tasks have been to establish a basic of socialism and then to carry out reform under that system. We have now already done a good job of this. From here on, our main historic tasks are to improve and develop socialism with Chinese characteristics and to provide a set of more complete, stable, and effective institutions for the development of the cause of the Party and the country, the wellbeing of the people, social harmony and stability, and the lasting political stability of the country."[1] In the strategy adopted at the 19th CPC National Congress for building a great modern socialist country, specific goals for institutional development and governance capacity building were clearly proposed.

The Resolution of the CPC Central Committee on Upholding and Improving the Socialist System with Chinese Characteristics and Modernizing the National Governance System and Capacity, adopted at the Fourth Plenary Session of the 19th Central Committee, not only reflects the consistency and continuity of the strategy but also, based on the development requirements of our country and the trends of the times, makes comprehensive planning and strategic deployment for achieving the historical tasks of the "second half." This has resulted in new theoretical, practical, and institutional achievements. Specifically, it accurately grasps the direction and laws of the evolution of our national system and national governance system, and places institutional development and governance capacity building in a more prominent position. It not only clarifies the direction and guiding principles but also sets out overall requirements and major tasks. It explains the 13 significant advantages of the system of socialism with Chinese characteristics and points out the main ways to transform these system advantages into governance efficacy. It proposes

---

1   Xi Jinping, *How to Comprehensively Deepen Reform*, Beijing, Central Party Literature Publishing House, 2014, p. 27.

a timetable and roadmap for the overall goals of the three-step strategy and outlines the major tasks of the 13 upholds and improves. It embodies the basic principles of scientific socialism and has distinct Chinese characteristics, national characteristics, and characteristics of the times. In summary, the Resolution creatively answers the significant question of "how to govern a socialist society," which concerns the future of the Party and the country. It enriches and develops the theory and practice of scientific socialism and has comprehensive, pioneering, and milestone significance.

II. Highlight the Great Superiority of the Socialist System

Since the 18th CPC National Congress, our Party has continuously improved and developed the system of socialism with Chinese characteristics through comprehensive deepening of reform, and has steadily enhanced the ability to effectively govern the country using this system. This not only paved a successful development path different from Western countries but also formed a successful institutional system distinct from the West, highlighting the great superiority of the socialist system. Socialism with Chinese characteristics in the New Era has become a landmark banner for the development of 21st-century world socialism. Its leading and exemplary role is continuously rising, becoming a milestone reference representing the development of the world socialist movement.

1. Basic characteristics of the system of socialism with Chinese characteristics

The Fourth Plenary Session of the 19th CPC Central Committee, standing at the overall and strategic height of the Party and the country's undertakings, focused on both the present and the long-term future.

It specially studied and deliberated on the major issues of upholding and improving the system of socialism with Chinese characteristics and modernizing the national governance system and capacity. It systematically answered the significant political question of "what to uphold and consolidate, and what to improve and develop" from the integration of firm institutional confidence and promotion of institutional innovation. For the first time, it comprehensively summarized the significant advantages of the system of socialism with Chinese characteristics, which are organically connected, complementary, and integrated as a whole. It systematically elaborated on the scientific institutional system, which is composed of fundamental institutions, basic institutions, and important institutions, with clear layers and comprehensive and systematic structures. It clearly put forward the guiding thought, overall requirements, overall goals, strategic approaches, and major measures for advancing the development of our country's system and national governance.

The Resolution of the CPC Central Committee on Upholding and Improving the Socialist System with Chinese Characteristics and Modernizing the National Governance System and Capacity, adopted at this plenary session, fully reflects the deepened understanding of the laws governing building socialism with Chinese characteristics by the Central Committee with General Secretary Xi Jinping at its core. It enriches and develops the theory and practice of scientific socialism and provides a profound institutional foundation and strong institutional guarantee for effective governance of China.

Historically, the main historical task of our socialist practice was to establish the basic socialist system and carry out reforms on this basis. The main historical task now and for a considerable period in the future is to improve and develop the system of socialism with Chinese characteristics, achieve institutional modernization, and provide a more complete, more stable, and more effective institutional system for the development of the Party and the country's undertakings, for the happiness and wellbeing of the people, for social harmony and stability, and for the long-term peace and stability of the country.

The resolution of the Fourth Plenary Session of the 19th CPC Central Committee states: "[G]uided by Marxism, the Chinese socialist system and state governance system have developed from the real conditions and culture of China, and they enjoy the full support of the people."[1] They embody significant vitality and strengths. General Secretary Xi Jinping also pointed out that our system and national governance system have been developed and gradually improved over time, evolving naturally on the basis of our country's historical heritage, cultural traditions, and economic and social development. This provides a fundamental basis for us to deeply understand the characteristics of the system of socialism with Chinese characteristics.

First, there is the unity of persistence and improvement.

The system of socialism with Chinese characteristics is the result of long-term development based on the economic and social development of our country. It is not something subjectively designed, static, or achieved overnight. General Secretary Xi Jinping pointed out: "The system of socialism with Chinese characteristics will not remain unchanged but will continue to develop and improve in the practice of reform."[2]

Great development inevitably calls for significant institutional reforms and adjustments. Over the past few decades, as China has rapidly advanced toward modernization, its institutional framework has also evolved swiftly. How should these institutions be improved? Through long-term practical exploration and reform innovation, our Party has derived a fundamental

---

1   Xi Jinping, *The Governance of China*, Beijing: Foreign Languages Press, 2020, vol. II, p. 146.
2   *Series of Speeches by General Secretary Xi Jinping (2016 Edition)*, Beijing: Xuexi Press and People's Publishing House, 2016, p. 27.

principle: the unity of persistence and improvement, consolidation and development, and building on past successes and making innovations. As General Secretary Xi Jinping emphasized: "We are comprehensively deepening reform not because socialism with Chinese characteristics is inferior, but rather to make it better. When we say we should have complete confidence in this system, we do not mean that we will rest on our laurels and keep the system just as it is; rather, we mean we should eliminate defects in our institutions and mechanisms in order to make our system more mature and ensure that it endures the test of time."[1]

For the fundamental systems, basic systems, important systems, basic principles, and fundamental theories that have been established and tested in practice, we must avoid making disruptive mistakes. We should always uphold, continuously consolidate, and adhere to their true nature. On this basis, we should also liberate our thoughts, seek truth from facts, and keep pace with the times. As economic and social development continues, we must resolutely eliminate all outdated ideas and institutional drawbacks, continuously enhancing and fully demonstrating the advantages of the system of socialism with Chinese characteristics. The Fourth Plenary Session of the 19th CPC Central Committee precisely revolved around the basic principle of "what to uphold and consolidate, and what to improve and develop," clearly defining the fundamental aspects that must be adhered to and the direction for improvement of various systems and frameworks, and made specific work arrangements accordingly.

Second, there is the unity of universality and particularity.

"The Chinese socialist system and state governance system did not fall out of the sky, but emerged from Chinese soil through a long process of revolution, economic development, and reform. They are the results of

---

1   Xi Jinping, How to Comprehensively Deepen Reform, Beijing, Central Party Literature Publishing House, 2014, p. 22.

a combination of the tenets of Marxism with China's conditions and the outcome of a range of innovations in theory, practice and system."[1] Just as General Secretary Xi Jinping stated: "Our Party integrates the fundamental tenets of Marxism with China's specific realities, organically combining its efforts to open up the right path, develop sound theories and establish effective systems and continuously exploring and advancing in practice."[2] The system of socialism with Chinese characteristics and the national governance system are the crystallizations of combining the fundamental tenets of Marxism with China's specific realities. The state system, political system, fundamental political system, basic political system, basic economic system, and various important systems established in our country all adhere to the basic principles of scientific socialism, creatively applying Marxist state theory, reflecting the general laws governing the development of human society, and possessing universality. At the same time, the system of socialism with Chinese characteristics and the national governance system are deeply rooted in China, with profound Chinese cultural roots and national characteristics. Based on the basic national conditions and the most important reality—the primary stage of socialism, they have gradually matured and become well-defined in practice, fully embodying the characteristics and advantages of socialism with Chinese characteristics, and thus possess particularity.

The significance of the system of socialism with Chinese characteristics in providing a Chinese approach for humanity's exploration of better social systems lies in governing a country and promoting its modernization. It requires adherence to the general laws governing the development of human society while also considering the specific characteristics of

---

1   Xi Jinping, *The Governance of China*, Beijing: Foreign Languages Press, 2020, vol. III, p. 144.
2   *Study Guide for the Resolution of the CPC Central Committee on Upholding and Improving the System of Socialism with Chinese Characteristics and Modernizing the National Governance System and Capacity*, Beijing: People's Publishing House, 2019, p. 180.

each country and nation, thereby choosing a system suited to one's own conditions and forging a modernization path with national characteristics.

Third, the unity of the Party's nature and the people's nature.

The unity of the Party's principles and the people's interests is the essential requirement of the nature, original aspiration and founding mission of a Marxist party. CPC leadership is the defining feature of socialism with Chinese characteristics and constitutes the greatest strength of the system of socialism with Chinese characteristics. The strong leadership of the CPC is the fundamental guarantee for achieving the overall goal of upholding and improving the system of socialism with Chinese characteristics and modernizing the national governance system and capacity. In the Resolution adopted at the Fourth Plenary Session of the 19th CPC Central Committee, the Party's leadership is emphasized across all areas, aspects, and stages of national governance. Strengthening the Party's leadership system is regarded as the "number one project" in the development of the socialist system with Chinese characteristics, the highest priority, and the most fundamental system, playing a pivotal role in guiding the development of all other systems.

Simultaneously, the Resolution is also permeated with the principle of putting people at the center, respecting the people's principal position, upholding the people's democracy, and realizing, maintaining, and developing the fundamental interests of the overwhelming majority of the people. It explicitly points out the need to uphold and improve the system of the people's democracy and develop socialist democracy. The organic unity of the Party's principles and the people's interests is the generative and developmental logic of the system of socialism with Chinese characteristics, and it is the value pursuit of upholding and improving the system of socialism with Chinese characteristics.

Fourth, the unity of scientific and holistic nature.

The system of socialism with Chinese characteristics is a summary and sublimation of the vivid practical experiences of our country's development, and a profound grasp and creative application of the laws governing social development. The system of socialism with Chinese characteristics is a scientific system formed by the Party and the people through long-term practical exploration. All work and activities of national governance in our country are carried out in accordance with this system. Our national governance system and capacity are the concentrated embodiment of the system of socialism with Chinese characteristics and its implementation capacity.

In the long-term practical development of revolution, development, and reform, our Party has always adhered to Marxism as a guide, proceeding from China's national conditions and gathering the wisdom and strength of the people to establish and develop a complete set of scientific and standardized systems. These systems conform to scientific theoretical logic, historical logic, and practical logic, providing institutional guarantees and support for national development.

Moreover, the system of socialism with Chinese characteristics is composed of a complete and integrated system of institutions, including the Party's leadership system, the system of people's democracy, the socialist rule of law system, the socialist administrative system, the basic economic system of socialism, the system of advanced socialist culture, the system of social security, the system of social governance, the system of eco-civilization, the system of the Party's absolute leadership over the people's army, the One Country, Two Systems framework, the system of foreign affairs, and the Party and state supervisory system. These encompass fundamental, basic, and important institutions across 13 areas, forming a comprehensive system of institutions and governance that covers all aspects and fields.

Fifth, the unity of creativity and openness.

The system of socialism with Chinese characteristics is the result of endogenous evolution, not an externally grafted product. General Secretary Xi Jinping pointed out: "Blindly copying the political systems of other countries will never work in China. They will never adapt to our country. Such a course of action will 'turn the tiger you are trying to draw into a dog.' It could even spell an end to the independent destiny of our country."[1] He also emphasized: "We should learn from all the beneficial achievements of human political civilization, but we will never blindly copy the Western political system model, nor will we abandon the fundamental socialist political system of our country."[2] The choice of a country's system is closely related to its level of economic and social development, national characteristics, and cultural traditions; it is a choice made through practice, history, and the will of the people.

The system of socialism with Chinese characteristics was created by the CPC, uniting and leading the people over a long period of practical exploration. It has grown out of China's longstanding cultural traditions, the struggles against foreign aggression, the pursuit of national independence and people's liberation since modern times, and the arduous creation and exploration of the socialist cause. It is a great creation in the history of human institutional civilization and a source of pride and confidence for the entire Party and the nation. Additionally, the system of socialism with Chinese characteristics takes neither the old path of being closed and inflexible, nor the erroneous path of abandoning socialism; it is a creative transformation and innovative development of both traditional systems and foreign systems. It inherits excellent traditions while also absorbing and learning from all the outstanding achievements of

---

1   *Series of Speeches by General Secretary Xi Jinping (2016 Edition)*, Beijing: Xuexi Press and People's Publishing House, 2016, p. 166.
2   *Ibid.*, p. 75.

institutional civilization created by other countries.

The CPC is a Marxist party with a high level of institutional awareness and outstanding governance capabilities. In its long-term practice and exploration, it has always organically unified the pioneering of the correct path, the development of scientific theory, and the development of effective institutions. It promptly transforms innovative theoretical principles and successful practical experiences into systematic institutional achievements. The political report of the 19th CPC National Congress emphasized the need to continue to comprehensively deepen reform, uphold and improve the system of socialism with Chinese characteristics, modernize China's system and capacity for governance, draw on the achievements of other civilizations, develop a set of institutions that are well conceived, and fully built, procedure based, and efficiently functioning to fully leverage the superiority of our socialist system.

In-depth research on the relationship between the particularity and universality of the system of socialism with Chinese characteristics, and how to transform "China's particularity" into "global generality," reflects the system's increasing international influence. Following the plans of the 19th CPC National Congress, our Party has continuously summarized the system of socialism with Chinese characteristics, its institutional features, advantages, and effectiveness, extracting a set of generally applicable, referable, and universally significant experiences. This provides a new option for the development of social systems in other countries and makes an original contribution to the development of human institutional civilization.

2. The remarkable advantages of the system of socialism with Chinese characteristics

China's institutional innovations are the most vivid and realistic versions that conform to China's current realities. Through continuous reform and innovation, socialism with Chinese characteristics has proven to be more efficient than the capitalist system in liberating and developing social productive forces, freeing and enhancing social vitality, and promoting well-rounded development of individuals. This efficiency enables it to gain comparative advantages in competition, fully demonstrating the superiority of the system of socialism with Chinese characteristics.

The superiority of the system of socialism with Chinese characteristics has been fully demonstrated. "The merits of a system should be assessed from a political and an overall perspective."[1] The key is to see whether it suits the national conditions, whether it is effective, and whether it has the support of the people. On this basis, it highlights the superiority of this system compared to others. Since the founding of the People's Republic of China, especially since the reform and opening up, the Party has led the people to achieve development and governance achievements that have astonished the world. In just a few decades, China has completed the modernization journey that took developed countries several hundred years, creating the miracle of rapid economic development and long-term social stability.

The system of socialism with Chinese characteristics transcends the Western dichotomies of market vs. government, state vs. society, centralized authority vs. democracy and freedom, and public vs. private spheres. This gives it a unique advantage compared to Western social systems. It has surpassed the middle-income trap, political chaos, and social unrest that some developing countries encounter during modernization. In addition, it has achieved rapid economic growth, social harmony, stability, and a vibrant reform spirit, becoming a model for many other developing

---

1   Xi Jinping, *The Governance of China*, Beijing: Foreign Languages Press, 2020, vol. III, p. 147.

countries in social systems and operational mechanisms. This has propelled the Chinese nation to achieve a tremendous transformation: it has stood up, grown rich, and is becoming strong. Therefore, whether we successfully respond to various crises or create development miracles, the reasons cannot be simply attributed to "latecomer advantage," nor can they be prejudicially attributed to "following the path paved by others," nor are they due to accidental luck or favorable circumstances. The secret of success lies precisely in the unique advantages of the system of socialism with Chinese characteristics, including the ability to unite all possible forces, strong mobilization capabilities, the advantage of concentrating forces to accomplish great tasks, and effectively promoting social fairness and justice. Thus, our confidence ultimately stems from the incomparable superiority of the system of socialism with Chinese characteristics.

The system of socialism with Chinese characteristics has many significant advantages. The Resolution of the Fourth Plenary Session of the 19th CPC Central Committee clearly pointed out that our national system and national governance system have many significant advantages, mainly:

- The significant advantage of adhering to the centralized, unified leadership of the Party, adhering to the Party's scientific theories, maintaining political stability, and ensuring that the country always advances in the direction of socialism;

- The significant advantage of adhering to the principle of the people running the country, developing people's democracy, maintaining close ties with the people, and relying closely on the people to promote national development;

- The significant advantage of adhering to comprehensive law-based governance, building a socialist rule of law country, and effectively ensuring social fairness, justice, and the rights of the people;

- The significant advantage of adhering to the principle of nationwide unity, mobilizing the enthusiasm of all sectors, and concentrating forces to accomplish great tasks;

- The significant advantage of adhering to the equality of all ethnic groups, forging a strong sense of community for the Chinese nation, and achieving common unity, struggle, and prosperity;

- The significant advantage of adhering to the public ownership as the mainstay, multiple forms of ownership developing together, the principle of distribution according to work as the mainstay, multiple forms of distribution coexisting, and organically combining the socialist system with the market economy to continuously liberate and develop social productive forces; an.

- The significant advantage of adhering to common ideals, values, and moral concepts, promoting the best elements of traditional Chinese culture, revolutionary culture, and advanced socialist culture, and uniting all people theoretically and culturally;

- The significant advantage of adhering to the people-centered philosophy of development, continually ensuring and improving people's livelihood, enhancing people's wellbeing, and pursuing the path of common prosperity;

- The significant advantage of insisting on reform and innovation, keeping pace with the times, being adept at self-improvement and development, and ensuring that society is always vibrant and dynamic;

- The significant advantage of upholding both integrity and talent, selecting and appointing capable individuals, assembling the best minds across the world, and cultivating more excellent talents;

- The significant advantage of the Party commanding the military, ensuring that the people's army is absolutely loyal to the Party and the people, and strongly safeguarding national sovereignty, security, and development interests;

- The significant advantage of adhering to One Country, Two Systems, maintaining long-term prosperity and stability in Hong Kong and Macao, and promoting the peaceful reunification of the motherland; an.

- The significant advantage of combining independence and self-reliance with opening up to the outside world, actively participating in global governance, and continuously contributing to the building of human community with a shared future.

These 13 significant advantages are interconnected and inseparable, forming an organic whole, and they are the necessary conditions and sufficient reasons for our firm confidence in the Four-Sphere Confidence.

Guidance by Marxism is the fundamental reason for the significant superiority of the system of socialism with Chinese characteristics. "One of the factors crucial to the strengths of our state and governance systems is that our Party, over many years, has combined Marxism with China's actual conditions, and integrated its efforts to open up the right path, develop sound theories and establish effective systems. The CPC has guided the development of the state and governance systems with dynamic Marxism adapted to the Chinese context."[1] In other words, only Marxism, and not any other doctrine, combined with China's realities, can achieve the organic unification of expanding the correct path, developing scientific theories, and building effective systems, thereby forming the comparative advantage of the system of socialism with Chinese characteristics and highlighting its superiority. Marxism, as "a doctrine about the general laws governing the development of nature, society, and human thinking, a doctrine about the inevitable replacement of capitalism by socialism and the ultimate realization of communism, a doctrine about the liberation of the proletariat, the liberation of all humanity, and the free and well-rounded development of every individual, and a guide to action for the

---

1   Xi Jinping, *The Governance of China*, Beijing: Foreign Languages Press, 2020, vol. III, pp. 147–148.

people to create a better life," provides the fundamental stance, viewpoint, and method for the establishment, adherence to, and improvement of the system of socialism with Chinese characteristics. For instance, communism, as the highest goal of Marxism, lays the fundamental basis for the superiority of the system of socialism with Chinese characteristics. "There are many ways to implement people's democracy, ensuring that the people run the country, so we must not be confined to just one particular rigid model, and there cannot be a single, universally applicable standard of judgment."[1] However, allowing for diversity does not mean there is no fundamental standard or basis. Communism, as the most ideal social system superior to capitalism, serves as the fundamental basis for upholding and improving the system of socialism with Chinese characteristics. It also endows the system with qualities of nobility, superiority, and advancement. The system of socialism with Chinese characteristics should continually expand communist elements through reform and innovation, more prominently reflecting the characteristics of a communist system. The new development philosophy proposed by our Party, which includes the vision of innovative, coordinated, green, open and shared development, and the insistence on and improvement of a social governance based on collaboration, participation, and common interests, as well as the harmony between humans and nature, and the establishment of a moderately prosperous society in all respects, all embody the directional guidance of communism. For instance, only by adhering to Marxism as a guide can we develop a socialist market economy that does not take capital as the fundamental standard but better reflects the people-centered philosophy of development, establishing a more advanced form of socialist market economy than that of capitalism. This approach better embodies the

---

1   *Series of Speeches by General Secretary Xi Jinping (2016 Edition)*, Beijing: Xuexi Press and People's Publishing House, 2016, p. 171.

community of destiny, the community of communication, and the community of production and life, creating conditions for the free and well-rounded development of every individual.

The leadership of the CPC is the fundamental guarantee for the significant superiority of the system of socialism with Chinese characteristics. "In the face of complex situations and arduous tasks, to effectively respond to risks and challenges, engage in the great struggle with many new historical features, and achieve the rejuvenation of the Chinese nation, the most fundamental guarantee is still the Party's leadership."[1] Therefore, in addressing the difficulties and challenges of misinterpretation or even stigmatization of the political party system of socialism with Chinese characteristics, we must uphold the leadership of the CPC as the fundamental guarantee. Moreover, consistently adhering to the Party's overall leadership ensures that the development of the system and governance system of socialism with Chinese characteristics advances continuously with direction, planning, steps, and strength.

Under the leadership of the CPC Central Committee with General Secretary Xi Jinping at its core, a scientific blueprint for building a modern socialist country and realizing the rejuvenation of the Chinese nation has been formulated. The overall goals of upholding and improving the system of socialism with Chinese characteristics and modernizing the national governance system and capacity have been proposed, pointing out the correct direction for the development of the system and governance system. It was proposed that, on the basis of completing the building of a moderately prosperous society in all respects, the objectives be achieved in two further 15-year stages. Additionally, it was suggested that the Party be built to be even stronger and more powerful in order

---

1   "Deeply Implement the Party's Organizational Line in the New Era—Study General Secretary Xi Jinping's Major Speech at the 21st Group Study Session of the CPC Central Committee's Political Bureau," www.gov.cn/xinwen/2020-07/01/content_5523340.htm.

to better unite and lead the people nationwide toward achieving these great goals. By deeply understanding the laws governing the Communist Party's governance, the laws governing socialist development, and the laws governing the development of human society, we can better elevate systematic understanding to the institutional level, more effectively modernizing the national governance system and capacity, and ensure the integration of the institutional system with the governance system, as well as the mutual promotion of institutional functions and governance capabilities. The nature and purpose of the CPC determine that it must strive for the happiness of the people, the rejuvenation of the nation, and the harmony of the world. The CPC consistently adheres to democratic centralism, focusing on enhancing its ability and determination to set the direction, plan the overall situation, formulate policies, and promote reforms, ensuring the scientific, reasonable, and effective implementation of the Party's line, principles, and policies. Modern history has fully proven that without the strong leadership of the CPC, China would become fragmented and lose the stable and united political environment and the long-term development of the economy and society.

"The fundamental reason that the Chinese nation has stood up, become better off and grown in strength ... is that the CPC has led the people in establishing and improving the Chinese socialist system."[1] To further enhance the superiority of the system of socialism with Chinese characteristics, General Secretary Xi Jinping pointed out: "We must eliminate all institutional obstacles and vested interests impeding our country's development, speed up the establishment of systems and mechanisms that are comprehensive, procedure-based and effective, and make the socialist system more mature and better-defined."[2] This provides

---

1   Xi Jinping, *The Governance of China*, Beijing: Foreign Languages Press, 2020, vol. III, p. 144.
2   *Ibid.*, p. 135.

a solid institutional guarantee for turning transforming our institutional advantages into better governance efficiency.

Furthermore, the miracle of China's modernization fully demonstrates that the system of socialism with Chinese characteristics is effective, practical, and endowed with strong vitality and significant superiority. It provides a robust guarantee for our political stability, economic development, cultural prosperity, national unity, people's happiness, social tranquility, and national unification. This system has contributed Chinese wisdom and Chinese approaches to exploring better social systems for human modernization. We must always adhere to the fundamental positions, principles, and directions that run through it, and steadfastly uphold the fundamental, basic, and important systems proven by practice. Certainly, as human society continues to progress and socialism with Chinese characteristics continues to develop, this system cannot be perfect and unchanging. We must firmly hold the Four-Sphere Confidence, maintain our composure, forge ahead with determination, innovate boldly, and strive to uphold and improve the system of socialism with Chinese characteristics, modernize the national governance system and capacity, and work toward building China into a great modern socialist country that is prosperous, strong, democratic, culturally advanced, harmonious and beautiful, and realizing the rejuvenation of the Chinese nation.

3. Fully demonstrate the superiority of the socialist system in comprehensive deepening of reform

Engels believed: "[T]he final causes of all social changes and political revolutions are to be sought, not in men's brains, not in men's better insights into eternal truth and justice, but in changes in the modes of production and exchange."[1] The superiority or inferiority of a social system,

---

1   https://www.marxists.org/archive/marx/works/1880/soc-utop/ch03.htm.

whether it is practical and effective, cannot be judged simply by subjective opinion, but must be tested and proven by practice. As General Secretary Xi Jinping profoundly pointed out: "Practice is the best touchstone of the efficacy of our systems."[1] After more than 70 years of exploration and development, our country has formed a set of "workable, practical, and efficient" systems. The most concentrated expression of practical success is found in the two miracles summarized on a macro level in the Resolution of the Fourth Plenary Session of the 19th CPC Central Committee: the miracle of rapid economic development and the miracle of long-term social stability. These two miracles are the tangible demonstration of the power of the socialist system with Chinese characteristics. Throughout history, most economic recessions and social unrest can ultimately be traced back to the failure to establish effective national systems, governance structures, and governing capacity. China's two miracles shine in tandem, complementing one another, and together, they have built the monumental achievement of effective governance of China. This is extraordinarily rare in the history of civilization, and no unbiased observer can deny this fact. Many foreign observers believe that China's remarkable accomplishments since the reform and opening up "owe much to its unique institutional advantages and development model."[2] The creation of such miracles in China "stems from the political and economic system that underpins them," and this "provides the institutional foundation for the long-term peace and stability of the ruling party and the nation."[3] Socialism with Chinese characteristics in the New Era fully showcases the superiority of the socialist system in the 21st century.

The significant achievements marking the resurgence of world

1   Xi Jinping, *The Governance of China,* Beijing: Foreign Languages Press, 2020, vol. III, p. 149.
2   "China's Modernization of Its National Governance System and Capacity Offers New Insights for the World," *People's Daily*, November 2, 2019.
3   "China's Miracles Stem from the Strengths of Its National Systems," *China Discipline Inspection and Supervision Daily*, October 21, 2019.

socialism in the 21st century are the broader institutional advantages that socialism has gained over capitalism. One of the most concentrated and prominent manifestations of the crisis of capitalism at the beginning of the 21st century is the inefficiency and decline of the capitalist system. Francis Fukuyama's shift from the "end of history" thesis to the "decay of capitalist institutions" thesis demonstrates the decline and dysfunction of capitalist political systems and mechanisms; Thomas Piketty's "Capital in the Twenty-First Century" discusses the decline and dysfunction of the capitalist economic system; and many Western theorists have described in various ways the collapse and decline of the values of democracy, freedom, and equality, which have long been regarded as "eternal laws" of capitalism, discussing the value crisis, institutional crisis, ecological crisis, and overall systemic crisis of capitalism. Therefore, in the mid-21st century, socialism's broader institutional advantages over capitalism will be the most important symbol of the revitalization of world socialism. If in the past we explained the superiority of the socialist system more theoretically based on historical laws, then in the 21st century, we must practically demonstrate the superiority of the socialist system through economic efficiency and governance capabilities that surpass those of the capitalist system. This is the enormous historical contribution of socialism with Chinese characteristics in the New Era to the development of human society and institutional civilization.

The founders of scientific socialism, based on historical materialism and the analysis of the fundamental contradictions of capitalist society, believed that the future social system that would replace capitalism has its inherent advancements and superiority. However, the socialist systems in reality have all been established in countries with relatively underdeveloped economies and cultures. Compared to developed capitalism, how the superiority of the socialist system can be realized and demonstrated in reality has become a major historical issue that Marxists must face and explore in the more than a century since the Russian October Revolution within the "one world, two systems" global structure. This is also a difficult problem to solve. The Soviet model of socialism once demonstrated the strong superiority of the socialist system in reality, but it also had many drawbacks. The reforms in the later socialist countries were efforts to eliminate these drawbacks and better demonstrate the superiority of the socialist system. After the demise of the Soviet Union, socialist countries, represented by China, continued to explore and solve this historical issue.

Reform and opening up are essential requirements of scientific socialism, inherent to socialist modernization, the source of vitality for contemporary China's development and progress, and an important tool for the Party and the people to catch up with the times in great strides. Engels pointed out long ago that socialist society "is not anything immutable. Like all other social formations, it should be conceived in a state of constant flux and change."[1]

Reform and opening up are processes of self-improvement and development for the socialist system. The experiences and lessons of world socialism indicate that a dogmatic attitude and rigid thinking toward Marxism and socialism are unworkable; only through reform and opening up can Marxism and socialism be upheld and developed. "We must keep abreast of the times; that is the purpose of our reform."[2] Following socialist transformation, China established the basic socialist system, achieving a profound transformation from thousands of years of feudalism to a system of people's democracy and socialism. At the beginning of the reform and opening up, Deng Xiaoping said, "The socialist revolution has greatly narrowed the gap in economic development between China

---

1   https://www.marxists.org/archive/marx/works/1890/letters/90_08_21.htm.
2   Deng Xiaoping, *Selected Works of Deng Xiaoping*, Beijing: Foreign Languages Press, 1994, vol. III, p. 239.

and the advanced capitalist countries. Despite our errors, in the past three decades we have made progress on a scale which old China could not achieve in hundreds or even thousands of years."[1] This is the initial manifestation and strong proof of the great superiority of the socialist system in China. Reform is China's second revolution, which essentially is the self-improvement and development of the socialist system, invigorating it through reform and innovation, and more fully demonstrating its superiority.

Over the past 40 years, reform and opening up has profoundly reshaped China, the Chinese nation, the Chinese people, and the CPC. It has served as a powerful driving force and an essential path for China's development, the advancement of socialism, and the evolution of Marxism. This process has enabled China to make a historic leap—from being behind the times, to catching up with them, and eventually to playing a leading role. General Secretary Xi Jinping pointed out: "What has our Party relied on to inspire the people, unify their thinking, and pool their energy? What has it relied on to stimulate the creative spirit and dynamism of all our people? What has it relied on to achieve rapid economic and social development in China and gain a comparative advantage in competition with capitalism? It has relied on reform and opening up."[2] For socialism to gain an advantage over capitalism, it must implement reform and opening up. On the basis of adhering to the fundamental principles of scientific socialism, it must reform all systems and mechanisms that do not meet the requirements of the times and the development of practice, absorb and learn from all advanced management methods and business practices that reflect the laws governing modern socialized production from countries around the world, including developed capitalist countries, and forge a new

1   Deng Xiaoping, *Selected Works of Deng Xiaoping*, Beijing: Foreign Languages Press, 1995, vol. III, p. 176.
2   Xi Jinping, "Explanation of the Central Committee of the Communist Party of China's Decision on Several Major Issues concerning Comprehensively Deepening Reform," *People's Daily*, November 16, 2013.

path of socialist modernization.

Over the past 70-plus years since the founding of the People's Republic of China, the socialist system has evolved from its basic establishment to consolidation and development, from institutional reform to innovation and improvement. While achieving historic accomplishments, it has continuously demonstrated its superiority and great advantages. Through ongoing reform and innovation, the system of socialism with Chinese characteristics has proven to be more efficient and able to gain a comparative advantage in competition compared to the capitalist system. The remarkable achievements of socialism with Chinese characteristics over the 40-plus years of reform and opening up are compelling evidence of the superiority of the socialist system in the great practice of strengthening the country, ensuring the happiness of the people, and achieving national rejuvenation.

Examples include the advantages of the leadership of the CPC, the ability to unite all forces that can be united, strong mobilization capabilities, the ability to concentrate resources to accomplish major tasks, and the effective promotion of social fairness and justice, among others. In the New Era, the CPC adheres to comprehensive deepening of reform, building a systematic, scientific, and effectively operating institutional system to more fully leverage the superiority of our socialist system. Through comprehensive deepening of reform, the system of socialism with Chinese characteristics is continuously improved and developed, enhancing the capacity to govern the country effectively using the socialist system. Specifically, our economic system effectively promotes the unity of efficiency and fairness, the political system ensures that the people run the country, the cultural system continuously promotes the prosperity and flourishing of socialist culture, the social system comprehensively ensures and improves people's livelihoods, and the eco-civilization system effectively achieves harmony and sustainable development between humans and nature.

In summarizing the experiences of reform and opening up, the Fourth Plenary Session of the 19th CPC Central Committee scientifically summarized the 13 significant advantages of the system of socialism with Chinese characteristics, covering all fields and aspects from productive forces to production relations, from the economic base to the superstructure. These advantages fully reflect the superiority, resilience, vitality, and potential of the system of socialism with Chinese characteristics, forming a "cluster of institutional advantages" led by the overarching advantage of the leadership of the CPC, with each advantage playing its strengths and the overall advantage being prominently displayed. This fully embodies the essential requirements and unparalleled superiority of the socialist system, indicating that the Party's understanding of the "three major laws" has reached an unprecedented height. At the beginning of the reform and opening up, Deng Xiaoping confidently foresaw, "Our system will improve day by day, it will absorb progressive elements from all countries in the world and become the best system in the world."

In reflecting on the achievements of reform and opening up, General Secretary Xi Jinping emphasized, "Improving and developing the Chinese socialist system is key to China's progress. It provides a strong guarantee for unlocking and developing productivity, for releasing and enhancing social vitality, for maintaining the vigor of the Party and the country...."[1] The Fourth Plenary Session of the 19th CPC Central Committee systematically outlined 13 key advantages of this system, encompassing areas from the forces of production to production relations, and from the economic base to the superstructure. These strengths demonstrate the inherent resilience,

---

1   Xi Jinping, "Speech at a Ceremony Marking the 40th Anniversary of Reform and Opening Up," *People's Daily*, December 19, 2018.

vitality, and potential of socialism with Chinese characteristics, presenting a "cluster of institutional advantages," led by the overarching advantage of CPC leadership, where each element complements the others, showcasing the system's unique benefits. This highlights the fundamental nature and unparalleled strengths of socialism, showing that the Party's grasp of the "three major laws" has reached new heights. As Deng Xiaoping predicted at the outset of reform and opening up, "Our system will improve more and more with the passage of time. By absorbing the progressive elements of other countries, it will become the best in the world."[1]

Today, the system of socialism with Chinese characteristics demonstrates strong vitality and continues to improve and develop. As Xi Jinping pointed out: "We need to rely on constant reform and innovation to ensure that socialism with Chinese characteristics is more efficient than capitalism in emancipating and developing the productive forces, emancipating and boosting social dynamism, and promoting individuals' well-rounded development. We also need to ensure that it sparks greater enthusiasm, initiative and creativity among all of our people, creates more favorable conditions for achieving social progress and gives us a competitive edge, thus giving full expression to the superiority of socialism with Chinese characteristics."[2]

Institutional advantage is the greatest advantage of a nation, and institutional competition is the most fundamental competition between countries. Stability in the system ensures the stability of the country, and strong governance ensures a strong nation. The world today is undergoing profound changes of a kind unseen in a century, making global institutional competition more complex and intense. There is a stark contrast between effective governance of China and the chaos in the West.

---

1 Deng Xiaoping, *Selected Works of Deng Xiaoping,* Beijing: Foreign Languages Press, 1995, vol. II, p. 335.
2 *Documents Produced since the 18th CPC National Congress,* Beijing: Central Party Literature Publishing House, 2014, vol. I, p. 550.

Some Western countries, including the United States, are unwilling to see the rise and strength of China, viewing our national system and governance system as challenges and alternatives to the Western institutional model. They spare no effort in distorting, slandering, containing, and suppressing our development path and social system. For instance, they label the system of socialism with Chinese characteristics as "capitalist socialism," "state capitalism," or "new bureaucratic capitalism," and malign China's rise and development as "new imperialism." They distort successful practices like the BRI as "new colonialism" and initiate trade wars to suppress our development of high-tech industries. Their fundamental aim is to undermine the leadership of the CPC and our socialist system, thereby hindering or interrupting the historical process of the rejuvenation of the Chinese nation. In response, we must remain clear-headed, maintain strategic resolve, and never lose our stance or get disoriented. At any time and under any circumstances, we must firmly uphold confidence in the path, theory, system, and culture of socialism with Chinese characteristics. "As socialism progresses, our institutions will undoubtedly mature, the strengths of our system will become self-evident, and our development path will assuredly become wider."[1] The increasingly mature and well-established system of socialism with Chinese characteristics not only provides institutional guarantees for realizing the rejuvenation of the Chinese nation but also offers new choices for some other countries in building their social systems, continuously enriching and innovating the civilization of human institutions.

---

1   Xi Jinping, *The Governance of China*, Beijing: Foreign Languages Press, 2018, vol. I, p. 24.

III. The Guiding Banner and Mainstay of 21st-Century World Socialism

1. New characteristics of world socialism development at the beginning of the 21st century

After the dramatic changes in Eastern Europe during the 1980s and 1990s, the development of world socialism fell into a significant decline. However, in just over 20 years—an instant in historical terms—the hands of history have made a "miraculous reversal." At the beginning of the 21st century, world capitalism plunged into a deep crisis, one from which it has yet to extricate itself. The longstanding "failure of communism," "obsolescence of socialism," and "decline of the Communist Party" narratives, while not entirely silenced, have lost much of their resonance and are now little more than outdated refrains. History always finds a way to carve a path for its inevitabilities amidst various contingencies. It is now justifiable to assert that capitalism is beginning to decline while socialism is starting to emerge from its trough. Compared to the period of the Soviet Union's demise and the Eastern European upheavals 30 years ago, the world has indeed undergone significant changes. People must now look at the world with fresh perspectives, re-examining and reassessing the global landscape, developments and changes, major events, and social systems. Against this backdrop, the fate of socialism and capitalism has once again become a fervent and serious topic of discussion.

Over the more than 30 years since the Eastern European upheavals, the surviving Communist parties worldwide have undergone crises, reorganization, renewal, and development. The Eastern European changes had an unprecedented impact on Communist organizations and the communist movement globally. On one hand, many Communist organizations were significantly affected, with some dissolving and disappearing, others changing their names and abandoning socialism, transforming into social-democratic types of parties, or becoming marginal radical groups with little influence on domestic politics. On the other hand, many Communist organizations tenaciously persisted in adversity, upholding the goals of socialism and communism, exploring theories and strategies suited to their national conditions, and achieving varying degrees of success, thus laying the foundation for the continuation of the international communist movement. Today, these Communist organizations that have persisted in their efforts have not vanished as some predicted. From defending their survival to seeking new achievements, they have propelled the development of the international communist movement in the 21st century.

According to relevant statistics, there are currently around 130 Communist or Marxist-oriented parties in over 100 countries worldwide. The total number of Communist Party members in existing socialist countries is approximately 99.5 million. Of these, the CPC has over 90 million members. Other socialist countries with ruling Communist parties include Vietnam, with about 4.5 million members in the Communist Party of Vietnam; the DPRK, with over 4 million members in the Workers' Party of Korea; Cuba, with about 1 million members in the Communist Party of Cuba; and Laos, with over 100,000 members in the Lao People's Revolutionary Party. Beyond these socialist countries, there are roughly 120 Communist organizations in other parts of the world, collectively having around 8.5 million members. Altogether, there are approximately 103 million Communist Party members worldwide. Among them, over 30 parties have more than 10,000 members, and nearly 30 parties are either currently in power, participating in government, or have recently done so.

Communist parties in various countries, operating under different social environments, national conditions, and social systems, explore diverse paths for revolution and development, each with its unique characteristics and achievements. However, it is undeniable that these Communist parties remain influential forces among modern political parties, significantly impacting political and economic landscapes on the global stage. They are also the main drivers of new developments in 21st-century world socialism.

Currently, the competition between the two major social systems is showing new features and trends, characterized by four main aspects:

1. The global surge of movements protesting and seeking to reform capitalism.

2. The simultaneous development of the trend toward the localization of Marxism and the strengthening of international cooperation.

3. The increasing role of socialism with Chinese characteristics as the banner of world socialism, with its leading and demonstrative effects becoming more evident.

4. The intensifying competition and struggle between a world capitalism experiencing a new downturn and a world socialism entering a new period of ascendance.

These new features and trends provide fresh perspectives and content for in-depth research into the theory and practice of 21st-century world socialism. For the development of 21st-century world socialism theory and practice, we must focus on the present while keeping an eye on the future. It is essential to deeply study the new characteristics and trends of contemporary socialism, the new changes and features of contemporary capitalism, the new content and methods of competition and cooperation between the two systems, the interconnections between contemporary capitalism, contemporary socialism, and socialism with Chinese characteristics, the overall situation and regular trends of the 21st-century world socialist movement, the relationship between socialism with Chinese characteristics and world socialism, and the pathways, methods, and significant implications of socialism with Chinese characteristics in leading the development of world socialism.

2. Socialism with Chinese characteristics as the mainstay of world socialism

Socialism with Chinese characteristics has become the most prominent highlight in the development of world socialism, serving as a significant reference and pillar. The rise of socialist China in the East is fully demonstrating the superiority, appeal, and attractiveness of socialism. China must fully understand and address the relationship between "keeping a low profile" and "making some contributions." Currently, the most important task is to focus on handling our own affairs well, continuously strengthening our composite national power, constantly improving people's lives, and persistently building a socialism that is superior to capitalism. This will lay a more solid foundation for us to gain initiative, advantages, and future success. Deng Xiaoping once confidently predicted that by the mid-21st century, China would have basically achieved modernization: "At that time the strength of China and its role in the world will be quite different. We shall be able to make greater contributions to mankind."[1]

Today, socialist China, still accounting for one-fifth of the world's population, has seen a significant enhancement in its composite national power. Now is the time for Chinese Communists to strive to realize the foresight and expectations of Deng Xiaoping. We must clearly recognize that "for a considerable period, the primary stage of socialism must continue to cooperate and struggle with the more developed productive forces of capitalism. We must earnestly learn from and draw upon the beneficial achievements of capitalist civilizations. We must also face the

---

1 Deng Xiaoping, *Selected Works of Deng Xiaoping*, Beijing: Foreign Languages Press, 1994, vol. III, p. 146.

reality that our socialist development may be compared with and criticized based on the strengths of Western developed countries. We must have strong strategic confidence, resolutely resist various erroneous proposals to abandon socialism, and consciously correct misconceptions that exceed our developmental stage."[1]

We can confidently assert that as long as socialism with Chinese characteristics continues to develop, the revitalization of world socialism will not be an empty talk.

The political report of the 19th CPC National Congress clearly elucidates the significant impact of socialism with Chinese characteristics on the development of world socialism. The entry of socialism with Chinese characteristics into the New Era holds great significance in the history of the development of the People's Republic of China, the history of the development of the Chinese nation, the history of the development of world socialism, and the history of the development of human society.

The New Era of socialism with Chinese characteristics has established a closer and more explicit connection with world socialism, signifying that scientific socialism in 21st-century China is brimming with vitality and prominently raising the great banner of socialism with Chinese characteristics on the global stage. This indicates that as China increasingly moves to the center stage of the world, and as its composite national power and international influence continue to grow and gradually lead, socialism with Chinese characteristics is no longer confined to China's own affairs. Instead, it stands as the most important and promising part of 21st-century world socialism, exerting significant influence and making original contributions. It is a great endeavor that provides a new choice for humanity's exploration of a better social system and contributes a Chinese

---

1   *Documents Produced since the 18th CPC National Congress*, Beijing: Central Party Literature Publishing House, 2014, vol. I, p. 117.

approach.

In the 21st century, as China offers its approaches for humanity's quest for a better social system, the cause of socialism with Chinese characteristics, led by the CPC, will increasingly impact the world. To a certain extent, socialism with Chinese characteristics represents the future of world socialism. This embodies the confidence in the path, theory, system, and culture of socialism with Chinese characteristics, and reflects the CPC's historical responsibility toward the cause of socialism and the development and progress of human advancement. According to the grand blueprint outlined by the Party's 19th National Congress, by the mid-21st century, China will have been built into a great modern socialist country that is prosperous, strong, democratic, culturally advanced, harmonious and beautiful, becoming a leading country in terms of composite national power and international influence. The Chinese nation will stand tall among the nations of the world with a more vigorous posture. With its great achievements in comprehensive development, the New Era of socialism with Chinese characteristics will undoubtedly become the mainstay of world socialism's revitalization.

IV. The Major Contributions of the CPC to the World Socialist Movement over the Past Century

The history of world socialism development is primarily a history of generations of Communists overcoming numerous difficulties, enduring tortuous tests, engaging in heroic and tenacious struggles, and achieving remarkable successes worldwide. It is also a history of Marxism and scientific socialism continuously enriching and developing through practice. The century-long development history of the CPC is an integral part of the international communist movement and the world socialist movement, holding a significant position and making substantial contributions. History eloquently proves that the CPC is a staunch believer and faithful practitioner of Marxism and scientific socialism, an active promoter and conscientious pioneer of the international communist movement and the world socialist movement, and a powerful leader and significant contributor to the innovative development of Marxism and world socialism in the 21st century.

Against the backdrop of the international communist movement, the CPC was gloriously born from the fusion of Marxism-Leninism with the Chinese workers' movement and grew stronger through persistent struggle. The sacred mission of the CPC is to seek happiness for the Chinese people and rejuvenation for the Chinese nation. Over the past century, the CPC has led the people in the Chinese revolution, development, and reform, guiding them to create one miracle after another. The CPC itself has become a large and powerful party globally, a mainstay of the world socialist movement. In its century-long development history, major milestones such as the founding of the CPC, the establishment of the People's Republic of China, the promotion of reform and opening up, and the pursuit of the cause of socialism with Chinese characteristics, the completion of the building of a moderately prosperous society in all respects, and the development of a great modern socialist country in all respects have all been landmark events for both Chinese socialism and world socialism. The century-long struggle led by the CPC has continually revitalized Marxism and scientific socialism, writing a magnificent Chinese chapter in the history of world socialism's development.

1. The Chinese revolution led by the CPC as an integral part of the international communist movement

The international communist movement is a historical activity led by Marxist parties, in which the proletariat and the working people worldwide oppose capitalism and all exploitative systems, carry out socialist revolution, development, and reform, establish a sound the socialist system, and ultimately achieve the goal of communism and the liberation of all humanity. The proletarian revolution is the most extensive, profound social transformation in human history, characterized by complexities, difficulties, and long-term struggles distinct from previous revolutions. The Chinese revolution led by the CPC represents the creative and concrete unfolding of the international communist movement in China, a large Eastern country with relatively underdeveloped economy and culture. It has distinct Chinese characteristics, forming a unique path of revolution.

From its inception, the CPC set its program to strive for socialism and communism, clearly inscribing it on its banner. The publication of the *Communist Manifesto* in 1848 marked the "magnificent sunrise" of scientific socialism, driving the development of world socialism in practice and profoundly altering the course of human history. The victory of the October Revolution in the early 20th century signified the transformation of scientific socialism from an ideal into a reality, facilitating the widespread dissemination of Marxism worldwide.

In China, a group of progressive intellectuals with early communist leanings began to adopt Marxism as a tool for understanding the fate of the nation and transforming society. Li Dazhao, a pioneer of the Chinese communist movement, pointed out that the October Revolution was a "revolution based on socialism," marking the beginning of a "new epoch" in human history, predicting that the future world "will be a world under the red flag."[1] In a series of writings, he systematically introduced and disseminated the fundamental principles of Marxist historical materialism, political economy, and scientific socialism. Cai Hesen, an

---

1 Li Dazhao, *Selected Works of Li Dazhao*, Beijing, People's Publishing House, 1999, vol. II, p. 217.

early important leader of the CPC, also remarked at the time that China's future transformation would "completely apply the principles and methods of socialism."[1] With the spread of Marxism-Leninism in China and its integration with the Chinese workers' movement, the CPC emerged, adopting the realization of communism as its highest ideal and ultimate goal. As Mao Zedong noted in "On the People's Democratic Dictatorship," "The salvoes of the October Revolution brought us Marxism-Leninism. The October Revolution helped," and "They [The Chinese] found Marxism-Leninism, the universally applicable truth, and the face of China began to change."[2] After the founding of the CPC, the Chinese revolution had a strong leadership core and a correct direction for advancement, the Chinese people had a backbone, and China's destiny had a bright developmental prospect. From then on, China's revolutionary movement also became an important part of the international communist movement.

The Chinese revolution led by the CPC was an anti-imperialist, anti-feudal new-democratic revolution, holding a significant position in the international communist movement. In semi-colonial, semi-feudal modern China, the primary social contradictions were those between the Chinese nation and imperialism, and between the people and feudalism. This determined that the Chinese people and the Chinese nation had to overthrow the rule of imperialism and feudalism, achieve national independence and the liberation of the people, and realize national prosperity and people's wealth. Fulfilling these two historical tasks and achieving the rejuvenation of the Chinese nation became the great dream unremittingly pursued by the Chinese people since modern times.

The CPC creatively applied the fundamental tenets of Marxism-Leninism to China, a large Eastern country with an underdeveloped

---

1   Cai Hesen, *Selected Works of Cai Hesen,* Beijing, People's Publishing House, 1980, p. 57.
2   Mao Zedong, *Selected Works of Mao Tse-tung,* Beijing, Foreign Languages Press, 1967, vol. II, p. 413.

economy and culture. They explored a new revolutionary path with Chinese characteristics, which involved surrounding the cities from the countryside, establishing independent regimes of the workers and the peasants by armed force, and eventually seizing national power. The CPC led the Chinese people in the country through 28 years of arduous struggle, establishing a state power of people's democratic dictatorship through the new-democratic revolution. This created the political preconditions for embarking on the socialist road and pioneered a diversified model of proletarian revolution in the history of the international communist movement. This greatly enriched and developed Marxism-Leninism, not only achieving the long-cherished dream of the Chinese nation for national independence and people's liberation, initiating a new epoch in Chinese history, but also becoming the most significant historical event in the international communist movement since the victory of the October Revolution. It was another great victory for the international proletarian struggle.

During the period of the new-democratic revolution, the founding of the CPC and its leadership of the Chinese revolution received guidance and assistance from the Communist International, which, to some extent, accelerated the process of the Chinese revolution. For example, when the CPC was exploring and formulating a revolutionary program suited to China's national conditions, Lenin's theory on national and colonial issues, and the Supplementary Theses on National and Colonial Questions formulated at the Second Congress of the Communist International played an important guiding role. From January 21 to February 2, 1922, during the First Congress of Communist and Revolutionary Organizations of the Far East convened by the Communist International, Lenin, while ill, met with the Chinese delegation. He hoped for cooperation between the CPC and the Kuomintang, urging the Chinese working class and revolutionary people to strengthen their unity and push the Chinese revolution forward. Similarly, in September 1938, during the Sixth Plenary Session of the Sixth CPC Central Committee, the process of establishing Mao Zedong's leadership position in the Party was positively influenced by the decisions conveyed by Wang Jiaxiang, the CPC representative to the Communist International. However, the guidance and assistance from the Communist International included both successful experiences and lessons from failures. The CPC combined the fundamental tenets of Marxism with the concrete realities of the Chinese revolution, pioneering the path of the new-democratic revolution, and forming and establishing Mao Zedong Thought. This was gradually advanced and realized through struggles against some erroneous guidance from the Communist International on the Chinese revolution. "The tendency to dogmatize Marxism and to sanctify the resolutions of the Communist International and the experiences of the Soviet Union almost led the Chinese revolution to the brink of disaster."[1]

The victory of the Chinese revolution led by the CPC is another successful example in the history of the international communist movement following the October Revolution. This victory strengthened the forces of the world's people's democratic front and the socialist camp, broke through the imperialist eastern front, struck a blow to the entire capitalist world, and weakened the imperialist global system. It fundamentally shifted the global balance of political power in favor of the international communist movement, significantly advancing its development. The founding of the People's Republic of China completely ended the history of semi-colonial and semi-feudal society in old China, achieving a great transformation from thousands of years of feudal autocratic politics to people's democracy. This change drastically altered the global balance of power between

---

1 *Annotated Edition of the Resolution on Certain Historical Issues of the Party since the Founding of the People's Republic of China*, Beijing: People's Publishing House, 1983, p. 47.

socialism and capitalism, bolstered the forces of world peace, democracy, and socialism, and greatly inspired and propelled the liberation struggles of colonized and semi-colonized peoples worldwide. It strongly facilitated the further disintegration of the imperialist colonial system, opening up broader avenues for the cause of liberation for the world's proletariat and all oppressed peoples.

2. The significant impact of the CPC's leadership in socialist development and reform on the development of world socialism

Lenin pointed out: "All nations will arrive at socialism—this is inevitable, hut all will do so in not exactly the same way, each will contribute something of its own to some form of democracy, to some variety of the dictatorship of the proletariat, to the varying rate of socialist transformations in the different aspects of social life."[1] Based on the victory of the new-democratic revolution, the founding of the People's Republic of China and its road toward socialism marked the development of scientific socialism from practice in a single country to practice in multiple countries, bringing the international communist movement into a new stage of development. Despite the dramatic changes in the Soviet Union and Eastern European countries in the late 1980s and early 1990s, the CPC has consistently adhered to the fundamental line of the primary stage of socialism. It has continued to advance the cause of reform, opening up, and socialist modernization, continuously pioneering and expanding the road of socialism with Chinese characteristics. Reform and opening up has made China a bright banner for the development and development of socialist countries and a strong bastion for the continued forward movement of the international communist and world socialist movements. As General Secretary Xi Jinping pointed out, "If socialism had not achieved today's

---

1   https://www.marxists.org/archive/lenin/works/1916/carimarx/6.htm.

success in China, if the leadership of the CPC and our socialist system had collapsed in the domino-like changes with the demise of the Soviet Union, the collapse of the Communist Party of the Soviet Union, and the dramatic changes in Eastern Europe, or had failed for other reasons, then the practice of socialism might have been wandering in the dark for a long time again, like Marx said, as a specter haunting the world."[1]

In the development and reform of socialism, the CPC has pioneered the socialist revolutionary path, the socialist development path, and the path of socialism with Chinese characteristics. These paths represent a great creative effort to combine the fundamental tenets of Marxism with China's specific realities, resulting in two major theoretical achievements of Chinese Marxism: Mao Zedong Thought and the theoretical system of socialism with Chinese characteristics. These achievements have continuously propelled the development of the international communist movement and the world socialist movement through practice.

The CPC creatively undertook socialist transformation, establishing a socialist system where the people run the country. the People's Republic of China transitioned from New Democracy to a socialist society, successfully achieving the most extensive and profound social transformation in Chinese history. Among these transformations, the socialist transformation of capitalist industry and commerce realized the peaceful redemption of the bourgeoisie, a concept once envisioned by Marx and Lenin. The formulation and implementation of the First Five-Year Plan led to the establishment of foundational industries necessary for national industrialization, which were previously very weak.

In the mid-20th century, when socialist forces were weaker than the Western capitalist forces, China formed a powerful socialist camp with the

---

1   Xi Jinping, *Stay True to the Original Aspirations and Founding Mission of the Party,* Beijing: Party Building Books Publishing House and Central Party Literature Publishing House, 2019, pp. 298–299.

Soviet Union and other people's democracies, significantly strengthening the international communist and world socialist forces. This alliance deeply changed the balance of international political power and the global landscape.

The CPC's exploration of a socialist development path suited to China's national conditions has provided a valuable reference model for the development of other socialist countries. Upon the basic completion of socialist transformation, the Party led the people to embark on comprehensive, large-scale socialist development. Mao Zedong's "On the Ten Major Relationships" emphasized learning from the Soviet Union while exploring an independent path to socialism. The Eighth CPC National Congress explicitly proposed to focus on developing social productive forces, achieving national industrialization, and gradually meeting the people's growing material and cultural needs.

In exploring the path of socialist development, the CPC proposed the need to correctly distinguish and handle two different types of social contradictions in socialist society, making the correct handling of contradictions among the people the theme of national political life. The Party also proposed shifting the focus of Party and state work to technological revolution and socialist development. During the Sino-Soviet split, the CPC effectively safeguarded the Party's independence and the country's sovereignty, upheld the fundamental principles of inter-party relations within the international communist movement, and promoted the healthy development of the international communist cause. The CPC actively supported the liberation struggles and just causes of oppressed nations, earning admiration and respect from around the world and solidifying unity and cooperation among communist parties and socialist countries.

During this period, although our Party experienced a series of twists and turns and hardships, including serious mistakes such as the Great Leap Forward and the People's Commune Movement, it withstood enormous international and domestic pressures. Despite these challenges, significant achievements were made in various aspects of development. An independent and relatively complete industrial system and national economic system were established. The material and cultural living standards of the people gradually improved, and significant progress was made in science, education, culture, and health. This solidified and developed the socialist regime of the People's Republic of China, laying the foundation for the comprehensive development of China's economy and society, and made important contributions to the development of world socialism and the progress of humanity.

The CPC has pioneered, adhered to, and developed socialism with Chinese characteristics, advancing the cause of reform, opening up, and the modernization of socialism with Chinese characteristics, greatly promoting the development of world socialism. Direction determines the path, and the path determines destiny. Whether in revolution, development, or reform, the path is the most fundamental issue. The CPC has steadfastly followed the path of socialism with Chinese characteristics, continuously expanding this path with the times. The CPC stands with the people, upholds the principle of serving the public and governing for the people, and practices the fundamental purpose of serving the people wholeheartedly. The basic line of the primary stage of socialism is the lifeline of the nation and the line for the happiness of the people. The CPC takes economic development as the central task to rejuvenate the country, upholding the Four Cardinal Principles as the foundation of the country, and taking reform and opening up as the path to strengthening the country. Reform and opening up is the crucial choice that determines the fate of contemporary China and is the important tool for the Party and the people to make great strides to catch up with the times. We will take neither the old path of being closed and inflexible, nor the erroneous path of abandoning socialism. The theory and practice of reform, opening up, and socialist modernization development clearly demonstrate that the path of socialism with Chinese characteristics is the only way to achieve socialist modernization and create a better life for the people.

The CPC has actively adjusted its policies and strategies in party diplomacy, adhering to the four principles of independence, complete equality, mutual respect, and non-interference in each other's internal affairs. It avoids disputes and supports fraternal parties in all countries to follow their own paths, restoring long-disrupted party-to-party relations with many communist parties. With the continuous enhancement of comprehensive national strength and international status, China's image as a responsible major country on the international stage is increasingly established.

The path of socialism with Chinese characteristics adheres to the fundamental principles of scientific socialism while distinctly reflecting Chinese characteristics. It embodies the general laws of building and consolidating socialism in a country with relatively underdeveloped economy and culture. The successful development of socialism with Chinese characteristics has provided valuable experiences for the global development of socialism. Despite the setbacks and twists in the development of the world socialist movement, the laws and overall trends of the development of human society revealed by Marxist science have not changed and will not change. During the significant historical juncture when dramatic changes occurred in the Soviet Union and Eastern Europe, leading to a downturn in the global socialist movement and a severe weakening of socialist forces worldwide, our Party overcame various interferences and obstacles, resolutely advanced reform and opening up, and continuously increased our composite national strength. This created a local upsurge amid the general downturn of global socialism, defending and revitalizing world socialism. As Deng Xiaoping pointed out, "[I] f China holds its ground and attains its goals for development, that will demonstrate the superiority of socialism.... As long as China doesn't collapse, one fifth of the world's population will be upholding socialism."[1]

After the outbreak of the global financial crisis in 2008, socialism with Chinese characteristics showcased its remarkable vitality and substantial advantages in addressing the crisis, effectively refuting the "end of socialism" and "decline of socialism" theories, as well as the "nihilism" surrounding communism that emerged following the drastic changes in Eastern Europe. While the global socialist movement, in general, remained in a downturn after this severe crisis, the significant achievements in the development of socialism with Chinese characteristics have become a pillar for the resurgence of the socialist movement worldwide. In addition, the Party's leadership in reform, opening up, and socialist modernization has accumulated a wealth of historical experience, offering valuable lessons and deep insights for developing countries on their paths to modernization. General Secretary Xi Jinping succinctly summarized this by stating: "The major success of socialism with Chinese characteristics in China demonstrates that socialism has not perished and will not perish; it is brimming with vitality and vigor."

3. The significant contributions of the CPC to the development of world socialism

Socialism with Chinese characteristics has entered the New Era, marking a new historical juncture for our country's development. "It

---

1 Deng Xiaoping, *Selected Works of Deng Xiaoping*, Beijing: Foreign Languages Press, 1994, vol. III, pp. 310–311.

means that scientific socialism is full of vitality in 21st century China, and that the banner of socialism with Chinese characteristics is now flying high and proud for all to see."[1] The New Era of socialism with Chinese characteristics has successfully addressed historic issues in the development of socialism, creating a new phase for the development of world socialism. It has become the guiding banner for 21st-century scientific socialism, the mainstay of world socialist development, and the leading force in promoting the progress and development of human society.

General Secretary Xi Jinping pointed out, "Due to the continuous success of socialism with Chinese characteristics, the bleak situation of world socialism after the end of the Cold War has been largely reversed. The passive position of socialism in its competition with capitalism has been significantly altered, and the superiority of socialism has been greatly demonstrated."[2] In the New Era, socialism with Chinese characteristics has developed even closer and more explicit connections with world socialism.

From the perspective of theoretical innovation and contribution, Xi Jinping Thought on Socialism with Chinese Characteristics for a New Era represents the scientific theoretical form of Marxism in the 21st century. It is the Marxism of contemporary China and the Marxism of the 21st century. Since the 18th CPC National Congress, under the leadership of General Secretary Xi Jinping, the Party has integrated the fundamental tenets of Marxism with the specific realities of contemporary China, thus establishing Xi Jinping Thought on Socialism with Chinese Characteristics for a New Era. This scientific theoretical system adheres to the Marxist stand, viewpoint and method, upholds the fundamental principles of scientific socialism, and scientifically summarizes the experiences and

1   Xi Jinping, *Secure a Decisive Victory in Building a Moderately Prosperous Society in All Respects and Strive for the Great Success of Socialism with Chinese Characteristics for a New Era: Report at the 19th National Congress of the Communist Party of China*, Beijing: People's Publishing House, 2017, p. 10.
2   Xi Jinping, *Stay True to the Original Aspirations and Founding Mission of the Party*, Beijing: Party Building Books Publishing House and Central Party Literature Publishing House, p. 331.

lessons of the world socialist movement. It enriches and develops Marxism with new theoretical content. This theoretical system is imbued with a firm belief in socialism and communism, making significant original contributions to the building of a human community with a shared future and safeguarding common human interests and values. It has generated broad appeal and influence worldwide, gaining widespread recognition and high praise.

Some believe that this thought has greatly altered the global balance of power between Marxism and anti-Marxism, socialism and capitalism, and that a new type of Marxist theory is taking shape. Others regard it as a landmark theoretical achievement amid the major changes of a kind unseen in a century, symbolizing the "rise of the East and the decline of the West." Furthermore, some view this thought as being rich with a century's worth of Chinese practice and exploration, providing valuable lessons and insights for the entire world.

Practice has fully proven that Xi Jinping Thought on Socialism with Chinese Characteristics for a New Era is not only the latest achievement of the adaptation of Marxism to the Chinese context and the scientific theory guiding the Chinese nation's rejuvenation, but also the latest theoretical form of 21st-century Marxism, making original contributions to the development of Marxism.

From the perspective of institutional contributions, socialism with Chinese characteristics in the New Era has fully demonstrated the superiority of the socialist system. A landmark achievement of 21st-century world socialism is that socialism has gained broader institutional advantages compared to capitalism. A prominent feature of current capitalist development is the inefficacy and decline of its various systems. As socialism with Chinese characteristics enters the New Era, the CPC has promoted comprehensively deepened reform, continuously improved and developed the socialist system with Chinese characteristics, and promoted the modernization of the national governance system and capacity. This has created unique governance and institutional advantages, while also accumulating rich experience on how to govern a socialist society. China's institutional innovations provide other developing countries with a valuable new option for system-building and contribute Chinese wisdom and approaches to the development of human institutional civilization. The achievements of building the socialist system with Chinese characteristics are not only China's but also the world's; they provide a safeguard for China's socialist modernization and national rejuvenation, while also contributing to human progress and the development of world civilization. Today, under the strong leadership of the CPC Central Committee with General Secretary Xi Jinping at its core, the entire Party and the Chinese people will undoubtedly write a brilliant chapter in the cause of socialism with Chinese characteristics in the New Era and usher in a new phase of world socialism in the 21st century.

From the perspective of human development, socialism with Chinese characteristics in the New Era has contributed Chinese approaches to the issues of human social development. The concept and practice of building a human community with a shared future is an important component of Xi Jinping Thought on Socialism with Chinese Characteristics for a New Era. Faced with profound changes of a kind unseen in a century, the CPC has scientifically understood and grasped the future of humanity, systematically addressing major questions that are crucial to human destiny: "What kind of world should we build, and how should we build it?" and "What is happening to the world, and where is it headed?" This represents a major innovation in the theory and practice of scientific socialism and embodies the Marxist value goal of human liberation and the grand ideal of achieving communism under the conditions of the New Era.

In his political report to the 19th National Congress of the CPC, General Secretary Xi Jinping pointed out: "The Communist Party of China strives for both the wellbeing of the Chinese people and human progress. To make new and greater contributions for mankind is our Party's abiding mission."[1] Based on the tremendous achievements and rich experience of the past century, the CPC will undoubtedly, from this new historical starting point, make new and greater contributions to the revival of world socialism and to the cause of human development and progress.

The tremendous success of socialism with Chinese characteristics in the New Era is a significant event in the history of world socialism and even in world history in the early 21st century. As history progresses and time passes, the profound global significance of socialism with Chinese characteristics will become increasingly evident. General Secretary Xi Jinping clearly summarized this significance: socialism with Chinese characteristics "placed the tenets of socialism, which go back 500 years, on a highly realistic, feasible, and correct path in the world's most populous country, allowing scientific socialism to display renewed vigor in the 21st century."[2] China must seize opportunities, employ great power wisdom, take on responsibilities, and fulfill its historical duties, making greater historical contributions.

In correctly understanding and evaluating the global significance of socialism with Chinese characteristics, several key points need to be emphasized.

First, it is essential to objectively and fully recognize that China has become the largest and most solid stronghold of world socialism. Socialism with Chinese characteristics has become the banner and weather vane of world socialism, serving as a new growth point for 21st-century global

1 *Documents from the 19th CPC National Congress*, Beijing: People's Publishing House, 2017, p. 46.
2 *Documents Produced since the 18th CPC National Congress*, Beijing: People's Publishing House, 2018, vol. II, p. 343.

socialism. This is an indisputable historical fact, regardless of whether people subjectively acknowledge it or not. We cannot avoid this reality; otherwise, we risk missing a once-in-a-lifetime historical opportunity, becoming laggards of history, or even being seen as obstructing historical development and the progress of civilization. The process of the rejuvenation of the Chinese nation is inseparable from the revitalization of world socialism.

Second, it must be acknowledged that China has undeniably become the banner and mainstay of world socialism in the early 21st century. China's path is fundamentally different from the past practices of the Soviet Union, which pursued a form of great-power hegemony, viewing itself as the "dominant" force in the international communist movement. It is entirely wrong to equate the two.

Third, China's greatest contribution to world socialism is simply doing its own work well. This was true in the past, is true in the present, and will remain true in the future. However, "not claiming leadership" does not mean "doing nothing." In today's world, where China has become a "waking lion" and a responsible global power, with composite national strength and influence that far surpasses the past, we must seriously study how to correctly balance "keeping a low profile" with "taking proactive action." We must carefully study the strategy, content, pathways, and methods by which China will contribute to the development of world socialism in the 21st century.

Fourth, we must thoroughly study the relationship between socialism with Chinese characteristics and world socialism, and examine the global significance of the theoretical system, path, and institutions of socialism with Chinese characteristics. We should summarize the important experiences and insights that most directly reflect the laws governing human social development, the laws governing socialist development, and the laws governing Communist Party governance, contributing even more to the theoretical and practical innovations of world socialism.

In the 21st century, a period of great change, transformation, and adjustment in the world, the CPC Central Committee, with General Secretary Xi Jinping at its core, has grasped the pulse of the times, aligned with global trends, and correctly understood the patterns and trends of development. By creatively maintaining the organic unity of the essence and characteristics of the times, the Party has led the Chinese people into the New Era of socialism with Chinese characteristics during a historic period of unprecedented global changes and intense competition between socialist and capitalist systems. This leadership has opened up a new phase in the development of scientific socialism, raising high the banner of socialism with Chinese characteristics and achieving great successes.

In 1893, Engels concluded the preface to the Italian edition of the *Communist Manifesto* with this hope and vision: "Will Italy give us the new Dante, who will mark the hour of birth of this new, proletarian era?"[1] Engels was looking forward to the new development of the Italian socialist movement in the early 20th century. The actual course of history was that, in the early 20th century, the Bolshevik Party and the Russian people, under Lenin's leadership, used the great victory of the October Revolution to transform socialism from theory and movement into a real, living system, thereby opening up a new era in the development of world socialism. Similarly, in the early 21st century, the CPC Central Committee, with General Secretary Xi Jinping at its core, has led the Chinese people in opening the New Era of socialism with Chinese characteristics, once again proving the superiority of socialism over capitalism and establishing China as the clear leading force and mainstay of global socialism. Today, we have every reason to believe and expect that the historical significance

---

1   https://publications.cpiml.net/book/communist-manifesto-prefaces/preface-to-the-1893-italian-edition.

of socialism with Chinese characteristics in the New Era, like the October Revolution in the early 20th century, will usher in a new phase of world socialist revitalization and a new stage of major development for 21st-century Marxism and scientific socialism.

Part Six

Pioneer a New Path to Modernization for Humanity

Achieving modernization has been the main theme pursued tirelessly by the Chinese nation to restore its former glory since modern times. It has been the central theme of the continuous struggle and determined progress of the Chinese people under the leadership of the CPC over the past century, and the consistent theme of socialist development and reform in the People's Republic of China for over 70 years.

On the journey toward modernization, generations of Chinese Communists have tirelessly sought and continuously fought. When the People's Republic of China was established, the CPC inherited a nation riddled with numerous problems and in urgent need of rebuilding from the Kuomintang government. In response to the daunting challenge of "seizing state power is easy, governing it is difficult," Mao Zedong confidently remarked, "Though seizing state power was not easy, governing it is not without solutions." The CPC, determined to lift the country from poverty and backwardness, directed its efforts toward industrialization and modernization.

After the founding of the People's Republic of China, the CPC embarked on the arduous path of socialist modernization, laying the fundamental political, institutional, and material foundations for the successful road to modernization initiated by the reform and opening up. They created a secure and stable domestic and international environments and provided valuable experiences and lessons. At the First Session of the First National People's Congress in 1954, Mao Zedong proposed that within several five-year plans, the People's Republic of China should be built into "an industrialized country with a high level of modern culture." In 1964, at the First Session of the Third National People's Congress, Zhou Enlai stated, "Within a relatively short period, we should build our country into a great socialist country with modernized agriculture, industry, national defense, and science and technology, catching up with and surpassing advanced world levels." At the First Session of the Fourth National People's Congress in 1975, Zhou Enlai reaffirmed the goal of Four Modernizations as the overall objective and task of socialist development.

Since the introduction of the reform and opening up policy, several generations of Chinese Communists have persistently explored, continually advanced, and innovatively developed the path of socialist modernization, centering around the question of "what kind of great modern socialist country to build and how to build it." As a result, the road to China's socialist modernization has been continuously improved.

At the beginning of the reform and opening up, Deng Xiaoping pointed out that the goal was to achieve the Four Modernizations by the end of the 20th century, which he termed "Chinese modernization," distinct from the Western concept. "Moderate prosperity" was identified as the minimum goal of the Four Modernizations, and he proposed the three-step development strategy. In 1987, the 13th National Congress of the CPC formally introduced this strategy for China's modernization. In 1997, the 15th National Congress proposed new three-step development goals and, for the first time, articulated the Two Centenary Goals as part of the development strategy. Subsequently, the 16th National Congress in 2002, the 17th National Congress in 2007, and the 18th National Congress in 2012 all reaffirmed this strategic goal, gradually enriching its content.

Since the 18th CPC National Congress, socialism with Chinese characteristics has entered the New Era. Under the leadership of the CPC Central Committee with General Secretary Xi Jinping at its core, significant emphasis has been placed on changes in the global, national, and party context. Responding to changes in the principal social contradiction, the CPC has promoted comprehensive deepening of reform and higher-level opening up to ensure the flourishing of the cause of socialist modernization with Chinese characteristics.

At the 19th CPC National Congress, General Secretary Xi Jinping articulated that the period between the 19th and the 20th CPC national congresses is the period in which the timeframes of the Two Centenary Goals converge. In this period, not only must we finish building a moderately prosperous society in all respects and achieve the First Centenary Goal; we must also build on this achievement to embark on a new journey towards the Second Centenary Goal of fully building a modern socialist country. A strategic arrangement for the 30 years following the achievement of a moderately prosperous society in all respects by 2020 was proposed, divided into two stages:

1. In the first stage from 2020 to 2035, we will build on the foundation created by the moderately prosperous society with a further 15 years of hard work to see that socialist modernization is basically realized.

2. From 2035 to the middle of the 21st century, having basically achieved modernization, we will work hard for a further 15 years and develop China into a great modern socialist country that is prosperous, strong, democratic, culturally advanced, harmonious, and beautiful.

This delineation provided a clearer timeline and roadmap for the Two Centenary Goals, closely aligning them with the realization of the Chinese Dream of National Rejuvenation.

The 19th CPC National Congress fully initiated a new journey toward building a modern socialist country. In exploring a modernization path that aligns with China's historical traditions, current conditions, and contemporary development trends, the CPC has deepened its scientific understanding of the laws governing the development of human society, socialist development, and Communist Party self-supervision and governance. By steadfastly following its own path while learning from the strengths of other development models, the CPC has carved out an unprecedented path to modernization in human history, breaking various paradoxes of modernization and creating a Chinese miracle of human modernization. This provides a valuable reference for the broad array of other developing countries and offers new choices for countries and peoples worldwide who seek to accelerate development while maintaining independence. This contribution of Chinese wisdom and approaches to global issues has landmark significance in the modernization history of human society.

I. Break the Paradoxes of Modernization

The modernization of human society is an unstoppable development trend. Countries and regions around the world, regardless of their historical traditions, social systems, or levels of development, will inevitably, sooner or later, embark on the path of modernization.

Modernization is a comprehensive term, and people from different social systems and fields have varied understandings and perspectives on the direction and methods of human society's modernization. Regardless of the country, modernization must occur within certain production relations and be connected with corresponding social systems. From the perspective of historical development, there have been two general paths to achieving modernization: one is through the capitalist route to modernizing human society, and the other is through the socialist route.

Historical practice shows us that while capitalism initiated the modernization process, it is neither a universal path nor the only option for achieving modernization. In fact, pursuing capitalist modernization alone makes it difficult to truly realize modern human society. In contrast, the socialist path to modernization aligns with the trends and laws of human development and is a viable choice for developing countries. However, if divorced from reality and reduced to dogma, socialist modernization will inevitably face setbacks and failures in the process of modernization. Faced with the contradictions and challenges encountered by Western modernization, China's modernization has achieved historic success, creating a miracle in the history of modernization. It has forged an unprecedented path, breaking the myths and paradoxes of modernization.

1. Capitalism cannot overcome the "modernization paradox"

Modernization was originally seen as an awakening from ignorance, barbarism, and backwardness that began in the Middle Ages. It was a long-term, revolutionary historical transformation across political, economic, social, and cultural domains, driven by the opening of new trade routes and the advancements of scientific and technological revolutions. Historically, it can be said that Western industrial civilization initiated and led the early stages of human modernization. Although Marx and Engels never explicitly coined the term "modernization," they clearly referred to the social and economic structures that emerged from the capitalist mode of production as "modern society." In the *Communist Manifesto*, they frequently used the term "modern" to describe capitalist society, such as "modern bourgeois society,"[1] "modern state power,"[2] "modern industry,"[3] and "modern laborer."[4] Marx made it clear that the ultimate purpose of *Capital* was "to reveal the economic laws of motion of modern society."[5] While the "modern" used by Marx and Engels may not carry exactly the same meaning as the term "modernization" as we use it today, there is a close connection. In the *Communist Manifesto*, their objective evaluations of the rise and development of capitalism inherently include a positive assessment of modernization. Similar statements include: capitalism advanced the industrial revolution, spurred technological progress and the growth of productive forces, generated immense material wealth, opened world markets, promoted urban development, established bourgeois democratic political systems and legal frameworks, opposed feudal despotism and privilege, triumphed over the ignorance and barbarism of Europe's Middle Ages, and shattered the feudal religious domination of human thought and spirit. Capitalist modernization not only marked the first step in humanity's journey toward modernization but also played a significant role in advancing human civilization and progress. Its successful experiences and positive outcomes hold historical significance for the development of human society. To deny this would not be the stance of a historical materialist.

However, capitalist modernization is not equivalent to the modernization of human society. True modernization is a universal pursuit that should benefit all humanity, involving several key aspects:

1. Quantitative Aspect: Modernization should enable all countries, regions, and peoples to enjoy its benefits, not just certain areas, countries,

---

1 https://www.marxists.org/archive/marx/works/download/pdf/Manifesto.pdf.
2 *Ibid.*
3 *Ibid.*
4 *Ibid.*
5 https://www.marxists.org/archive/korsch/19xx/introduction-capital.htm.

regions, or groups.

2. Qualitative Aspect: Modernization should allow all countries and peoples to truly escape poverty, ignorance, oppression, exploitation, and other backward, unequal, and unjust social conditions.

3. Productivity Aspect: Modernization should continuously advance productivity and technological levels, driving industrialization, intelligence, and IT application to better meet the production and living needs of all people worldwide.

4. Realistic Aspect: Modernization should provide all countries and peoples with the conditions, paths, and opportunities to achieve it. They should be able to build a modern state through their own efforts and advantages without being suppressed or marginalized in the modernization process.

Human society's journey toward modernization requires the positive contributions of commodities, profit, and capital. However, the fundamental contradiction in capitalist society between socialized production and private ownership of the means of production dictates that Western modernization will inevitably center on capital and pursue the maximization of surplus value. This pursuit inevitably leads to repeated economic crises. While promoting the modernization and liberalization of capital, it also objectively generates a series of problems and contradictions, hindering the modernization process and disrupting the healthy development of human society. The inherent contradictions, systemic limitations, and historical constraints of capitalist modernization make it impossible to fundamentally resolve its paradoxes. As Marx observed, " In bourgeois political economy – and in the epoch of production to which it corresponds—this complete elaboration of what lies within man, appears as the total alienation, and the destruction of all fixed, one-sided purposes as the sacrifice of the end in itself to a wholly external compulsion."[1]

Therefore, the belief that the Western path is the only "universal path" to modernization, and that other countries have no choice but to imitate and follow suit, is completely erroneous. The current chaos in Western countries, such as the widening wealth gap, refugee crises, rampant populism, terrorism, and de-globalization movements, further highlights the crisis of Western modernization. These issues underscore a series of paradoxes that deviate from the values of "freedom, democracy, equality, rule of law, and human rights" that capitalism espouses. In short, the Western path to modernization has hit a dead end due to its internal contradictions, and the historical limitations of the capitalist system prevent it from resolving these contradictions and overcoming the paradoxes of modernization.

(1) The paradox in the development of democracy

Western countries are often hailed as "beacons of democracy," with democracy being the most significant hallmark of capitalist modernization. The series of value concepts promoted by Western democracy, such as "sovereignty of the people," "separation of powers," "natural rights," and "social contract," appear to be perfect political ideas. These concepts played a significant role in the revolutionary overthrow of feudal landlords and nobles by the bourgeoisie. However, once the bourgeoisie gained power, democracy based on private ownership of the means of production largely manifested as electoral democracy. This form of democracy is driven by the pursuit of personal interest maximization, fundamentally serving individual wealth and fame rather than the public, the collective, or everyone.

The voting rights held by the broad working class and the people cannot change the capitalist ownership of the means of production, nor can they cast a substantive democracy that serves the people. Moreover,

---

1   https://www.marxists.org/archive/marx/works/1857/precapitalist/ch01.htm.

Western elections are often manipulated by money, media, criminal forces, political oligarchs, and financial oligarchs, becoming entirely a game for the wealthy, a puppet controlled by group interests, and a means for capital to manipulate public opinion, which is diametrically opposed to substantive democracy. Western-style democracy is increasingly becoming a political tool for a few Western countries to achieve hegemonic rule. In recent years, Western-style democracy has fostered the rise of populist forces. Some countries that have undergone Western-style democratization have fallen into political turmoil and social unrest, with people displaced. Some countries that have blindly copied Western democratic systems ended up in great chaos and severe damage, even becoming vassals of developed Western countries. As the world's superpower, the United States, under the banner of "democracy," practices hegemonism in other countries and regions. Western-style democratization has become a major source of global chaos, social division, and national instability. These points fully illustrate the drawbacks and paradoxes of Western democracy.

(2) The paradox in economic development

In the colonial expansion aimed at maximizing profits and wealth, capital formed a world system dominated by Western developed capitalist countries. In this system, a few European and American countries developed through imperialism and colonialism, while the vast majority of countries in the world were colonized and exploited, remaining in a developing state. A tiny fraction of people became wealthy, while the vast majority fell into poverty. A few developed countries, benefiting from the advantage of early modernization, enjoy a life of "high income, high welfare, and high consumption," and have become models for many developing countries to emulate. At one time, the ideas that "Western modernization" is the only path to modernization and that history ends with capitalism were rampant.

Under capitalist conditions, "The worker becomes all the poorer the more wealth he produces, the more his production increases in power and size. The worker becomes an ever cheaper commodity the more commodities he creates. The *devaluation* of the world of men is in direct proportion to the *increasing value* of the world of things."[1] Capitalism's inherent inability to overcome periodic economic crises repeatedly exposes the paradox of capitalist economic development.

Since the beginning of the new century, especially since the global financial crisis of 2008, with the saturation of capital expansion, financial crises have erupted frequently, and economic stagnation has become normalized in Western capitalist economies. The gap between developed and undeveloped capitalist countries has widened, as has the gap between the rich and the poor. United Nations Secretary-General António Guterres pointed out that the world's 26 richest individuals control half of the world's wealth. Welfare systems are on the brink of collapse, and government debt burdens are increasingly heavy, with US government debt reaching nearly US$27 trillion. The developed countries' virtual economies are disconnected from their real economies, resulting in a loss of competitiveness in the real economy, making economic recovery difficult and new prosperity far off, while high unemployment rates persist. These factors have severely weakened the material productive capacity of capitalism, causing the entire economy to fall into a state of prolonged stagnation, bringing many uncertainties and instabilities to the world economy. Some developing countries that follow the West and adopt its "modernization plans" either fall into the "middle-income trap" and stagnate for a long time, become dependent on and controlled by "core countries," losing their independence, or fall into bankruptcy under the harsh "structural adjustment programs."

---

1   https://www.marxists.org/archive/marx/works/1844/manuscripts/labour.htm.

(3) The paradox in culture and civilization

Individualism is the core value of capitalist culture, expressed in forms such as "freedom, democracy, equality, fraternity, and human rights." These values removed intellectual barriers to promote capitalist modernization by opposing feudal despotism and medieval religious theocracy. Capitalist culture, as a form of ideological consciousness, reflects the development of the capitalist mode of production and the needs of bourgeois rule, serving as a value system for capital appreciation and capital domination. Currently, capitalist culture is an important strategic resource for Western developed countries to maintain their world hegemonic status, advocating cultural hegemonism in cultural exchanges. They use their powerful cultural "soft power" to promote cultural infiltration, and even cultural colonialism, conducting "peaceful evolution" and "color revolutions" in other countries, attempting to subvert other social systems or state regimes, fostering pro-Western forces to maintain the hegemonic status of developed Western countries. Due to the extremely covert means and paths, this brings strong deception to the public who blindly pursue "freedom, democracy, and human rights." Numerous events have proven that Western forces, through cultural infiltration, promote "peaceful evolution" and "color revolutions," bringing not the so-called "democracy, freedom, and equality" they claim, but real, tangible, and severe disasters such as social unrest, national division, and frequent violence.

There exists a profound contradiction between the highly developed material world and the weakened spiritual world in developed capitalist countries. In these materially advanced capitalist countries, the populace is driven by strong material desires, with money-worshipping rampant. True human needs and psychology are severely distorted, with widespread spiritual emptiness and frequent criminal activity. The United States, the most developed country today, has the largest prison population in the world. These phenomena, which run counter to the genuine human values of "freedom, democracy, equality, fraternity, rule of law, and human rights," highlight that capitalist civilization is trapped in an irreversible vicious cycle.

(4) The paradox in national governance

The development of the capitalist economy and bourgeois rule also requires a stable social environment. So far, after each economic crisis, the bourgeoisie either reluctantly adopts some conciliatory or concessionary policies to ease domestic class contradictions, or they directly shift these contradictions abroad to maintain domestic social order and normal development.

Many developing countries often focus solely on the outward appearance of Western modernization, viewing the capitalist nations of Europe and the United States as an ideal "paradise on earth" and a "promised land" for immigration. However, the relative social stability and surface-level prosperity of a few developed countries cannot conceal the inherent greed and profit-driven nature of capital today. In this era of peaceful development, although Western nations make every effort to avoid discussing, and even attempt to whitewash, the violent history of brutal plunder and colonial aggression that led them to modernization—what can only be described as "dripping ... with blood and dirt"[1]—the contradictions and conflicts between the bourgeoisie and the working class have not disappeared, either domestically or internationally. Instead, they have taken on new forms, such as increasingly acute ethnic, racial, and religious tensions, which are sometimes expressed in violent and even terroristic ways.

Even within Western capitalist countries, groups such as refugees, illegal immigrants, the poorly educated, proletarians, and semi-

---

1   https://www.marxists.org/archive/marx/works/1867-c1/ch31.htm.

proletarians—the so-called "lower classes"—struggle to access fair and equitable public services, increasingly becoming marginalized in society. Their conflicts with the elite upper classes continue to deepen, making social tensions more complex and severe, occasionally erupting into violent incidents and social unrest. All of this demonstrates the inherent and insurmountable problems within the capitalist system when it comes to effective social governance.

(5) The paradox in the ecological environment

Capital's pursuit of profit is inseparable from natural resources, but the greedy nature of capital inherently makes it an enemy of nature. The development of human society is inseparable from nature, and the modernization of human society must necessarily be a harmonious coexistence between humans and nature. "The worker can create nothing without *nature,* without the *sensuous external world.*"[1] "Nature is man's *inorganic* body."[2]

However, capitalism has been destroying the natural ecological environment in its modernization process. In the capitalist modernization model, the unrestrained pursuit of profit by capital leads to the over-exploitation of natural resources and the ecological environment. The relationship between humans and nature is alienated by capital into a relationship of conquest and control, which has given rise to a series of "civilizational diseases" that violate and damage nature. This has resulted in global ecological problems such as resource depletion, environmental degradation, consumption alienation, the greenhouse effect, and sharp declines in biodiversity.

In the contemporary world system dominated by developed capitalist countries, these countries utilize the global division of labor to transfer

---

1   https://www.marxists.org/archive/marx/works/1844/manuscripts/labour.htm.
2   https://www.marxists.org/archive/marx/works/1844/manuscripts/labour.htm.

high-energy-consuming and highly polluting industries to developing countries. Western countries, leveraging their capital and technological advantages, practice ecological imperialism and ecological colonialism, shifting environmental pollution and disorderly resource exploitation to developing countries. They view the vast developing countries as providers of raw materials, primary products, or low- to mid-end products, and as dumping grounds for all their commodities. For a period, this helps alleviate the ecological crisis in developed countries, but the mitigation of environmental problems in Western countries comes at the expense of the environments of developing countries. Today, Western countries drink clean water, breathe clean air, and enjoy beautiful environments because they have transferred polluted water, air, and harsh environments to the vast developing countries and their people. Even so, when Donald Trump was President of the United States, he withdrew from the Paris Climate Agreement and refused to sign the Kyoto Protocol on reducing greenhouse gas emissions, a typical act of ecological hegemonism. This Western modernization development model, which sacrifices the ecological environment of developing countries for its own economic growth and improved quality of life, is increasingly being questioned and criticized. These questions and criticisms indicate that ecological and environmental issues are not only insurmountable problems in the capitalist modernization process but also global problems.

From the democratic political paradox, economic development paradox, cultural exchange paradox, social governance paradox, and ecological environment paradox present in capitalist modernization, we can see that capitalist modernization has four distinct characteristics:

1. Modernization is achieved through the greedy nature of unrestrained capital expansion.

2. Modernization is realized by widening the gap between the rich

and the poor, as well as the gap between "core countries" and "peripheral countries."

3. Modernization is attained through internal exploitation and plunder, and externally through hegemonism and power politics.

4. Modernization is achieved at the expense of the natural ecological environment.

Such a modernization process is inherently unsustainable and incompatible with the current era of peaceful development and the reality that most countries have embarked on independent paths. It is also unreplicable for developing and underdeveloped countries that are at a disadvantage in global competition. It is no wonder that the vast majority of countries that chose the Western modernization path after World War II have been unable to overcome the "middle-income trap." Therefore, for China and many developing countries, modernization does not mean "Westernization." It must not follow the crowd, nor blindly imitate the West. Instead, it should combine their unique characteristics and advantages to pursue a modernization development path that suits their own realities and national conditions.

2. The distinct advantages of the Chinese path to modernization

Modernization is both a hallmark of human civilization and progress and an enduring goal pursued by societies throughout history. For generations, the Chinese people have aspired to this vision, striving tirelessly since modern times to realize it. Since the founding of the People's Republic of China, the Party has led the Chinese people in relentless exploration and innovation, achieving remarkable socialist modernization and creating the world-renowned miracle of Chinese modernization. This transformation has enabled the long-suffering Chinese nation to experience a profound rebirth. Today, we stand closer than ever to achieving national rejuvenation, with unprecedented confidence and capability.

The establishment of the People's Republic of China in 1949 holds great historical significance, providing the Chinese nation with the social conditions and institutional foundation necessary for modernization, and setting the course for building a modern state. Shortly after its founding, the Party incorporated goals such as the "modernization of agriculture and transportation" and the "establishment of a solid modern national defense" into its general policy for the transition period. In 1956, the Party's Eighth National Congress adopted the Party Constitution, which set forth the goal of achieving the Four Modernizations in industry, agriculture, transportation, and national defense.

In December 1964, during the government work report delivered at the First Session of the Third National People's Congress, Zhou Enlai proposed that by the end of the 20th century, China should become a great socialist country with modern agriculture, modern industry, modern national defense, and modern science and technology. He outlined a two-step approach: first, within 15 years, establish an independent and relatively complete industrial and national economic system, bringing Chinese industry close to the world's advanced level; second, by the end of the century, strive to make Chinese industry a global leader while fully modernizing agriculture, industry, national defense, and science and technology. In 1975, the Fourth National People's Congress reaffirmed this two-step strategy for realizing the Four Modernizations in full.

In 1978, the Third Plenary Session of the 11th CPC Central Committee adhered to the socialist direction and path of modernization, corrected some previous unrealistic practices regarding modernization, decisively shifted the focus of the Party and the country's work to economic development, and implemented reform and opening up, achieving a great historical turning point for the Party and the country's endeavors. Since the Third Plenary Session of the 11th Central Committee, every National Congress of the Party has, from different angles and with different emphases, focused on and highlighted the issue of socialist modernization, consistently advancing the historical process of building a great modern socialist country.

As socialism with Chinese characteristics entered the New Era, and based on this new historical context, the 19th CPC National Congress made new top-level designs for advancing socialist modernization in China. It explicitly proposed that, on the basis of building a moderately prosperous society in all respects, China should be built into a great modern socialist country that is prosperous, strong, democratic, culturally advanced, harmonious and beautiful by the middle of the 21st century, thus clearly outlining the timetable and roadmap for China's socialist modernization.

Having finished built a moderately prosperous society in all respects, China has now embarked on a new journey toward building a great modern socialist country in all respects.

It can be said that a major conclusion drawn from the long-term practical exploration of socialist modernization by the entire Party and the people nationwide is to build China into a great modern socialist country that is prosperous, strong, democratic, culturally advanced, harmonious and beautiful. Undoubtedly, the realization of this blueprint will expand the pathways to modernization for human society, offering new choices for those countries and nations that wish to accelerate development while maintaining their independence. It will break through various paradoxes inherent in the Western modernization process and will be a significant historical event in the history of human development, bearing landmark significance.

(1) Build a modern prosperous and strong country and break the economic development paradox of capitalist modernization

"Prosperous and strong" means achieving national wealth and strength, which is the ideal state and material foundation for building a great modern socialist country. Throughout the CPC's century-long struggle, it has united and led the Chinese people through arduous efforts, enabling the historically oppressed Chinese nation to achieve a tremendous transformation: it has stood up, grown rich, and is becoming strong. In the New Era, the principal contradiction in Chinese society has shifted to the contradiction between unbalanced and inadequate development and the people's ever-growing need for a better life. China's economy has transitioned from long-term rapid growth to a new normal of high-quality development.

Since the 18th CPC National Congress, under the strong leadership of the Party Central Committee with General Secretary Xi Jinping at its core, the Party has put forward a series of new ideas, strategies, initiatives, and deployments for China's economic development in the New Era. These include:

- Adhering to the centralized, unified leadership of the Party over economic work and the people-centered philosophy of development.

- Striving to build a modern economic system, firmly implementing the concepts of innovative, coordinated, green, open and inclusive development.

- Prioritizing quality and efficiency, focusing on supply-side structural reform as the main line to promote changes in the quality, efficiency, and drivers of economic development, and enhancing total factor productivity to continually boost China's economic innovation and competitiveness.

- Improving the socialist market economy, correctly managing the relationship between the government and the market to let the market play a decisive role in resource allocation and better leverage the role of the government, innovating and improving macroeconomic regulation.

- Upholding the basic economic system where public ownership is the mainstay and various forms of ownership develop together, further advancing state-owned enterprise reform, and stimulating the vitality of all market entities.

- Developing the real economy, accelerating the implementation of the innovation-driven development strategy, the rural revitalization strategy, and the regional coordinated development strategy.

- Promoting the formation of a new pattern of comprehensive openness, with China opening its doors wider during a period of major global development, transformation, and adjustment, advancing the BRI, and implementing high-level opening up.

These new ideas, strategies, initiatives, and deployments have ensured the continuous, healthy, and rapid development of China's economy amid sluggish global economic growth, intensified international trade frictions, and increasing domestic economic downward pressure. In 2019, China's GDP reached 99.1 trillion yuan, solidifying its position as the world's second-largest economy, accounting for over 16% of the global economy. Despite the outbreak of the COVID-19 pandemic in 2020, China not only withstood the impact but also became a global model for pandemic control. It was the only major economy to achieve positive growth, with a 2.3% increase, pushing its total economic output past 100 trillion yuan and its share of the global economy to 17.5%.

In terms of per capita GDP, China's sustained high growth during the reform period allowed it to enter the ranks of lower-middle-income countries in 1993, followed by upper-middle-income countries in 2009, while simultaneously becoming the world's second-largest economy by total economic output.

Per Capita GDP Exceeds US$10,000 for Two Consecutive Years

In 2019, China's per capita GDP reached approximately US$10,300, and in 2020, it rose to about US$10,500. According to World Bank data, China is nearing the threshold for high-income countries, defined in July 2020 as those with a per capita GNI exceeding US$12,535.

Comparison of Economic Development between China and the US in 2020

In 2020, China's GDP amounted to US$14.73 trillion. Despite the United States experiencing a GDP contraction of 3.3%, its GDP remained at US$20.95 trillion. This brought China's GDP to 70.3% of the US figure, marking the first time in history it surpassed the 70% mark. By comparison, at its peak following World War II, the Soviet Union's GDP was only slightly above 40% of the US level. Japan's GDP during its growth peak reached about 30% of the US GDP, though it appeared to be 70% due to the sudden appreciation of the yen before the Plaza Accord. Thus, China became the first country since World War II to reach 70% of the US GDP—a milestone in global economic history.

Comparison of Economic Development between China and the EU in 2020

Preliminary Eurostat data indicated that in 2020, GDP in the 19 Eurozone countries fell by 6.8%, while GDP in the 27 EU countries declined by 6.4%. Excluding the UK, the nominal GDP of the 27 EU countries in 2019 was approximately US$15.58 trillion. According to Eurostat, by 2020, this figure had dropped to US$14.58 trillion. For the first time in history, China's GDP surpassed that of the European Union, marking another significant event in the annals of global economic development.

The historic achievements in the Three Critical Battles preventing and defusing major risks, targeted poverty alleviation, and pollution control and the successful realization of the goal of building a moderately prosperous society in all respects have laid a solid foundation for building a great modern socialist country in all respects. These accomplishments fully demonstrate the advantages of the socialist economic system. They also declare to the world that China's modernization path avoids the "enclosures" modernization of the West "sheep eating people" and the colonial expansion model. The success of the Chinese path breaks the economic development paradox for late-developing countries, which, by following the Western modernization footsteps, often become "peripheral countries," fall into dependency, or get trapped in the "middle-income trap."

(2) Build a modern democratic country and break the democratic paradox of capitalist modernization

The people are the creators of history, and true democracy is when the people run the country. People's sovereignty is the essence of socialist democracy, and people's democracy is the broadest and most genuine democracy. Developing socialist democracy is the inevitable result of the historical, theoretical, and practical logic of the Chinese people's long struggle since modern times. It is inherent in promoting the modernization of the national governance system and capacity and is a necessary requirement for building a great modern socialist country.

Without democracy, there can be no socialism; without democracy, there can be no socialist modernization. The establishment of the People's Republic of China and the fundamental socialist system not only made it possible for the people the run the country for the first time in Chinese history but also ensured the institutional design for this practice. The system of people running the country has continually developed, matured, and been systematized through the long-term exploratory practice of socialism with Chinese characteristics. Consequently, socialist democracy has been constantly improved, forming a unique path of democratic political development with Chinese characteristics. The key to this path lies in the unity of Party leadership, the running of the country by the people, and law-based governance.

Since the 18th CPC National Congress, the country has consistently adhered to the correct direction of the development of socialist democracy. The institutional development of the unity of Party leadership, the running of the country by the people, and law-based governance has been comprehensively strengthened. The Party's leadership system and mechanisms have been continually improved, intra-Party democracy has become more widespread, socialist consultative democracy has been fully implemented, the modernization level of the national governance system and capacity has significantly improved, and the development of socialist democracy has entered a new realm. In his political report at the 19th CPC National Congress, General Secretary Xi Jinping pointed out: "The very purpose of developing socialist democracy is to give full expression to the will of the people, protect their rights and interests, spark their creativity, and provide systemic and institutional guarantees to ensure the people run the country."[1]

Faced with the goal of building a great modern socialist country that is democratic, the 19th CPC National Congress proposed higher requirements and comprehensive plans for the development of socialist democracy in the New Era of socialism with Chinese characteristics. It clearly articulated that China should not just mechanically copy the political systems of other countries; instead, it is necessary to uphold the unity of Party leadership, the running of the country by the people, and law-based governance, strengthen institutional guarantees to ensure the people run the country, give play to the important role of socialist consultative democracy, advanced law-based governance, deepen reform

---

1   Xi Jinping, *Secure a Decisive Victory in Building a Moderately Prosperous Society in All Respects and Strive for the Great Success of Socialism with Chinese Characteristics for a New Era: Report at the 19th National Congress of the Communist Party of China*, Beijing: People's Publishing House, 2017, p. 36.

of Party and government institutions and the system of government administration, and consolidate and develop the patriotic united front.

Practice has proven that there is no single model for political systems in the world. Political systems cannot be abstractly judged without considering specific social and political conditions and historical and cultural traditions. They cannot be rigidly copied from foreign political systems. Practice has also proven that socialist democracy with Chinese characteristics embodies the fundamental will of the overwhelming majority of the people, genuinely ensures long-term social harmony and stability and national enduring peace, and possesses great vitality. It fully demonstrates the significant political advantages of "China's effective governance," breaking the paradox of Western democracy that leads to "Western chaos."

(3) Build modern, culturally advanced country and break the paradox of capitalist modernization

Civilization is a significant marker of social progress and a key characteristic of a modern socialist nation. It represents the cultural state that a modern country should aspire to, embodying a socialist culture that is geared to the needs of modernization, the world, and the future. It is also a crucial pillar for realizing the rejuvenation of the Chinese nation. Without cultural confidence and prosperity, it is impossible to build a modern, culturally advanced country or to achieve national rejuvenation.

The Chinese nation boasts a civilization that spans over 5,000 years, making it the only uninterrupted civilization in the world and a significant contributor to global civilization. However, we must not overlook the historical fact that in modern times, traditional Chinese civilization, primarily feudal in nature, was once defeated by Western civilization, represented by capitalist culture. We must also remember that the transformation of our thinking became proactive only after the introduction of Marxism, which allowed Chinese civilization to rise anew from its decline, like a phoenix reborn from the ashes. The CPC, founded on Marxism, has always placed great importance on the development of socialist culture.

Since the introduction of the reform and opening up policy, especially since the 18th CPC National Congress, our Party has creatively addressed a series of significant theoretical and practical issues in the development of socialist culture with Chinese characteristics. Significant progress has been made in theoretical and cultural development, cultural confidence has been highlighted, the nation's cultural soft power and the influence of Chinese culture have been greatly enhanced, and the entire Party and society have become more intellectually united.

A country's strength lies in its cultural strength; the foundation of a nation lies in its civilization. To better transition from "growing rich" to "becoming strong," the 19th CPC National Congress, while outlining the correct direction for advancing the cause of socialism with Chinese characteristics in the New Era, also clarified the development goals of socialist culture in the New Era. It emphasized the need to consistently adhere to the path of cultural development with Chinese characteristics, to inspire the cultural innovation and creativity of the entire nation, and to build a strong socialist culture. It stressed the importance of firmly grasping the leadership of ideological work, building a socialist ideology with strong cohesion and leading power, fostering and practicing core socialist values to unite people's hearts and efforts, promoting the creative transformation and innovative development of the best elements of traditional Chinese culture, and adhering to a people-centered creative orientation to produce socialist literature and art worthy of the times. It also called for the development of cultural undertakings and industries to provide rich intellectual nourishment to meet the people's new expectations for a better life.

However, socialist culture with Chinese characteristics is unique without being isolated, and strong without being hegemonic.

Chinese traditional culture has always embodied inclusiveness, akin to the vast ocean that embraces countless streams. It is a multifaceted and integrated culture, primarily based on Han culture while amalgamating the cultural essences of various ethnic groups. The culture of socialism with Chinese characteristics, guided by Marxism, originates from the outstanding traditional culture nurtured by the 5,000-year civilization of the Chinese nation. It is forged from the revolutionary culture and advanced socialist culture created by the Party leading the people in revolution, development, and reform, and it is rooted in the great practice of socialism with Chinese characteristics. This culture inherently absorbs all the advanced cultural achievements of humanity, making it international in nature. areas with concentrations of ethnic minorities What is successful in one country is of significance to the world. Chinese culture has never engaged in cultural hegemony, looking down on others; instead, it has always viewed other cultures as equals—this was true in the past, remains true today, and will be true in the future, regardless of the level of development.

On May 15, 2019, at the Conference on Dialogue of Asian Civilizations held in Beijing, Xi Jinping delivered a major speech, in which he stated: "Diversity spurs interaction among civilizations, which in turn promotes mutual learning and further development."[1] He emphasized, "Civilizations vary from each other only as human beings differ in terms of skin color and the language used. No civilization is superior to others."[2] "Such exchanges and mutual learning [between civilizations] should be reciprocal, equal-footed, diverse, and multidimensional; they should not

---

1   Xi Jinping, *The Governance of China*, Beijing: Foreign Languages Press, 2020, vol. III, p. 543.
2   *Ibid.*, p. 544.

be coercive, imposed, one-dimensional, or one-way."[1] Addressing the need to strengthen exchanges and mutual learning among different countries, ethnic groups, and cultures, Xi Jinping proposed four key points: First, we need to respect each other and treat each other as equals. Second, we need to uphold the beauty of each civilization and the diversity of civilizations around the world. Third, we need to stay open and inclusive and draw on each other's strengths. Fourth, we need to advance with the times and explore new ground. These Chinese propositions contribute Chinese wisdom and approaches to promoting global civilizational exchanges and mutual learning. They break the paradox embedded in Western culture—the so-called "nobility" that underpins "Western centrism," "universal values," and even "cultural hegemony."

(4) Build a harmonious modern country and break the paradox of social governance in capitalist modernization

Social governance is a crucial aspect of national governance, and social harmony is an important criterion for evaluating the effectiveness of social governance. Social harmony is the organic unity of relationships among people, between people and society, and between people and nature. It is the unification of democracy and the rule of law, fairness and efficiency, vitality and order. Fundamentally, social harmony is closely related to whether the relations of production are compatible with the level of productive forces. When relations of production lag behind the level of productive forces, social problems arise; likewise, when they surpass the level of productive forces, social problems also occur. Valuing harmony is a traditional virtue of the Chinese nation. The concepts of unity between humanity and nature, harmonious coexistence of all countries, and diversity in harmony reflect the intellectual pursuit and social ideals of the Chinese people.

---

1   *Ibid.*, p. 545.

The Chinese Communists adhere to the fundamental principles of scientific socialism and have established a socialist system on Chinese soil, realizing the ideal society long dreamed of by the Chinese people. In national governance, the Party has always upheld the principle of putting the people first, taking solid steps on the path to social fairness and justice, and achieving common prosperity for all. While creating the rare miracle of rapid economic development, China has also created a miracle of long-term social stability, resulting in a society that is both vibrant and orderly.

Since the 18th CPC National Congress, the Party has thoroughly implemented the people-centered philosophy of development. A series of measures benefiting the people have been carried out, social welfare development has steadily advanced, and the lives of the people have continually improved. The people's sense of fulfilment, happiness, and security has significantly increased, and society has maintained long-term stability and development. People are increasingly living in peace and contentment, and society is becoming more stable and orderly. A social governance system led by the Party, with the government taking responsibility, democratic consultation, social collaboration, public participation, legal guarantees, and technological support has been increasingly perfected. Social governance based on collaboration, participation, and common interests is gradually being formed. A social governance model based on collaboration, participation, and common interests is gradually being completed. China is progressing toward a higher level of safety and security.

On the other hand, the profound changes in the principal contradiction in Chinese society have brought about a series of new challenges in social governance and social development. The 19th CPC National Congress and the Fourth Plenary Session of the 19th Central Committee made important arrangements for strengthening and innovating social governance and establishing a sound social governance system with Chinese characteristics, both from the perspectives of action plans and institutional guarantees. Practice has proven that China's social governance system and institutions can continuously meet the people's growing needs for a better life, promote social fairness and justice, and ensure good social order.

Chinese social governance is currently one of the most effective governance models in the world, breaking the paradox in Western social governance that focuses only on material aspects and benefits only a minority rather than the vast majority. Chinese social governance not only provides a harmonious social environment for the development of socialist modernization and reform and opening up, ensuring long-term stability and vitality, but also offers Chinese wisdom and approaches for other developing countries to improve their social governance systems and solve social problems.

(5) Build a modern beautiful country and break the ecological paradox of capitalist modernization

Humans and nature are part of a life community, and humanity must respect, adapt to, and protect nature. Nature becomes more beautiful through human care and will generously repay humanity; conversely, if nature is destroyed by human greed, it will ruthlessly retaliate. Only by following natural laws can humanity effectively avoid pitfalls in the development and utilization of nature. The harm humans inflict on nature ultimately harms humanity itself—this is an inescapable law. Promoting eco-civilization is a millennial plan concerning the sustainable development of human society and the wellbeing of future generations. Sacrificing the environment for the sake of modernization reflects human shortsightedness and selfishness. Socialist modernization is about harmony between humans and nature. It involves creating more material and cultural-ethical wealth to meet the people's growing needs for a better life, as well as providing more high-quality ecological products to meet the people's increasing demand for a beautiful ecological environment.

Since the 18th CPC National Congress, the Central Committee, with General Secretary Xi Jinping at its core, has placed unprecedented emphasis on ecological advancement, integrating it with economic, political, cultural, and social development to form the Five-Sphere Integrated Plan for the New Era of socialism with Chinese characteristics. Significant efforts have been made to promote ecological advancement, implementing the strictest possible ecological and environmental protection systems, advocating the concept that lucid waters and lush mountains are invaluable assets, and protecting the ecological environment as one would protect one's eyes. Comprehensive measures have been taken to address prominent environmental issues that concern the people, resulting in significant improvements in ecological governance and the overall state of the environment. China is increasingly becoming an important participant, contributor, and leader in global ecological advancement.

Our country is currently in a critical period of ecological advancement, aiming to provide more high-quality ecological products to meet the people's growing needs for a beautiful environment. We are also at a pivotal moment where we have the capability and conditions to address prominent ecological and environmental issues. The 19th CPC National Congress, from the strategic perspective of speeding up reform of the system for developing an ecological civilization and building a beautiful China, has made specific arrangements and plans in promoting green development, solving prominent environmental problems, intensifying the protection of ecosystems, and reforming the environmental regulation system, thereby accelerating the development of a beautiful China. As the largest developing country, China's endeavor to build a beautiful China is also a significant contribution to building a beautiful world.

Unlike the ecological selfishness of capitalism, China, while addressing its domestic environmental issues, actively participates in global environmental governance. The United Nations Environment Programme has praised China as a model for global desertification control and has promoted the formation of the Belt and Road desertification control cooperation mechanism, providing important references for global sustainable development and contributing to the shared goal of building a beautiful planet. China's green development concept of harmony between humans and nature, its eco-civilization institutional system that implements this concept, and the corresponding policies and measures are fundamentally different from the ecological colonialism and ecological imperialism practiced during the modernization processes of Western capitalism, where they kept the beautiful environment for themselves while shifting environmental problems and ecological crises onto others. This breaks the ecological paradox of Western modernization.

In summary, since the founding of the People's Republic of China, especially since the reform and opening up, we have achieved in decades what took Western developed countries hundreds or even several hundred years to accomplish. China's modernization is an unprecedented transformation in human history. So far, fewer than 30 countries with a combined population of less than one billion have achieved industrialization. China's successful exploration of the path to modernization, as the world's largest developing country, means that the Chinese people, who outnumber the total population of all current developed countries, will join the ranks of modernized countries, and this will have a global impact. When China becomes the first major modernized country to succeed without following the capitalist path but rather through the socialist road, the great social revolution led by the CPC in reform and opening up will more fully demonstrate its global significance. The achievements of socialist modernization with Chinese characteristics provide ironclad proof that the Western model is not the only path to modernization. Ultimately, developing countries will break free from the dilemma of either falling into development traps by following the West or becoming dependent in their development and will find their own paths to modernization.

3. China successfully pioneers an unprecedented path to modernization in human history

The principle of fundamental social contradictions is a core tenet of historical materialism, encompassing the dialectical movement between productive forces and relations of production, as well as between the economic base and the superstructure. The interaction and movement of these contradictions together constitute the fundamental laws governing the movement of society, scientifically explaining the "two inevitabilities" and "two impossibilities" in the development of human society. This provides a scientific theoretical basis for fully understanding the direction, path, and laws of social historical movement and modernization, and for recognizing the superiority of socialist modernization over capitalist modernization.

Modernization, as a great revolution in human society sparked by the industrial, technological, and information revolutions, has significantly advanced social productive forces, prompting profound changes in the relations of production and the superstructure. To adapt to the continuously developing productive forces, the capitalist system has undergone continuous self-adjustment during the modernization process, resulting in many new changes. Although these adjustments and changes have some progressive significance, they cannot fundamentally alter the capitalist private ownership of the means of production, nor can they resolve the basic contradictions of capitalism. Therefore, issues such as polarization and class antagonism arising in the capitalist modernization process cannot be thoroughly solved, leading to the gradual decline and increasing difficulties of capitalist modernization.

What is the direction and future of the progress of human society? What are its trends and currents? The development of productive forces has advanced significantly during the process of capitalist modernization, continually pushing beyond the limits set by capitalist production relations. Amid this breakthrough, a distinct form of socialist modernization has emerged, demonstrating increasing superiority over its capitalist counterpart. Socialist modernization not only represents the direction of the progress of human society but also reflects the currents and trends of both current and future social development.

To advance Chinese modernization, it is necessary to adhere to the organic unity between the general laws governance human social progress and the specific realities of China. Only by aligning with the broader direction of the progress of human society and the trends of the era can China's modernization proceed smoothly and successfully.

Since the founding of the People's Republic of China, the country has fundamentally established a basic socialist system. The CPC has united and led all of its members and the people in consistently standing at the forefront of the times, advancing socialist modernization, building a great modern socialist country, and achieving the rejuvenation of the Chinese nation. Since the initiation of the reform and opening up policy, China has steadfastly adhered to the Four Cardinal Principles, ensuring that its modernization continues to progress along the correct path of socialism. Deng Xiaoping insightfully noted, "We are a socialist country. The basic expression of the superiority of our socialist system is that it allows the productive forces of our society to grow at a rapid rate unknown in old China, and that it permits us gradually to satisfy our people's constantly growing material and cultural needs."[1] The facts have proven that socialism, especially within the framework of reform and opening up, increasingly demonstrates its advantages over capitalism. The international community has also come to better understand and appreciate the merits of socialism with Chinese characteristics.

Particularly since the 18th CPC National Congress, General Secretary Xi Jinping has, from the perspective of historical materialism, emphasized, "It is necessary to grasp the movement of the contradictions between the productive forces and production relations, and between the economic base and the superstructure, in order to fully understand the fundamental aspects and direction of societal development."[2] He has repeatedly stressed that socialism with Chinese characteristics is fundamentally socialism, and not any other doctrine. He further noted that harmony between scientific socialism cannot be abandoned harmony between—to do so would be to abandon socialism itself. The Eight Principles outlined in the political report of the 19th CPC National Congress focus on the essential attributes of the socialist system and deeply explore the profound connotations of socialism with Chinese characteristics in the New Era, clarifying its nature and direction.

Moreover, upholding socialism does not mean rigidly adhering to dogma or remaining complacent. Rather, it requires advancing social development in response to changes in the movement of fundamental social contradictions, and actively promoting comprehensive reform and opening up. Xi Jinping has pointed out, "To uphold and develop socialism with Chinese characteristics, we must constantly adjust the relations of

---

1   Deng Xiaoping, *Selected Works of Deng Xiaoping*, Beijing: Foreign Languages Press, 1995, vol. III, p. 139.
2   Xi Jinping, *The Party's Work to Improve Publicity and Guide People in Their Thinking*, Beijing: Central Party Literature Publishing House, 2020, p. 34.

production to suit the development of the productive forces and improve the superstructure to suit the development of the economic base."[1] The fundamental social contradictions are dynamic and continuously evolving, and thus the process of reform and opening up is ongoing and never truly complete. The overall goal of this reform is to improve and develop the system of socialism with Chinese characteristics, and to modernize the national governance system and capacity.

In today's world, the unstoppable wave of modernization, marked prominently by the reform of global governance systems and economic globalization, continues to surge forward. Peace and development remain the irreversible trends and the direction of human progress. The world today faces profound changes of a kind unseen in a century, with various modernization ideas competing. Some of these ideas can learn from each other and develop together, while others are mutually exclusive and self-centered. Amidst severe challenges and complex situations, how to firmly uphold socialism with Chinese characteristics in the New Era and unwaveringly achieve the goal of "building a great modern socialist country in all respects" is a significant contemporary issue facing the Chinese Communists. Our Party has proposed the Five-Sphere Integrated Plan and the Four-Pronged Comprehensive Strategy, comprehensively opening new horizons for the modernization of contemporary China.

China's modernization is an unprecedented transformation in human history. Against the backdrop of profound global changes, adjustments, and turbulence, China, standing at the center stage of the world, provides new directions, approaches, and options for addressing major global issues such as the world economy, international security, and global governance. The attractiveness and influence of China's development concepts, development path, and development model have significantly increased.

1 *Ibid.*

China is increasingly playing an important role as a builder of world peace, a contributor to global development, and a maintainer of international order. It is promoting the establishment of a new international economic and political order and the development of economic globalization in a fair and reasonable direction. Adhering to new development philosophy, China contributes new ideas of "scientific development, peaceful development, inclusive development, and win-win development" to the development of human society. It actively fulfills the role of a responsible major country, leads the reform of the global governance system, practices the global governance concept of achieving shared growth through discussion and collaboration, and actively promotes the building of human community with a shared future. Through the solid advancement of the BRI, China ensures that the people of the countries and regions along the route gain tangible benefits. It promotes the transcendence of civilizational barriers through civilizational exchanges, the transcendence of civilizational clashes through mutual learning, and the transcendence of civilizational superiority through civilizational coexistence. In the New Era, China has not only achieved significant development for itself but also brought benefits to the world, continuously contributing Chinese wisdom and approaches to global issues.

II. What Is New about Chinese Modernization

The path of modernization with Chinese characteristics follows the laws governing the development of human society and the laws governing socialist development. It is a brand new path of modernization that is entirely different from capitalism. This Chinese path to modernization offers Chinese wisdom, experience, and approaches for humanity's journey toward modernization.

What is new about the modernization path with Chinese characteristics as a novel and distinctive road from the existing capitalist modernization road?

The Chinese Communists, with their proud tradition and great spirit of independence, self-reliance, and self-strengthening, have always emphasized the "Chinese" characteristics and essential requirements for achieving modernization. At the beginning of the reform and opening up, Deng Xiaoping pointed out the need to "create better and newer things with Chinese characteristics," explicitly proposing "Chinese-type modernization." He stated, "The modernization we are striving for is modernization of a Chinese type. The socialism we are building is a socialism with Chinese characteristics."[1] General Secretary Xi Jinping repeatedly emphasized, "There is no one-size-fits-all development model in the world, nor is there a development path that remains unchanged. The diversity of historical conditions determines the diversity of development paths chosen by different countries."[2] The 19th CPC National Congress set the overall task of realizing socialist modernization and the rejuvenation of the Chinese nation. The Fifth Plenary Session of the 19th Central Committee upheld the integration of inheritance and innovation, elucidating the guiding thought, principles, and basic connotations of China's modernization, fully demonstrating the distinctive features and essential requirements of Chinese modernization. Chinese modernization adheres to the general laws governance modernization while fully reflecting the country's historical traditions, fundamental national conditions, institutional attributes, and actual development.

1. The modernization of a huge population

1 Deng Xiaoping, *Selected Works of Deng Xiaoping*, Beijing: Foreign Languages Press, 1994, vol. III, p. 39.
2 *Documents Produced since the 18th CPC National Congress*, Beijing: Central Party Literature Publishing House, 2014, vol. I, p. 699.

A huge population is a fundamental national condition of China. In a country with such a vast population, bringing the entire population into modernization is an extraordinarily challenging task. Since the 18th National Congress, the CPC Central Committee, with General Secretary Xi Jinping at its core, has adhered to the fundamental principles of scientific socialism, combined them with China's reality and the characteristics of the times, exercised overall leadership, coordinated the efforts of all sides , and coordinated efforts to pursue the Five-Sphere Integrated Plan and the Four-Pronged Comprehensive Strategy, thus making solid strides in the modernization of a huge population.

According to the International Monetary Fund, in 2019, there were 35 developed economies globally that had achieved modernization, with a total population of less than one billion. As the world's largest developing country, China, through continuous efforts, has built a moderately prosperous society in all respects benefiting over 1.4 billion people. This will further elevate one fifth of the world's population to the level of moderately developed countries, creating a great miracle in human history and making a significant contribution to human development and progress.

2. The modernization of common prosperity for all

Whose modernization is it, and who drives and realizes modernization? These are the most direct practical issues and fundamental positions in advancing modernization, determining its nature and whether it can achieve ultimate success. Marxism holds that the people are the creators of history and the primary force determining the historical development of human society. The mass line is our Party's fundamental political position, the mass viewpoint is a basic perspective of historical materialism, and the mass line method is our Party's fundamental working method.

Chinese modernization is centered on the people. Unlike Western capitalist modernization, which serves a minority of the bourgeoisie and is centered on capital, the ultimate goal of socialist modernization with Chinese characteristics is to achieve national prosperity, national rejuvenation, and people's happiness. Being people-centered has been a consistent and prominent feature of over 70 years of China's modernization. After the founding of the People's Republic of China, the Chinese Communists, with Mao Zedong as the main representative, proposed the grand goal of achieving the Four Modernizations to transform the country from poverty and backwardness and to improve people's lives. In the new period of reform and opening up, the Chinese Communists, with Deng Xiaoping as the main representative, proposed the goal of building a moderately prosperous society, closely linking national modernization with the improvement of people's living standards, greatly mobilizing the enthusiasm of the people to build a great modern socialist country. Since the 18th National Congress, the CPC Central Committee, with General Secretary Xi Jinping at its core, has proposed and adhered to the people-centered philosophy of development, focusing on the people's new expectations for a better life, making new top-level designs for socialist modernization in the New Era, and advancing the historical process of China's socialist modernization, continuously enhancing people's sense of security, happiness, and fulfillment.

Chinese modernization is a modernization jointly created by the people, not one involving only a few. The people are the true heroes: "The magnificent history of the Chinese nation has been written by the Chinese people. The extensive and profound Chinese civilization has been created by the Chinese people. The spirit of the Chinese nation, kept fresh and alive throughout history, has been cultivated by the Chinese people. The endeavor of the Chinese people has led to a tremendous transformation of the Chinese nation: It has stood up, become better off and grown in strength."[1] "The people are our Party's greatest strength in governance. They are the solid base of our republic, and the foundation of a well-built Party and a prosperous nation. Our Party is from the people, for the people, and successful because of the people. It must always be close to the people, and work vigorously by their side through thick and thin."[2] The path of socialist modernization with Chinese characteristics is the only way to build a strong socialist country and realize the rejuvenation of the Chinese nation. This endeavor is not only a monumental national undertaking but also a great project in human history, bearing significant and profound implications for the development of both the Chinese nation and human society. The CPC's original aspiration and founding mission are to seek happiness for the people, rejuvenation for the nation, and harmony for the world. "The roc soars not merely because of the lightness of one of its feathers; the steed gallops not merely because of the strength of one of its legs."

The path to modernization with Chinese characteristics is neither quick nor easy. It faces significant challenges, including resistance and exclusion from the Western model of modernization, as well as risks across various fields such as economics, politics, culture, society, ecology, military affairs, science, technology, and security. Achieving this grand vision of modernization requires drawing upon the collective strength and wisdom of the people. As it is often said, "Before the people, we are always students in the primary school."

In leading the people toward socialist modernization, the Party has consistently emphasized the importance of firmly establishing the people's

---

1 *Thirty Lectures on Xi Jinping Thought on Socialism with Chinese Characteristics for a New Era,* Beijing: Xuexi Press, 2018, p. 88.
2 Xi Jinping, *The Governance of China,* Beijing: Foreign Languages Press, 2020, vol. III, p. 163.

principal status. It stays committed to doing everything for the masses and relying on them, following the principle of "from the masses, to the masses." It respects the people's pioneering spirit and strives to fully unleash their creative potential. The ultimate measure of the Party's work is the support, approval, happiness, and satisfaction of the people.

3. The modernization of material and cultural-ethical advancement

The concept of overall planning, coordination, comprehensive development, and harmony reflects the fundamental requirements of Marxist dialectical materialism, an important ideological and methodological approach in Marxism. Dialectical materialism reveals the universal interconnectedness and eternal development of the material world, advocating for objective, relational, developmental, comprehensive, systematic, and dialectical analysis and resolution of problems rather than subjective, isolated, static, partial, fragmented, and absolute analysis. This approach allows for truly understanding the essence, mastering the laws, and properly handling various significant relationships.

Chinese modernization is characterized by overall planning, coordination, comprehensive development, and harmony. The Western path to modernization is built on the private ownership of the means of production and the free competition of market mechanisms, where the goal of the production material owners is to maximize surplus value. This inherently leads to a modernization ideology centered on self-priority, self-superiority, and capital and profit-centric values.

This type of modernization, focused purely on economic growth and short-term gains, leads to a narrow, distorted development that struggles to achieve overall planning, coordination, comprehensive development, and harmony. In contrast to Western modernization, over the past 70 years since the founding of the People's Republic of China, China has gradually established a sound basic economic system centered on public ownership of the means of production, while also allowing for the development of multiple forms of ownership within a socialist market economy. This institutional foundation has supported our consistent commitment to overall planning, coordination, comprehensive development, and harmony in our modernization efforts.

The Chinese Communists, represented mainly by Mao Zedong, proposed the Four Modernizations—modernizing agriculture, industry, national defense, and science and technology—which encompass the basic aspects of modernization. Successive central committees since the beginning of reform and opening up has continuously inherited and developed the goals of the Four Modernizations. Deng Xiaoping emphasized, "From the very first year of the 1980s, we must devote our full attention to achieving the four modernizations and not waste a single day"[1] and insisted, "[T] he political line of the Party at the present stage is to work with one heart and one mind for our country's four modernizations. This should be done resolutely and wholeheartedly despite all interference."[2]

From the early focus on achieving both material and cultural-ethical progress, to the three-pronged approach of political, material, and cultural progress, to the fourfold strategy of economic, political, cultural, and social development, and ultimately to the Five-Sphere Integrated Plan introduced at the 18th CPC National Congress—which encompasses economic, political, cultural, social, and ecological advancement—the strategies for socialist modernization with Chinese characteristics have continuously matured through development and refinement. This Five-Sphere Integrated Plan fully embodies the methodology and philosophy of overall planning, coordination, and comprehensive development that has guided the entire

---

1   Deng Xiaoping, *Selected Works of Deng Xiaoping*, Beijing: Foreign Languages Press, 1995, vol. II, p. 243.

2   *Ibid.*, p. 274.

modernization process.

Since the 18th CPC National Congress, the Central Committee, with General Secretary Xi Jinping at its core, has put forward several key strategic frameworks, including the Five-Sphere Integrated Plan for advancing economic, political, cultural, social, and ecological development; the Four-Pronged Comprehensive Strategy of making comprehensive moves to finish building a moderately prosperous society in all respects (build a modern socialist country in all respects), deepen reform, advance law-based governance, and strengthen Party self-governance; the five development concepts of innovative, coordinated, green, open and inclusive development. These frameworks uphold and strengthen the Party's major strategic concepts and significant theoretical viewpoints. They demonstrate, on one hand, that overall planning, coordination, comprehensive development, and harmony are defining features of the governance approach under the leadership of the Central Committee with General Secretary Xi Jinping at its core. On the other hand, they reflect the Party's deep understanding and scientific grasp of the laws governing socialist modernization.

The CPC Central Committee, with General Secretary General Secretary Xi Jinping at the core, has skillfully integrated the concepts of overall planning, coordination, comprehensive development, and harmony into the methods of governance, ensuring that these principles guide the country's progress in a balanced and sustainable manner.

First, the Central Committee has stressed both major and minor problems and both major and minor aspects of a problem, while focusing on major issues and major aspects of a problem. It has emphasized both coordinated advancement and overall planning, as well as identifying key priorities and tackling critical issues, coordinating efforts to pursue the Five-Sphere Integrated Plan and the Four-Pronged Comprehensive

Strategy. As General Secretary Xi Jinping pointed out: "In every aspect of our work, we should address both major and minor problems and both major and minor aspects of a problem, while focusing on major issues and major aspects of a problem. Different problems cannot be solved by undifferentiated measures."[1] For example, he often emphasized that in finishing building a moderately prosperous society in all respects, no one should be left behind. We must promote overall progress while targeting precise points, implementing targeted poverty alleviation and eradication.

Second, the Central Committee has stressed the art of playing the piano with ten fingers. Socialist modernization is a comprehensive modernization. It is essential to coordinate and balance economic, political, cultural, social, and ecological advancement, considering every aspect, sector, and level comprehensively. As General Secretary Xi Jinping profoundly noted: "We must base our actions on a clear understanding of the situation, balance various factors comprehensively, highlight key points to drive the overall situation. Sometimes we need to focus on the big picture while letting go of minor details, and other times we need to address small details to reveal the broader context. Figuratively speaking, we need to play the piano with ten fingers."[2]

Third, the Central Committee has emphasized the need to have the broader picture in mind and maintain the broadest perspective. The cause of socialism with Chinese characteristics in the New Era is one of comprehensive development and progress. The ability to properly balance personal interests with collective interests, and local interests with national interests, is crucial for the success of modernization. General Secretary Xi Jinping repeatedly stressed the need to "be adept at grasping the overall picture and making major plans and consciously think and act in line

---

1 Xi Jinping, "Dialectical Materialism as the Worldview and Methodology of the Chinese Communists," *Qiushi*, Chin. ed., 2019, no. 1.
2 "Xi Jinping's Interview with Russian Television," *People's Daily*, February 9, 2014.

with the bigger picture," to "enhance the ability to observe trends, set the overall direction, and plan major tasks," and to "strategize the big picture, focusing both on individual moves and the overall strategy." Under the scientific guidance and strong promotion of these concepts and methods, China's socialist modernization in the New Era has achieved historic accomplishments and undergone historic changes.

4. The modernization of harmony between humanity and nature

As humans transform nature and society, they also continuously transform themselves. In the process of transforming the objective world, they are also transforming their subjective world.

A socialist society lays the institutional foundation for the organic integration of these elements and opens up broad prospects. The integration is specific and historical; the coordinated and comprehensive development of the economy and society provides economic, political, and cultural conditions for the well-rounded development of individuals. In turn, the well-rounded development of individuals promotes more coordinated and comprehensive economic and social development. In the process of achieving modernization, China adheres to its national conditions and the current level of productivity, continuously liberating and developing productive forces to provide a material foundation for the well-rounded development of individuals. Through developing socialist democracy, ensuring a high level of cultural-ethical progress, and establishing new types of social relations, institutional guarantees are provided for the well-rounded development of individuals. By ensuring a high level of cultural-ethical progress, cultural dynamism is provided for the well-rounded development of individuals. By properly managing the relationship between humans and nature, a sustainable and favorable environment is provided for the well-rounded development of individuals.

The Fifth Plenary Session of the 19th CPC Central Committee proposed the goal of achieving substantive progress in ecological advancement during the 14th Five-Year Plan period, with a widely established green production and lifestyle by 2035, a fundamental improvement in the ecological environment, and the basic realization of the "Beautiful China" objective. Specific plans were made to "promote green development and facilitate harmony between humans and nature." This entails adhering to the principle that "lucid waters and lush mountains are invaluable assets," respecting nature, conforming to nature, and protecting nature, while maintaining natural ecological boundaries. Implementing a sustainable development strategy, establishing an eco-civilization system, and promoting a comprehensive green transformation of economic and social development are major measures to build China into a great modern socialist country that is prosperous, strong, and beautiful. a prosperous and beautiful great modern socialist country. This path of modernization ensures that economic and social development remains aligned with the people-centered philosophy and requirements, acknowledges the people as the creators of history and the beneficiaries of material and cultural-ethical wealth, and continuously promotes the goal of the well-rounded development of individuals.

Modernization characterized by harmony between humans and nature is rooted in China's reality, encompassing comprehensive, coordinated, and sustainable development. This approach can effectively transition China's economic and social development onto a green, coordinated, and sustainable trajectory. Coordinated development involves balancing urban and rural areas, regions, the economy and society, humans and nature, and domestic development and opening up, promoting the coordinated development of all social aspects. Sustainable development aims to achieve harmony between humans and nature, aligning economic development with population, resources, and the environment, ensuring the perpetual development of the economy and society across generations. This development path, while adhering to the general laws governing modern socialized production and economic development, also fits China's national conditions and realities, helping to solve current development challenges. It considers both the present and the long-term, maintaining unity between the Party's highest and fundamental programs. It aims to develop for the fundamental interests of the overwhelming majority of the people in China and contributes to building a human community with a shared future characterized by lasting peace and common prosperity.

5. The modernization of peaceful development

"Peace is the eternal hope of the people. Like air and sunshine, people hardly notice peace when they have it, but life without it is impossible. Without peace, development is out of the question."[1] Without peace, smooth development is impossible, and without development, lasting peace cannot be maintained. In an era where human society possesses abundant social wealth, advanced science and technology, and close international exchanges, we are more equipped than ever to move toward the goals of peace and development. The key to maintaining peaceful development is to recognize the trends of the times and keep pace with its progress.

After the founding of the People's Republic of China, the country proposed the Five Principles of Peaceful Coexistence, pursued an independent foreign policy of peace, and made solemn commitments never to expand or seek hegemony. At the beginning of the reform and opening up period, to create favorable domestic and international environments for China's modernization, Deng Xiaoping scientifically analyzed the domestic

---

1   Xi Jinping, "Working Together toward a Better Future for Asia and the World: Keynote Speech at the Boao Forum for Asia Annual Conference 2013," *People's Daily*, April 8, 2013.

and international situation and the requirements of the development of human society, proposing that "peace and development are the themes of the times." On the basis of the Five Principles of Peaceful Coexistence, China established and developed friendly and cooperative relations with countries worldwide, effectively maintaining overall international peace and stability and promoting common development among countries nations. Over the past 40-plus years of reform and opening up, China has consistently adhered to the following principles and concepts:

- Regardless of its level of development, China will always be a staunch force for maintaining world peace, developing itself through a peaceful international environment and creating more development opportunities for the world through its own development.

- China opposes hegemonism and power politics, does not indiscriminately copy foreign models, nor does it require other countries to copy its practices. On the path of development, China neither "imports" nor "exports" models.

- China adheres to an open strategy of mutual benefit, mutual respect, equal consultation, mutual learning, and seeking common ground while reserving differences with other countries and nations.

- China advocates resolving disputes and conflicts between countries through dialogue and cooperation and proposes important concepts such as building a human community with a shared future and initiatives like the Belt and Road that benefit people worldwide.

It is precisely because of this favorable international environment and consistent adherence to these principles and concepts that China has created the globally admired "Chinese miracle" on its modernization path.

As the world enters the new century and socialism with Chinese characteristics enters the New Era, the world today faces profound changes of a kind unseen in a century, marked by significant development, transformation, and adjustment. Yet, peace and development remain the themes of our times. Maintaining and adapting to peaceful development remains an important principle that the world and China should continue to uphold in the new century. "[O]ne cannot live in the 21st century while thinking in the old fashion, lingering in the age of colonial expansion or with the zero-sum mentality of the Cold War."[1] "China's pursuit of peaceful development is not an act of expediency, still less diplomatic rhetoric. Rather, it is the conclusion drawn from an objective assessment of China's history, its present and future."[2] The Chinese nation has always been peace-loving. Traditional Chinese culture emphasizes ideas such as "the common good reigns over all under Heaven," "harmony under Heaven," and "harmony in relations with all other countries." The love of peace, as a cherished tradition, is deeply embedded in the cultural fabric and heritage of the Chinese nation, profoundly and subtly influencing every individual.

China's path of peaceful development is grounded in a profound understanding of the laws governing the modernization of human society. From a guiding perspective, both pacifism and the notion that a rising power will inevitably seek hegemony are inconsistent with these laws; they are unsustainable and reflect historical idealism that contradicts the foundational principles of Marxism. The CPC views the pursuit of happiness for the people, national rejuvenation, and global harmony as its historical mission. The CPC has consistently opposed imperialism, colonialism, hegemony, and power politics, advocating for a more equitable international political order and aligning itself with the broad populace and developing countries.

Importantly, since modern times, China has endured colonial invasion and exploitation by Western powers, gaining a deep understanding

---

1   Xi Jinping, *The Governance of China*, Beijing: Foreign Languages Press, 2018, vol. I, p. 299.
2   *Ibid.*, p. 293.

of the suffering and devastation that hegemony inflicts on developing countries and their peoples. This historical experience heightens China's appreciation for the importance of peaceful development and reinforces its commitment to maintaining a peaceful environment both domestically and internationally, firmly rejecting the path of hegemony. General Secretary Xi Jinping has eloquently stated, "China is now on the road to development and prosperity, but we reject the logic that a country which grows strong is bound to pursue hegemony," adding, "a warlike country, however big it might be, is bound to perish."[1]

The practices since the founding of the People's Republic of China, particularly since the reform and opening up, have demonstrated that peaceful development is the right choice, harmonizing with China's social system, basic national conditions, historical experiences, cultural traditions, and the aspirations of people worldwide.

Of course, China has always adhered to the path of peaceful development, but this is not a form of pacifism. Rather, it is the consistent unification of independence, self-determination, and peaceful development, with a firm commitment to safeguarding the country's core interests. General Secretary Xi Jinping emphasized, "We should keep to the path of peaceful development, but we must not relinquish our legitimate rights and interests or sacrifice our country's core interests. No foreign country should expect us to sell off our core interests, or to accept damage to our sovereignty, security or development interests."[2]

China's path of peaceful development has clear boundaries. It will never achieve its modernization at the expense of other countries' interests, nor will it blindly abandon its core national interests and legitimate rights

---

1   Xi Jinping, "Forging a Strong Partnership to Enhance Prosperity of Asia: Speech at the National University of Singapore," *People's Daily*, November 8, 2015.
2   "Xi Jinping Emphasizes Better Coordination of Domestic and International Situations to Solidify the Foundation of the Path of Peaceful Development during the Third Group Study Session of the Political Bureau of the CPC Central Committee," *People's Daily*, January 30, 2013.

for the sake of modernization. No country or bloc should expect China to accept damage to its sovereignty, security or development interests. China will resolutely defend its core national interests.

6. The socialist modernization path under the leadership of the Communist Party

Since human society entered the Western-dominated capitalist world system, especially in the era of imperialism, late-developing countries have found it impossible to achieve modernization by spontaneously adopting privatization, capital, market, and free competition as Western developed countries did. In other words, late-developing countries can only achieve modernization by integrating into the Western-led capitalist world system. Moreover, such modernization is either a restrictive modernization that involves forfeiting some sovereignty or an attached form of "modernization," as seen in many developing countries today. These two types of so-called "modernization" are pseudo-modernizations in name only, essentially embedding themselves passively within the Western modernization system and bearing differentiated roles in a differentiated form of modernization. Different developing countries are assigned different "modernization models" based on their resource endowments—some as raw material suppliers, others as producers of primary products, some as producers of mid- to high-end products, and others as market providers, etc.

The socialist modernization path is different from the Western modernization path. Compared to the spontaneous capitalist modernization, socialist modernization is a conscious modernization that requires strong political leadership. Without this, it is unimaginable to carve out a socialist modernization path distinct from the Western-dominated capitalist world system. A strong political leadership must be guided by advanced theories and composed of the advanced class. Only an advanced political party guided by advanced theories and composed of the advanced class can form a powerful political force, leadership force, cohesive force, mobilization force, and organizational force, ensuring unity and consciousness in all actions. Only such an advanced political party can unite the people's hearts, stabilize the situation, gather the wisdom of the people, mobilize the people's enthusiasm, seize fleeting development opportunities, and lead the socialist modernization development with goals, plans, steps, and guidance.

Building China into a modern country and achieving the rejuvenation of the Chinese nation has been the relentless dream of countless devoted individuals since modern times. However, despite various explorations and experiments, the backward semi-colonial and semi-feudal state of our society and the miserable fate of the Chinese people were not fundamentally changed. "With the advent of modern times, Chinese society became embroiled in intense upheavals; this was a time of fierce struggle as the Chinese people resisted feudal rule and foreign aggression. It was in the midst of this, in 1921, as Marxism-Leninism was integrated with the Chinese workers' movement, that the Communist Party of China was born. From that moment on, the Chinese people have had in the Party a backbone for their pursuit of national independence and liberation, of a stronger and more prosperous country, and of their own happiness; and the mindset of the Chinese people has changed, from passivity to taking the initiative."[1]

Only under the leadership of the CPC can socialist modernization become a reality. After its founding, the CPC united and led the Chinese people in the country. Through prolonged and bloody struggles, it achieved the victory of the new-democratic revolution, established the People's

---

1   *A Guide to the Political Report of the 19th National Congress of the Communist Party of China*, Beijing: People's Publishing House, 2017, p.

Republic of China, completed the socialist transformation, established the basic socialist system, and successfully realized the most profound and greatest social transformation in Chinese history. This laid the fundamental political premise and institutional foundation for all contemporary development and progress in China, cleared the obstacles for achieving socialist modernization in the People's Republic of China, opened up the path, and created the conditions.

Under the strong leadership of the CPC, generation after generation has continuously promoted the new great social revolution of reform and opening up, providing the Party and the people's cause with powerful momentum for progress, eliminating all theoretical and institutional barriers to national and ethnic development, and opening up the path of socialist modernization with Chinese characteristics.

In our country, the political conscious force that plays a core leadership role has always been the CPC under the guidance of Marxism. As Deng Xiaoping pointed out: "In a big country like ours, it is inconceivable that unity of thinking could be achieved among our several hundred million people or that their efforts could be pooled to build socialism in the absence of a Party whose members have a spirit of sacrifice and a high level of political awareness and discipline, a Party that truly represents and unites the masses of people and exercises unified leadership. Without such a Party, our country would split up and accomplish nothing."[1] It is precisely under the unified and strong leadership of the party, through more than 70 years of relentless efforts and continuous struggle, overcoming countless difficulties, that our socialist modernization development has achieved great success. Our country has undergone earth-shaking changes, overcoming one seemingly insurmountable challenge after another, and creating one remarkable human miracle after another. The Chinese nation

---

1   Deng Xiaoping, *Selected Works of Deng Xiaoping*, Beijing: Foreign Languages Press, 1995, vol. II, p. 560.

has achieved a tremendous transformation: it has stood up, grown rich, and is becoming strong. Today, we are closer to, more confident in, and more capable of achieving the goal than ever before and fully building a socialist modernized nation.

Since the 18th CPC National Congress, our party has positioned itself at a new historical juncture in the New Era, giving the leadership of the CPC a correct definition. It has pointed out that CPC leadership is the defining feature of socialism with Chinese characteristics and constitutes the greatest strength of the system of socialism with Chinese characteristics. Moreover, it has emphasized that the Party exercises overall leadership over all areas of endeavor in every part of the country. It has proposed that we should unwaveringly uphold and improve Party leadership and make the Party still stronger. It has stressed the following:

▪ Uphold and strengthen overall Party leadership and ensure that the Party exercises effective self-supervision and practices strict self-governance in every respect;

▪ Take strengthening the Party's long-term governance capacity and its advanced nature and purity as the main thrust; take enhancing the Party's political building as the overarching principle; take holding dear the Party's ideals, convictions, and purpose as the underpinning; and take harnessing the whole Party's enthusiasm, initiative, and creativity as the focus of efforts;

▪ Make all-round efforts to see the Party's political building enhanced, its theory strengthened, its organizations consolidated, its conduct improved, and its discipline enforced, with institution building incorporated into every aspect of Party building;

▪ Step up efforts to combat corruption and continue to improve the efficacy of Party building;

▪ Build the Party into a vibrant Marxist governing party that is always at the forefront of the times, enjoys the wholehearted support of the people, has the courage to reform itself, and is able to withstand all tests."[1]

This provides the fundamental political guarantee for building a great modern socialist country on a new starting point and realizing the rejuvenation of the Chinese nation.

From the Four Modernizations goals proposed in the early years of the founding of the People's Republic of China, to the three-step strategy proposed after the reform and opening up, and then to the two-step goal of building a great modern socialist country put forward at the 19th CPC National Congress, it fully reflects our Party's increasingly deep, profound, and scientific understanding of the laws governing socialist modernization. To ensure that our modernization drive proceeds smoothly in the right direction and follows scientific laws, over the more than 70 years since the founding of the People's Republic of China, the system of Party leadership has gradually been established and continuously matured and become well-defined in the process of socialist modernization.

III. Provide a New Option for Other Developing Countries to Achieve Modernization

A small number of developing countries first embarked on modernization around the mid-19th century, such as Argentina and Brazil. However, after a period of medium- to high-speed development, these countries quickly entered a phase of stagnation and decline, even falling into the "middle-income trap," commonly referred to as the "Latin American trap." The vast majority of developing countries embarked on modernization after World War II, choosing the Western development model under the demonstrative effect of Western modernization. From

---

1 *Documents from the 19th CPC National Congress*, Beijing: People's Publishing House, 2017, pp. 49–50.

their perspective, as long as they strive to follow and emulate Western Europe and North America, they will surely be able to modernize their own countries. However, over the past 70 years, the vast majority of these developing countries that chose the Western path to modernization have not achieved their desired outcomes. Instead, they have paid a heavy price, with most countries falling into development difficulties, experiencing widespread economic stagnation, political disorder, social decay, and widening wealth gaps. In some cases, individual countries in certain geopolitical regions have frequently faced wars. This situation has shattered the mythicized worship of the Western modernization path that they previously chose, leaving many developing countries at a historical crossroads.

The current development difficulties faced by many developing countries have both internal and external causes. Internally, the main issues lie in the initial choice of development path and the timely transformation of development strategies after that choice. Externally, the main issues include: first, most developing countries entered the then-modernization wave as weaker groups; second, they actively joined the Western-led economic globalization and world system, which not only restricted their development but also integrated them into the Western-arranged "vertical division of labor" in the international economic system, to some extent making them appendages of Western modernization. Under the combined effects of these internal and external factors, many developing countries have been locked into a state of "underdeveloped development" from the very start of their modernization journey to ensure Western prosperity.

The modernization of developing countries is destined to undergo a long historical process because, from the outset of their modernization efforts, they were placed under the constraints of international monopoly capital groups, which delineated a very narrow development space for them. Practice has shown that only a very few developing countries have achieved Western modernization, and even then, their modernization is somewhat dependent. From a long-term historical perspective, developing countries will ultimately need to embark on a modernization path that aligns with the direction of the development of human society. Should they continue on the Western path, or choose an alternative route? If they choose an alternative, which path should they take? Undoubtedly, the path of socialist modernization with Chinese characteristics provides a new option for many other developing countries that are experiencing development difficulties and feeling uncertain about the future. Of course, this option does not mean copying China exactly or treating China's "specificity" as "universality." Instead, it means extracting and learning from some of the common and beneficial experiences formed in China's path to modernization.

1. Properly balance reform, development, and stability

Reform, development, and stability are major issues that developing countries, including China, must manage well. These three elements are intrinsically linked. For many developing countries, development is the absolute principle and the key to solving all problems; reform is the driving force behind development and the only way to modernization; stability is the fundamental prerequisite for both reform and development, without which nothing can be achieved. It can even be said that the key to solving all problems in many developing countries lies in reform, development, and stability. These three elements are like three interrelated strategic pieces on the chessboard of modernization. If each move is well made and they mutually promote each other, the overall situation will thrive. If one move fails, the other two will also face difficulties, potentially leading to setbacks in the overall situation.

From a practical perspective, the main reason why many developing countries are currently in a modernization dilemma is that they have not properly balanced these three elements. Particularly for some developing countries, social instability has become the overriding issue. Economic development or reform efforts are often accompanied by political and social turmoil, which in turn restricts healthy and stable economic development. This situation, where reform, development, and stability are difficult to reconcile, is largely due to the interference, intervention, and disruption by Western developed countries, which severely limits the policy choices of many developing countries, putting them in a dilemma. Most developing countries frequently encounter social conflicts and upheavals in their modernization process, with their progress often being disrupted or interrupted.

China has found a balance in balancing reform, development, and stability. Maintaining social stability has always been a major issue in the process of reform and opening up. By adhering to the premise of stability, China has promoted reform, opening up, and economic development, achieving unprecedented long-term and large-scale development in modern Chinese history and laying a solid foundation for China to become a truly powerful country. Entering the New Era, China's economy has shifted from a phase of rapid growth to a stage of high-quality development, deepening supply-side structural reform, and transforming the mode of economic development. In 2020, despite the impact of the COVID-19 pandemic, China's economy still maintained positive growth, while the global economy experienced negative growth. History tells us that without a stable political environment, nothing can be accomplished.

Reform is for the sake of development, stability is also for the sake of development, and development is for the people. For a long time, poverty has been the fundamental problem hindering the progress of many developing countries and has been a concern of the international community, but it has not yet been significantly improved.

Africa is the poorest region in the world and also has the highest concentration of developing countries. According to statistics provided by relevant United Nations departments, out of the 48 poorest countries in the world, 34 are in Africa. The extremely poor population in Africa accounts for 43% of its total population, making poverty the most challenging issue in Africa's economic development. According to the United Nations Economic Commission for Latin America and the Caribbean's report "Social Panorama of Latin America 2018," in 2017, the number of poor in Latin America reached 184 million, equivalent to 30.2% of the population, while the number of extremely poor stood at 62 million, or 10.2% of the population. Preliminary statistics show that in 2018, the number of poor people in Latin America was 182 million, a decrease of 2 million from 2017; however, the number of extremely poor people rose to 63 million, an increase of 1 million from 2017.

China, the world's largest developing country, is also widely recognized by the international community as the most effective in poverty eradication. In 1978, China had 770 million rural poor, which decreased to 30.46 million by 2017. Over the 40 years of reform and opening up, China reduced its rural poor population by 740 million, accounting for 60% of the global reduction in poverty during this period. In 1978, China's poverty incidence rate was 97.5%, which dropped to 3.1% by 2017. By 2020, China had eliminated absolute poverty under its current standards. The successful balancing of reform and development provided the material foundation for solving the poverty issue; the gradual resolution of poverty, in turn, created a stable political and social environment for further reform and development.

On their path forward, developing countries should:

- Effectively manage their reforms to promote social progress and national strength.

- Focus on development as the central task to address all problems encountered in their progress.

- Maintain social stability to foster reform and development.

- Address poverty through reform and development to solve issues of polarization and wealth disparity, thereby maintaining social stability.

2. Properly balance independence and openness

The Western countries that first entered modernization indeed have many aspects worth learning from. However, many developing countries, in their efforts to follow and learn from Western modernization, adhered to dogmatism and took a path of outright imitation. Unfortunately, this approach caused many developing countries to lose their independence to a large extent. In their comprehensive adoption of the Western model, they failed to grasp the general principles it embodied, and even more so, did not integrate it with their own historical and cultural conditions.

In fact, the Western model of modernization itself does not conform to the value orientations of the development of human society. Its modernization process is accompanied by external exploitation and plunder. One of the main reasons why many developing countries fall into difficulties in their modernization process is that their governments, in unconditionally accepting and implementing the Western model of modernization, fail to properly balance independence and openness in the modernization process.

The modernization of developing countries has been carried out from the beginning under the premise of losing a significant part of their independence, with openness being one of its important attributes. However, openness without complete independence is a double-edged sword. In practice, the great cost that many developing countries have paid in openness is the loss of independent development capabilities and development rights. Some Western countries, by using bank loans, direct investments, and economic aid as bait, have made many developing countries open their doors to international capital. These countries then act in accordance with the rules set by the West, becoming passive links in the global capitalist chain. This leads to difficulties in making independent decisions in fiscal policy, monetary policy, and major decisions affecting national livelihood, effectively losing their economic sovereignty and other forms of sovereignty. The long-term dependence of some Latin American countries on foreign capital, where their economies face collapse once the foreign capital withdraws, is a typical example of this.

In retrospect, what American scholar Francis Fukuyama called the "end of history" is far from over. Developing countries should and can open up better paths to modernization. The path of socialist modernization with Chinese characteristics is a road that is different from, superior to, and has infinitely bright prospects compared to the Western path. On the road ahead, developing countries should firstly promote the modernization process based on their own conditions. Every country has its unique resource endowments, historical background, and cultural foundation. Modernization should not aim to eliminate these differences but to find ways to transform these national characteristics into development drivers. Secondly, they should dialectically learn from the advanced experiences of other countries and independently explore modernization paths with their own characteristics. Thirdly, they should actively participate in the globalization process and follow an independent path of open development. In the face of globalization, developing countries should neither close themselves off, missing development opportunities, nor become dependent on others, falling into the lower end of the division of labor system.

Instead, they should maintain their independence while actively integrating into the globalization process to promote continuous development of productive forces.

3. Properly remain dependent or break free

Western developed capitalist countries have established and dominate the world system, while many developing countries in Asia, Africa, and Latin America have passively entered this system. These peripheral developing countries are in a disadvantaged or even dependent position within the world system. The modernization of peripheral countries is strictly constrained and limited by the world system.

Almost all developing countries have been unable to shed their dependence on the Western center during their modernization processes. Faced with the Western-dominated world system, the strong inertia of Western development, the powerful control exerted by major Western countries, and the enticing yet toxic "fruits" of Western modernization, many developing countries have had no choice but to opt for dependent development. While this choice has brought some limited development to these countries, it has also resulted in a loss of some degree of independence. Have developing countries not thought about breaking away from the West to pursue independent development? Of course, they have. In fact, quite a few countries have even taken action. However, those countries that acted soon faced various forms of suppression from Western countries, leading them to either abandon their efforts or stagnate, as seen in some Latin American countries.

Do developing countries truly have no choice but to remain dependent or attempt to break free? As the largest developing country in the world, China, through its own path to modernization, has shown many other developing countries that it is possible to neither completely break away from the West nor be entirely dependent on it. Instead, China has chosen to actively integrate into the international community without sliding into the Western development track. China has boldly drawn on the advanced achievements of capitalist countries without losing its independence. It is precisely because China has integrated into the world and international society on the premise of maintaining its independence that it has been able to achieve such remarkable development success and remain uniquely prominent. Furthermore, China has repeatedly managed to insulate itself from the economic crises brought about by the capitalist world.

On the road ahead, developing countries should first establish the belief that "there are multiple routes to modernity."[1] They must believe that there are other paths to modernization beyond the Western model. For example, the Chinese modernization path, which has created the Chinese miracle, successfully broke away from dependence on international capitalism and is an independent modernization path. Second, they need to theoretically overcome the abstract dichotomy of "development-dependence" and "poverty-independence" and, in practice, create a "development-independence" type of modernization path. Modernization is not simply a process of identifying with the Western countries; it inherently contains different value orientations and mode choices for development within the historical, social, and cultural context of each country. If developing countries do not break away from the "center-periphery" system of dependent development dominated by international capital and developed countries, it will be difficult for them to truly embark on the path of modernization.

---

1   Alberto Martinelli, *Global Modernization: Rethinking the Project of Modernity*, translated by Li Guowu, Beijing: The Commercial Press, 2010, p. 122.

4. Properly balance government and market

Planning and market mechanisms are both economic tools used by all economies, with some prioritizing planning and supplementing with market mechanisms, some prioritizing the market and supplementing with planning, and some advocating for laissez-faire, pursuing absolute marketization. Practice has shown that, up to now, the best means of resource allocation is the market. However, the market has inherent flaws, such as spontaneity, unpredictability, and delays, which necessitate government intervention to mitigate and resolve. In practice, many developing countries, during their marketization processes, have almost entirely abandoned the responsibilities that the state and government should assume in fostering economic and social development. This has led to extreme wealth polarization, widening regional disparities, social instability, and, consequently, economic and social stagnation, with modernization efforts experiencing significant setbacks. In contrast, during China's reform and opening up, the government and the market were properly balanced. China not only established a socialist market economy but also, through practical experience, developed a theoretical framework for a socialist market economy with Chinese characteristics, offering valuable insights to address global economic challenges. The establishment of China's socialist market economy has greatly mobilized the productive energies of all sectors, significantly liberated and developed the country's productive forces, spurred rapid economic growth, elevated China's international standing, and consistently improved the living standards of its people.

Looking forward, developing countries must first dispel the illusion of laissez-faire and absolute marketization. Governments must take on an active and effective role in development, using state power to formulate economic plans, set clear development goals and directions, create a favorable environment for economic growth, and efficiently manage resources to prevent the waste and social disruption caused by unchecked market forces. This will foster healthy and sustainable economic development. Secondly, they must move beyond the myth of industrial catch up. Since embarking on the path of modernization, many developing countries have adopted an industrial catch-up strategy, believing that only industrialization can secure national independence and prosperity. However, many of these nations are still in the agricultural stage of development, with insufficient social advancement. Attempts at rapid industrialization often lead to increased social disorder and are unlikely to succeed. Experience has shown that the relentless pursuit of industrial catch up has hindered modernization in developing countries: the single-minded focus on industrialization has resulted in unbalanced economies, the reckless exploitation of natural resources has caused severe ecological damage, making growth unsustainable, and neglecting agricultural development in favor of industry has created internal economic imbalances. These imbalances, exacerbated by food crises, poverty, and hunger, have sparked serious political crises. Finally, the state-owned sector should be expanded while encouraging the joint development of both state-owned and private sectors. The state-owned sector exist to varying degrees under different social systems.

Developing countries should, while fully leveraging the role of the market, enhance the government's macro-control functions and capabilities over both state-owned and private sectors, thereby effectively mitigating the negative impacts of the market.

IV. The Chinese Path to Modernization as a New Form of Human Advancement

In his major speech at a ceremony marking the centenary of the CPC in 2021, General Secretary Xi Jinping proposed a series of significant ideas, viewpoints, and assertions. He elevated the valuable experiences accumulated by our Party over the past century to innovative conclusions and insights into development laws, thereby advancing our Party's understanding of the "three major laws" to a new height, with significant theoretical, practical, and global implications. Among these, General Secretary Xi Jinping made new summaries about the major theoretical and practical significance of socialism with Chinese characteristics from the perspective of pioneering new paths for human development and creating new forms of human advancement. He profoundly pointed out: "As we have upheld and developed socialism with Chinese characteristics and driven coordinated progress in material, political, cultural, ethical, social and eco-environmental terms, we have pioneered a new and uniquely Chinese path to modernization, and created a new model for human progress."[1] This major assertion indicates that the path, theory, system, and culture of socialism with Chinese characteristics are continuously developing, forging an unprecedented path to modernization for humanity. Chinese modernization not only has its distinctive features and unique advantages but also opens up a new form and vast space for the progress of human advancement. It is an organic unity of particularity and universality as well as Chinese characteristics and global significance.

---

1   Xi Jinping, *Speech at a Ceremony Marking the Centenary of the Communist Party of China,* Beijing: People's Publishing House, 2021, p. 14.

1. Distinctive features and unique advantages of Chinese modernization

The new path of Chinese modernization follows the general laws governing modernization development while fully reflecting the country's historical traditions, basic national conditions, institutional attributes, and practical development. Chinese modernization aligns with China's realities, reflecting the laws governing socialist development and the laws governing the development of human society.

First, it fully leverages the significant advantages of the leadership of the CPC and the system of socialism with Chinese characteristics. Achieving modernization has been the persistent dream of the Chinese people since modern times. The original aspiration and founding mission of the Chinese Communists are to seek happiness for the Chinese people and rejuvenation for the Chinese nation. Since the founding of the People's Republic of China, especially since the reform and opening up, the CPC has made a series of institutional arrangements for the country's economic and social development. By continuously improving the system of socialism with Chinese characteristics, the advantages generated by the socialist system—such as the ability to unite all forces that can be united, strong mobilization capabilities, the advantage of concentrating efforts on major tasks, and effectively promoting social fairness and justice—have been fully demonstrated. General Secretary Xi Jinping pointed out: "The defining feature of socialism with Chinese characteristics is the leadership of the Communist Party of China and the greatest strength of the system of socialism with Chinese characteristics is the leadership of the Communist Party of China."[1]

The leadership of the CPC and the system of socialism with Chinese characteristics transcend the mechanical dichotomies of the West regarding market and government, state and society, centralized authority and

---

1   *Documents from the 19th CPC National Congress*, Beijing: People's Publishing House, 2017, p. 16.

democratic freedom, public and private sectors. This has resulted in significant advantages such as rapid economic growth, social harmony and stability, and abundant reform vitality. These advantages not only provide successful experiences for achieving modernization but also stand in stark contrast to the political chaos and social unrest encountered by some countries during their modernization process.

Under the centralized, unified leadership of the CPC, the significant advantages of the system of socialism with Chinese characteristics are vividly demonstrated and integrated into the great practice of realizing the rejuvenation of the Chinese nation. The Chinese people continuously achieve brilliant accomplishments in socialist modernization, creating a world miracle in Chinese modernization. General Secretary Xi Jinping pointed out, "Our greatest strength lies in our socialist system, which enables us to pool resources in a major mission. This is the key to our success."[1] Chinese modernization emphasizes leveraging the political advantage of the socialist system to concentrate resources on major tasks, mobilizing all positive factors to form a common will and collective action for modernization. Whether it is establishing an independent and relatively complete industrial system, independently developing the nuclear bombs, missiles and the artificial earth satellite, addressing a series of major risks and challenges in the modernization process, or completing the arduous task of poverty alleviation, it all requires leveraging the advantages of the new framework of pooling nationwide effort and resources for major missions, with everyone working in unison and concentrating resources to tackle key challenges together.

The battle against poverty is a vivid embodiment of the new

---

1   Xi Jinping, "Strive to Build China into a Scientific and Technological Leader: Speech at the Joint Session of the National Conference on Scientific and Technological Innovation, the 18th Meeting of the Academicians of the Chinese Academy of Sciences and the 13th Meeting of the Academicians of the Chinese Academy of Engineering, and the Ninth National Congress of the China Association for Science and Technology," *People's Daily,* June 1, 2016.

framework of pooling nationwide effort and resources for major missions. In this battle, the central, local, and various sectors fully demonstrated their enthusiasm and the entire country worked together to tackle challenges. This included strengthening east-west poverty alleviation cooperation, promoting the flow of talent, funds, and technology to impoverished areas, and organizing targeted poverty alleviation efforts in accordance with local conditions. Central Party and government departments and different industries and sectors have brought their specializations to bear to fight poverty through the development of local businesses, science and technology, education, cultural programs and health services, and by boosting the consumption of products and services from poor areas. The facts have fully proven that only by concentrating resources and efforts can we effectively overcome difficult problems in a short period.

Second, the practical goal of Chinese modernization is to achieve well-rounded development of individuals and common prosperity for all. Our modernization is one of common prosperity for all, not one of increasing polarization and social fragmentation. Achieving common prosperity is an inherent requirement for realizing the lofty ideal of communism, the historical mission of the CPC, and the essential characteristic of socialism. General Secretary Xi Jinping emphasized, "The development we pursue is development that benefits the people; the wealth we seek is common prosperity for all."[1] Continuously creating a better life and gradually achieving common prosperity for all is a distinctive feature of socialism with Chinese characteristics in the New Era. The 19th CPC National Congress clearly outlined the goal of basically achieving socialist modernization by 2035. By then, significant strides toward common prosperity for all will have been made, and the Chinese people will enjoy

---

1   "The CPC Central Committee Holds Forum with Non-CPC Individuals, and Xi Jinping Presides the Meeting and Delivers a Key Speech," *People's Daily,* November 2, 2015.

a wealthier, fairer, and happier life. Making common prosperity for all an important aspect of building a great modern socialist country showcases the scientific, advanced, and superior nature of Chinese modernization. It aligns with the laws governing socialist development and the developmental trends of human society.

Since the 18th CPC National Congress, the Central Committee with General Secretary Xi Jinping at its core adopted the Five-Sphere Integrated Plan for promoting coordinated economic, political, cultural, social, and ecological advancement, coordinated efforts to pursue the Four-Pronged Comprehensive Strategy and the concepts of innovative, coordinated, green, open and inclusive development. These new development philosophies, along with the integrated plan and comprehensive strategy, demonstrate two key points:

1. They fully reflect that promoting coordinated of material, political, cultural-ethical, social, and ecological advancement is a distinctive feature of the governance of the CPC Central Committee with General Secretary Xi Jinping at its core.

2. They show that Chinese modernization is comprehensive modernization of both people and objects, ultimately aiming to achieve national strength, national rejuvenation, and people's happiness. This is fundamentally different from Western capitalist modernization, which serves only a small bourgeoisie and centers around capital. This also reflects our Party's profound understanding and scientific grasp of the laws governing socialist modernization.

Third, Chinese modernization pursues a path of peaceful development, benefiting both China and the world. General Secretary Xi Jinping pointed out: "Pursuing a path of peaceful development is a strategic decision made by our Party based on the trend of the times and our fundamental interests," and "Pursuing a path of peaceful development is the inheritance and development of the best elements of cultural Chinese traditions and the inevitable conclusion drawn by the Chinese people from their sufferings since modern times."[1] The CPC has always firmly opposed imperialism, colonialism, hegemonism, and power politics, as well as the unequal international political order. It has always stood with the people and other developing countries. Since the founding of the People's Republic of China, our country has never initiated a war, never occupied an inch of others' land, and has resolved border issues with 12 out of 14 neighboring countries through peaceful negotiations. Moreover, "adhering to the path of peaceful development" was written into the newly revised Constitution in 2018, making China the only country in the world to do so. All these facts indicate that China's path to modernization is one of peaceful development. It has completely transcended the logic that "a rising power will inevitably seek hegemony" and avoided the Thucydides Trap, and it stands in stark contrast to the modernization paths of capitalist countries, which were built through colonial plunder and aggressive wars.

2. Expand the broad space for the development and progress of human advancement with a new form of civilization

General Secretary Xi Jinping once stated: "Our country is the largest socialist country in the world. When we build a great modern socialist country and become the first modern country to be successfully built not on a capitalist road but on a socialist road, the great social revolution led by our Party in China will more fully demonstrate its profound historical significance."[2] On the journey to modernization, today we have achieved the First Centenary Goal, finishing building a moderately prosperous

---

1   Xi Jinping, *On Building a Human Community with a Shared Future,* Beijing: Central Party Literature Publishing House, 2018, p. 1.
2   Xi Jinping, *Stay True to the Original Aspirations and Founding Mission of the Party,* Beijing: Party Building Books Publishing House and Central Party Literature Publishing House, 2019, p. 7 Beijing: Party Building Books Publishing House and Central Party Literature Publishing House, 2019, pp. 322–323.

society in all respects on Chinese soil and for the first time, eliminated extreme poverty. The rejuvenation of the Chinese nation has taken a crucial step forward. By the mid-21st century, we aim to build China into a great modern socialist country that is prosperous, strong, democratic, culturally advanced, harmonious and beautiful. This will allow the Chinese nation to stand tall among the nations of the world with even greater vigor, making new and greater contributions to the development of human society and the progress of civilization, with far-reaching historical and global significance.

First, for the first time, eliminating absolute poverty that has plagued the Chinese people for thousands of years constitutes a great contribution to human development.

General Secretary Xi Jinping pointed out: "The history of China is a chronicle of the Chinese people's struggle against poverty." For thousands of years, the Chinese people have had a strong desire to live a moderately prosperous life and escape poverty. Eliminating poverty, enhancing people's wellbeing, and ultimately achieving common prosperity are not only essential requirements of socialism but also the relentless pursuit of the Communists. After the founding of the People's Republic of China, our Party led the entire nation in declaring war on poverty. Since the introduction of the reform and opening up policy, in accordance with current poverty standards, 770 million rural poor people in China have been lifted out of poverty. In accordance with the World Bank's international poverty standards, China's reduced poverty population accounts for more than 70% of the global reduced poverty population during the same period. Especially since the 18th CPC National Congress, the Central Committee has implemented a series of poverty alleviation plans. In 2015, a decision was made to win the battle against poverty, and in 2016, the 13th Five-Year Plan for Poverty Alleviation was issued. These measures effectively promoted innovation in poverty alleviation methods, raised standards, and expanded content. The scope, depth, and intensity of poverty alleviation were unprecedented. As of February 2021, all of the 98.99 million rural residents, who were lying below the current poverty line, had emerged from poverty, all regional poverty had been eliminated, and the task of eliminating absolute poverty had been completed, achieving the United Nations 2030 Agenda for Sustainable Development poverty reduction target 10 years ahead of schedule. This created a human miracle that will go down in history and won widespread acclaim from the international community. China also initially established the world's largest social security system covering the most people, including areas such as pensions, medical care, subsistence allowances, housing, and education. In accordance with the "Global Wealth 2018: Seizing the Analytics Advantage" released by the Boston Consulting Group, China has risen 25 places in the past 10 years, the fastest progress among the 152 surveyed countries. China's remarkable achievements in poverty alleviation have provided Chinese wisdom and Chinese approaches to global poverty reduction and the protection of human rights. As Xi Jinping pointed out: "China's development, viewed through the lens of history, is an integral part of the lofty cause of human progress."[1]

Second, leading over 1.4 billion Chinese people into the ranks of modern countries completely rewrites the global modernization map.

Chinese modernization is a modernization of a huge population. Enabling all people to enter modernization in such a populous country as ours is an extremely challenging task. At a ceremony marking the centenary of the CPC, General Secretary Xi Jinping solemnly declared that we have realized the First Centenary Goal of building a moderately prosperous society in all respects. For our country, the largest developing country in

---

1   Xi Jinping, *The Governance of China*, Beijing: Foreign Languages Press, 2020, vol. III, p. 250.

the world with a population of over 1.4 billion, achieving modernization means that more Chinese people will enter the ranks of modernization than the combined population of all current developed countries. This will fundamentally rewrite the global map of modernization, marking a great miracle in human history and making a significant contribution to human development and progress, with a global impact.

Third, reshaping the nature and direction of modernization and expanding the pathways to human modernization provide new options for many other developing countries.

Since the late 19th century, human society has entered a Western-dominated capitalist world system. Many developing countries found themselves in colonial or semi-colonial conditions and were forced into this system, making it difficult to achieve national independence, social development, and modernization while being oppressed, restricted, and exploited by modern Western powers. The modernization of developing countries has often taken the form of constrained modernization, requiring the cession of full or partial sovereignty, or a form of dependent "modernization." These so-called forms of "modernization" carry the name but not the substance of true modernization. In essence, they are passively integrated into the Western modernization framework, playing different roles in a hierarchical process. Depending on their resource endowments, various developing countries were assigned different "modernization models"—some as suppliers of raw materials, others as producers of primary products, manufacturers of low- to mid-tier goods, or as markets for consumption.

Under the leadership of the CPC and guided by the new path of Chinese modernization, our country has achieved remarkable economic and social development milestones. In a few decades, we have completed the industrialization process that took developed countries several centuries. China has become the world's largest manufacturing country and the second-largest economy, creating rare economic growth and long-term social stability miracles. From 1979 to 2020, China's GDP grew at an average annual rate of 9.2%, significantly higher than the world economy's average annual growth rate of 2.7% during the same period. Especially since the 18th CPC National Congress, our economic output has successively crossed the thresholds of 60 trillion yuan, 70 trillion yuan, 80 trillion yuan, 90 trillion yuan, and 100 trillion yuan. Even in 2020, when the COVID-19 pandemic had a severe impact, China quickly brought the epidemic under control, resumed work and production ahead of others, and achieved a GDP growth of 2.3% for the year, becoming the only major economy in the world to achieve positive growth. The new path of Chinese modernization and the new form of human advancement created by socialism with Chinese characteristics offer a new choice for many developing countries that are struggling and feeling uncertain about their future.

The successful pioneering of the new path of Chinese modernization serves as a global demonstration and guiding example, indicating that there is no fixed model or single path for modernization. Each country must independently explore a modernization path that suits its own national conditions, based on its history and realities. Every country's exploration and efforts should be respected. As China gradually achieves its development goals, history and practice will prove that the Chinese path to modernization has created a new form of human advancement, increasingly highlighting its profound historical and global significance.

Part Seven

Provide New Approaches to Global Problems

The world today faces profound changes of a kind unseen in a century. Peace and development remain the themes of our times, yet instability and uncertainty are becoming more pronounced. Humanity is in an era of emerging challenges and increasing risks, entering a period of turbulence and transformation. Serious global issues such as insufficient growth momentum, lagging global governance, and imbalanced global development are becoming increasingly prominent. Forces like trade protectionism, isolationism, and populism are reasserting themselves. In his keynote speech at the opening of the 2017 World Economic Forum Annual Meeting, General Secretary Xi Jinping quoted British writer Charles Dickens: "It was the best of times, it was the worst of times," to describe the contradictory world we live in today. Facing such a world of contradictions, severe global challenges, and the crossroads of human development, General Secretary Xi Jinping posed the question "What has happened to the world and how should we respond?" in his speech at the United Nations Office in Geneva in 2017.

In the New Era, China is increasingly moving to the center stage of the world. The Chinese path, theory, system, and culture are profoundly influencing and changing the world. The famous British historian Arnold Toynbee predicted that if China can blaze a new trail in terms of social and economic strategic choices, it will prove its ability to offer a gift that both China and the world need. In response to the question "What has happened to the world and how should we respond?" posed by the world and the times, the Chinese Communists, with General Secretary Xi Jinping as the principal representative, proposed the great concept and grand vision of building a human community with a shared future. They creatively answered the question of "What kind of world should we build, and how should we build it?" This deepened the understanding of the laws governing the development of human society, provided Chinese approaches to address global challenges and common human problems, and made new and greater contributions to the development and progress of human society.

I. What's Going on in This Turbulent World?

The first 20 years of the 21st century have passed, and in this short span, the world has witnessed a series of remarkable changes. At the beginning of the century, one of the world's largest energy service companies and the 7th-ranked company in the "Fortune 500" list of American companies, Enron Corporation, suddenly filed for bankruptcy protection in the New York Bankruptcy Court on December 2, 2001. This event did not make people realize that the US subprime mortgage problem was accumulating even more destructive energy. It wasn't until April 2007, with the bankruptcy of New Century Financial Corporation, the second-largest subprime mortgage company in the US, that the risks of subprime mortgage bonds were exposed. In 2008, the financial storm triggered by the US subprime mortgage crisis quickly swept through the world's major financial markets. In an era of deep economic globalization, the impact of the crisis was no longer confined to a single country or region but rapidly spread, severely affecting the development of the global economy and evolving into an global financial crisis.

History is never a simple repetition. Since the establishment of the capitalist system over 300 years ago, although it seems to have experienced an unchanging cycle of alternation between prosperity and crisis, the dialectics of historical development always relentlessly drive substantial changes, the realization of inevitable laws, and stage-specific qualitative changes amid seemingly unchanging appearances, sudden contingencies, and continuous quantitative changes. The periodic nature of the alternation between capitalist prosperity and crisis is precisely what Marx profoundly revealed as "The world trade crises must be regarded as the real concentration and forcible adjustment of all the contradictions of bourgeois economy."[1] "[A]s this cannot produce any real solution so long as it does not break in pieces the capitalist mode of production, the collisions become periodic."[2] Each crisis adds new insights to the examination of the fate of capitalism and adds new significance to the historical solutions that transcend the capitalist system itself. Over a decade since the outbreak of the crisis, its deep-seated impacts continue to manifest: global economic growth is sluggish, development gaps are increasingly prominent, various forms of protectionism are significantly rising, armed conflicts occur from time to time, Cold War mentality, hegemonism, power politics, and new interventionism persist, while arms races, terrorism, refugee crises, cybersecurity, climate change, and other traditional and non-traditional security threats are intertwined, leading to many chaotic phenomena

1   https://www.marxists.org/archive/marx/works/1863/theories-surplus-value/ch17.htm.
2   https://www.marxists.org/archive/marx/works/1877/anti-duhring/ch24.htm.

in some Western countries. The "Western chaos" has also plunged the maintenance of world peace and the promotion of common development into uncertainty and unpredictable panic. So, what can we see from this "Western chaos"?

1. The deep-rooted causes of the "Western chaos"

Firstly, the "Western chaos" represents a new outbreak of the inherent maladies of capitalism. Since the first comprehensive economic crisis in Britain in 1825, capitalism has experienced periodic crises every few years. Capitalists always believe that capitalism itself can overcome these crises, referring to them as normal "cyclical adjustments" of the capitalist economy. They want people to believe that the cycles of prosperity, recession, depression, and recovery are inevitable in a capitalist economy, as natural as the changing seasons or the ebb and flow of tides. They call on people to tighten their belts, endure sacrifices, and give up some of the benefits and living conditions enjoyed during prosperous times to overcome the difficulties, all in the hope of ushering in a new period of prosperity. Some even claim that each crisis allows capitalism to "renew itself" and "be reborn," while some defenders of capitalism argued that the 2008 financial crisis would make capitalism "reborn from the ashes" like a "phoenix rising from the flames." At that time, to mitigate the impact and consequences of the crisis, economists invented various anti-crisis theories and measures, including fiscal policies, monetary policies, state intervention, macroeconomic regulation, stimulating consumption, and balancing supply and demand.

However, the unshakable "curse" of capitalism is that, on one hand, it repeatedly navigates through crises, narrowly escaping disaster, changing its form of existence, and continuing its wanton expansion. On the other hand, no matter how much it disguises itself or how aggressively it expands, capitalism inevitably falls into the web of crisis over and over again.

In fact, through the historical fog shrouding capitalism and unveiling its mysterious veil, Marx revealed the fundamental contradiction of capitalist society: the contradiction between the socialization of production and the private ownership of the means of production. This fundamental contradiction is the unremovable "curse" of capitalism and always manifests through the outbreak of crises. Economic crises serve a dual role for capitalism.

On one hand, attempts to resolve and adjust to crises can temporarily restore productivity and may even achieve greater development than before the crisis. But on the other hand, determined and constrained by this fundamental contradiction, the inevitable demise of capitalism is a "terminal illness" it is born with, always demonstrating its destined historical fate through increasingly severe outbreaks. As Marx pointed out, in crises, "Capitalist production seeks continually to overcome these immanent barriers, but overcomes them only by means which again place these barriers in its way and on a more formidable scale."[1]

However, capitalist economists, historians, and politicians always intentionally or unintentionally avoid or erase this contradiction within capitalism. Like some cancer patients who either do not wish to directly mention their "terminal illness," or avoid treatment and refuse to acknowledge their condition, or always believe they have hope and a chance to continue living, they often view crises not as inevitable but as repeated "errors" of capitalism. The most representative of this "error theory" is the American economist Arthur Okun, who discovered "Okun's Law." In his book *The Political Economy of Prosperity*, he states that recessions are fundamentally preventable; they are like plane crashes rather than hurricanes. But we have never been able to eliminate plane crashes from the

---

[1] https://www.marxists.org/archive/marx/works/1894-c3/ch15.htm.

earth, and of course, it is unclear whether we have the wisdom and ability to eliminate recessions. The dangers have not disappeared; the factors that can lead to cyclical recessions still lurk on the wings of the plane, waiting for some error by the pilot.

When discussing the causes of this crisis, various individuals have proposed different reasons: inadequate regulation, financial fraud, excessive speculation, the greed of a few, and so on. Among these, the most interesting and thought-provoking are the doubts cast by the heads of state or nominal heads of state of the UK and the US on the "collective intelligence" of capitalist economists and politicians during the crisis.

(1) At the end of 2008, during a visit to the London School of Economics, Queen Elizabeth II questioned some top economists: why had none of them noticed or predicted the coming crisis? It was reported that the economists collectively fell silent. Some time later, a group of top economists collectively signed a letter to Her Majesty, stating: "Sorry, Your Majesty, we failed to foresee the global financial crisis," and "In short, the failure to predict the timing, extent, and severity of this crisis was a collective failure of many learned people, both domestically and internationally, who did not see systemic risk as a whole." This perfectly echoes Okun's "error theory."

(2) The then-US President Barack Obama expressed a similarly "brilliant" doubt and helplessness. He said: "Our economy is badly weakened, a consequence of greed and irresponsibility on the part of some, but also our collective failure to make hard choices and prepare the nation for a new age."

What a "systemic risk"! What "hard choices in a new age"!

Such expressions are highly ironic: another example of top capitalist politicians and economists collectively "cheating" and "evading" during a critical crisis. Even the best "elites" still use cunning professional jargon to deceive the public and the world. However, the term "collective," mentioned in both statements, actually refers to the inherent maladies of the entire capitalist system resurfacing. This kind of self-deceptive explanation also reveals the helplessness, avoidance, and concealment of capitalism's defenders regarding its fundamental contradictions. However, without addressing the essence and core of the issue, all efforts to resolve the crisis are no different from Don Quixote fighting windmills in Cervantes' work.

Secondly, the "Western chaos" is an inevitable product of the capitalist mode of production. Marx and Engels believed that capitalist economic crises are unique products of the capitalist mode of production, which expose all the contradictions of the capitalist economy and society. Since the beginning of the 21st century, economic globalization has developed rapidly, accompanied by the swift expansion of the capitalist mode of production globally. Economic globalization is an inevitable product of the highly developed social productive forces and social division of labor. In addition, it is itself a globalization dominated by international monopoly capitalism, an expansion of the capitalist mode of production and social relations worldwide. This is determined by the inherent nature of capital and the capitalist mode of production.

The basic characteristics of the capitalist mode of production are: the pursuit of capital appreciation at all costs, the expansion of capital and production completely detached from social needs, and the disregard for human life as long as there are conditions to reduce wage costs. In short, it is a production model that disregards all consequences to achieve private profit. In the *Communist Manifesto*, Marx and Engels profoundly discussed the endless expansion and accumulation nature of capital and the global development of capitalism: "The bourgeoisie cannot exist without constantly revolutionizing the instruments of production, and thereby the relations of production, and with them the whole relations of society," and "The need of a constantly expanding market for its products chases the bourgeoisie over the entire surface of the globe. It must nestle everywhere, settle everywhere, establish connections everywhere."[1]

The unrestricted impulse and demand of capital to pursue profit require it to continuously break through various limitations and boundaries and to promote a production dominated by the capitalist mode of production. Today, with the aid of advanced means from the information technology revolution, the speed at which the bourgeoisie and their profit-chasing capital "travel" is instantaneous, fleeting, and unpredictable.

What it pursues is no longer limited to "product sales," but encompasses a comprehensive selection of markets, raw materials, labor, investment environments, and profit environments. Increasingly, it seeks excessive speculative profits from financial capital detached from commodities and the real economy. Transnational capital moves from one country to another, from one region to another, seeking so-called "competitive advantages" with boundless freedom. The boundaries it seeks to break through are the "spaces" of various nation-states that it once relied on historically. It treats the globe as its free realm for unrestrained shuttling and frenzied profiteering.

No wonder the prominent American investor Grantham laments, "Capitalism threatens even our own survival," and that this "unbridled pursuit of growth at all costs" can lead to the destruction of the entire system, adding that "globalization will provide more opportunities for capitalists to self-destruct."[2] No wonder the veteran strategist of capitalism, Zbigniew Kazimierz Brzeziński, says, "The financial catastrophe of 2008 nearly precipitated a calamitous economic depression, jolting America and

---

1   https://www.marxists.org/archive/marx/works/1848/communist-manifesto/ch01.htm.
2   "Grantham is uncertain whether Marx's theories on capitalism are correct," US MarketWatch, http://bookmark.people.com.cn/toViewBookmark.do? id=209520, March 12, 2012.

much of the West into a sudden recognition of their systemic vulnerability to unregulated greed."[1] No wonder Klaus Schwab, founder of the World Economic Forum, states that "the current form of the capitalist system is no longer fit for the world today."[2] No wonder the current French President Emmanuel Macron is deeply concerned, pointing out that the contemporary capitalist model faces four insurmountable crises: social inequality, democratic crisis, sustainability crisis, and climate crisis, stating that "the modern capitalist model can no longer work in this environment."[3]

Facing the crisis of capitalism and the resulting "Western chaos," we can derive at least the following insights from the standpoint of Marxist theory and methodology:

First, the "Western chaos" indicates that Western capitalism is gradually losing its capacity and space for self-regulation and innovation. Reviewing the history of capitalism, in order to free itself from one crisis after another and seek new development and greater profits, capitalists have always kept the capitalist system in a state of constant change and renewal. As Marx revealed: "The bourgeoisie cannot exist without constantly revolutionizing the instruments of production, and thereby the relations of production, and with them the whole relations of society."[4] These means of rescue and regulation include strategies of technological innovation, geographical expansion, and industrial upgrading. Capitalists have indeed proven to be "excellent innovators," with each strategy driven to its extreme by capital and the pursuit of profit.

Technological innovation allows capital to always grasp the most

---

1   https://mo.tnu.tj/wp-content/uploads/2020/11/strategic_vision__america_and_the_crisis_of_global_power.pdf.

2   Klaus Schwab, "The Capitalist System Is No Longer Fit for the World," *Financial Times Deutschland,* January 25, 2012.

3   Emmanuel Macron, "The Modern Capitalist Model Can No Longer Work," *Reference News*'s Baidu Baijia account, February 8, 2021.

4   https://www.marxists.org/archive/marx/works/1848/communist-manifesto/ch01.htm.

advanced human science and inventions; geographical expansion enables capital to fully control the pulse of globalization, spreading to every corner of the world; industrial adjustment ensures that capital occupies the most profitable industrial sectors as quickly as possible. Precisely because capital tends to move to its limits, it has historically allowed capitalism to escape from one crisis after another and rapidly develop. However, this same movement of capital also leads to more comprehensive and intense crises, leaving fewer means to prevent them. Every weapon used to respond to a crisis eventually turns against itself. As Marx stated a century and a half ago: "Modern bourgeois society, with its relations of production, of exchange and of property, a society that has conjured up such gigantic means of production and of exchange, is like the sorcerer who is no longer able to control the powers of the nether world whom he has called up by his spells."[1]

For example, continuous technological innovation leads to a constant increase in the organic composition of capital, making the law of the tendency of the rate of profit to fall more pronounced. Consequently, capital is forced into a frenzy of financialization to seek profits, with the virtual economy becoming significantly detached from the real economy, turning into an uncontrollable "demon." This "demon" conjured through the magic of "financial innovation" is even more "deadly," and capitalism finds it increasingly difficult to control and manage it.

As capital expands globally without restraint, its fundamental contradictions and various other conflicts also intensify on an international scale. Western countries' methods of transferring crises abroad are now met with global resistance, causing these contradictions to rebound domestically, leading to intense protests like the Western "Occupy Wall Street movement." Thus, it is evident that the capacity and space for

---

1   *Ibid.*

capitalism's self-regulation and innovation have become serious issues.

Second, the "Western chaos" indicates that Western capitalism is gradually losing its developmental diversity. Looking back at the history of capitalism over several centuries, it can be said that, like other social formations, capitalism is a unity of diversity. In different historical periods, different countries and regions have produced different models of capitalism. For example, the "Anglo-Saxon model" in the UK and the US, characterized by a free market; the "Rhine model" in Germany and other continental European countries, characterized by a social market economy; and the "Swedish model" in Sweden and other Nordic countries, characterized by labor-capital coordination and social security.

However, after more than 30 years of global expansion of international monopoly capitalism and the rampant rise of neoliberalism, overall capitalism has tended to return to its primitive forms of accumulation and domination. Especially in this crisis, the serious drawbacks of capitalism's tendency toward a single development model have been exposed. The neoliberal model has become notorious, and aside from a few extreme defenders, other bourgeois supporters are eager to distance themselves from it. Even Francis Fukuyama, who once proclaimed the "end of history," now believes that this libertarian form of capitalism must change. As for other forms of capitalist models, having been gradually eroded and assimilated by neoliberalism over the past 30 years, they have lost their unique foundations, ideologies, and advantages. For instance, the social-democratic model, through its so-called "Third Way" innovation, has gradually adapted to, accepted, and moved toward the neoliberal model, betting its development means and fate on the neoliberal path. With the collapse of neoliberalism in the crisis and the loss of credibility of mainstream Western economics, there is currently confusion and entanglement about the future direction of capitalism and the adjustments it will make post-crisis. This is the adverse result of the long-term dominance of a single capitalist model and the gradual loss of developmental diversity. The loss of diversity means the extinction of vitality and dynamism.

In reflecting on capitalism, many people, including left-wing critics of capitalism and right-wing supporters, have made judgments and predictions about the future fate of capitalism. Some representative viewpoints include those of left-wing individuals, such as the renowned founder of world-systems analysis, Immanuel Wallerstein, who believes that the development of capitalism has reached its limit and that the impetus for further expansion has been exhausted. He predicts that the capitalist world-system has another 40 to 50 years of life left, after which there will be a divergence with two possible developmental directions: one characterized by a more hierarchical and oppressive world-system, and the other more inclined toward equality and justice. He expresses a preference for the latter.

Moderate right-wing individuals, such as the seasoned American journalist Michael Schuman, believe that capitalism will undergo a makeover following the "Great Recession." From Los Angeles to London to Athens, the public's outburst of dissatisfaction cannot be ignored. However, regardless of how loud the calls for change may be, capitalism will not disappear. The challenge ahead is how to reform capitalism, and the outcome will determine its fate over the next two to three decades. Conservative right-wing figures, like former Federal Reserve Chairman Alan Greenspan, argue in his article "The Consequences of Poor Market Intervention," that despite the flaws of free-market capitalism, none of the systems tried as alternatives—from Fabian socialism to Soviet-style communism—have successfully met the needs of their respective populations. Capitalism needs adjustment, but its model should not be arbitrarily "improved."

This crisis has caused capitalism, as a comprehensive social system, to face large-scale questioning or opposition worldwide for the first time since World War II. The "Occupy Wall Street" movement is the first large-scale mass movement in over half a century to target capitalism as a whole for critique. This has sharpened various contradictions within capitalism, exposing its inherent flaws, especially the deepest ones. Hence, Lenin's revelations about the parasitic, decaying, and dying nature of capitalism a century ago are once again prominently displayed in the era of global capitalism.

It is crucial here to emphasize how to scientifically understand the parasitic, decaying, and dying nature of capitalism. This first requires adopting a historical perspective, a global scale, and dialectical thinking. When we speak of the parasitic and decaying nature of capitalism, it is not to be simplistically understood as its complete inability to develop. Rather, as Lenin understood imperialism a hundred years ago, it is about the coexistence of stagnation trends and rapid development trends. Evaluating its decay on a global scale does not mean judging it like a terminally ill patient in daily life who is on the brink of death today and will die tomorrow. It should be correctly understood that capitalism is gradually losing its historical rationality and vitality as a social formation. Its historical limitations and temporality are often highlighted by comprehensive crises, while the perfection and eternity touted by its proponents are repeatedly shattered by historical tests.

2. The effective governance of China stands out

In sharp contrast to the "Western chaos," characterized by stark wealth gaps, social governance failures, incessant party disputes, rising protectionism, rampant populism, and pervasive terrorism, is the effective governance of China.

Since the 18th CPC National Congress, under the strategic leadership of the Party Central Committee with General Secretary Xi Jinping at its core, China has creatively advanced the governance of the country based on its traditions, current national conditions, and long-term governance experience. This has resulted in the formation of new concepts, thoughts, and strategies for governance. The governance model developed is distinct from those of historical socialist countries and Western capitalism, showcasing unique advantages compared to Western social governance. A new landscape of governance has emerged, leading to a highly stable political climate, and continuous advancements in economic standards, technological capabilities, defense power, and international influence.

The stark contrast between the effective governance of China and the chaos in the West highlights the distinct and superior development of socialism with Chinese characteristics. Our comprehensive deepening of reform has made the socialist system with Chinese characteristics more mature and well-defined. This has provided a complete, stable, and effective system for the development of the Party and the country, the wellbeing of the people, social harmony and stability, and the long-term peace and order of the nation. The superiority of this system has been recognized and endorsed by many insightful individuals worldwide. Some historically-minded foreign scholars have keenly observed the significant role and status of socialism with Chinese characteristics in the new phase of the 21st-century world socialist movement. Although their perspectives and conclusions may differ from ours, their global vision and historical trend predictions are of inspirational value to us.

The effective governance of China has created a Chinese miracle, prominently reflected in the "two major miracles" of rapid economic development and long-term social stability. These two miracles, interwoven and mutually reinforcing, are practical demonstrations of the power of the socialist system with Chinese characteristics, together constituting a monument to the effective governance of China. The Fourth Plenary Session of the 19th CPC Central Committee scientifically summarized the 13 significant advantages of the socialist system with Chinese characteristics, covering all areas from productivity to production relations, and from the economic base to the superstructure. This fully reflects the superiority, resilience, vitality, and potential of the socialist system with Chinese characteristics, forming a "system advantage group" led by the greatest advantage of the leadership of the CPC, with various advantages being fully showcased and combined to demonstrate overall superiority. This indicates that our Party's understanding of the "three major laws" has reached an unprecedented height.

The world today faces profound changes of a kind unseen in a century, making global institutional competition more complex and intense. We must remain clear-headed, maintain strategic resolve, and never lose our bearings or become disorganized. Under any circumstances, we must firmly uphold our confidence in the path, theory, system, and culture of socialism with Chinese characteristics.

"If a dynasty cannot continue to rise, it will fall; if a country cannot improve its governance, the state of order will deteriorate." We must adhere to the guidance of Xi Jinping Thought on Socialism with Chinese Characteristics for a New Era, advancing institutional development and innovation through comprehensive deepening of reform, opening up a new future for the effective governance of China.

II. What Should China Do as It Moves to the Center of the World Stage

The political report of the 19th CPC National Congress pointed out that with decades of hard work, socialism with Chinese characteristics has crossed the threshold into a new era. This is a new historic juncture in China's development. It will be an era that sees China moving closer to center stage and making greater contributions to humanity.

1. Contribute to global governance and peaceful development

China is an active contributor to the concept of global governance. Since the 18th CPC National Congress, it has actively promoted major-country diplomacy with Chinese characteristics, building on the fine traditions of Chinese diplomacy while continuously exploring and advancing. General Secretary Xi Jinping proposed a series of new concepts, propositions, and initiatives rich in Chinese characteristics, reflecting the spirit of the times and leading the trend of human progress, forming his diplomatic thinking. The core ideas of these new concepts include: promoting the democratization of international relations, advocating and practicing a correct view of justice and interests, establishing new types of international relations, particularly new major-country relations, and advocating for a sense of human community with a shared future, promoting the building of such a community. Gennady Zyuganov, leader of the Communist Party of the Russian Federation, wrote: "The international relations model proposed by China is becoming increasingly attractive. All the principles in the concept of 'human community with a shared future' advocated by China are highly promising—people of all countries cooperate equally for common wellbeing."[1]

(1) Upholding the principle of achieving shared growth through discussion and collaboration, advocating for the democratization of international relations

---

[1] "Article by Communist Party of Russia Leader Zyuganov: The US Has Sinister Motives in Sowing Discord between China and Russia," *Reference News*, August 3, 2020.

The democratization of international relations is a principle actively advocated by China, Russia, and other countries. In the New Era, as international relations undergo profound changes, the external living environment for humanity is becoming increasingly complex, with uncertain risk factors continually increasing: major infectious diseases, climate change, and other non-traditional security threats are spreading; humans face many common challenges. In the face of hegemony and unilateralism, which greatly impact multipolarity and multilateralism, humanity faces many issues that require collective resolution, such as development deficits, environmental deficits, and governance deficits. No single country can solve these global problems alone.

Moreover, the notion of "America First" prioritizes US national interests above all else, leading to the US frequently breaking agreements and withdrawing from international organizations. This arbitrary behavior harms the interests of other countries and international public interests, and the US no longer provides public goods to the international community. In such a context, the demand for the democratization of international relations is growing louder. Xi Jinping has frequently addressed the issue of democratizing international relations in his speeches. He pointed out that international affairs should be handled through consultation among all parties, not dictated by a single country or a few countries.

In his keynote speech titled "Toward a Community of Shared Future for Mankind" at the United Nations Office at Geneva on January 18, 2017, Xi Jinping emphasized the need to promote the democratization of international relations, rejecting dominance by just one or a few countries. He asserted that the destiny of the world should be determined by all countries collectively, the rules of international relations should be written by all countries, global affairs should be managed by all countries, and development outcomes should be shared by all countries.

The political report of the 19th CPC National Congress also stated that China follows the principle of achieving shared growth through discussion and collaboration in engaging in global governance. China stands for democracy in international relations and the equality of all countries, big or small, strong or weak, rich or poor. China supports the United Nations in playing an active role in international affairs, and supports the efforts of other developing countries to increase their representation and strengthen their voice in international affairs.

(2) Uphold the greater public good while pursuing shared interests and advocate for a mutually beneficial open strategy

The principle of upholding the public good while pursuing shared interests is a new concept in international relations proposed by Xi Jinping during his visit to Africa in 2013. It is one of the core ideas of Xi Jinping's diplomatic thinking and embodies the essence of China's national view on the greater public good and shared interests. This concept runs through the theory and practice of major-country diplomacy with Chinese characteristics. Over the past eight years, Xi Jinping has frequently mentioned in important domestic and international speeches that China sticks to the sound values of upholding the greater good and pursuing shared interests, with high priority given to the greater good. He emphasized that in international cooperation, while we must consider shared interests, we should prioritize the public good even more. The principle of upholding the greater good while pursuing shared interests has both significant practical relevance and long-term historical significance for promoting the building of a human community with a shared future.

The principle of upholding the greater good while pursuing shared interests represents China's approach to national interests in international relations, balancing both its own interests and those of other countries and the global community. This concept is a significant contribution to the theory of international relations, reflecting distinct Chinese characteristics and embodying the value orientation that humanity should collectively aspire to. It "exemplifies the ethical practice of integrating the greater good with shared interests and assisting those in need."[1] During his visit to Africa, Xi Jinping proposed the principles of sincerity, amity, good faith, real results for China-Africa cooperation, emphasizing the mutually beneficial nature of this cooperation. He stated that China will fully implement its commitments without attaching any political conditions, focusing on helping African countries transform their resource advantages into development advantages and achieve diversified, independent, and sustainable development. The proposal to establish the Silk Road Economic Belt is a concrete manifestation of achieving mutual benefit and common development with developing countries.

During Xi Jinping's visit to the Republic of Korea in 2014, he further elaborated on China's concept of cooperative development and the principle of upholding the public good while pursuing shared interests in international relations in his speech at Seoul National University. "A country does not seek interests as its goal, but rather the public good." In international relations, the proper handling of the public good and shared interests is crucial. Politically, countries should abide by international law and basic principles of international relations, uphold fairness and justice, and treat each other with equality. Economically, they should take a comprehensive and long-term perspective, adhering to mutual benefit, mutually beneficial cooperation, and common development. These ideas about the relationship between "the public good" and "shared interests" embody the best elements of traditional Chinese culture, reflect profound changes in international relations and the international situation, and

---

1   "Wang Yi, "'Deeply Study and Implement Xi Jinping's Diplomatic Thinking to Continuously Open Up New Horizons for Major-Country Diplomacy with Chinese Characteristics," *Qiushi*, Chin. ed., no. 15, 2020.

serve as new guiding principles for managing relations between different countries.

The Treaty of Westphalia, signed by European countries in 1648, laid the foundation for the international political system of inter-state relations, forming the Westphalian system. It has been a significant international political system since modern times, based on independent nation-states, with states as the main actors in international politics, and it continues to play an important role today. Therefore, respecting the independence, sovereignty, and equality of nation-states is a fundamental principle of international relations. However, influenced by the traditional realist view of national interests, Western hegemonic countries regard their sovereignty and territorial integrity as the fundamental principles of national interests but do not respect the national interests, sovereignty, and territorial integrity of weaker and smaller nations, engaging in colonial aggression.

In the era of globalization, these countries even openly engage in armed aggression against sovereign states under the pretext of combating terrorism for their national interests. For example, the war on Iraq was launched under the pretext of Iraq possessing weapons of mass destruction, missile strikes on Syria were conducted under the pretext of Syria possessing chemical weapons, and military strikes were carried out in Afghanistan and Libya under the pretext of combating terrorism. These actions have resulted in over a decade of turmoil and warfare in these countries and regions, with terrorism and extremism becoming more rampant and spreading, causing the people in these areas to suffer immensely from the brutal devastation of war, terrorism, and extremism.

Western hegemony also blatantly interferes in the internal affairs of other countries, using methods such as color revolutions and armed interventions to exert political, economic, and cultural hegemony over West Asia, North Africa, and the Middle East, aiming to maximize their national interests.

China has consistently advocated that the highest principle of national interest is to respect and uphold national sovereignty and territorial integrity. The fundamental principle of foreign relations is to abide by international law and the Five Principles of Peaceful Coexistence. China's view of national interest also includes peacefully building its homeland, conducting foreign trade and cooperation on the basis of equality and mutual benefit, reasonably considering the interests of other countries while safeguarding its own national interests, striving to promote world peace, and maintaining the common interests of all peoples. The 18th CPC National Congress emphasized that China will continue to keep in mind both the interests of the Chinese people and the common interests of the people of all countries, get more actively involved in international affairs, play its due role of a major responsible country, and work jointly with other countries to meet global challenges. China will unwaveringly follow a win-win strategy of opening up and promote robust, sustainable and balanced growth of the global economy through increased cooperation. The 19th National Congress solemnly promised that the CPC strives for both the wellbeing of the Chinese people and human progress. To make new and greater contributions for mankind is our Party's abiding mission. The CPC calls on the people of all countries to work together to build a community with a shared future for mankind, to build an open, inclusive, clean, and beautiful world that enjoys lasting peace, universal security, and common prosperity.

In his speech at a ceremony marking the 60th anniversary of the Five Principles of Peaceful Coexistence, Xi Jinping stated: "We must uphold sovereign equality. Sovereignty is the fundamental mark of a country's independence, the fundamental embodiment of national interests, and a reliable guarantee. Sovereignty and territorial integrity are inviolable.

Countries should respect each other's core interests and major concerns. These are absolute principles that cannot be discarded or shaken at any time."[1] This is also a basic theory and viewpoint of Marxism regarding international issues. Engels believed, "It is historically impossible for a great people even to discuss internal problems of any kind seriously, as long as it lacks national independence."[2] In discussing whether Poland could gain independence and liberation from Tsarist Russia, Engels said, "[I] independence is the basis of any common international action."[3]

Clearly, the fundamental difference between our advocated principle of upholding the public good while pursuing shared interests and the traditional Western realist view of interests lies in how national interests are perceived and the ways and means of achieving or realizing national interests. Therefore, the principle of upholding the public good while pursuing shared interests transcends the traditional Western view of national interests.

(3) Adhere to the concept of common development and advocate the establishment of a new type of international relations

The establishment of a new type of international relations, especially a new type of major-country relationship with the United States, is a new concept and proposition in international relations put forward by General Secretary Xi Jinping.

The democratization of international relations and the realization of equal consultation in international affairs between large and small countries have significant practical and historical implications for constructing a fair and just new international order. The establishment of new types of international relations, especially new types of major-country relations,

---

1   Xi Jinping, *On Building a Human Community with a Shared Future*, Beijing: Central Party Literature Publishing House, 2018, pp. 130–131.
2   https://www.marxists.org/archive/marx/works/1882/letters/82_02_07.htm.
3   *Ibid.*

refutes the Thucydides Trap theory. The political report of the 18th CPC National Congress explicitly stated: "We will improve and grow our relations with developed countries by expanding areas of cooperation and properly addressing differences with them; and we will strive to establish a new type of relations of long-term stability and sound growth with other major countries."[1] The inclusion of "establishing new types of major-country relations" in the report of the 18th National Congress and important documents of the First Session of the 12th National People's Congress marked it as a significant new concept in China's foreign policy and guidance for foreign relations. Thus, establishing new types of major-country relations has become a crucial aspect of China's diplomatic strategy. The political report of the 19th National Congress emphasized that China will continue to hold high the banner of peace, development, cooperation, and mutual benefit and uphold its fundamental foreign policy goal of preserving world peace and promoting common development. China remains firm in its commitment to strengthening friendship and cooperation with other countries on the basis of the Five Principles of Peaceful Coexistence, and to forging a new form of international relations featuring mutual respect, fair-ness, justice, and win-win cooperation.

In the 2014 Central Conference on Foreign Affairs, Xi Jinping explicitly pointed out the need to advance major-country diplomacy with Chinese characteristics. The concept of major-country diplomacy with Chinese characteristics posits that major countries are decisive forces influencing world peace. Therefore, we actively manage relations with major countries such as Russia, the United States, and the European Union. In his address at the opening ceremony of the sixth round of the China-US Strategic and Economic Dialogue, Xi Jinping noted: "Building

---

1   *Documents Produced since the 18th CPC National Congress*, Beijing: Central Party Literature Publishing House, 2014, vol. I, p. 38.

a new type of major-country relationship is a significant strategic choice jointly made by both sides based on summarizing historical experiences, considering the national conditions of both countries and the world situation. It aligns with the fundamental interests of the peoples of both countries and all other countries and reflects the political responsibility of both sides to break the traditional pattern of major-country conflicts and confrontations and create a new model for the development of major-country relations."[1] Xi Jinping proposed that China and the United States should "maintain cooperation, avoid confrontation, benefit both countries, and contribute to the world," adding new connotations to the new type of major-country relationship between China and the United States. On November 12 of the same year, in a meeting with President Obama at the Great Hall of the People, Xi Jinping proposed advancing China-US relations in six key areas. Furthermore, China attaches great importance to relations with other developing countries, promoting neighborhood diplomacy based on the policy of amity, sincerity, mutual benefit, and inclusiveness, and advancing the development of new types of international relations. Significant progress has been made in pragmatic cooperation between China and Africa, China and Arab countries, and China and Latin America, with joint development of the BRI, providing financial support and project cooperation for infrastructure development in other developing countries. The establishment of new types of international relations unfolds in all aspects.

General Secretary Xi Jinping's proposal to establish new types of international relations, especially new types of major-country relations with the United States, received a positive response from the US and was

---

1   Xi Jinping, "Strive to Build a New Model of Major-Country Relations between China and the United States: Speech at the Joint Opening Ceremony of the Sixth Round of the China-US Strategic and Economic Dialogue and the Fifth Round of the China-US High-Level Consultation on People-to-People Exchange," *Guangming Daily*, July 10, 2014.

actively endorsed by then-President Obama. Obama expressed that the US hoped for a peacefully developing China to play an active and constructive role internationally, stating that China and the US could entirely avoid the Thucydides Trap. This proposal also garnered positive affirmation from honest American experts and scholars. Henry Kissinger described it as a vision of a strategic, long-term partnership between China and the US.

On January 22, 2014, the *World Post* published an exclusive interview with Xi Jinping, in which Xi specifically discussed the need to avoid falling into the Thucydides Trap when handling relations between major countries in today's world. On September 22, 2015, during a speech at a reception jointly hosted by the Washington State government and friendly communities in Seattle, Washington State, the United States, Xi Jinping reiterated: "We want to deepen mutual understanding with the US on each other's strategic orientation and development path. We want to see more understanding and trust; less estrangement and suspicion in order to prevent misunderstanding and miscalculation. We should strictly base our judgement on facts, lest we become victim to hearsay, paranoid, or self-imposed bias. There is no Thucydides Trap in the world. Should major countries time and again make the mistakes of strategic miscalculation, they might create such traps for themselves.

Then-President Obama responded positively to this notion, also expressing the belief that China and the US were not destined to fall into the Thucydides Trap. As a result, significant consensus was reached between China and the US on this issue.

China's vision for a new type of major-country relationship with the US advocates for non-conflict, non-confrontation, mutual respect, mutual trust, inclusiveness, mutual learning, and mutually beneficial cooperation. Such a relationship, based on trust and collaboration, is fully capable of avoiding the so-called Thucydides Trap. Therefore, the establishment of new forms of international relations—particularly among major countries—directly challenges the validity of the Thucydides Trap theory.

However, after President Trump took office, he introduced the "America First" doctrine, framing China-US and US-Russia relations as major-power competitions. In a move contrary to international law and the fundamental principles of international relations, the Trump administration frequently withdrew from international organizations, terminated or abandoned key international agreements and treaties, and acted in opposition to mainstream global values. It launched a comprehensive strategy aimed at suppressing and containing China.

In 2020, the US and its allies, particularly Japan and Australia, conducted frequent military exercises in the South China Sea. On July 6, the US Navy deployed two aircraft carrier strike groups—the *USS Nimitz* and *USS Ronald Reagan*—in a show of force in the region. Within the span of six months, US ships and aircraft carried out 2,000 close reconnaissance missions near China's southeastern coast. On July 21, the US abruptly announced the closure of the Chinese consulate in Houston, further escalating tensions and increasing the risk of a direct conflict between China and the US. This marked the most challenging period for China-US relations since the establishment of diplomatic ties.

Thus, building a new type of major-country relationship between China and the US remains a long and difficult process. The US must fully recognize that China-US relations extend beyond bilateral concerns—they affect the global landscape, the peace and wellbeing of people around the world, and the sustainable peace and development of the international community.

2. Adhere to independence and innovation

Independence and openness are closely intertwined and dialectically unified; they cannot be separated or opposed. Marxism teaches that the material world is universally interconnected, with each entity exhibiting its own unique characteristics, representing the dialectical unity of universality and particularity, commonality and individuality. Internal factors are the fundamental drivers of a thing's development, while external factors provide the conditions for that development. However, external factors can only exert influence through internal factors.

Adhering to independence means recognizing one's own characteristics and individuality, valuing internal factors, and promoting development through self-driven efforts. Adhering to openness means recognizing the universal connections and common features of things, maintaining a global perspective, and actively utilizing favorable external conditions to foster growth. Thus, independence and openness are mutually supportive and closely linked. Only by adhering to independence can one better engage in openness; the stronger the capacity for independence, the greater the potential for openness. Likewise, by adhering to openness, one can better develop and enhance the ability to pursue self-reliant growth.

One must not reject openness in the name of independence and self-reliance, thereby falling into isolationism, arrogance, stagnation, and rigid dogmatism. Nor should one reject independence in the name of openness, leading to dependency, blind imitation, the loss of self-identity, and the abandonment of core principles. Both approaches are unsustainable and lack vitality.

Since the introduction of the reform and opening up policy, a misguided belief has emerged that reform and opening up means following the Western path to modernization. This view suggests that China's socialist modernization during this period merely involved "walking on roads built by Western developed countries," with the assumption that doing so leads to faster progress. It claims that China's economy is "essentially a parasitic economy" and that China's development achievements, "scoring high by copying others' work," do not demonstrate China's superiority, nor do they reflect the strength of its system or the ingenuity of its people.

These views are deeply flawed, prejudiced, and rooted in arrogance. They ignore the colonial and exploitative methods employed during the Western modernization process—methods that cannot be replicated by later-developing countries. Moreover, the contemporary Western-promoted paths of capitalization, marketization, privatization, and liberalization leave little room for others to grow. Looking at the development trajectories of countries today, the modernization process for developing nations is riddled with difficulties and traps. Many countries are treated as mere objects for periodic exploitation, labeled as rogue states, or subjected to sanctions, deprivation, enslavement, and even military intervention.

There is no universal, one-size-fits-all development model in the world, nor is there a fixed path to modernization. No country has achieved strength and revitalization by relying solely on external forces or by following others step by step. China, which has risen to prominence without dependence on developed nations, following its own path, relying on self-development and hard work, is a unique case. It has achieved strength and revitalization not by copying others or relying on external forces, but by charting its own course.

In his major speech at a ceremony marking the centenary of the CPC, Xi Jinping confidently declared:

"The Chinese nation has fostered a splendid civilization over more than 5,000 years of history. The Party has also acquired a wealth of experience through its endeavors over the past 100 years and during more than 70 years of governance. At the same time, we are also eager to learn what lessons we can from the achievements of other cultures, and welcome helpful suggestions and constructive criticism. We will not, however, accept sanctimonious preaching from those who feel they have the right to lecture us. The Party and the Chinese people will keep moving confidently forward in broad strides along the path that we have chosen for ourselves, and we will make sure the destiny of China's development and progress remains firmly in our own hands."[1]

For thousands of years, the Chinese nation has endured hardships, worked diligently, and innovated. The achievements we enjoy today were neither stolen nor taken by force, nor were they gifts from other nations. They were earned through the hard work, blood, and sweat of people from all ethnic groups across the country, over decades of effort. The Chinese people deeply understand that, as the most populous country in the world, no one is in a position to grant us favors. If we want to develop, we must rely on our own hard work and perseverance. Since the founding of the People's Republic of China, Mao Zedong emphasized the importance of "walking our own path," independently exploring the road to building socialism.

Since the introduction of the reform and opening up policy, the Chinese people and the CPC have firmly adhered to independence and innovation. With clear goals and full confidence, they have forged ahead, pioneering a new path of socialist modernization with Chinese characteristics—distinct from the Western model—that has created a "Chinese miracle" in the history of human modernization. China has established the world's most complete industrial system, become the second-largest economy, and for years has been the largest contributor to global economic growth, benefiting the world through its development.

Since the 18th CPC National Congress, the Party has continued to lead the nation on its own path, focusing on its own affairs. General

---

Secretary Xi Jinping has repeatedly emphasized: "The most important thing is to do our own things well." Practice has proven that China has discredited several flawed theories with undeniable facts: the "end of history" theory, the "China collapse" theory, and the "socialism failure" theory. On the one hand, China has adhered to reform and opening up while maintaining independence, pursuing both innovation and the principle of seeking truth from facts. On the other hand, China has upheld peaceful development, opposed hegemonism, and safeguarded its own development interests. This has led modern China down a path of self-reliance, self-respect, self-improvement, and self-awareness.

The path, theory, system, and culture of socialism with Chinese characteristics continue to advance, expanding the path for developing countries to modernize. China provides a new option for nations that wish to accelerate their development while maintaining independence, contributing Chinese wisdom and approaches to addressing global challenges.

3. Actively assume major-country responsibilities

Since the 18th CPC National Congress, socialism with Chinese characteristics has entered the New Era, and China is increasingly moving toward the center of the world stage, actively taking on the responsibilities of a major country. In September 1988, China formally applied to join the United Nations Special Committee on Peacekeeping Operations. In 1989, China sent personnel for the first time to participate in the United Nations Transition Assistance Group in Namibia, contributing to Namibia's independence from South Africa.

China began participating in global peacekeeping missions in 1990, sending military observers to United Nations operations annually. Chinese peacekeeping forces are now a vital branch of the United Nations peacekeeping mission. In April 1992, China sent an engineering battalion of 400 officers and soldiers to the United Nations Transitional Authority in Cambodia, marking the first organized deployment of Chinese military personnel in UN peacekeeping operations. Between April 1992 and September 1993, China dispatched two engineering battalions, totaling 800 officers and soldiers, to support peacekeeping efforts in Cambodia. This was the first instance of the Chinese government deploying troops for United Nations peacekeeping missions.

Over the past 30 years, Chinese peacekeeping officers and soldiers have made outstanding contributions to maintaining local security, quelling violent conflicts in turbulent regions, restoring social stability, and supporting regional and global peace efforts. In recognition of their contributions, they have been awarded the United Nations Peace Medal.

Today, China has more than 2,000 peacekeepers stationed overseas, actively contributing to global peace. As of July 2020, China has sent over 40,000 peacekeepers, making it the largest contributor of peacekeepers among the five permanent members of the United Nations Security Council. This commitment to world peace and development is a tangible demonstration of China's willingness to fulfill its responsibilities as a major country. China will continue to actively assume these responsibilities, working to maintain regional stability, security, and global peace and development.

China has also actively proposed and implemented strategic concepts and values for global governance. It has been a key participant in global governance initiatives, notably through the BRI, collaborating with countries along the route. This cooperation includes improving infrastructure in developing countries by building roads and railways, establishing the AIIB, and providing funding through the Silk Road Fund. These efforts represent China's proactive approach to shouldering major-country responsibilities and effectively aligning national interests with global responsibilities, as well as national interests with international priorities.

China's engagement in global governance is evident not only in its introduction of innovative ideas and initiatives but also in the BRI's governance plan. This plan offers a public platform for regional and global cooperation, providing global public goods that benefit all participants.

The BRI opens new avenues for international cooperation, representing a beneficial exploration of diverse paths to global collaboration. It encompasses bilateral, multilateral, regional, and global cooperation. Some experts believe that the "New Silk Road" concept transcends traditional models of regional economic cooperation by advocating for an open and inclusive system. It encourages the active participation of all parties with an open mindset, reducing operational barriers, expanding the support base, and fully mobilizing various resources.

Notably, the Silk Road Economic Belt does not rely on exclusive institutional designs. Instead, it promotes regional economic cooperation while seeking broad global economic interconnections. Its highly open character allows for effective coordination with global economic organizations such as the World Trade Organization (WTO), the International Monetary Fund (IMF), and the World Bank, attracting more countries and regions into its growing network of economic cooperation. Moreover, the Silk Road Economic Belt demonstrates a high degree of inclusiveness and pragmatism, enabling development at both bilateral and multilateral levels.[1]

The BRI pioneers a new model of global governance, representing significant theoretical and practical advancements in major-country

1   Mali Li and Ren Baoping, *Report on the Development of the Silk Road Economic Belt (2014)*, Beijing: China Economic Press, 2014, p. 19.

diplomacy with Chinese characteristics. It is a grand vision aimed at promoting exchanges and cooperation among nations, reshaping the international political and economic order, and creating a new framework for global governance. The BRI works toward building a global community with a shared future, an unprecedented endeavor in human history. The initiative is already benefiting, and will continue to benefit, people across the world. Over time, the BRI will help improve the international order, making it more just and equitable.

The BRI follows the principle of achieving shared growth through discussion and collaboration. At its core, the BRI emphasizes mutually beneficial cooperation, promoting the common economic development of countries along its route and fostering the exchange and mutual learning of diverse civilizations. The principle of achieving shared growth through discussion and collaboration is the foundation of the theoretical essence of the BRI.

The BRI upholds openness and inclusiveness. During General Secretary Xi Jinping's visit to the UK in 2015, he addressed the China-UK Business Summit, explaining that the BRI is open to all, forming a broad "circle of friends" across Africa, Asia, and Europe. Any country interested in participating is welcome to join. The BRI is diverse, encompassing various fields of cooperation and offering flexible forms of collaboration. It is a win-win initiative, where countries work together, following the principles of extensive consultation, joint contribution, and shared benefits, to achieve common development and prosperity. As Xi Jinping aptly described, "This road is not a private path for any one party, but a broad avenue for everyone to advance together."[1]

---

1   Xi Jinping, *The Belt and Road Initiative*, Beijing, Central Party Literature Publishing House, 2018, p. 80.

4. Keep to the path of peaceful development

Rooted in historical trends, cultural heritage, and fundamental national interests, China has made a strategic choice to follow the path of peaceful development. General Secretary Xi Jinping emphasized: "China's path of peaceful development is not an expedient measure or mere diplomatic rhetoric, but a conclusion drawn from objective judgments of history, reality, and the future. It represents a unity of confident thought and conscious practice."[1]

The commitment to peaceful development has become a core national strategy, enshrined in the Constitution of the People's Republic of China, and it profoundly influences the country's development planning and major policies. By keeping to this path, China aims to develop itself while maintaining world peace and, in turn, contribute to global peace through its own development.

China's adherence to peaceful development is a continuation and promotion of its millennia-old cultural tradition of valuing peace. The Chinese nation has long been a peace-loving people, with the pursuit of peace deeply embedded in the nation's cultural heritage and woven into the fabric of its civilization Throughout its millennia-long history, the Chinese nation has developed concepts such as "universal love and non-aggression," "benevolence and good neighborliness," "seeking harmony among nations," "valuing harmony above all," "unity in diversity," "turning hostility into amity," "a prosperous nation and peaceful people," "harmony among all nations," "friendly relations with neighboring and allied countries," "all within the four seas are brothers," "world peace," and "universal harmony."

General Secretary Xi Jinping once remarked, "The deepest cultural pursuit of a nation must be embedded in the genes of its enduring national spirit." Historically, China has held the belief that "A warlike nation,

---

1   Xi Jinping, "Speech at the Körber Foundation in Germany," *People's Daily*, March 30, 2014.

however big it may be, will eventually perish." This sentiment is reflected in Sun Zi's famous military treatise, *The Art of War*, which begins by stating: "Warfare is the greatest affair of state, the basis of life and death, the Dao to survival or extinction. It must be thoroughly pondered and analyzed." The essence of this teaching is to approach war cautiously and, whenever possible, avoid it.

For thousands of years, the values of peace have been ingrained in the Chinese nation's identity, etched into its collective memory, and passed down through generations. Peace is not only a guiding principle but also deeply embedded in the genes of the Chinese people.

From the Opium War in 1840 to the founding of the People's Republic of China in 1949, over a span of more than 100 years, our country suffered repeated invasions and endured the misery of war and turmoil. The war of aggression launched by Japanese militarism alone caused over 35 million casualties among our military and civilian population. This tragic history has left an indelible mark on the memory of our people. These unbearable sufferings have made our people deeply realize that what we need most is a harmonious and stable domestic environment and a peaceful and tranquil international environment. Only peace and tranquility can lead to prosperity and development, and any upheaval and war are against the fundamental interests of our people.

Adhering to the path of peaceful development is conducive to realizing our development goals. Currently, with the continuous development of economic globalization and regional economic integration, maintaining world economic stability and development aligns with our interests; our destiny is closely linked with that of the world. Our country is striving to achieve the rejuvenation of the Chinese nation, known as the Chinese Dream. The 19th CPC National Congress clearly outlined the Two Centenary Goals. Our goal is to basically achieve socialist modernization by 2035. The vision is that by the end of this stage, the following goals will have been met:

- China's economic and technological strength has increased significantly. China has become a global leader in innovation.

- The rights of the people to participate and to develop as equals are adequately protected. The rule of law for the country, the government, and society is basically in place. Institutions in all fields are further improved; the modernization of China's system and capacity for governance is basically achieved.

- Social etiquette and civility are significantly enhanced. China's cultural soft power has grown much stronger; Chinese culture has greater appeal.

- People are leading more comfortable lives, and the size of the middle-income group has grown considerably. Disparities in urban-rural development, in development between regions, and in living standards are significantly reduced; equitable access to basic public services is basically ensured; and solid progress has been made toward prosperity for everyone.

- A modern social governance system has basically taken shape, and society is full of vitality, harmonious, and orderly.

- There is a fundamental improvement in the environment; the goal of building a Beautiful China is basically attained.

We will, building on having basically achieved modernization by 2035, work hard for a further 15 years to develop China into a great modern socialist country that is prosperous, strong, democratic, culturally advanced, harmonious, and beautiful by 2050. By the end of this stage, the following goals will have been met:

- New heights are reached in every dimension of material, political, cultural and ethical, social, and ecological advancement.

- Modernization of China's system and capacity for governance is achieved.

- China has become a global leader in terms of composite national strength and international influence.

- Common prosperity for everyone is basically achieved.

- The Chinese people enjoy happier, safer, and healthier lives.

- The Chinese nation will become a proud and active member of the community of nations.

To achieve these goals, we need both a harmonious and stable domestic environment and a peaceful and tranquil international environment. Only by adhering to the path of peaceful development and maintaining world peace together with all countries can we achieve our development goals.

Adhering to the path of peaceful development aligns with the global trend. The world economy is undergoing profound adjustments, with protectionism and unilateralism reasserting themselves, setbacks in economic globalization, and impacts on multilateralism and the free trade system, increasing risks and challenges. Moreover, we must see that the current trend of openness and connectivity in the world is rolling forward, and the historical trend of economic globalization is irreversible. The old paths of colonialism and hegemonism are not viable; only the path of peaceful development is feasible.

General Secretary Xi Jinping pointed out, "There is only one trend in today's world, and that is peace, development, cooperation, and win-win outcomes. History and reality both prove that those who follow the trend will prosper, while those who go against it will perish."[1]

We are currently facing a marked increase in instability and uncertainty on the international stage. The only way to effectively meet

---

1   Xi Jinping, *On Building a Human Community with a Shared Future,* Beijing: Central Party Literature Publishing House, 2018, p. 191.

these challenges is to align ourselves with the broader trends of global development and embrace deeper, wider, and more vigorous openness. In this New Era, for our economy to thrive, we must continue to swim in the vast ocean of the global marketplace—weathering storms, broadening our horizons, and actively participating in and leading the process of economic globalization, all while advancing a higher level of open economy. As General Secretary Xi Jinping remarked, "It is impossible and against the tide of history to retreat the ocean of the world economy back into isolated lakes and rivers."[1]

We must resolutely follow the path of peaceful development. Only by adopting a more open stance can we strengthen our engagement and interaction with the world, fostering mutual understanding and friendship with people from all nations. Our commitment to peaceful development, while working hand-in-hand with other countries to build a world of lasting peace and shared prosperity, does not mean we will forgo our legitimate rights, nor will we compromise on our core national interests. Instead, we will steadfastly uphold the unity of our sovereignty, security, and development interests, navigating the complex global landscape to safeguard both world peace and stability.

III. A New Proposal for Building the Human Community with a Shared Future

Humanity has only one Earth, which is the sole home for humans so far. The most straightforward understanding of the human community with a shared future is that the interests and destinies of all countries and nations are closely intertwined. We should strive to make our planet a harmonious home for all and turn the aspirations of people worldwide for a

---

1 *Ibid.,* pp. 402–403.

better life into reality. Historically, globalization is an objective requirement of the development of social productive forces and an inevitable result of technological advancement. As globalization progresses, every country now faces the issue of how to manage its relationship with the external world. With the goal of realizing the aspirations of people worldwide for a better life and addressing current global issues, Xi Jinping has insightfully grasped the trends, rhythms, and tides of our era, profoundly understood the historical changes in the fate of humankind and the relationship between China and the world, and proposed a new solution for building a human community with a shared future to tackle common global challenges and issues.

1. Creatively propose the concept of building a human community with a shared future

The concept of building a human community with a shared future can be traced back to Xi Jinping's speech at the Moscow State Institute of International Relations on March 23, 2013, where he first presented the idea to the world. At that time, Xi Jinping emphasized that humanity is increasingly becoming a community with a shared future, where everyone's fate is intertwined. He called on all countries to jointly promote the establishment of a new type of international relations centered on mutually beneficial cooperation. He stated: "It is a world where countries are linked with and dependent on one another at a level never seen before. Mankind, by living in the same global village in the same era where history and reality meet, has increasingly emerged as a community of common destiny in which everyone has in himself a little bit of others."[1]

Subsequently, Xi Jinping delivered two more major speeches at United Nations conferences, outlining a beautiful vision for building a

---

1   Xi Jinping, *The Governance of China*, Beijing: Foreign Languages Press, 2018, vol. I, p. 298.

human community with a shared future. He proposed the overall path for creating this community and expressed a strong desire to work with other countries to promote world peace, stability, prosperity, and progress. On September 28, 2015, at the United Nations Headquarters in New York, Xi Jinping attended the general debate of the 70th Session of the United Nations General Assembly and delivered a speech. He proposed to jointly build a new partnership of mutually beneficial cooperation and to work together to create human community with a shared future. He emphasized building partnerships in which countries treat each other as equals, engage in extensive consultation, and enhance mutual understanding, create a security environment featuring fairness, justice, joint efforts, and shared interests, promoting open, innovative and inclusive development that benefits all, increasing inter-civilization exchanges to promote harmony, inclusiveness, and respect for differences, and building an ecosystem that puts Mother Nature and green development first. This 20-minute speech received 15 rounds of enthusiastic applause, the most and warmest applause of that session. On January 18, 2017, at the United Nations Office in Geneva, Xi Jinping attended the high-level meeting on "building a human community with a shared future together" and delivered a keynote speech. He advocated jointly advancing the great process of building of a global community of shared future by following the principles of extensive consultation, joint contribution, mutual benefit, mutual learning, and green and low-carbon development. He called for building a world of lasting peace, universal security, common prosperity, openness and inclusiveness, and cleanliness and beauty.

In addition, Xi Jinping has repeatedly emphasized the awareness of human community with a shared future in a series of important bilateral and multilateral diplomatic occasions, such as his speech to the Indonesian Parliament in 2013, the first World Internet Conference in

2014, the Central Conference on Foreign Affairs in 2014, his speech to the Pakistani Parliament in 2015, the Paris Climate Conference in 2015, the second World Internet Conference in 2015, the fourth Nuclear Security Summit in 2016, the CPC in Dialogue with World Political Parties High-Level Meeting in 2017, the Shanghai Cooperation Organization Qingdao Summit in 2018, the Beijing Summit of the Forum on China-Africa Cooperation in 2018, the first Conference on Dialogue of Asian Civilizations in 2019, and the CPC and World Political Parties Summit in 2021. He proposed building a China-ASEAN community with a shared future, a China-Pakistan community with a shared future, an Asian community with a shared future, a cyberspace community with a shared future, a China-Latin America community with a shared future, and a China-Africa community with a shared future, enriching and developing the theoretical connotation of the concept of building a human community with a shared future. In his major speech at the ceremony marking the centenary of the CPC, General Secretary Xi Jinping pointed out: "On the journey ahead, we will remain committed to promoting peace, development, cooperation, and mutual benefit, to an independent foreign policy of peace, and to the path of peaceful development. We will work to build a new model of international relations and a global community of shared future, promote the high-quality development of the Belt and Road Initiative through joint efforts, and use China's new achievements to provide the world with new opportunities."[1]

2. The theoretical logic of the concept of building a human community with a shared future

The concept of building a human community with a shared future

---

1   Xi Jinping, *Speech at a Ceremony Marking the Centenary of the Communist Party of China,* Beijing: People's Publishing House, 2021, p. 16.

not only inherits and promotes the Marxist goal of establishing a "union of free individuals" but also deeply integrates the traditional Chinese cultural ideal of "universal unity and all under Heaven being of one family."

The idea of building a human community with a shared future inherits the Marxist goal of establishing a "union of free individuals." In the long historical period before the advent of capitalist society, constrained by backward productivity and production methods, humanity existed in relatively isolated and closed environments. During that time, social relations and individual freedom were confined within narrow spaces. However, to cope with natural challenges and various external threats, humans often formed small collective units such as clans, tribes, families, and communes based on kinship, geographical ties, and religion. Marx and Engels, the founders of Marxism, made scientific predictions about the future direction of societal development based on an in-depth study of the general laws of social history. They anticipated that with the advancement of productivity, human society would inevitably move toward a communist society, where the union and liberation of free individuals would be realized, and communities would naturally emerge. They predicted that on the basis of developed productive forces, human history would shift from a regionally limited history to a world history. Marx stated: "The further the separate spheres, which interact on one another, extend in the course of this development, the more the original isolation of the separate nationalities is destroyed by the developed mode of production and intercourse and the division of labor between various nations naturally brought forth by these, the more history becomes world history."[1]

Indeed, as Marx and Engels observed, after entering capitalist society, with the advent of large-scale social production, social productivity rapidly increased. The isolated human social system was gradually broken by

---

1   https://www.marxists.org/archive/marx/works/1845/german-ideology/ch01b.htm.

international division of labor and intercourse, and the world began to establish extensive connections. Particularly, the globalization of capitalist production drew all nations into the capitalist world market system. The connections between peoples became increasingly close, and cooperation and exchanges deepened, showing a trend of development from isolation to expanded contact. As stated in the *Communist Manifesto*: "The bourgeoisie has through its exploitation of the world market given a cosmopolitan character to production and consumption in every country.... In place of the old local and national seclusion and self-sufficiency, we have intercourse in every direction, universal inter-dependence of nations. And as in material, so also in intellectual production. The intellectual creations of individual nations become common property."[1]

The high development of productivity is a necessary condition for community formation. Engels explicitly pointed out in the 1892 Polish edition preface of the *Communist Manifesto*, over 40 years after its original publication, that "A sincere international collaboration of the European nations is possible only if each of these nations is fully autonomous in its own house."[2] He further emphasized in the 1893 Italian edition preface of the *Communist Manifesto,* "Without restoring autonomy and unity to each nation, it will be impossible to achieve the international union of the proletariat, or the peaceful and intelligent cooperation of these nations toward common aims."[3] From this, it is evident that the prerequisites for realizing the union and liberation of free individuals include both the high development of productivity and the establishment of universal connections in world intercourse based on this productivity development. Only in this way can a communist society, as a world-historical existence, be realized. Marx stated, "Only in community [with others has each]

---

1   https://www.marxists.org/archive/marx/works/1848/communist-manifesto/ch01.htm.
2   https://www.marxists.org/archive/marx/works/1848/communist-manifesto/preface.htm.
3   https://www.marxists.org/archive/marx/works/1848/communist-manifesto/preface.htm#preface-1893.

individual the means of cultivating his gifts in all directions; only in the community, therefore, is personal freedom possible.... In a real community the individuals obtain their freedom in and through their association."[1]

Marx and Engels believed that the "communities" formed in pre-capitalist societies could not provide sufficient material conditions for the well-rounded development of individuals. Although capitalist society created unprecedented productivity development and rich material conditions in human history, it led to the alienation of human development, which does not constitute a real "community." A real "community," or a union of free individuals, can only be formed in a socialist society, especially a communist society. This real "community" is a union based on highly developed productivity and the equal collective ownership of social resources by all its members. It is a union that serves people rather than being alienated by material things and is formed by the voluntary and conscious association of individuals, rather than being dominated by oppressive forces. In such a union, each individual voluntarily unites and gains freedom through this union, achieving comprehensive development. This is the future society that Marx and Engels firmly believed in: "In place of the old bourgeois society, with its classes and class antagonisms, we shall have an association, in which the free development of each is the condition for the free development of all."[2]

As the connections between countries become closer, there is an objective requirement to make the ultimate goal of human development the realization of individual freedom, comprehensive development, and the liberation of all humanity. Only in this way can it align with the common interests of all countries and humanity.

General Secretary Xi Jinping, from the perspective of benefiting all

---

1   https://www.marxists.org/archive/marx/works/1845/german-ideology/ch01d.htm
2   https://www.marxists.org/archive/marx/works/1848/communist-manifesto/ch02.htm.

of humanity, proposed the concept of building a human community with a shared future, which is directed toward caring for the common destiny of all humanity. This concept aligns, in terms of its value goals, with the Marxist idea of establishing a "union of free individuals," highlighting the CPC's unwavering commitment to strengthening unity, cooperation, mutual benefit, and common development with countries worldwide. It represents the latest theoretical achievement of Marxism regarding the establishment of a "union of free individuals."

The concept of building a human community with a shared future incorporates the ideal societal pursuit found in traditional Chinese culture of "universal unity and all under Heaven being of one family." Looking back on history, the Chinese nation has a long history and splendid culture. The profound and extensive traditional Chinese culture, with its deep roots and longstanding heritage, represents the unique cultural identity of the Chinese nation, providing rich nourishment for its continuous growth and development, and will support the Chinese nation in creating a bright future. Traditional Chinese culture contains a rich system of ideas and methods related to "universal unity and all under Heaven being of one family." In the history of human advancement, the social ideal of "universal great unity" appeared early in China, where the Chinese people aspired to build a beautiful world as described in the statement, "When the Grand course was pursued, a public and common spirit ruled all under the sky." *The Book of Rites'* "Liyun" states:

When the Grand course was pursued, a public and common spirit ruled all under the sky; they chose men of talents, virtue, and ability; their words were sincere, and what they cultivated was harmony. Thus men did not love their parents only, nor treat as children only their own sons. A competent provision was secured for the aged till their death, employment for the able-bodied, and the means of growing up to the young. They showed kindness and compassion to widows, orphans, childless men, and those who were disabled by disease, so that they were all sufficiently maintained. Males had their proper work, and females had their homes. (They accumulated) articles (of value), disliking that they should be thrown away upon the ground, but not wishing to keep them for their own gratification. (They labored) with their strength, disliking that it should not be exerted, but not exerting it (only) with a view to their own advantage. In this way (selfish) schemings were repressed and found no development. Robbers, filchers, and rebellious traitors did not show themselves, and hence the outer doors remained open, and were not shut. This was (the period of) what we call the Grand Union.

Beyond the pursuit of the social ideal of "universal unity," the Chinese people have always emphasized "all under Heaven are of one family" and adhered to the principles of "harmony between humanity and nature," "unity of the public good and shared interests," "working together with one heart," "harmonious coexistence," "valuing harmony," "being kind to others," and "do not impose on others what you do not desire." They advocate for caring for all people and living things, promoting harmony among nations, and achieving great unity in the world. They hope not only for their own wellbeing but also for the wellbeing of people in other countries. The Chinese nation is also a peace-loving nation, having pursued and upheld the ideals of peace and harmony throughout its over 5,000 years of civilization. These principles and beliefs have been passed down through generations in China, deeply rooted in the Chinese spirit and reflected in Chinese behavior. They constitute the foundation and essence of traditional Chinese culture and collectively reflect the common value pursuits of all humanity, preparing the cultural core for the proposal of the concept of building a human community with a shared future.

The inheritance of China's traditional cultural ideals of "universal unity and all under Heaven being of one family" has provided a vital cultural foundation for the concept of building a human community with a shared future. Since assuming the role of General Secretary, Xi Jinping has repeatedly reinterpreted the contemporary relevance of China's profound cultural heritage. For instance, he has noted that "Chinese culture values harmony, and the concept of 'harmony' in Chinese civilization has a long history, embodying a cosmological view of harmony between heaven and humanity, an international outlook of harmony among countries, a social philosophy of unity in diversity, and a moral perspective that emphasizes the goodness of the human heart."[1] The rich philosophical thought, humanistic spirit, ethical teachings, and moral principles of Chinese traditional culture, he has said, "can provide valuable insights for understanding and transforming the world, offer useful guidance for governance, and serve as inspiration for moral development."[2]

The advocacy for building a human community with a shared future reflects Xi Jinping's vision from both a historical and contemporary perspective, as he inherits and innovatively extends the traditional Chinese ideal of "universal unity and all under Heaven being of one family." Xi emphasizes: "We should seek common ground while setting aside differences, and work together to build a new type of international relations based on cooperation and mutual benefit. Regardless of their size, strength, or wealth, all nations should treat each other as equals, ensuring both their own development and helping others to develop as well. Only when everyone prospers will the world be a better place."[3] He further elaborates:

---

1   Xi Jinping, *On Building a Human Community with a Shared Future,* Beijing: Central Party Literature Publishing House, 2018, p. 152.
2   *Ibid.,* p. 143.
3   *Ibid.,* p. 371.

"Although countries have their differences and occasional conflicts, the people of the world all live under the same blue sky and share the same home. We should regard each other as family. The people of all countries should embrace the idea that "all under Heaven are of one family," open their hearts, understand one another, seek common ground while respecting differences, and work together to build a human community with a shared future."[1]

The idea of building a human community with a shared future, as advocated by Xi Jinping, is imbued with profound Chinese wisdom. It reflects the deep thinking of the CPC in the New Era about the future of humanity, highlights the broad global vision of "benefiting all under heaven," and enhances China's cultural voice within the diverse cultures of the world. This vision has earned widespread international praise. In an interview with *People's Daily* in 2018, former Spanish Prime Minister Felipe González remarked: "China's rich cultural heritage, spanning thousands of years, continues to be passed down to this day. In my view, China is steadfast in establishing good international relations, addressing shared human concerns, and building a human community with a shared future. I am confident that through its efforts, China will realize the Chinese Dream."[2]

3. The practical logic of the concept of building a human community with a shared future

Xi Jinping pointed out, "In today's world, interaction and interdependence is the general trend with cross-border flows of goods, capital, information, and personnel, regardless of distance, size, and level of development, countries are increasingly finding themselves to be part

---

1 *Ibid.*, p. 510.
2 "Xi Jinping's Thought: A Source of Inspiration," *People's Daily*, April 12, 2018.

of a community of common interests and a shared future that is based on intertwined interests and common challenges."[1] The concept of building a human community with a shared future upholds the principles of extensive consultation, joint contribution, mutual benefit, mutual learning and green and low-carbon development. Its goal is to build an open, inclusive, clean and beautiful world that enjoys lasting peace, universal security, and common prosperity, which aligns with the sincere wishes and common pursuits of all countries for peace, development, cooperation, and progress. Achieving this noble pursuit will inevitably break the notion that a nation's strength is anonymous with hegemonic behavior, promote the development of a beautiful world characterized by mutually beneficial cooperation and democratic relations, and provide practical guidance for the comprehensive development of human society.

(1) China's approach for achieving human peace and development

The world today is undergoing momentous changes of a kind not seen in a century, but the trend of the times for peace, development, cooperation, and win-win outcomes remains unchanged. In the face of the unprecedented changes in the world and the global pandemic of COVID-19, the world has entered a period of turbulence and transformation. However, the aspirations of people from all countries for development, peace, unity, and progress have become even stronger.

At the beginning of the reform and opening up period, to create favorable domestic and international environments for China's modernization, Deng Xiaoping scientifically analyzed the domestic and international situations and the requirements for the development of human society, proposing that peace and development are the themes of the times. On the basis of the Five Principles of Peaceful Coexistence, China established and developed friendly cooperative relations with countries

---

1   *Op. cit.,* p. 271.

around the world, effectively maintaining overall international peace and stability and promoting common development. Over the past 40-plus years of reform and opening up, China has consistently pursued a strategy of mutual benefit and win-win outcomes, advocating for resolving disputes and conflicts between countries through dialogue and cooperation. The CPC and socialist China have gradually become leading forces in achieving human peace and development.

The world now stands at a new historical starting point, with humanity facing more problems that require joint solutions. Amid the great changes in the world, the trend of "the East rising and the West declining" is becoming increasingly prominent. China's continued rapid development has become a major force driving the evolution of the global landscape. At the same time, it must be recognized that hegemonism and power politics still persist, undermining international fairness and justice, which not only fails to fundamentally resolve various contradictions and conflicts but also erodes the foundation of world peace.

Hegemonism and an unfair global political and economic order are the roots of global chaos. Only by truly breaking the old world political and economic order that is unjust, unreasonable, and based on the strong bullying the weak, and by establishing a new world political and economic order of peace, development, cooperation, and win-win outcomes, can we fundamentally solve global governance issues. This will also create a better international environment for China to achieve the rejuvenation of the Chinese nation.

Promoting the building of a human community with a shared future is the Chinese approach to build a world of peace, development, cooperation, and win-win outcomes and achieve sustainable peace and development for humanity. Looking around the world today, globalization is facing headwinds, economic growth is persistently sluggish, development gaps are increasingly evident, wealth distribution is severely imbalanced, and global inequality is worsening. In addition, regional conflicts and wars continue, terrorism is on the rise, and non-traditional security threats are spreading. Faced with such complex problems and severe challenges, Western capitalist countries have clearly shown their inability to cope effectively. Meanwhile, the trend of openness and connectivity in the world is surging forward, the historical trend of economic globalization is irreversible, and the old path of colonialism and hegemonism is untenable. Only by conforming to the trend of world development, strengthening the ties and interactions among countries, and deepening the understanding and friendship among peoples, can we effectively address global risks and challenges. Only by building a human community with a shared future can we fundamentally solve the issues of peace and development in the 21st century.

(2) The right way forward for humanity is build a better world

No one expected that the third decade of the 21st century would begin with a global public health crisis as countries around the world fight against the COVID-19 pandemic. In the past year or so, over three million people worldwide have died from COVID-19. COVID-19 is the most widespread global pandemic humanity has encountered in the past century, posing a severe crisis and serious test to the entire world, and threatening the people's lives and safety. The global spread of the COVID-19 pandemic has shown that humanity is a community with a shared future, where everyone's fate is intertwined. Since the outbreak, China has consistently upheld the concept of building a human community with a shared future. With a lawful, open, transparent, and responsible attitude, China promptly informed the international community about the pandemic, shared prevention and treatment experiences without reservation, and provided assistance to international organizations and other countries to the best of its ability. The CPC, together with 240 political parties from over 110 countries, issued a joint appeal, urging all parties to prioritize human safety and health, uphold the concept of building a human community with a shared future, and work together to strengthen international cooperation in combating the pandemic.

Between January and April 2020, Xi Jinping repeatedly mentioned during conversations or meetings with foreign leaders and heads of international organizations, "The virus knows no borders, and the epidemic does not distinguish between races. In responding to this global public health crisis, the urgency and importance of building a human community with a shared future have become even more apparent."[1] This assessment has received widespread recognition and praise from the international community.

The COVID-19 pandemic has severely impacted the world economy, making recovery difficult and complicated. Various contradictions have become prominent or even intensified, including those between fairness and efficiency, growth and distribution, and technology and employment. The wealth gap has widened, and for the first time in 20 years, the global extreme poverty rate has increased. In accordance with the World Bank, by the end of 2021, about 150 million people will have fallen into extreme poverty due to the COVID-19 pandemic. Currently, developing the economy, improving livelihoods, and achieving common security are the primary and shared tasks faced by most countries. However, some Western countries have politicized the pandemic, leading to severe disruptions in the flow of people and goods and impacting global industrial and supply chains.

Since the outbreak of COVID-19, Xi Jinping has profoundly

---

1   Xi Jinping, *Coordinate Epidemic Prevention and Control with Economic and Social Development*, Beijing: Central Party Literature Publishing House, 2020, p. 154.

articulated the concept of building a global community of health for all at various multilateral summits, including the 2020 Extraordinary G20 Summit on COVID-19, the 73rd World Health Assembly, the series of high-level meetings marking the 75th anniversary of the United Nations, the BRICS leaders' summit, and the APEC informal leaders' meeting. He has proposed a series of significant initiatives and measures and actively committed to making vaccines a global public good. At the Global Health Summit video conference held in Beijing, Xi Jinping put forward five key points to promote international cooperation in fighting the pandemic, including "sticking together in solidarity and advocating cooperation," and announced five major measures, including providing an additional US$3 billion in international aid for a period of three years to support developing countries in fighting the pandemic and restoring economic and social development. These efforts aim to guide the world toward an early end to the pandemic and toward a rapid economic recovery.

The practice has fully demonstrated that whether it is to curb the spread of the virus or to resist the global economic recession caused by the pandemic, promoting the building of a human community with a shared future is essential. Strengthening international solidarity and cooperation is crucial for the world to accelerate economic recovery and safeguard our shared home.

Xi Jinping pointed out, "It is the expectation of the people of all countries and the responsibility of our generation of politicians to let the light of civilization shine brightly. To see this fulfilled, China's solution is this: to build a human community with a shared future."[1] "We should together promote the democratization of international relations. The world's destiny must be determined by the people of all countries together, and world affairs should be managed through discussion by the

---

1   *Op. cit.*, p. 416.

governments and peoples of all countries."[1] To achieve win-win and shared benefits, globalization can no longer follow the old path of the law of the jungle and zero-sum games. The concept of building a human community with a shared future upholds the principles of extensive consultation, joint contribution, mutual benefit, mutual learning and green and low-carbon development. Its goal is to build an open, inclusive, clean, and beautiful world that enjoys lasting peace, universal security, and common prosperity. This aligns with the sincere wishes and common pursuits of all countries for peace, development, cooperation, and progress, and it will undoubtedly promote the development of a beautiful world characterized by mutually beneficial cooperation and democratic relations, providing practical guidance for the comprehensive development of human society.

Great times call for a grand strategy, and a grand strategy calls for great vision. China will do well only when the world does well, and vice versa. Advocating the building a human community with a shared future, proposing new principles for the international order, and envisioning new relationships for human society fundamentally aim to make the world a better place and the people happier. Facing the complex problems and severe challenges of today's world, no country can tackle the various challenges facing humanity alone, nor can any country retreat into self-isolation. The CPC is a party committed to the cause of human progress. The practical significance of the concept of building a human community with a shared future, advocated by our Party, has once again been confirmed. It requires the joint efforts of all countries to maintain and promote world peace and development.

---

1 *Ibid.,* p. 133.

IV. Make New and Greater Contributions to Humanity

The CPC has always regarded making new and greater contributions to humanity as its mission. Making new and greater contributions to humanity is also the solemn commitment and consistent pursuit of the Chinese Communists. As socialism with Chinese characteristics enters the New Era, China's influence on the world has never been as comprehensive, profound, and long-lasting as it is today. Faced with the tremendous and profound changes occurring in the economic, political, cultural, and various other fields at the beginning of the 21st century, and in response to the question of "What has happened to the world and how should humanity responds?" China, as a responsible major country, has issued the call of the times: "China should make greater contributions to human society and assume greater responsibilities." It has proposed the beautiful initiative to "Let the torch of peace be passed from generation to generation, let the driving force of development be continuously generated, and let the light of civilization shine brightly."

1. Always regard making new and greater contributions to humanity as our mission

Over the more than 70 years since the founding of the People's Republic of China, our Party has led the Chinese people in the historical process of striving for national prosperity, the happiness of the people, and national rejuvenation. This process is also the continuous history of socialist China making contributions to the cause of human progress. In 1956, Mao Zedong said, "China is a large country, accounting for one-quarter of the world's population, but its contribution to humanity does not match its population proportion," and "China should make greater contributions to humanity."[1] Therefore, transforming the backward situation and building a prosperous and strong socialist China is essential for making the necessary contributions to the cause of human progress. The establishment of the People's Republic of China laid the political and institutional foundations for China's path to the world. The tremendous achievements in various economic and social aspects have strengthened the forces of world socialism and greatly advanced the cause of human progress.

Since the introduction of the reform and opening up policy, making more contributions to humanity has become an intrinsic requirement for the development of socialist China. In 1978, during a meeting with foreign guests, Deng Xiaoping said, "To measure whether we are truly a socialist country, we must not only develop ourselves and achieve the Four Modernizations but also, as we develop, contribute more to humanity."[2] Reform and opening up not only dramatically changed China but also profoundly altered the world.

At a CPC in Dialogue with World Political Parties High-Level Meeting, Xi Jinping emphasized that everything the CPC does is to seek happiness for the Chinese people, rejuvenation for the Chinese nation, and peace and development for humanity. During his meeting with UN Secretary-General António Guterres, Xi Jinping further stated that all our efforts are aimed at seeking happiness for the people, rejuvenation for the nation, and great harmony for the world. Currently, tens of thousands of Chinese scientists, engineers, entrepreneurs, technicians, medical personnel, teachers, ordinary workers, and volunteers are working side by side with local people in many developing countries, helping them change

---

1   Mao Zedong, *Collected Works of Mao Zedong*, Beijing: People's Publishing House, 1999, vol. VII, p. 124, 125.
2   *Chronology of Deng Xiaoping 1975–1997*, Beijing: Central Party Literature Publishing House, 2004, vol. I, p. 325.

their destinies. All these actions are concrete measures of China practicing the concept of building a human community with a shared future.

The century-long international practice of the CPC has demonstrated to the world our country's major-country responsibility and historical commitment to promoting common human development. It reflects our determination to strive to build an open, inclusive, clean, and beautiful world that enjoys lasting peace, universal security, and common prosperity. This has been highly praised by recipient countries and the international community.

2. Make great contributions to world peace

In today's chaotic and disorderly world, where turmoil is frequent, a rising China is committed to building an open, inclusive, clean, and beautiful world that enjoys lasting peace, universal security, and common prosperity. On the basis of seeking common ground while reserving differences, China seeks to develop itself by maintaining world peace and, in turn, maintains world peace through its own development. In the New Era, China is advancing along the path of peaceful development, making significant contributions to global prosperity and stability.

Strengthen the forces maintaining regional and world peace through China's own development

The peace and stability of the world depend on the strength of the forces maintaining world peace. Historically and currently, China should be considered a trustworthy and reliable force for peace on the international stage. The stronger we are, the stronger the forces of world peace will be. This is because the Chinese nation has always been peace-loving, and the pursuit of peace is deeply rooted in the cultural world of our people. Xi Jinping stated, "Our forebears knew that "Regardless of size, a state partial to war will perish." Since ancient times, the Chinese nation has actively engaged in foreign trade and communication, and not in invasion and expansion. It has devoted its energies to protecting its country in patriotism, and not to grabbing more land in colonialism."[1]

Historically, China has been one of the world's most powerful countries for long periods, but it has no record of colonizing or invading other countries. Even when China's GDP accounted for more than 30% of the world's total centuries ago, it did not engage in external aggression or expansion. As early as the 1980s, Deng Xiaoping pointed out, "[I]f China, with its one billion people, keeps to socialism and adheres to the policy of peace, it will be following the right course and will be able to make greater contributions to humanity."[2]

Since the introduction of the reform and opening up policy, China has voluntarily reduced its military personnel by over 4 million, actively participated in international arms control, disarmament, and non-proliferation processes, opposed arms races, maintained global strategic balance and stability, and signed or joined over 20 multilateral arms control, disarmament, and non-proliferation treaties, including the Treaty on the Non-Proliferation of Nuclear Weapons.

China has achieved unprecedented economic development and social progress, surpassing both its pre-revolutionary past and the capitalist West, through self-reliance rather than colonial exploitation. This has led to the fastest large-scale poverty reduction in human history to date. Notably, following the global financial crisis in late 2008, when major world economies experienced significant slowdowns or even faced recessions, China's economy maintained high growth rates and was the first to recover. From 2013 to 2017, China's average annual contribution to global economic growth exceeded 30%, surpassing the combined contributions

---

1   Xi Jinping, *On Building a Human Community with a Shared Future,* Beijing: Central Party Literature Publishing House, 2018, p. 107.
2   Deng Xiaoping, *Selected Works of Deng Xiaoping,* Beijing: Foreign Languages Press, 1994, vol. III, p. 161.

of the United States, the Eurozone, and Japan, making China the leading contributor globally.[1] China's economic development has become a vital engine driving the recovery of the world economy, serving as a key stabilizer and source of momentum for global economic growth.

In recent years, China has actively participated in addressing major international and regional hotspot issues, engaging in dialogue and negotiations on issues like the Iran nuclear deal and the Syrian conflict, playing a constructive role in promoting political solutions. Since 2015, China has announced the establishment of the China-UN Peace and Development Fund, with a commitment of US$1 billion over ten years, which officially began operations in 2016. To date, almost all intergovernmental international organizations have seen China's involvement. China is also the second-largest contributor to the UN budget and the largest troop-contributing country to UN peacekeeping missions. As the world's largest developing country, "Having always promoted world peace, contributed to global development, and safeguarded the international order, China is ready to seek a broader convergence of interests with all countries, with a view to establishing a new model of international relations based on mutually beneficial cooperation, and forming a community of shared future and interests for all humankind."[2] Xi Jinping's words clearly articulate that in the New Era, China, with a spirit of responsibility, will work together with countries worldwide to strive for the development of a world of lasting peace and universal security.

Foster an international order that is fairer, more equitable, and more rational to contribute wisdom and approaches for world peace

---

1 "Statistical Communiqué of the People's Republic of China on the 2017 National Economic and Social Development," National Bureau of Statistics of China, February 28, 2018.
2 *Documents Produced since the 18th CPC National Congress*, Beijing: People's Publishing House, 2018, vol. II, pp. 353–354.

The world today is undergoing momentous changes of a kind not seen in a century. International relations are undergoing profound transformations, the international landscape is continuously evolving, and global uncertainties are increasing.

Especially, the United States, driven by its national strategic interests, has proposed national security policies such as "America First," frequently tearing up international treaties, agreements, and withdrawing from international organizations. For example, in 1982, to maintain its maritime hegemony, the US refused to sign the United Nations Convention on the Law of the Sea and still has not joined it. In 1984, dissatisfied with its cultural dominance being gradually eroded by developing countries, the US formally withdrew from UNESCO, only to rejoin in 2003 during the George W. Bush administration. In 2017, citing reasons such as saving money, urging reform, and protesting anti-Israel bias, the US again announced its withdrawal from UNESCO. In 2001, claiming that fulfilling environmental obligations did not align with its national interests, the US refused to sign the Kyoto Protocol and still hasn't. In 2001, to strengthen its military advantage, the US officially withdrew from the Anti-Ballistic Missile Treaty signed with the Soviet Union in 1972. In 2017, believing that multilateral trade agreements were not in America's best interests and hindered the "America First" policy, the US announced its withdrawal from the Trans-Pacific Partnership (TPP). In 2017, the US government claimed that the Paris Agreement impeded American economic development and announced its withdrawal from the accord. In 2018, despite the International Atomic Energy Agency (IAEA) confirming that Iran had fulfilled its commitments under the nuclear agreement and without clear evidence that Iran violated the agreement by conducting nuclear tests, the US insisted on withdrawing from the Joint Comprehensive Plan of Action (JCPOA) endorsed by the UN Security Council and imposed economic sanctions on Iran. In 2018, citing the alleged inability of the United Nations Human Rights Council to effectively protect human rights, the US announced its withdrawal from the Council. In 2018, the it announced its withdrawal from the Optional Protocol to the Vienna Convention on Diplomatic Relations concerning the Compulsory Settlement of Disputes, which involved issues of international court jurisdiction. In 2019, to freely develop intermediate-range missile capabilities, the US announced its withdrawal from the Intermediate-Range Nuclear Forces Treaty (INF) on August 2. In 2020, using the pretext of alleged Russian violations, the US announced it would begin the process of withdrawing from the Open Skies Treaty on May 22, 2020. On July 6, 2020, as a means to find a scapegoat for its poor handling of the COVID-19 pandemic, the US announced its withdrawal from the World Health Organization, currently still owing over US$200 million in membership dues.[1] These actions by the US to withdraw from agreements and organizations have severely undermined key components of the international order that it once actively promoted and led in establishing. Consequently, the world order is also undergoing evolution, and establishing a new world order is a pressing issue facing the people of the world today.

In contrast, China has always aimed for the wellbeing of all humanity, demonstrating an internationalist spirit. We unite with all nations that treat us as equals, transcending ideological differences, value disparities, civilizational conflicts, and social system contradictions. We reject the law of the jungle and do not seek hegemonic dominance. From advocating the Five Principles of Peaceful Coexistence to promoting the concept of "building a human community with a shared future," from proposing "One Country, Two Systems" and "shelving disputes and pursuing joint development" to initiating the BRI, China continually contributes its

---

1 "America's 'Withdrawals' over the Years," *Global Times*, July 8, 2020.

wisdom in handling major issues in international relations, national unification, and regional development. We have consistently emphasized that we are beneficiaries and upholders of the current international order, only seeking to rectify its unreasonable aspects rather than establishing a completely new system. We advocate for the democratization of international relations, where global affairs are deliberated collectively. Our goal is to reform the unreasonable phenomena in international relations, fostering an international order that is fairer, more equitable, and more rational and striving to establish a new world order characterized by fairness, justice, and mutually beneficial cooperation.

China also provides the world with insights and approaches for addressing developmental challenges, overcoming governance difficulties, and exploring better social systems. This has earned widespread praise from the international community. Noted American China expert and Harvard University emeritus professor Ezra Feivel Vogel has remarked that "the historical task of China and the United States is to shape a new international order, which is a shared responsibility of both countries." He believes that "the era of American unipolar dominance is coming to an end. The United States can no longer exert the same level of influence as before and lead global affairs unilaterally. This means that China needs to cooperate with the United States and other countries to provide a comprehensive new order for the world. In this new order, the world should not be divided into hostile blocs, as that would be disastrous for all countries. Instead, the world should unite under an overall framework."[1]

Therefore, building a new world order that is fair, just, and based on mutually beneficial cooperation is the aspiration of people worldwide. It is the path to achieving the democratization of international relations,

---

1   "Harvard Emeritus Professor and 'China Hand' Ezra Vogel: The Era of American Unipolar Dominance Is Ending," *Global Times,* July 20, 2020.

equality among nations large and small, and the realization of mutual benefit through bilateral or multilateral international cooperation. This requires joint consultation and formulation by major countries like China, the United States, Russia, and the peoples of the European Union, Asia, Africa, and Latin America. This is the historical responsibility bestowed upon us by the unprecedented changes of the past century and the historical mission through which China will make even greater contributions to humanity.

3. Make great contributions to global development

Our Party not only benefits the Chinese people but also the people of the world. Xi Jinping emphasized: "The CPC has its origin in the people and has relied on the people for its growth and development. It has always cared about the people, Chinese and others, and is committed to working for their wellbeing."[1] Since the founding of the People's Republic of China, we have adhered to the philosophy of developing ourselves while benefiting the world. In our development journey, we have provided substantial aid and preferential loans to many other developing countries, along with significant personnel, intellectual, and technical support. We have also helped many developing countries complete numerous projects aimed at economic and social development and improving people's livelihoods.

Since the 18th CPC National Congress, Xi Jinping has announced a series of pragmatic aid initiatives and measures at major international events, including the high-level meetings marking the 75th anniversary of the UN, the Paris Climate Conference, the Johannesburg Summit of the Forum on China-Africa Cooperation, the G20 Hangzhou Summit, and

---

1   Xi Jinping, *The Governance of China*, Beijing: Foreign Languages Press, 2020, vol. III, p. 507.

the BRICS Xiamen Summit. These include the Eight Major Initiatives,[1] the Ten Cooperation Plans for China-Africa relations, the establishment of the South-South Cooperation Assistance Fund and the Institute of South South Cooperation and Development, and the launch of the Economic and Technical Cooperation Plan for BRICS Countries. China has proposed approaches and contributed wisdom on global and regional issues such as poverty alleviation, disease control, climate change, and refugee assistance, leading the trend for peace and development and promoting the reform of the global governance system.

China's open development brings benefits to countries around the world and promotes global development. China's growth has provided numerous benefits to neighboring countries and the world. When the Asian financial crisis erupted in 1997, China maintained a stable yuan exchange rate, significantly contributing to economic stability in Asia. During the global financial crisis of 2008, China was a major contributor to the global economic recovery, creating new growth points for the economic development of various countries. Since 2013, against the backdrop of a slow global economic recovery and prolonged low growth, China's economy has maintained a high growth rate, providing new impetus for global economic recovery. By supplying a large number of low-cost goods and services, the Chinese people have not only reduced the living costs of people in other countries using Chinese-made products but also played a crucial role in controlling global inflation and mitigating global economic fluctuations.

Moreover, China's rapidly growing middle-income population is becoming an increasingly important consumer group for global goods and

---

1   Securing a national fund worth tens of billions, signing 100 investment attraction projects, hosting 100 forums and business events, launching 100 first releases, debuts, and premieres, establishing a global digital trade alliance for 100 companies, selecting 100 exemplary digital trade cases, releasing the Forbes Global Top 100 Digital Trade Companies list, and unveiling the CCID National Top 100 Digital Trade Companies list.

services, providing a vast market for countries around the world.

While striving for its own development and poverty eradication, China actively engages in South-South cooperation, offering aid to many other developing countries without attaching any political conditions, and supports them in their efforts to eliminate poverty. China actively participates in discussions on the United Nations 2030 Agenda for Sustainable Development, fully commits to domestic implementation, and has been the first to release national plans and progress reports on the agenda, achieving early results in multiple areas. Within the framework of South-South cooperation, China assists other developing countries in implementing the agenda. Over the past three years, the China-UN Peace and Development Fund's 2030 Agenda for Sustainable Development Sub-Fund has successfully implemented 27 projects, benefiting 49 countries in Asia, Africa, and Latin America, injecting strong momentum into the global implementation of the agenda.

For global development, China always upholds the banner of peace, development, cooperation, and mutual benefit, adhering to the diplomatic policy of maintaining world peace and promoting common development. China actively advocates for creating more cooperation opportunities worldwide, promotes the establishment of a new international economic and political order, fosters healthy economic globalization, addresses global challenges facing human society, and strives to promote common development and prosperity among all countries. By following the new development philosophy, China contributes new ideas of "scientific development, peaceful development, inclusive development, and win-win development" to human society. Transitioning from the "world's factory" to the "world's market," China's vast market provides numerous employment opportunities for various countries, and its strong consumer capacity opens up more "imaginative space" for global goods and services.

With solid advancement of the BRI, in May 2017, Xi Jinping announced a series of development cooperation measures at the Belt and Road Forum for International Cooperation, including offering 60 billion yuan in aid to participating developing countries and international organizations. These measures highlight China's determination and actions to eliminate the global governance deficit, bringing tangible benefits to the people of the countries and regions along the Belt and Road and promoting shared development and prosperity.

4. Make great contributions to human progress

As socialism with Chinese characteristics enters the New Era, China, with its broad-mindedness of seeking common ground while reserving differences and being open and inclusive, actively promotes the flourishing of world civilizations and human progress. Chinese culture, the Chinese path, and the Chinese system are becoming more vibrant, continuously making new and greater contributions to human advancement. Advocating for the diversity of civilizations, China promotes exchanges, mutual learning, and harmony among different civilizations. Xi Jinping pointed out: "Civilization cannot exist without diversity, and this diversity will endure as far into the future as we can imagine. The mere existence of differences should not cause alarm. What truly raises concern are arrogance, prejudice, and hatred, as well as attempts to impose a hierarchy on civilizations or force one's own history, culture, or social system onto others. The right path is for nations to pursue peaceful coexistence based on mutual respect, expand common ground while setting aside differences, and foster exchanges and mutual learning. This is how we can drive the progress of civilization forward."[1] "Civilizations become more

---

1   Xi Jinping, "Let the Torch of Multilateralism Light up Humanity's Way Forward: Special Address at the World Economic Forum Virtual Event of the Davos Agenda the World Economic Forum Virtual Event of the Davos Agenda," *People's Daily,* January 26, 2021.

colorful through exchange and richer through mutual learning."[1] Through continuous efforts, we should encourage countries to "transcend cultural misunderstandings with intercultural exchanges, overcome cultural clashes through mutual learning, and rise above ideas of cultural supremacy to embrace coexistence."[2] Although the discourse of civilizational clash and superiority occasionally resurfaces in today's world, China steadfastly advocates for the diversity of civilizations as an inexhaustible driving force for human progress. Together with the international community, China promotes mutual respect and harmony among different civilizations, making mutual learning a positive force in building a human community with a shared future. The various civilizations created by humanity will shine together, weaving a vibrant and colorful tapestry. By engaging in diverse dialogues and exchanges, Chinese civilization will reach out to the world, and ancient Chinese concepts such as "universal unity," "harmony among countries," and "working together with one heart" will become crucial elements in promoting world peace, development, and fostering a just and reasonable international order. These concepts play a significant role in building a human community with a shared future.

Make great contributions to global poverty eradication

Since the 18th CPC National Congress, General Secretary Xi Jinping placed poverty alleviation at the forefront of governance, uniting and leading the Chinese people in the largest, most intense, and most inclusive poverty alleviation campaign in human history. By the end of 2020, after eight years of arduous efforts by the entire Party and the nation, China had lifted out of poverty all of the 98.99 million rural residents, who were lying below the current poverty line, as had the 832 counties and 128,000 villages, thus addressing regional poverty and completing the daunting task

---

1　Xi Jinping, *On Building a Human Community with a Shared Future,* Beijing: Central Party Literature Publishing House, 2018, p. 76.
2　*Ibid.,* p. 491.

of eradicating absolute poverty.

International public opinion generally acknowledges that China's achievements in eradicating extreme poverty are immense, accounting for the largest proportion of poverty reduction worldwide. In accordance with Matteo Marchisio, the representative of the International Fund for Agricultural Development in China, China's significant accomplishments in poverty reduction are due to the formulation of development plans and pragmatic policies tailored to its national conditions. He added that targeted poverty alleviation is an effective measure in China's decisive battle against poverty, providing important insights for other developing countries in their efforts to escape poverty.

The President of the World Economic Forum, Børge Brende, highly praised China's poverty alleviation efforts, stating that this is an unprecedented great achievement in the history of human poverty reduction. Chea Monyrith, Project Planning Director of the Civil Society Alliance Forum in Cambodia, stated: "China has created a miracle in the history of global poverty reduction," and "China has enabled the fruits of development to benefit more people, lifting hundreds of millions out of poverty. China has made significant contributions to global poverty reduction." Humphrey Moshi, Director of the Center for Chinese Studies at the University of Dar es Salaam in Tanzania, remarked that China has fully leveraged its institutional and political advantages, mobilizing resources from all sectors of society for poverty alleviation, and adopting targeted, sustainable policies that have achieved remarkable poverty reduction results. He stated that as the country with the largest number of people lifted out of poverty, China accounts for over 70% of the global poverty reduction, instilling confidence in the global fight against poverty.[1] José Graziano da Silva, Director-General of the United Nations Food and Agriculture Organization, also noted that China's efforts are the biggest factor in reducing the global population of poverty and hunger. Klaus Rohland, director of the World Bank's China office, specifically mentioned that without China's achievements in poverty alleviation, the UN Millennium Development Goals would have been difficult to achieve.

The significant achievements in the development of the socialist system with Chinese characteristics are a great creation in the history of human institutional civilization. The CPC not only benefits the Chinese people but also the people of the world. The achievements of the development of the socialist system with Chinese characteristics belong not only to China but also to the world; they not only provide a guarantee for China's socialist modernization and national rejuvenation but also contribute to the progress of humanity and the development of world civilization. Xi Jinping pointed out: "Only after solving national problems will we be in a better position to solve international problems. And by reviewing domestic practices we will develop a greater ability to offer suggestions and solutions for global issues."[2] China, as a developing country with over 1.4 billion people, sees every major progress and achievement in its institutional development and innovation having a broad and far-reaching impact on the entire world. Deng Xiaoping once confidently envisioned: "Our system will improve more and more with the passage of time. By absorbing the progressive elements of other countries, it will become the best in the world."[3]

In the 21st century, as the CPC seeks to provide a Chinese approach for humanity's exploration of better social systems, Xi Jinping emphasized

---

1 "China's Significant Contribution to Global Poverty Reduction Efforts: International Comments on China's Decisive Battle against Poverty," *People's Daily,* June 2, 2020.

2 Xi Jinping, *The Governance of China*, Beijing: Foreign Languages Press, 2017, vol. II, p. 369.

3 Deng Xiaoping, *Selected Works of Deng Xiaoping*, Beijing: Foreign Languages Press, 1995, vol. II, p. 335.

that we firmly believe, "As socialism progresses, our institutions will undoubtedly mature, the strengths of our system will become self-evident, and our development path will assuredly become wider."[1] The influence of China's development path on the world will inevitably grow. This is a concentrated expression of confidence in our path, theory, system, and culture, and it represents our historical responsibility for the socialist cause and the development of human society and the progress of human advancement.

With a sense of historical responsibility and a global perspective, General Secretary Xi Jinping explicitly stated: "China's transition from new democracy to socialism, the creation and expansion of the socialist path with Chinese characteristics, has turned the beautiful ideal of socialism into a vibrant and successful path and system on the ancient land of China. This not only provides an important institutional guarantee for the rejuvenation of the Chinese nation but also offers a compelling path and system choice for humanity's pursuit of a better future."[2] He added, "The CPC and Chinese people have every confidence in their ability to provide a Chinese solution to aid the exploration of a better social system for humanity."[3] This offers a new option for other developing countries in their institutional development and contributes Chinese wisdom and approaches to the development of human institutional civilization. Former Mexican President Felipe Calderón noted, "China's development achievements greatly inspire other developing countries.... China has found a development path that suits itself and continues to innovate in national governance and economic development. China adheres to a people-centered approach, promoting social fairness and justice, and is committed to ensuring that the benefits

---

1 Xi Jinping, *The Governance of China*, Beijing: Foreign Languages Press, 2018, vol. I, p. 24.
2 *Documents Produced since the 18th CPC National Congress*, Beijing: Central Party Literature Publishing House, 2016, vol. II, pp. 79–80.
3 Xi Jinping, *The Governance of China*, Beijing: Foreign Languages Press, 2017, vol. II, p. 37.

of development are shared more equitably among all people. In such a healthy and positive social environment, the Chinese people are full of enthusiasm, striving hard for personal and national dreams. People of all ethnic groups work together, creating a united, vibrant, and prosperous social landscape."[1] We firmly believe that under the leadership of the CPC, through comprehensive deepening of reform, the socialist system with Chinese characteristics will become more mature, well-established, and improved. Its superiority and advantages will be fully demonstrated and utilized, making it the best system in the world and enriching the treasure trove of institutional civilization with its unique achievements.

At a ceremony marking the centenary of the CPC, Xi Jinping declared to the world: "The Party will continue to work with all peace-loving countries and peoples to promote the shared human values of peace, development, fairness, justice, democracy and freedom. We will continue to champion cooperation over confrontation, to open up rather than closing our doors, and to focus on mutual benefits rather than zero-sum games. We will oppose hegemony and power politics, and strive to keep the wheels of history rolling toward bright horizons."[2]

At the CPC and World Political Parties Summit in July 2021, Xi Jinping profoundly stated: "Proceeding from reality in all it does, the CPC has led the Chinese people in finding, through trial and error, the path of socialism with Chinese characteristics. History and practice have proven and will continue to prove that this is not only the correct path that works, but also the sure path that pays off. We will unswervingly follow the path leading to a bright future to ensure that development is pursued

---

1   Felipe Calderón, "Tell Personal Stories and Witness a Glorious Journey: China's Development Achievements Greatly Inspire Other Developing Countries," *People's Daily*, January 6, 2020.
2   Xi Jinping, *Speech at a Ceremony Marking the Centenary of the Communist Party of China,* Beijing: People's Publishing House, 2021, p. 16.

for both our own good and the benefit of the world."[1] The transformative changes in China in the New Era have not only laid a solid foundation for building a great modern socialist country in all respects but also provided other developing countries with valuable experience in modernization, contributed Chinese approaches to improving global governance, and created an inclusive and symbiotic global civilization. China's development has revitalized global socialism, offered a Chinese alternative to the Western logic that "a nation's strength is anonymous with hegemonic behavior," and made significant contributions to world economic development and human advancement. China has become a builder of world peace, a contributor to global development, and a defender of international order. By the middle of the 21st century, China aims to have comprehensively built a great modern socialist country that is prosperous, strong, democratic, culturally advanced, harmonious, and beautiful. This will enable one-fifth of the world's population to achieve common prosperity under socialism and enjoy a better life, fully demonstrating the immense superiority of the socialist system. This will be a monumental contribution to the new development of 21st-century world socialism and a significant contribution to the progress of human history.

---

1   Xi Jinping, "Strengthening Cooperation among Political Parties to Jointly Pursue the People's Wellbeing: Keynote at the CPC and World Political Parties Summit," *People's Daily*, July 7, 2021.

References

Chinese References

1. *Selected Works of Marx and Engels*, Volumes 1–4, Beijing: People's Publishing House, 2012.

2. *Collected Works of Marx and Engels*, Volumes, 1–10, Beijing: People's Publishing House, 2009.

3. *Collected Works of Marx and Engels*, Volume 23, Beijing: People's Publishing House, 1965.

4. *Collected Works of Marx and Engels*, Volume 31, Beijing: People's Publishing House, 1998.

5. *Collected Works of Marx and Engels,* Volume 44, Beijing: People's Publishing House, 2001.

6. *Selected Works of Lenin*, Volumes 1–4, Beijing: People's Publishing House, 2012.

7. *Special Collected Works of Lenin*, Beijing: People's Publishing House, 2009.

8. *Collected Works of Lenin*, Volume 20, Beijing: People's Publishing House, 1989.

9. *Collected Works of Lenin*, Volume 27, Beijing: People's Publishing House, 1990.

10. *Collected Works of Lenin*, Volume 36, Beijing: People's Publishing House, 1985.

11. *Selected Works of Mao Tse-tung*, Volumes 1–4, Beijing: People's Publishing House, 1991.

12. *Collected Works of Mao Zedong*, Volumes 1–8, Beijing: People's Publishing House, 1993–1999.

13. *Special Compilation of Mao Zedong's Works*, Beijing, Central Party Literature Publishing House, 2003.

14. *Chronology of Mao Zedong* (1949–1976), Beijing: Central Party Literature Publishing House, 2013.

15. *Selected Works of Zhou Enlai*, Volume II, Beijing: People's Publishing House, 1997.

16. *Selected Works of Deng Xiaoping*, Volumes I–III, Beijing: People's Publishing House, 1993-1994.

17. *Chronology of Deng Xiaoping 1975-1997*, Volumes I–III, Beijing: Central Party Literature Publishing House, 2004.

18. *Selected Works of Jiang Zemin*, Volumes I–III, Beijing: People's Publishing House, 2006.

19. *Selected Works of Hu Jintao*, Volumes I–III, Beijing: People's Publishing House, 2016.

20. Xi Jinping, *The Governance of China*, Beijing: Foreign Languages Press, 2014.

21. Xi Jinping, *The Governance of China*, Volume II, Beijing: Foreign Languages Press, 2017.

22. Xi Jinping, *The Governance of China*, Volume III, Beijing: Foreign Languages Press, 2020.

23. *An Introduction to Xi Jinping Thought on Socialism with Chinese Characteristics for a New Era*, Beijing: Xuexi Press and People's Publishing House, 2019.

24. *An Introduction to Xi Jinping's Diplomatic Thinking*, Beijing: People's Publishing House and Xuexi Pres, 2021.

25. *An Introduction to Xi Jinping's Thinking on the Rule of Thinking*, Beijing: People's Publishing House and Xuexi Pres, 2021.

26. Xi Jinping, *The Chinese Dream of National Rejuvenation*, Beijing: Central Party Literature Publishing House, 2013.

27. Xi Jinping, *The Campaign to Heighten Awareness of and Implement the Mass Line*, Beijing: Central Party Literature Publishing House, 2014.

28. Xi Jinping, *How to Comprehensively Deepen Reform*, Beijing, Central Party Literature Publishing House, 2014.

29. Xi Jinping, *Comprehensive Law-Based Governance,* Beijing, Central Party Literature Publishing House, 2015.

30. Xi Jinping, *Implement the Four-Pronged Comprehensive Strategy*, Beijing, Central Party Literature Publishing House 2015.

31. Xi Jinping, *Improve Party Conduct, Ensure Clean Government, and Combat Corruption*, Beijing: Central Party Literature Publishing House and China Fangzheng Press, 2015.

32. Xi Jinping, *Strengthen Party Discipline and Uphold Party Regulations*, Beijing: Central Party Literature Publishing House and China Fangzheng Press, 2016.

33. Xi Jinping, *Promote Technological Innovation*, Beijing: Central Party Literature Publishing House, 2016.

34. Xi Jinping, *Promote Socialist Economic Development,* Beijing: Central Party Literature Publishing House, 2017.

35. Xi Jinping, *Promote Socialist Political Development,* Beijing: Central Party Literature Publishing House, 2017.

36. Xi Jinping, *Promote Socialist Cultural Development*, Beijing: Central Party Literature Publishing House, 2017.

37. Xi Jinping, *Promote Socialist Social Development,* Beijing: Central Party Literature Publishing House, 2017.

38. Xi Jinping, *Promote Socialist Eco-Civilization*, Beijing: Central

Party Literature Publishing House, 2017.

39. Xi Jinping, *Adopt a Holistic Approach to National Security*, Beijing: Central Party Literature Publishing House, 2018.

40. Xi Jinping, *Stay True to the Original Aspirations and Founding Mission of the Party*, Beijing: Party Building Books Publishing House and Central Party Literature Publishing House, 2019.

41. Xi Jinping, *Eliminate Pointless Formalities and Bureaucratic Constraints*, Beijing: Central Party Literature Publishing House, 2020.

42. Xi Jinping, *Pursue Major-Country Diplomacy with Chinese Characteristics*, Beijing: Central Party Literature Publishing House, 2020.

43. Xi Jinping, *Coordinate Epidemic Prevention and Control with Economic and Social Development*, Beijing: Central Party Literature Publishing House, 2020.

44. Xi Jinping, *Ensure Full and Rigorous Self-Governance of the Party, 2021*, Beijing: Central Party Literature Publishing House, 2021.

45. Xi Jinping, *On Building a Human Community with a Shared Future*, Beijing: Central Party Literature Publishing House, 2018.

46. Xi Jinping, *Comprehensively Deepen Reform*, Beijing: Central Party Literature Publishing House, 2018, p. 187.

47. Xi Jinping, *The Belt and Road Initiative*, Beijing, Central Party Literature Publishing House, 2018.

48. Xi Jinping, *Uphold the Party's Leadership over All Work*, Beijing: Central Party Literature Publishing House, 2019.

49. Xi Jinping, *The Party's Public Communication Work*, Beijing: Central Party Literature Publishing House, 2020.

50. Xi Jinping, *Ensure Comprehensive Law-Based Governance*, Beijing: Central Party Literature Publishing House, 2020.

51. Xi Jinping, *On Grasping the New Development Stage, Implementing the New Development Philosophy, and Building a New Development Dynamic*,

Beijing: Central Party Literature Publishing House, 2021.

52. Xi Jinping, *Up and Out of Poverty,* Fuzhou: Fujian People's Publishing House, 1992.

53. Xi Jinping, *Zhejiang, China: A New Vision for Development*, Hangzhou: Zhejiang People's Publishing House, 2007.

54. Xi Jinping, *Do Real Work and Be a Pioneer: Reflections and Practices on Promoting Zhejiang's New Development*, Beijing: Central Party School Press, 2013.

55. Xi Jinping, *Speech at the Seminar on Philosophy and Social Sciences,* Beijing: People's Publishing House, 2016.

56. Xi Jinping, *Speech at the Ceremony Marking the 95th Anniversary of the Founding of the CPC,* Beijing: People's Publishing House, 2016.

57. Xi Jinping, *Secure a Decisive Victory in Building a Moderately Prosperous Society in All Respects and Strive for the Great Success of Socialism with Chinese Characteristics for a New Era: Report at the 19th National Congress of the Communist Party of China*, Beijing: People's Publishing House, 2017.

58. Xi Jinping, *Speech at the Preparatory Meeting for the Education Campaign on CPC History,* Beijing: People's Publishing House, 2021.

59. Xi Jinping, *Speech at a Ceremony Marking the Centenary of the Communist Party of China,* Beijing: People's Publishing House, 2021.

60. *Documents Produced since the 18th CPC National Congress*, Volume I, Beijing: Central Party Literature Publishing House, 2014.

61. *Documents Produced since the 18th CPC National Congress*, Volume II, Beijing: Central Party Literature Publishing House, 2016.

62. *Documents Produced since the 18th CPC National Congress*, Volume III, Beijing: Central Party Literature Publishing House, 201 2018.

63. *Documents Produced since the 19th CPC National Congress*, Volume I, Beijing: Central Party Literature Publishing House, 2019.

64. *Documents Produced since the 19th CPC National Congress*, Volume II, Beijing: Central Party Literature Publishing House, 2021.

65. *Documents from the 18th CPC National Congress,* Beijing: People's Publishing House, 2012.

66. *Documents from the 19th CPC National Congress,* Beijing: People's Publishing House, 2017.

67. *Documents from the Fifth Plenary Session of the 19th CPC Central Committee,* Beijing: People's Publishing House, 2020.

68. *Resolution on Historical Issues and Resolution on Historical Issues of the Party since the Founding of the People's Republic of China,* Beijing: Publishing House for the History of the Communist Party of China, 2010.

69. *Resolution of the Central Committee of the Communist Party of China on the Major Achievements and Historical Experience of the Party over the Past Century,* Beijing: People's Publishing House, 2021.

70. Central Publicity Department Theory Bureau, *Five Hundred Years of World Socialism*, Beijing: Xuexi Press, 2016.

71. *History of the Communist Party of China*, Volume I and II, Beijing: Publishing House for the History of the Communist Party of China, 2011.

72. A Brief History of the Communist Party of China, Beijing: People's Publishing House, CPC Party History Publishing House, 2021.

73. *A Brief History of the People's Republic of China,* Beijing: People's Publishing House and Contemporary China Publishing House, 2021.

74. *A Brief History of Reform and Opening Up*, Beijing: People's Publishing House and China Social Science Press, 2021.

75. *A Brief History of Socialist Development,* Beijing: People's Publishing House and Xuexi Press, 2021.

76. *A History of the People's Republic of China* (in five volumes), Beijing: People's Publishing House and Contemporary China Publishing House, 2012.

77. *Ninety Years of the Communist Party of China* (in three volumes), Beijing: Publishing House for the History of the Communist Party of Chin and Party Building Books Publishing House, 2016.

78. *14th Five-Year Plan for Economic and Social Development and Long-Range Objectives through the Year 2035*, Beijing: People's Publishing House, 2020.

79. *Basic Issues of Xi Jinping Thought on Socialism with Chinese Characteristics for a New Era*, Beijing: People's Publishing House and Central Party School Press, 2020.

80. Institute for Contemporary China Studies, *70 Years of the People's Republic of China,* Beijing: Contemporary China Publishing House, 2019.

81. National Bureau of Statistics of the People's Republic of China, *China Statistical Yearbooks* and other statistical materials from various years.

82. National Bureau of Statistics of the People's Republic of China, *Statistical Communiqué of the People's Republic of China on the 2017 National Economic and Social Development.*

83. Hu Sheng (eds.), *A Concise History of the Communist Party of China*, Beijing: Publishing House for the History of the Communist Party of Chin, 1991.

84. Wang Weiguang (eds.), *New Mass Philosophy (Concise Edition),* Beijing: China Social Science Press, 2017.

85. Leng Rong, *Socialism with Chinese Characteristics and the Building of of a Moderately Prosperous Society in All Respects,* Beijing: China Social Science Press, 2008.

86. Jiang Hui, New Characteristics of World Socialism in the 21st Century, Beijing: Social Sciences Academic Press, 2016.

87. Jiang Hui, *Banner and Road, Essays on Socialism with Chinese Characteristics,* Beijing: China Social Science Press, 2020.

88. Jiang Hui, *World Socialism in Momentous Changes: A Collection of*

Essays on World Socialism, Beijing: China Social Science Press, 2020.

89. Jiang Hui *et al.*, *A General Survey of Contemporary World Socialism,* Beijing: China Social Science Press, 2020.

90. Jiang Hui (eds.), *Foreigners' Views on the International Contribution and Global Significance of China's Fight against the COVID-19 Pandemic,* Beijing: Contemporary China Publishing House, 2020.

91. Jiang Hui (eds.), *Witnessing the Centenary of a Great Party Together: Narratives from a Hundred Foreign Communists,* Beijing: Contemporary China Publishing House, 2021.

92. Jin Chongji, *Outline of Twentieth-Century Chinese History,* Beijing: Social Sciences Academic Press (China), 2009.

93. Pang Xianzhi, *The Glorious Road,* Beijing: SDX Joint Publishing Company, 2019.

94. Li Jie, *Struggle and Dreams: The Century-Long Journey of the Chinese People's Pursuit of Dreams in Modern Times,* Beijing: China Social Science Press, 2021.

95. Chen Xianda, *A Compulsory Course for Communists, Mastering and Utilizing Marxism,* Beijing: Orient Press, 2020.

96. Ezra F. Vogel, *Deng Xiaoping and the Transformation of China,* Beijing: SDX Joint Publishing Company, 2013.

97. Egon Krenz, *China, as I See It* (CHINA, wie ich es sehe), Beijing: World Affairs Press, 2019.

98. Graham Allison (translated by Chen Dingding and Fu Qiang), *Destined for War, Can America and China Escape Thucydides's Trap?,* Shanghai: Shanghai People's Publishing House, 2018.

99. John J. Mearsheimer (translated by Wang Yiwei and Tang Xiaosong), *The Tragedy of Great Power Politics,* Shanghai: Shanghai People's Publishing House, 2014.

100. Samir Amin (translated by Ding Kaijie *et al.* and edited by Li

Zhi), *Capitalism in the Age of Globalization,* Beijing: Renmin University of China Press, 2013.

101. David Harvey (translated by Zhang Yin), *The Limits of Capital,* Beijing: CITIC Press Group, 2017.

102. Thomas Piketty (translated by Hong Hui and Zhang Chenqi), *The Long Crisis: The Decline and Revival in Europe* (Peut-on sauver l'Europe? Chroniques 2004-2012), Beijing: CITIC Press Group, 2018.

103. Philip Kotler (translated by Guo Jinxing *et al.*), *Confronting Capitalism, Real Solutions for a Troubled Economic System*, Beijing: China Machine Press, 2016.

104. Samuel Bowles *et al.* (translated by Meng Jie *et al.*), Understanding Capitalism, Competition, Command, and Change, Beijing: Renmin University of China Press, 2013.

English references

I. Monographs

1. David Shambaugh, *Power Shift: China and Asia's New Dynamics,* California: University of California Press, 2005.

2. David Shambaugh, *China's Future,* UK: Polity Press, 2016.

3. Daniel Koss, *Where the Party Rules, The Rank and File of China's Communist State,* Cambridge: Cambridge University Press, 2018.

4. Elizabeth Economy: *The Third Revolution: Xi Jinping and the New Chinese State*, Oxford: Oxford University Press, 2018.

5. Elizabeth J. Perry & Mark Selden, *Chinese Society, Change, Conflict and Resistance,* London: Routledge Taylor & Francis Group, 2010.

6. Jeffrey N. Wasserstrom, *Popular Protest and Political Culture in Modern China,* London: Routledge Taylor & Francis Group, 2018.

7. James Mann, *The China Fantasy, How Our Leaders Explain Away*

Chinese Repression, New York: Viking, 2007.

8. Ka-ho Mok, *Social and Political Development in Post-Reform China,* London: Palgrave Macmillan, 2000.

9. Susan L. Shirk, *The Political Logic of Economic Reform in China,* California: University of California Press, 1993.

10. Vivienne Shue & Patricia M. Thornton (eds.), *To Govern China, Evolving Practices of Power,* New York: Cambridge University Press, 2017.

11. Marta Harnecker, *A World to Build: New Paths toward Twenty-First Century Socialism,* New York City: Monthly Review Press, 2015.

II. Academic papers

1. Balla, S. J. (2017), "Is consultation the 'new normal?,'" Online policymaking and governance reform in China, *Journal of Chinese Political Science,* 22 (3), 375-392.

2. Bandeira, E. M. (2017), "Political reforms in a global context: some foreign perspectives on constitutional thought in late imperial China," *Contemporary Chinese Political Economy and Strategic Relations,* 3 (1), 139-185.

3. Creemers, R. (2015), "China's constitutionalism debate, content, context and implications," *The China Journal,* (74), 91-109,244.

4. Cao, C., & Suttmeier, R. P. (2017), "Challenges of S&T system reform in China," *Science,* 355 (6329), 1019-1021.

5. Dorn, J. A. (2019), "China's future development, challenges and opportunities," *Cato Journal,* 39 (1), 173-188.

6. Guo, B. (2017), "China's administrative governance reform in the era of 'new normal,'" *Journal of Chinese Political Science,* 22 (3), 357-373.

7. Guo, Y., & Li, S. (2015), "Anti-corruption measures in China: suggestions for reforms," *Asian Education and Development Studies,* 4 (1), 7-23.

8. Joseph Fewsmith (2018), "The 19th Party Congress, Ringing in Xi Jinping's New Age," *China Leadership Monitor,* No. 55.

9. Lampton, D. M. (2015), "Introduction to the special issue-mainland China's reform and transition? the opportunities and challenges of the Xi-Li administration, Chinese political system change, pluralization, and learning," *Issues and Studies,* 51 (1), 1-22.

10. Legiędź, T. (2019), "The economic consequences of the recent political changes in China: the new institutional economics perspective," *Ekonomia i Prawo,* 18 (2), 197-208.

11. Li, H. (2017), "Chinese discourse on constitutionalism and its impact on reforms," *Journal of Chinese Political Science,* 22 (3), 407-427.

12. Naughton, B. (2017), "Is China socialist?," *The Journal of Economic Perspectives,* 31 (1), 3-24.

13. Naughton, B. (2015), "Reform retreat and renewal: how economic policy fits into the political system," *Issues and Studies,* 51 (1), 23-54.

14. Noakes, S. (2018), "A disappearing act: The evolution of China's administrative detention system," *Journal of Chinese Political Science,* 23 (2), 199-216.

15. Noesselt, N. (2017), "Governance change and patterns of continuity: assessing China's 'new normal,'" *Journal of Chinese Political Science,* 22 (3), 341-355.

16. Semenov, A. A. (2016), "Development of democratic processes in the People's Republic of China: prospects of transformation of the political regime," *Contemporary Chinese Political Economy and Strategic Relations,* 2 (1), 351-XII.

17. Teets, J. C. (2015), "The politics of innovation in China: local officials as policy entrepreneurs," Issues and Studies, 51 (2), 79-109.

18. Taylor, J. R. (2015), "The China dream is an urban dream:

assessing the CPC's national new-type urbanization plan," *Journal of Chinese Political Science*, 20 (2), 107-120.

19. Teets, J. C. (2015), "The politics of innovation in China: local officials as policy entrepreneurs," *Issues and Studies,* 51 (2), 79-109.

20. Xia, Z., Tian, S., & Yan, X. (2019), "Mapping the knowledge domain: research on service-oriented government in China," *Journal of Chinese Political Science*, 24 (2), 341-360.

21. Winberg Chai and May-lee Chai, "The Meaning of Xi Jinping's Chinese Dream," *American Journal of Chinese Studies,* Vol. 20, No. 2 (October 2013).

22. John Garrick and Yan Chang Bennett, "Xi Jinping Thought: Realization of the Chinese Dream of National Rejuvenation?," *China Perspectives*, No. 1-2 (113), (2018).

Afterword

The New Era of Socialism with Chinese Characteristics: Global Relevance represents the culmination of my many years of research into the historical achievements and transformative changes of this New Era, as well as its theoretical, practical, contemporary, and global implications. Anchored in the advancements of both practical and theoretical innovation, this book delves into the profound contributions and historical status of this New Era within the annals of Marxism, world socialism, human society's development, and the progress of human advancement. Through comprehensive and systematic exploration, it aspires to foster deeper and broader research on this pivotal subject.

As this manuscript goes to print, I would like to seize this opportunity to extend my heartfelt gratitude to You Daoqin, the editor-in-chief of Jiangxi People's Publishing House, along with the dedicated editors Wang Yimu, Chen Caiyan, Zhang Zhigang, and others. Their unwavering support and diligent efforts have been instrumental in bringing this book to fruition. My sincere thanks also go to researchers Yu Haiqing and Chen Zhigang from the Institute of Marxism at the Chinese Academy of Social Sciences, Professor Zhuang Wencheng from the School of Marxism at Beijing International Studies University, and Chen Xueqiang from the Personnel and Education Bureau of the Chinese Academy of Social Sciences. Their meticulous assistance with data collection and editing has been invaluable, and I am deeply grateful.

Given the limitations of my academic perspective and research capabilities, there are inevitably errors and oversights in this book. I earnestly welcome and appreciate the critiques and corrections from experts, scholars, and readers in the relevant fields.

Jiang Hui

November 2021

Beijing

www.ingramcontent.com/pod-product-compliance
Lightning Source LLC
Chambersburg PA
CBHW041428270326
41932CB00031B/3490

* 9 7 8 1 9 1 7 1 4 3 4 9 3 *